D1559284

Praise for *The Terrorization of Dissent*

"This chilling, well-researched book lays out precisely how our own government, right here in these United States, acts against the interests of its citizens to protect the often illegal conduct of private businesses; how U.S. agencies have infiltrated social movements and invaded individuals' lives and homes, harassing, harming, and even destroying people and groups who pose a threat by exposing institutional wrongdoing. This book is a public service that will shock you into realizing that we live in a banana republic."

— **Ingrid Newkirk**, founder of PETA
and author of *Free the Animals*

"*The Terrorization of Dissent* opens the curtain on how corporate greed and political bankruptcy collided to create the Animal Enterprise Terrorism Act. This intelligent compendium offers legal, political, and theoretical analyses of how one law has vilified and punished an entire social justice movement. It's crucial reading for anyone who cares about our constitutional rights and the committed individuals whose only crime was drawing attention to the exploitation and cruel treatment of animals."

— **Heidi Boghosian**, executive director
of the National Lawyers Guild

"This analysis of the AETA is a must-read for those who seek to understand how and why forms of protest against structural and institutionalized oppression (everything from civil rights to antiwar) are criminalized, pathologized, and constructed as 'terrorism.' *The Terrorization of Dissent* shows how the AETA is not a singular issue, but joins a long history of repressing social movements that seek to disrupt the machinery of capitalism and its commodification of sentient beings (human and nonhuman animals) to benefit a privileged demographic of consumer citizens."

— **A. Breeze Harper**, editor of *Sistah Vegan: Food, Identity,
Health, and Society—Black Female Vegans Speak*

"An excellent and very important book. It's vital that all those who are concerned for the protection of our fellow creatures understand why this appalling Act has come about and work together to try to circumvent and challenge it."

— **Ronnie Lee**, founder of the Animal Liberation Front

"As laws targeting specific social movements continue to be executed, *The Terrorization of Dissent* offers a timely and urgent challenge to the blatant unconstitutionality of the Animal Enterprise Terrorism Act. The chapters in this collection should interest anyone who is concerned about freedom of expression, the United States's growing plutocracy, and the continued exploitation of nonhuman animals."

—**Dr. Kim Socha**, author of *Women, Destruction, and the Avant-Garde: A Paradigm for Animal Liberation*

"The law serves primarily to enforce hegemonic consensus and to criminalize those in society who would dissent from the same. In a more perfect world there could be a participatory set of legal institutions that tend toward justice. But in contemporary America, we have instead generated a massive legal-industrial complex that results in new threats to democracy, freedom, justice, and peace. At the very nadir of this nightmare sits the Animal Enterprise Terrorism Act. This book is therefore a welcomed jurisprudence with an attitude—a bellwether critique of how 'terrorism' is defined, investigated, and prosecuted post-9/11."

—**Dr. Richard Kahn**, core faculty in Education at Antioch University Los Angeles

"Animal rights and the humane treatment of animals continues to slip by the societal radar. Most of the public assumes that animals have some types of law in place that protect animals. Thus, *The Terrorization of Dissent* is a timely book that challenges us to not only be aware of this issue, but to engage in it. Anyone serious about any dimension of activism needs to read this book."

—**Dr. Daniel White Hodge**, director of the Center for Youth Ministry Studies at North Park University and author of *The Soul of Hip Hop: Rimbs, Timbs and a Cultural Theology*

"In the United States, we have become entangled in a shared mentality and enforced amnesia that enshrines injustice in the name of justice and that exalts inhumanity and torture in the name of national security. The Animal Enterprise Terrorism Act forbids acts of liberation, acts of mercy, and acts of social justice, thereby enforcing and legitimizing the most heinous acts against nonhuman life, shackling humanity in a locked cage of cutthroat barbarism and savagery. This book is a powerful weapon in the struggle for justice."

—**Dr. Peter McLaren**, professor in the Division of Urban Schooling at University of California, Los Angeles

"Today, arrays of corporate, political, and police force actors have worked in a concerted effort to criminalize a broad range of activities which could be construed to be part of an animal rights movement. This effort constitutes a war on dissent against institutions of animal cruelty, and it has been subsumed by the fictional 'war on terror,' in what are essentially attempts to normalize the terror felt by the animals which constitute the raw materials of animal-using industries. In reviewing this war on dissent, *The Terrorization of Dissent* focuses on the 2006 Animal Enterprise Terrorism Act, a Bush-era statute, while providing the reader with a comprehensive picture of the use of police power on behalf of enshrined corporations. It's an essential text for anyone wishing to broaden their knowledge of U.S. government repression in this era."

—**Dr. Samuel Fassbinder**, coeditor of *Greening the Academy:*
Ecopedagogy through the Liberal Arts

"For decades, 'animal enterprises' have been teaming up and crying victim to Congress in efforts to create special protections against those of us struggling for animal liberation. One result is the Animal Enterprise Terrorism Act—a bold step deeper into fascism where the thought crime of animal liberation earns us extraordinary attention from law enforcement and disproportionate legal consequences. Bringing together several essential voices and spanning the divide between activist and academic, this volume puts an important focus on the deplorable lengths a sadistic industry will go to in efforts to satisfy its greed."

—**Leslie James Pickering**, author of *Mad Bomber Melville*

"This is the most important book about the Animal Enterprise Terrorism Act. If you are concerned at all about social justice, activism, or the U.S. constitution, then you must read this book now. *The Terrorization of Dissent* should be required reading for every law school."

—*Journal for Critical Animal Studies*

The Terrorization of Dissent

Corporate Repression, Legal Corruption, and the Animal Enterprise Terrorism Act

EDITED BY

JASON DEL GANDIO AND ANTHONY J. NOCELLA II

LANTERN BOOKS • NEW YORK

A Division of Booklight, Inc.

2014
LANTERN BOOKS
128 Second Place, Brooklyn, NY 11231
www.lanternbooks.com

Copyright © 2014 by Jason Del Gandio and Anthony J. Nocella II

All rights reserved. No part of this book may be reproduced, stored in a retrieval system, or transmitted in any form or by any means, electronic, mechanical, photocopying, recording, or otherwise, without the written permission of Lantern Books.

Printed in the United States of America

LIBRARY OF CONGRESS CATALOGING-IN-PUBLICATION DATA

The terrorization of dissent : corporate repression, legal corruption, and the animal enterprise terrorism act / edited by Jason Del Gandio and Anthony J. Nocella II.
    pages cm
ISBN 978-1-59056-430-1 (pbk. : alk. paper) —
ISBN 978-1-59056-431-8 (ebook)
1. United States. Animal Enterprise Terrorism Act. 2. Animal rights activists—Legal status, laws, etc.—United States.
3. Ecoterrorism—United States. 4. Terrorism—Prevention—Law and legislation—United States. 5. Animal rights movement—United States. I. Del Gandio, Jason, editor of compilation. II. Nocella, Anthony J., editor of compilation.
KF3841.A3282006A2 2014
345.73'02317—dc23

2013029887

CONTENTS

Foreword by Piers Beirne   xi

Preface by Will Potter   xv

Introduction: Situating the Repression and Corruption of the AETA   xix
Jason Del Gandio and Anthony J. Nocella II

PART I: EXAMINING THE LEGALITIES OF THE AETA   1

The Animal Enterprise Terrorism Act: Protecting the Profits
of Animal Enterprises at the Expense of the First Amendment   3
Kim McCoy

Who is the Real "Terrorist"?   35
Dara Lovitz

Kangaroo Court: Analyzing the 2006 "Hearing" on the AETA   51
Vasile Stanescu

The Disconnect between Politics and Prosecution under the AETA   68
Lillian M. McCartin and Brad J. Thomson

PART II: POLITICAL REPRESSION AND CORPORATE COLLUSION   89

The "Green Scare" and "Eco-Terrorism:" The Development of U.S.
"Counterterrorism" Strategy Targeting Direct Action Activists   91
Michael Loadenthal

Terrorizing Dissent and the Conspiracy Against "Radical" Movements   120
Scott DeMuth and David Naguib Pellow

Interest Group Politics, the AETA, and the
Criminalization of Animal Rights Activism   139
Wesley Shirley

Terrorism, Corporate Shadows, and the AETA: An Overview   161
John Sorenson

Part III: Theorizing the AETA   175

A Green Criminologist Perspective on Eco-Terrorism   177
Anthony J. Nocella II

The Rhetoric of Terrorism   203
Jason Del Gandio

Critiquing the AETA: A Foucauldian Reading   220
Sarat Colling, Eric Jonas, and Stephanie Jenkins

Stop Huntingdon Animal Cruelty: A Queer Critique of the AETA   236
Jennifer D. Grubbs

Part IV: Interviews and Personal Reflections   253

Interview with Joseph Buddenberg of the AETA 4   255
Dylan Powell

Interview with Scott DeMuth, Former ALF Political Prisoner   263
Brad J. Thomson

Interview with Walter Bond, Current ALF Political Prisoner   277
Carol L. Glasser

Interview with Josh Harper of the SHAC 7   287
Dylan Powell

A Personal Story and a Plea to Other Activists   294
Aaron Zellhoefer

Blum v. Holder   300
Sarahjane Blum, Jay Johnson, and Ryan Shapiro

Afterword by Heidi Boghosian   307

Acknowledgments   315

About the Contributors   317

About the Publisher   327

This book is dedicated to all of those who have been politically repressed for speaking out against corporate domination and organizing for social justice

FOREWORD

Piers Beirne

I wrote this foreword deeply saddened by the news of the great soci-
ologist and criminologist Stanley Cohen's passing in January 2013.
I had known Stan since the early 1970s from our time together at Durham University in the Department of Sociology (on Old Elvet, across
the street from the infamous "F Wing," Durham's maximum security
facility for long-term prisoners). From his earliest book, *Folk Devils and
Moral Panics: The Creation of the Mods and the Rockers* (1972), to one of
his most recent, *States of Denial: Knowing about Atrocities and Suffering*
(2001), Stan Cohen had a longstanding concern with political repression and human rights. He was a fearless, if soft-spoken, activist for
social justice—first as a student in apartheid South Africa, then as a
lecturer and professor of sociology in Britain and afterward in Israel,
and eventually again in Britain at the Mannheim Centre for Criminology at the London School of Economics.

I mention Stan Cohen here because it was he who created the hugely
influential concept of "moral panic." The concept, which was quickly
popularized through *Folk Devils and Moral Panics*, was required reading
at colleges and universities and the inspiration for many a dissertation
on deviance and social control, on the dramatization of evil, and on the
marginalization of certain "out groups." Cohen initially deployed the
concept of moral panic to weave together the different threads of his
research on oppositional youth gangs in England of the 1960s—on the
Mods and the Rockers, in particular—and on the spiraling out-of-con-
trol process of societal reaction whereby the fears of elderly and conservative populations about hooligans in south coast seaside resorts were

stoked by the mass media and amplified by repressive state and police apparatuses. The key point about moral panics, Cohen insisted, is that every society episodically creates these eruptions.

In the United States, historically, moral panics of varying intensity have been constructed around and against communism, anarchism, women's suffrage, desegregation of schools and the military, same-sex marriage, drug use, serial murder, child kidnapping, sex offenses, and terrorism. Now enter: activism in the movement for animal rights. *The Terrorization of Dissent: Corporate Repression, Legal Corruption, and the Animal Enterprise Terrorism Act* is a collection of essays by lawyers, scholars, and activists and includes interviews with some who have suffered from the AETA's conspiracy provisions (famously, members of the Stop Huntingdon Animal Cruelty campaign). The editors, Jason Del Gandio and Anthony J. Nocella II, do a wonderful job of assembling a book that documents not only how the Animal Enterprise Terrorism Act (AETA) is a clear violation of the First Amendment but also, chiefly, how corporate America and the U.S. government have conspired to use law and naked force to tarnish animal rights activism (i.e., vandalism and property damage) and civil disobedience around environmental issues with the brush of terrorism. Under the terms of the AETA—signed into law by President George W. Bush on November 27, 2006—the predictable *ka-ching!* of corporate profit is nowadays the ultimate arbiter of what can and can't be done to animals in intensive rearing regimes, in laboratory vivisection, and in factories that transform animals' lives, bodies, flesh, and skin into food, entertainment, clothing, toiletries, glue, and so on.

From the early 1990s through the terrible tragedies of 9/11 and up to the present, the history of the AETA raises disturbing questions about how suffocating and prejudiced the tentacles of panic are in the post-9/11 homeland. Who has the power to draw and enforce a line between freedom of expression and terrorism? How does that terrorism differ from the terrorism of the State, of xenophobia, and of speciesism? As someone who regularly labors at the intersection of animal abuse and criminology, I welcome the publication of this book. Relatively little indeed has been written by progressive scholars on the Animal Enterprise Terrorism Act. That omission is considerably relieved here.

Will Potter's wonderful catchphrase "green is the new red" may downplay the fact that, just as there were and are many shades of "red" (communism, Stalinism, Trotskyism, anarchism, anarcho-syndicalism, the New Left, and so on), some of which have been as much at war with each other as with capitalism and imperialism, so, too, are there many shades of green. Whatever their particular hue, however, to my knowledge every major tendency within today's green movement has an interest in (1) free speech (which the AETA threatens to suppress and dismiss as terrorism) and (2) respect for all life on tiny planet Earth, including a nonviolent route to the achievement of green nonspeciesist futures.

In the relative safety of a foreword, I would like to relate a story that I have long been saving for just such an occasion as this. (The story is drawn from a liberal combination of Geoffrey Chaucer's "Parliament of the Birds" and Cyrano de Bergerac's "Story of the Birds.") Once upon a time there was a man named Drycona. He was persecuted in his homeland for his progressive ideas. He left the land where he was born and he traveled to many places, among which were the sun and the moon.

On one of his voyages, unexpectedly, he was captured and detained by two birds, a phoenix and a magpie. Some of the strongest soldier birds then escorted Drycona to a forest in the Kingdom of the Birds, where he was imprisoned in the hollow trunk of a large oak tree. In prison, he awaited trial. Eventually, Drycona the human was brought before a Tribunal of the Birds. On the tribunal sat magpies as solicitors, jays as counsel, and starlings as judges.

Drycona was charged with the most heinous of crimes—being a (hu)man. The official indictment stated that the human kills us without being attacked by us . . . he eats us when he might satisfy his hunger with more suitable food . . . and most cowardly of all, he debauches the natural disposition of hawks, falcons, and vultures by teaching them to massacre their kind, to feed upon their like, or to deliver us into his hands.

In his defense Drycona claimed that he was in fact not a human. Actually, he asserted, he was a monkey. In order to survive in the company of humans without being a human, he had learned as a youngster to walk on two legs and to speak a human language. He was a monkey, in other words, who merely looked like a human.

At this, Drycona was ordered to appear for examination by the syndics. For a whole day and night the syndics paraded up and down and in front of Drycona, performing numerous tricks, such as walking with nutshells on their heads. Drycona was quite unmoved by all of this.

The next day the syndics testified to a special committee that Drycona could not be a monkey because not once had he copied any of their tricks, as a real monkey would have done. He was therefore found guilty of being a human. Sentencing, however, was to be postponed until good weather arrived. (The solicitor general informed the human that at the end of a criminal prosecution they never pronounced sentence in bad weather, as they did not want their minds to be clouded by an overcast day or by rain.)

A week later, the king, a dove, read out the sentence. Death! Drycona was to be executed in a fitting and very undeceiving way: by being eaten by the weakest creatures in the kingdom—bees, midges, gnats, and fleas. Just as the insects approached Drycona, ready to devour him, he was given a reprieve.

"Though as a man you deserve to die simply because you were born," he was told, "pardon, pardon, pardon!" This late and, for Drycona, very welcome turn of events happened as a result of the testimony of a parrot who, in an earlier phase of his life, had been named Caesar by Drycona's cousin. The parrot testified that a long time ago Drycona, the man, feeling pity for a poor caged bird, had released him and set him free. Even though humans may be unable to reason, sometimes they have good hearts!

PREFACE

Will Potter

When I testified before the U.S. House Judiciary Committee about the Animal Enterprise Terrorism Act in 2006, I argued that such sweeping legislation criminalizes First Amendment activity, whistle-blowing, and nonviolent civil disobedience as "terrorism" and would have a chilling effect on free speech. Members of the committee, including Representative Bobby Scott (D-VA) and Representative James Sensenbrenner (R-WI), dismissed my concerns and promised that the law would only target property destruction and violence. This has been the major talking point from supporters of this legislation for years: the law is only about "extremists," and as long as you aren't part of the Animal Liberation Front, you have nothing to worry about. Lawmakers went so far as to respond to my concerns by including empty rhetoric in the rules of construction promising that the bill "does not include any lawful economic disruption (including a lawful boycott) that results from lawful public, governmental, or business reaction to the disclosure of information about an animal enterprise."

Since that time, the true scope of this legislation has been exposed by prosecutions, uncovered FBI documents, and new campaigns by industry groups. It has become undeniably clear that members of Congress were either duped by corporations and the FBI or they intentionally lied to the American people about their intentions. The true targets of the AETA are not arsonists or underground activists. Instead, the people most at risk are undercover *investigators* and *aboveground* activists.

The very first AETA arrests were four animal rights activists in California who were never accused of property destruction or violence.

The government argued that their conduct—which included "chalking defamatory slogans," protesting while wearing masks, distributing fliers, and attending a home protest—amounted to a campaign of terrorism. In a major blow to the government's overzealous use of the new law, a U.S. District Court threw out the indictment because prosecutors did not clearly explain what, exactly, the protesters did. "In order for an indictment to fulfill its constitutional purposes, it must allege facts that sufficiently inform each defendant of what it is that he or she is alleged to have done that constitutes a crime," Judge Ronald M. Whyte said in his ruling. "This is particularly important where the species of behavior in question spans a wide spectrum from criminal conduct to constitutionally protected political protest."

Even more disturbing is the fact that the FBI Joint Terrorism Task Force has kept files on activists who expose animal welfare abuses on factory farms and has recommended prosecuting them as terrorists. This information was revealed in documents that were uncovered through the Freedom of Information Act (FOIA) and has been reported on my website, GreenIsTheNewRed.com. The 2003 FBI file details the work of several animal rights activists who used undercover investigation to document repeated animal welfare violations. The FBI special agent who authored the report said they "illegally entered buildings owned by [redacted] Farm . . . and videotaped conditions of animals." The animal activists caused "economic loss" to businesses, the FBI says. And they also openly rescued several animals from the abusive conditions. This was not done covertly in the style of underground groups like the Animal Liberation Front; instead, it was an act of nonviolent civil disobedience and, as the FBI agent notes, the activists distributed press releases and conducted media interviews taking responsibility for their actions.

Based on these acts—trespassing in order to photograph and videotape abuses on factory farms—the agent concludes that there "is a reasonable indication" that the activists "have violated the Animal Enterprise Terrorism Act, 18 USC Section 43 (a)." The file was uncovered through a FOIA request by Ryan Shapiro, a doctoral candidate at MIT who is one of the activists mentioned as being in violation of the law. "It is deeply sobering to see one's name in an FBI file proposing terrorism charges," Shapiro told me. "It is even more sobering to realize the supposedly terroristic activities in question are merely exposing the horrific cruelty of factory farms, educating the public about what goes on behind those closed doors, and openly rescuing a few animals from one of those farms as an act of civil disobedience."

The FBI file, it should be noted, was dated 2003. That is three years before the Animal Enterprise Terrorism Act was passed. In other words, the FBI argued that such prosecutions were possible under the previous and narrower version of the law. If that was the case, why was the AETA even necessary? The FBI knew that the existing law was already vague and overly broad, but joined industry groups in grasping for even more power.

In recent years a legislative trend has developed that, prior to the AETA, I never would have thought possible. More than a dozen states have considered legislation that explicitly criminalizes undercover investigations by nonprofit animal welfare groups like The Humane Society and Mercy for Animals. At the time of this writing, Iowa and Utah have passed "Ag Gag" bills into law, and others are expected to follow.

These investigations have exposed systemic animal cruelty at factory farms and completely changed the national dialogue about animal agriculture. The video footage has led to criminal convictions in Iowa, voter referendums in Florida, and consumer outrage at the most egregious animal welfare abuses. The threat that they pose to factory farming is unmistakable. When a California slaughterhouse was shut down for egregious animal welfare violations, industry groups put pressure on Congress. Three lawmakers then sent a letter to the USDA urging the department to take action against "the onslaught of attacks" by animal welfare groups. The lawmakers and industry groups compared the video investigation to arson and called it "economic terrorism."

This is the political climate since the passage of the AETA. In the years after it was signed into law, industry groups and law enforcement have only grown more ambitious. There has been a widening of the net, which risks ensnaring more and more activists as "terrorists." Such repression of political activists is certainly not new; for instance, the FBI used both legal and illegal tactics against civil rights, antiwar, and other activists during COINTELPRO in the 1960s. But in post-9/11 America, the power of "terrorism" rhetoric, combined with corporate efforts to manufacture and manipulate government repression, has created a unique and incredibly powerful culture of fear.

However, the political climate within the animal rights movement has changed as well. During the 2006 hearing, I testified as the only opposing witness. The vast majority of activists were completely unaware of the legislation, and most organizations were unwilling to speak up about it. This chilling effect still exists, in many ways, but the movement's response has radically changed. The Center for Constitutional Rights is challenging the Animal Enterprise Terrorism Act on behalf of activists who have felt silenced. A diverse coalition of animal, environmental, civil liberties, and legal organizations is fighting Ag Gag bills across the country. National media have slowly but steadily become more willing to shine a light on these issues.

This current collection of essays—written by activists, lawyers, and scholars, and finely edited by Jason Del Gandio and Anthony J. Nocella II—adds critical voices to the growing chorus of opposition. *The Terrorization of Dissent* should be viewed not as a historical examination, but as a contemporary toolkit. The authors chart the legal and political history of the law and include the personal stories of those affected.

These texts should be read with the understanding that this repression is dynamic. The AETA, as a legal and corporate tactic, is expanding to other social movements, and it is evolving as it appears internationally: Corporations have ushered in nearly identical crackdowns in Austria, Spain, Finland, and many other countries. This book is a toolkit not just for animal rights activists, but for all social movements around the world who are effectively challenging corporate power, and who want to better prepare themselves for the backlash that is an inevitable part of that struggle.

INTRODUCTION

SITUATING THE REPRESSION AND CORRUPTION OF THE AETA

Jason Del Gandio and Anthony J. Nocella II

Congress shall make no law . . . abridging the freedom of speech, or of the press; or the right of the people peaceably to assemble, and to petition the Government for a redress of grievances.
  —First Amendment to the U.S. Constitution

I disapprove of what you say, but I will defend to the death your right to say it.
  —Evelyn Beatrice Hall (summarizing the thought of Voltaire)

The only way in which a human being can make some approach to knowing the whole of a subject is by hearing what can be said about it by persons of every variety of opinion and studying all modes in which it can be looked at by every character of mind. No wise man [or woman] ever acquired his [or her] wisdom in any mode but this.
  —John Stuart Mill

To view the opposition as dangerous is to misunderstand the basic concepts of democracy. To oppress the opposition is to assault the very foundation of democracy.
  —Aung San Suu Kyi

BACKGROUND AND CONTEXT OF THE AETA

The 2006 Animal Enterprise Terrorism Act (AETA) is intended to equip law enforcement agencies with the tools to apprehend, prosecute, and convict individuals who commit "animal enterprise terror." But this Act does not concretely define or properly explain what is actually meant by that phrase—"animal enterprise terror." The first part, "animal enterprise," can refer to any endeavor that uses nonhuman animals for earning a profit. The second part, "terror," can refer to any action that interferes with that profit-seeking enterprise. Thus, in brief, anyone interfering with a company's ability to make a profit from the exploitation of animals can be considered a terrorist. Everything from simple graffiti ("save the animals!") to boycotting particular corporations ("don't buy company X's animal-tested products") to advocacy campaigns ("we are educating the public about animal abuse and asking people to lobby against these companies") can now be prosecuted as acts of terrorism. If this is true, then the AETA is less about "fighting terrorism" and more about safeguarding corporate profit.

The AETA had been in the making for over twenty years. Corporate industries earning their money from animal and environmental enterprises began lobbying Congress in the 1980s. This was, at least in part, a response to the effectiveness of the animal rights and environmental movements that began in the 1970s. Those movements had become more effective in raising awareness about such issues as animal abuse, safety, and care; the legal rights and ethical concerns of animals; the danger of overconsuming natural resources; the importance of eco-friendly lifestyles; the use of sustainable energies; and so on. Such campaigns obviously challenge the profit motives of private industries. Those industries thus began lobbying Congress in the hopes of legally quarantining the effectiveness of these movements. The Animal Enterprise Protection Act (AEPA) was passed in 1992. Animal rights activism went on the rise in the mid- and late-1990s. Private industries then sought a more draconian approach to their legal quarantine. The events of September 11, 2001, provided the perfect context. The United States had just been attacked, people were understandably afraid, and anything referencing "terrorism" received high priority. The AETA was then signed into law five years later.

Given this history, we believe that the AETA is a clear example of how corporations are capable of hijacking United States law and cajoling Congress to criminalize dissent and activism. This criminalization is best understood as the *terrorization of dissent*. "Terrorization" refers to the ability of those in power to stigmatize activists as terrorists (Nocella 2013). This is essentially a propagandistic smear campaign that demonizes activists and undermines their causes. The general public, as well as law enforcement agencies and institutional authorities (judges, lawyers, political pundits, and mass media), begin to see the targeted activists not just as criminals, but as violent sociopaths to be feared, captured, and imprisoned. A political logic is suddenly deployed throughout society in which activists are understood to be criminals and enemies while power holders are understood to be victims and allies. But the question must be asked, who is really a greater threat to society: activists fighting for justice and equality or corporations that exploit human labor, pillage natural resources, and abuse nonhuman animals? The answer is obvious. But the fact that most people readily accept, without critical thought, the logic of terrorization demonstrates the effectiveness of terrorization campaigns.

We argue that the terrorization of dissent is a form of *corporate repression* undergirded by *legal corruption*. "Corporate repression" refers to the ability of corporate industries to prevent and/or restrain the open and honest debate, discussion, and critique of particular laws, practices, procedures, beliefs, and/or values that are deemed by some, if not by many, as unjust, immoral, and/or ill-willed. "Legal corruption" refers to the distortions and perversions of the legal process in which laws are passed or revoked for personal gain and political opportunity rather than to serve a greater good. When presented in this light, the AETA is an extension rather than aberration of the political system.

For example, so-called "right-to-work" laws actually *undermine* the ability of labor unions to fight for better wages and working conditions while enabling corporations to earn higher profits. Barack Obama's 2010 Affordable Care for America Act seems wonderful, as it enables 30 million new people to get health care. But this Act forwent the possibility of a public option health care plan (i.e., government-based low-income health insurance) and granted the health care industry 30 million new profit-generating customers. Emissions cap-and-trade proposals provide monetary incentives for corporations to lower their pollution emissions. But corporations can simply factor in the cost of buying and/or trading emission permits. That cost can then be passed on to consumers while maintaining current levels of pollution. Bill Clinton's 1996 Telecommunications Act was lauded as increasing competition among mass media corporations. But as of 2010, approximately six corporations own almost all of the media in this country: The Walt Disney Company, 21st Century Fox/News Corp, Time Warner, CBS Corporation/Viacom, Comcast/NBCUniversal, and Sony Corporation of America. Economic free trade agreements like NAFTA (North American Free Trade Agreement) are presented in similar ways, espoused as benefiting workers, consumers, and the environment. The exact opposite is true. Wages are decreased and sweatshops are increased, product safety regulations are lowered, environmental standards are weakened, and under Chapter 11 of NAFTA, private corporations can sue national governments if said corporations can demonstrate that either state or federal laws hinder corporate profits. The laws must then be overturned and the corporations compensated.

To understand the nature of these legal corruptions, one has to look no further than the 2010 *Citizens United v. Federal Election Commission* case, in which the Supreme Court argued that the First Amendment prohibits the government from restricting political spending. In brief, the argument states that corporations are natural persons; natural persons have freedom of speech; freedom of speech includes political spending; corporations are thus allowed to contribute to political campaigns like other citizens. The only problem is that corporations are not like other citizens. Corporations are collections of people dedicated to the accumulation of private wealth. Considering that we live in a capitalist society, wealth equals power. And if money equals speech, which is what the Supreme Court essentially argued, then the large majority of *actual people* are systematically excluded from expressing their political speech: 1 percent of the U.S. population owns 34 percent of the wealth; 10 percent of the population owns 71 percent of the wealth; and 1 out of 7 Americans live in poverty (Haugen, Musser, and Klamabakal 2010, 15; DeNavas-Walt, Bernadette, and Smith 2012, n.p.).

But what about the activists who dare to speak out, critique, and challenge these legal corruptions? Political pundits and mainstream mass media portray them as out of touch fringe extremists;

communication strategists are hired to devise anti-activist propaganda; corporate-funded think tanks draft model legislation to criminalize dissent; and the revolving door between public service and private industry spins around, endlessly. None of this is necessarily new, of course. The profit motive, and the corruptions stemming from it, cut to the core of the American project—genocide of Native Americans, enslavement of Africans, indentured servitude of poor Europeans, the military-industrial complex and the prison-industrial complex, structural inequalities, class discrimination, etc. Running parallel to these atrocities is the repression of social movements and progressive causes. The abolitionist movement was framed as a potential threat to tobacco and cotton industries. The suffrage movement, which lasted nearly seventy years, had to fight tooth and nail for the right to vote. The U.S. labor movement was demonized as a communist takeover and unpatriotic. Dr. Martin Luther King, Jr. and Malcolm X were surveilled and harassed by the government. The FBI's COINTELPRO (Counterintelligence Program) sought to infiltrate, divide, and dismantle the Black Power movement, the American Indian movement, the anti–Vietnam War movement, the countercultural movement, and the New Left in general. Members of the women's liberation movement were labeled as "man-haters." The gay liberation movement, the AIDS activist movement, and today's same-sex marriage movement are cast as threats to traditional America. And most recently, the Occupy Wall Street movement has been stigmatized as a bunch of spoiled college kids and wannabe hippies with no direction, goals, or solutions. Given this history, it is obvious that the corporate repression and legal corruption of the Animal Enterprise Terrorism Act is an extension of the past, and, unfortunately, a glimpse into a possible future. Consequently, the AETA should be analyzed and resisted by everyone who believes in a better world.

It should be noted, though, that the experiential background of animal rights activists is not necessarily the same as most of the activists just mentioned. Most, but surely not all, animal rights activists are white, able-bodied, and economically affluent. Many of them are also men. Such activists are endowed with certain privileges and cultural capital, and tend not to be direct targets of systemic prejudice, endemic poverty, police brutality, mass incarceration, or hate crimes. It is also much easier for such individuals to live "normal" lives once repression hits. Highlighting these kinds of privileges neither invalidates the work and experience of animal rights activists nor creates some kind of essential wedge between the animal rights movement and other movements. Instead, it points to the importance of acknowledging difference, diversity, and the intersectionality of varying oppressions. This kind of work can be difficult, but it can strengthen the relations among different movements and concretize the possibility of "total liberation."

An Overview of the Chapters

This book serves as a cross-disciplinary critique of the AETA. It brings together scholars, lawyers, and activists with the intent of exposing the problematic history and chilling effects of this law. The book is organized into four parts with a total of eighteen chapters.

In "Part I: Examining the Legalities of the AETA," authors address the legal problems and inconsistencies of the AETA. Kim McCoy's "The Animal Enterprise Terrorism Act: Protecting the Profits of Animal Enterprises at the Expense of the First Amendment" is a close reading of the AETA, and argues that its language is impermissibly vague and its intent is based on political ideology rather than sound legal concerns. Given her expertise as a lawyer, she firmly believes that the AETA is unconstitutional and an utterly flawed piece of legislation. Dara Lovitz's "Who Is the Real 'Terrorist'?" unpacks the legal, academic, and political relativity of the term *terrorism* and demonstrates that the profit-seeking activities of the animal industries are closer to "terrorism" than the activities of animal advocates. She provides a wealth of evidence to support her case. Vasile Stanescu's "Kangaroo Court: Analyzing the 2006 'Hearing' on the AETA" analyzes the rhetorical inconsistences of the actual courtroom hearing that led to passage of the AETA. His analysis suggests that the hearing was not a fair, open, and democratic inquiry. Instead, it was a deliberately orchestrated piece of "political theater" intended to demonize all animal rights activists, thus making for easy passage of the AETA. Finally, Lillian M. McCartin and Brad J. Thomson's "The Disconnect between Politics and Prosecution under the AETA" concludes this section. McCartin and Thomson compare and contrast the statements made by congressional proponents of the AETA with the actual realities of AETA prosecutions and convictions. In doing so, they demonstrate how the AETA violates the First Amendment and censors constitutionally protected animal advocacy activities.

In "Part II: Political Repression and Corporate Collusion," authors highlight the repressive nature of the AETA and the collusion between private interests and political legislation. In "The 'Green Scare' and 'Eco-Terrorism': The Development of U.S. 'Counterterrorism' Strategy Targeting Direct Action Activists," Michael Loadenthal traces the historical and legal development of the AETA while also highlighting the contradictions between the government's depictions and the actual realities of animal liberationists. He focuses specifically on the "counterterrorism strategy" used to target the Animal Liberation Front and the Earth Liberation Front. In "Terrorizing Dissent and the Conspiracy Against 'Radical' Movements," Scott DeMuth and David Naguib Pellow situate the crackdown on animal rights activists within a broader context of repression. They emphasize that animal rights activists are neither the first nor the last to be legally targeted. Consequently, the AETA is not a concern for only animal rights activists, but for *all* activists. The following two chapters by Wesley Shirley and John Sorenson, titled, respectively, "Interest Group Politics, the AETA, and the Criminalization of Animal Rights Activism" and "Terrorism, Corporate Shadows, and the AETA: An Overview," provide detailed accounts of the collusion between corporate industries and the political/legal system. Most people would like to think that Congress passes impartial laws to benefit the overall good of society. But Shirley and Sorenson demonstrate in no uncertain terms that is not the case with the AETA.

In "Part III: Theorizing the AETA," authors provide theoretical frameworks for understanding a variety of issues related to the AETA. Anthony J. Nocella's chapter, "A Green Criminologist Perspective on Eco-Terrorism," articulates the nature of "green criminology." In brief, green criminology argues that crimes can be committed against the natural world. This perspective counters the legalities of the AETA: environmental and animal rights advocates are *not* "terrorists"; instead, they act in defense of vulnerable victims while the backers of the AETA—private industries—commit criminal acts on a daily basis. Private industries should, therefore, be charged with crimes against nature and animal and environmental advocates should be applauded. Jason Del Gandio's "The Rhetoric of Terrorism" approaches the AETA from a rhetorical perspective. He points out that rhetoric—defined as well-crafted communication—is basic to all human interactions. He demonstrates how Congress and private industries have rhetorically manipulated the public into believing that animal advocates are "terrorists" and that billion-dollar corporations are "innocent victims." In "Critiquing the AETA: A Foucauldian Reading," Sarat Colling, Eric Jonas, and Stephanie Jenkins apply the work of French philosopher Michel Foucault to the controversies of the AETA. They argue, in brief, that the AETA accomplishes a discursive distortion: it simultaneously constructs non-violent activists as violent terrorists and animal-abusing industries as faultless victims in need of special legal and political protection. The last chapter of this section, "Stop Huntingdon Animal Cruelty: A Queer Critique of the AETA" by Jennifer D. Grubbs, theorizes from the perspective of an activist, arguing that the Stop Huntingdon Animal Cruelty campaign (SHAC) "queers" our understanding of both the AETA and animal rights activism. She demonstrates how SHAC's use of direct action, performance, and "play" challenge the normative boundaries of many preestablished assumptions about the world. People are thus called to critically reflect upon their own beliefs and habits, which is a necessary step for social change.

In "Part IV: Interviews and Personal Reflections," animal advocates who have been convicted and/or directly affected by the AETA are given an opportunity to speak for themselves. Dylan Powell provides two interviews—one with Joseph Buddenberg of the AETA 4 and one with Josh Harper of the SHAC 7. Brad J. Thomson interviews Scott DeMuth, a former ALF political prisoner. And Carol Glasser interviews Walter Bond, a current ALF political prisoner. These interviews, both sobering and inspiring, give voice to those who have lost their freedom due to the legalities of the AETA. In the second to last chapter, "A Personal Story and a Plea to Other Activists," Aaron Zellhoefer narrates how his life was turned upside down when law enforcement agencies raided his living quarters and arrested his romantic partner and roommates. His partner served five years in a federal correction institution. Zellhoefer provides a clear warning that the AETA affects all activists. If Congress is willing to pass the AETA, what other activists will be targeted next? The final chapter, "Blum v. Holder," by Sarahjane Blum, Jay Johnson, and Ryan Shapiro explains how the authors, in conjunction with the New York City–based Center for Constitutional Rights, have filed a lawsuit in federal court against the AETA. The suit, *Blum v. Holder*, challenges the AETA as an unconstitutional infringement on free speech. We believe it is fitting to end the book on this note as it demonstrates that the AETA—and other laws like it—can be brought to light and challenged.

CONCLUDING REMARKS: TRADITIONS, LOGISTICS, AND CLARIFICATIONS

It is important to locate all texts—books, essays, or otherwise—in particular theoretical traditions and disciplines. This allows readers to better understand the context, methodology, and framework that shapes the information provided. Broadly speaking, this book is grounded in the tradition of critical studies. Criticality is the dual act of critiquing systems of power and providing alternative perspectives, values, and practices. The tradition of critical studies includes, but is not limited to, Marxism, hermeneutics, psychoanalytical theory, the Frankfurt School, postmodernism and poststructuralism, feminism, critical race, gender, and queer studies, cultural studies, postcolonial studies, critical rhetoric, and critical legal theory.

More specifically, though, this book emerges from critical animal studies, which is a new field, beginning around 2006–07 (for more information, see the Institute for Critical Animal Studies and Best, Nocella, Kahn, Gigliotti, and Kemmerer 2007). Critical animal theory, like the numerous other subdisciplines, challenges such predominant systems of power as racism, sexism, ableism, homophobia, capitalism, imperialism, etc.; but it *also* argues for the inclusion of anti-speciesist perspectives in fighting for global social justice. Unlike animal rights, advocacy, or liberation, critical animal theory argues for liberation of both humans and nonhumans, which might include everything from animals to plants, insects, nature, and beyond (Nocella, Sorenson, Socha, and Matsuoka 2013). This theory promotes direct democracy and mutual aid and is therefore critical of representative democracy, which often aids in the corporatization of law and the silencing of dissent. This theoretical framework also challenges anti-intellectualism, dogmatism, and anti-progressivism while stressing the need for learning, listening, discussing, reflecting, strategizing, and openly debating. Finally, critical animal theory privileges intersectional academic-activist action and scholarship over detached, apolitical contemplation. In this way, then, this book champions the spirit of critical animal studies.

Before closing out this introduction, it is important to note a few logistics and clarifications. First, the editors want to acknowledge that there is no "lead editor" for this project. Jason Del Gandio and Anthony J. Nocella II equally contributed to the completion of this project. Jason's name appears first due to alphabetical order. Second, all the chapters follow a similar format and style except for the McCoy chapter. That chapter was adapted from a law journal and we agreed to retain some of the original legalese for clarity and specificity of argument. Third, all online material was accessible at the time that each chapter was originally completed, but some chapters were completed as far back as two or more years ago. Consequently, we cannot guarantee that access at this time. Fourth, this book is a collection of differing viewpoints. The individual editors and individual contributors are obviously unified in their concern that the AETA is a problematic and even unlawful piece of legislation. But it should be noted, too, that we do not all agree with one another on each and every point. That is the beauty of free speech—to enable and even encourage different opinions to converse and collide. Fifth, these pieces were independently written; consequently, there may be some repetition in recounting the history of the AETA and its predecessor, the AEPA, as well as cases related to the AETA. And sixth, common terms used throughout this book include "radical," "activist," and "social movement." Unless otherwise noted, "radical" refers to a political orientation that focuses on challenging and overturning *root* (rather than surface) problems, thereby laying groundwork for a more just, humane, and egalitarian world. "Activist" refers to an individual who acts in the name of some social, cultural, political, and/or economic justice. Included within this broad definition are those who act in defense of nonhuman animals and the natural environment. "Social movement" refers to an organized collectivity that coordinates actions over an extended period of time in the fight for a better world. A social movement can be tightly organized around a specific goal (like the civil rights movement fighting for African Americans' rights) or it can be loosely organized around a set of common themes (like the Occupy movement fighting for a cluster of varying though overlapping goals and ideologies). We emphatically argue that these terms—"radical," "activist," and "social movement"—have *nothing* to do with "terrorism." The people, groups, actions, ideologies, and worldviews discussed in this book are in no way, shape, or form related to, or definable according to standards of, "terrorism." That is a major impetus for this book: to challenge the erroneous mislabeling of particular activists and to expose the corrupt and unconstitutional underpinnings of the Animal Enterprise Terrorism Act.

References

Best, Steven, Anthony J. Nocella II, Richard Kahn, Carol Gigliotti, and Lisa Kemmerer. "Introducing Critical Animal Studies." *Journal of Critical Animal Studies* 5, no. 1 (2007): 1–2.

DeNavas-Walt, Carmen, Bernadette D. Proctor, and Jessica C. Smith. "Income, Poverty, and Health Insurance Coverage in the United States: 2011." U.S. Census Report issued September 2012. www.census.gov/prod/2012pubs /p60-243.pdf.

Haugen, David M., Susan Musser, and Vickey Klamabakal. "Introduction." In *Social Justice: Opposing Viewpoints*, edited by David M. Haugen, Susan Musser, and Vickey Klamabakal, 14–18. Detroit: Greenhaven Press, 2010.

Institute for Critical Animal Studies, The. www.criticalanimalstudies.org.

Nocella, Anthony J. II. "The Rise of the Terrorization of Dissent." In *The End of Prisons: Reflections from the Decarceration Movement,* edited by Mechthild E. Nagel and Anthony J. Nocella II, 13–30. New York: Rodopi, 2013.

Nocella, Anthony, J. II., John Sorenson, Kim Socha, Atsuko Matsuoka. *Defining Critical Animal Studies: An Intersectional Social Justice Approach for Liberation.* New York: Peter Lang Publishing, 2013.

PART I
EXAMINING THE LEGALITIES OF THE AETA

THE ANIMAL ENTERPRISE TERRORISM ACT

PROTECTING THE PROFITS OF ANIMAL ENTERPRISES
AT THE EXPENSE OF THE FIRST AMENDMENT

Kim McCoy

First they came for the terrorists,
and I didn't speak up because I wasn't a terrorist.
Or so I thought . . . [1]

Despite its own admissions that animal rights activists have taken no lives,[2] the United States Federal Bureau of Investigation (FBI) categorizes animal advocates as "one of today's most serious domestic terrorism threats."[3] The FBI's admissions demonstrate the contradictory nature of its proclamation. This contradiction also denigrates the experience of those who have lost loved ones or suffered actual physical

---

1   The opening statement is the author's adaptation of a poem attributed to pastor Martin Niemöller.

2   FBI, "When Talk Turns to Terror: Homegrown Extremism in the U.S.," (May 23, 2005), http://fbi.gov/page2/may05/jlewis052305.htm; Terry Frieden, "FBI, ATF Address Domestic Terrorism: Officials: Extremists Pose Serious Threat" (May 19, 2005), www.cnn.com/2005/US/05/19/domestic.terrorism /index.html ("No deaths have been blamed on attacks by [animal rights groups]."); FBI, Congressional Testimony: Statement of John E. Lewis, Deputy Assistant Director: Counterterrorism Division Before the Senate Committee on Environment and Public Works (May 18, 2005), www.fbi.gov/congress /congress05/lewis051805.htm ("Most animal rights . . . extremists have refrained from violence targeting human life") [hereinafter Lewis Testimony]; Senate Committee on Environment and Public Works, Statement of Senator James M. Inhofe: "Oversight on Eco-terrorism Specifically Examining the Earth Liberation Front ('ELF') and the Animal Liberation Front ('ALF')" (May 18, 2005), http:// epw.senate.gov/hearing_statements.cfm?id=247266 ("Experts agree that [animal rights groups] have not killed anyone to date . . .").

3   FBI, *Lewis Testimony, supra* n. 2.

violence or threats of real terrorism from a multiplicity of other groups that the FBI fails to elevate to the top of its domestic terrorism agenda. Going one step further, the Department of Justice (DOJ) and, previously, the Department of Homeland Security have labeled the Animal Liberation Front (ALF) as "the most serious domestic terrorist threat."[4] The classification of animal advocates as terrorists encourages a disproportionate and predominantly unfounded element of fear in the American public. This unjustified fear has contributed to the enactment of federal legislation—namely, the Animal Enterprise Terrorism Act (AETA)[5]—that targets individuals based solely upon their political ideology.

Robert Mueller, Director of the FBI, stated that the FBI would continue to "investigate and bring to justice the animal rights...extremist movements whose criminal acts threaten the American *economy* and American lives."[6] When financial interests are mentioned ahead of human lives, one must wonder exactly whose interests are being protected by this legislation, and at what price to American civil liberties?

The contradiction is nowhere more apparent than in the AETA, which protects business interests and profits at the expense of civil liberties and the right to dissent under the First Amendment. To better understand the AETA, this article discusses the climate of "terrorism" in which the AETA was born, as well as the AETA's legislative precursors, several case studies, inherent social policy flaws, and unconstitutionality. The AETA is unconstitutional because it is vague, overbroad, and impermissibly content- and viewpoint-based. It is redundant because existing laws already cover every crime included in its language. It detracts from efforts against true terrorism, chills social discourse and activism, and impedes the investigation of abusive animal enterprises. Finally, the AETA should be struck down by the courts in its entirety, or immediately repealed.

---

4   Senate Committee on Environment and Public Works, *supra* n. 2.

5   Animal Enterprise Terrorism Act, 18 U.S.C.A. § 43 (West 2007) (formerly known as the Animal Enterprise Protection Act; amended by Pub. L. No. 109-374 (November 27, 2006)).

6   FBI, "Major Executive Speeches: Prepared Remarks of Robert S. Mueller, III: Director, Federal Bureau of Investigation: Operation Backfire Press Conference" (Jan. 20, 2006), www.fbi.gov/pressrel/speeches/mueller012006.htm (emphasis added).

BACKGROUND INFORMATION

Terrorism Defined

To understand the AETA, it must be examined within the broader context of what the U.S. government considers to be "terrorism." In a nation obsessed with waging "war on terror," especially during the Bush Administration, it is important to know exactly what constitutes terrorism. However, there exists no one universally accepted definition of this powerful and provocative word.[7] For some people, the word *terrorism* may conjure up images of commercial airplanes being flown into buildings, killing thousands. Others may picture secret compounds in the wilderness, full of homemade bombs and chemical weapons. Apparently, some people would also include nonviolent ALF-type actions, such as the rescue of innocent animals from the unmitigated horrors of laboratories and factory farms, in their definition of terrorism. Such a notion is absurd, given that the ALF adheres to "strict nonviolence guidelines" and specifically instructs its members to take every available precaution to prevent harm to any animal, human or nonhuman.[8]

Individuals, corporations, and government departments—all of which arguably stand to profit in some way from the confusion—have exploited the ambiguity of the word *terrorism* to the extent that it "is commonly used as a term of abuse, not accurate description."[9]

---

7   Steven Best and Anthony J. Nocella II, "Appendix 3: Defining Terrorism," in *Terrorists or Freedom Fighters? Reflections on the Liberation of Animals*, ed. Steven Best and Anthony J. Nocella II (New York: Lantern Books, 2004), 361, 369–76.

8   ALF, "Introducing the Animal Liberation Front," in *Terrorists or Freedom Fighters? supra* n. 7, at 7 (reprinted from *The ALF Primer*) ("Take all necessary precautions against harming any animal, human and nonhuman."); *The ALF Primer*, http://animalliberationfront.com/ALFront/ALFPrime.htm#ALF%20Guidelines (noting that "the ALF does not, in any way, condone violence against any animal, human or nonhuman. Any action involving violence is by its definition not an ALF action, and any person involved is not an ALF member. [The principle of nonviolence] must be strictly adhered to. In over 20 years, and thousands of actions, nobody has ever been injured or killed in an ALF action.").

9   Interview by Sabahattin Atas with Noam Chomsky, Prof. of Linguistics and Philosophy, MIT (September 2003), http://www.chomsky.info/interviews/200309 --.htm.

Consistent with the prevalent with-us-or-against-us mentality,[10] the distinction "between good and bad varieties of terrorism...is determined by the *agent* of the crime, not its character."[11] This line of thinking has created a political climate rich in McCarthyite propaganda and ripe for unconstitutional legislation such as the AETA.

Animal Enterprise Protection Act

To better understand the AETA, one must first consider its predecessor, the Animal Enterprise Protection Act (AEPA),[12] and the legislative efforts leading to it. During the late 1980s and early 1990s, Representative Charles W. Stenholm (D-TX) tried repeatedly to enact federal legislation "to prevent, deter, and penalize crimes...against U.S. farmers, ranchers, food processors, and agricultural and biomedical researchers."[13] Representative Stenholm's attempts included the Farm Animal and Research Facilities Protection Act of 1989 (House Bill 3270), the Farm Animal and Research Facilities Protection Act of 1991 (House Bill 2407 1H), and the Animal Rights Terrorism Act of 1992 (House Bill 2407 RH).[14] These bills, designed to amend the Food Security Act of 1985,[15] offered steep penalties, required no element of interstate travel, and included provisions for a private right of action by animal facility owners.[16] None was enacted into law.

Prior to the passage of the AEPA, a number of states already had laws in place that "specifically criminalized economic sabotage by animal

---

10   President George W. Bush, "Address to a Joint Session of Congress and the American People" (Sept. 20, 2001), http://www.whitehouse.gov/news/releases/2001/09/20010920-8.html. ("Either you are with us, or you are with the terrorists.").

11   Interview, *supra* n. 9 (emphasis added).

12   Animal Enterprise Protection Act of 1992, 18 U.S.C. § 43 (2000) (enacted Aug. 26, 1992; amended by Public Law No. 109-374) [hereinafter, AEPA].

13   135 Cong. Rec. E3079 (daily ed. Sept. 19, 1989) (statement of Hon. Charles W. Stenholm).

14   H.R. 3270, 101st Cong., 1st Sess. (Sept. 13, 1989); H.R. 2407, 102nd Cong., 2nd Sess. (May 20, 1991).

15   135 Cong. Rec. E3079; Food Security Act of 1985, 7 U.S.C. § 1281 (2006) (1985 amendment to the Agricultural Adjustment Act of 1938).

16   *Id.* at E3080.

liberators."[17] In fact, Paul L. Maloney, the Deputy Assistant Attorney General for the DOJ's Criminal Division, testified in 1990 that the DOJ "[could] not endorse the creation of new federal legislation which, in [the DOJ's] view, would add nothing to the prosecution of [animal rights motivated] offenses."[18] Nevertheless, on March 5, 1991, Senator Howell Heflin (D-AL) introduced Senate Bill 544, which ultimately passed in lieu of related House Bill 2407 and was signed into law on August 26, 1992 as the AEPA.[19] Congress amended the AEPA's restitution provisions in 1996[20] and increased its maximum penalties in 2002.[21]

The AEPA created a special offense—beyond existing criminal provisions—for any person traveling or using the mail in "interstate or foreign commerce...for the purpose of causing a *physical* disruption to the functioning of an animal enterprise."[22] Penalties included fines and the possibility of imprisonment, ranging from a maximum of one year to life.[23] However, it soon became clear that these provisions were not enough to satisfy certain special interest groups.

In 2003, the American Legislative Exchange Council (ALEC)—supported by tobacco, petroleum, pharmaceutical, and transportation companies—proposed new model legislation targeting animal and environmental advocates.[24] This proposed legislation, known as the Animal and

---

17 Laura G. Kniaz, *Animal Liberation and the Law: Animals Board the Underground Railroad*, 43 Buff. L. Rev. 765, 818, n. 296 (Winter 1995).

18 *Id.* at 819 (quoting testimony from the Animal Research Facility Protection: Joint Hearing Before the Subcommittee on Department Operations, Research, and Foreign Agriculture and the Subcommittee on Livestock, Dairy, and Poultry of the House Committee on Agriculture, 101st Cong., 2d Sess. 2 (Feb. 28, 1990).

19 Sen. 544, 102nd Cong., 1st Sess. (March 5, 1991).

20 AEPA, 18 U.S.C. § 43 (as amended by Pub. L. No. 104-294 (1996)); Will Potter, "Animal Enterprise Protection Act" (July 29, 2006), http://www .greenisthenewred.com/blog/aepa/.

21 AEPA, 18 U.S.C.A. § 43 (Supp. IV 2006) (as amended by Pub. L. No. 107-188, title III, § 336).

22 *Id.* at § 43(a)(1) (emphasis added).

23 *Id.* at §§ 43(a)–(c).

24 For a comprehensive analysis of ALEC's failed legislation, see Andrew N. Ireland Moore, *Caging Animal Advocates' Political Freedoms: The Unconstitutionality of the Animal and Ecological Terrorism Act*, 11 *Animal L.* 255 (2005); American Legislative Exchange Council, "Animal Rights and Ecological Terrorism Act

Ecological Terrorism Act, was flawed in many of the same ways as the AETA. In 2004, the FBI testified before the Senate Judiciary Committee, claiming the need for stronger legislation to protect against secondary and tertiary targeting of animal enterprises.[25] Attempting to justify this alleged need, the FBI pointed to Stop Huntingdon Animal Cruelty (SHAC), an animal advocacy group maintaining a website that reported on direct actions—both legal and illegal—taken by independent third parties against companies doing business with Huntingdon Life Sciences, a notorious animal testing facility.[26]

Animal Enterprise Terrorism Act

In November 2006, the FBI got what it wanted.[27] Following two unsuccessful related bills,[28] Senator James M. Inhofe (R-OK) introduced Senate Bill 3880—now the AETA—to amend and rectify purported gaps and loopholes in the existing AEPA.[29] The AETA served the primary func-

---

Fact Sheet," http://www.alec.org/2/criminal-justice/animal-rights-and-ecological -terrorism-act.html (proposing that the bill addresses "forms of terror" committed in the name of animal rights and does not inhibit one's right to speak or protest); see also Press Release, American Legislative Exchange Council, "ALEC Offers Legislation to Fight Domestic Terror by Animal and Eco-Extremist Groups: 'Let's Call a Terrorist, a "Terrorist,"' Says ALEC" (September 13, 2003), http://www.alec.org/news/press-releases/press-releases-2003/september/alec -offers-legislation-to-fight-domestic-terror-by-animal-rights-and-eco-extremist -groups.html (offering ALEC's position that legislation will assist in fighting acts of what they deemed to be domestic terror by animal rights groups).

25 Senate Judiciary Committee, "Animal Rights: Activism vs. Criminality. Statement of John E. Lewis, Deputy Assistant Director, Counterterrorism Division. Federal Bureau of Investigation," (May 18, 2004), http://judiciary .senate.gov/testimony.cfm?id=1196&wit_id=3460.

26 Id.

27 Pub. L. No 109-374, 120 Stat. 2652 (2006) (amended AEPA, changed title to AETA).

28 Sen. 1926, 109th Cong. (Oct. 27, 2005) (sponsored by Senator James M. Inhofe (R-OK); not enacted into law); H.R. 4239, 109th Cong. (Nov. 4, 2005) (sponsored by Representative Thomas E. Petri (R-WI); not enacted into law).

29 As noted in Will Potter's testimony at the May 23, 2006 (H.R. 4239), the DOJ emphasized how its "hands [we]re tied" from protecting the targets of animal rights advocates under existing law, but failed to mention the successful prosecution and conviction of the SHAC 7 only months earlier using the very law it now claimed was inadequate. Will Potter, "An Analysis of the Animal Enterprise Terrorism Act," http://www.greenisthenewred.com/blog/aeta-analysis-109th/ (Oct. 10, 2006).

tion of expanding the AEPA to cover secondary and tertiary targets, such as family members or any "person or entity having a connection to, or relationship with, or [business] transactions with an animal enterprise."[30] It also disproportionately increases penalties and permanently brands alleged perpetrators—even those who are *not* accused of instilling fear, inflicting bodily injury, or causing any economic damage—as terrorists.[31]

The AETA was strongly supported by industry-backed advocacy groups such as ALEC,[32] the Center for Consumer Freedom (CFC),[33] and the United States Sportsmen's Alliance (USSA).[34] However, the driving force behind the AETA was the Animal Enterprise Protection Coalition (AEPC).[35] Founded by the National Association of Biomedical Researchers (NABR),[36] the AEPC comprises a multitude of deep-pocketed animal-exploiting industries, including furriers, ranchers, hunters, biomedical researchers, rodeos, circuses, and pharmaceutical companies.[37] Another staunch supporter of the AETA is the ironically named National Animal Interest Alliance (NAIA) and its counterpart, the NAIA Trust, which "was created in order to focus more resources on influencing legislation and defending the victims of animal and environmental extremism."[38]

---

30   120 Stat. at 2653–2654 (amending 18 U.S.C.A. § 43(a)(2)(A)).

31   *See id.* at § 43(b)(1) (penalties apply "if the offense does not instill in another the reasonable fear of serious bodily injury or death").

32   Press Release, National Lawyers Guild, *National Lawyers Guild Opposes Animal Enterprise Terrorism Act* (Oct. 30, 2006), http://www.nlg.org/news/statements /AETA_Act.htm.

33   Center for Consumer Freedom, *New Law Scares the Animal Rights Fringe. It Should.,* www.consumerfreedom.com/news_detail.cfm?headline=3179 (Nov. 14, 2006).

34   U.S. Sportsmen's Alliance, *Federal Bills Crack Down on Animal Rights Terrorism,* www.ussportsmen.org/ Read1.cfm?ID=1825&programdocs=AH (July 24, 2006).

35   National Association for Biomedical Research, *Animal Enterprise Protection Coalition,* www.nabr.org/AEPC/OnePager.htm.

36   *Id.*

37   Fur Commission. USA, *Animal Enterprise Protection Coalition: Supporting Groups,* www.furcommission.com/resource/pressSFbills.htm.

38   "Our members are pet owners, dog and cat clubs, obedience clubs and rescue groups as well as breeders, trainers, veterinarians, research scientists, farmers, fishermen, hunters and wildlife biologists. The membership roster of NAIA includes some of America's most respected animal professionals, advocates and enthusiasts," www.naiaonline.org/about/index.htm.

The NAIA Trust "advances the well-being of animals [yes, you read that correctly] and the rights of responsible animal owners by . . . urging passage of strong laws that target vandalism, harassment, arson, bombing, and *other types of domestic terrorism* committed in the name of animal rights and environmentalism."[39] Members of AEPC and NAIA have a vested financial interest—as the types of enterprises afforded unprecedented special protection under the AETA—as well as the resources and political clout necessary to push legislation like the AETA through Congress.

On the other side of the field—voicing direct opposition to the AETA—stands a very different coalition. The Equal Justice Alliance (EJA), formed in response to this legislative assault on animal advocates, lists more than 250 social advocacy groups that are allied with the EJA in their opposition to the AETA.[40] Despite opposition from these hundreds of groups and concerned individuals, the controversial AETA was stealthily pushed through the House of Representatives with minimal debate and passed by a voice vote of only five representatives on November 13, 2006.[41] Ironically, this vote took place mere hours after a groundbreaking ceremony for a national memorial honoring Martin Luther King, Jr., during which congressional representatives praised King's once-controversial civil rights tactics—similar to those currently employed by animal advocates—as "good [and] necessary trouble."[42] The AETA was officially signed into law later that month on November 27, 2006.[43]

---

39   National Animal Interest Alliamce. www.naiatrust.org/ (emphasis added).

40   Equal Justice Alliance, "AETA Opposition List," http://noaeta.org/allies.htm. The Equal Justice Alliance continues to monitor the application of the AETA and fight for its repeal. *Id.*

41   Will Potter, "Animal Enterprise Terrorism Act Signed into Law," 27:2 *Earth First! J.* 8, 8–9 (Jan. 2007), www.earthfirstjournal.org/article.php?id=1&PHPSESSID =ab319fd6fbce5fdc0c7fe92af6cde736. Congressman and 2008 presidential candidate Dennis Kucinich (D-OH) provided the only voice of dissent. *See* Equal Justice Alliance, *AETA Report*, http://www.noaeta.org/report .htm (Nov. 13, 2006) (eye witness account of Kucinich's participation by Dr. Alex Hershaft, founder of Farm Animal Rights Movement).

42   Public Broadcasting Service, "Thousands Attend Groundbreaking for MLK Memorial: Leaders Reflect on King's Work," http://www.pbs.org/newshour/bb /social_issues/july-dec06/mlk_11-13.html (Nov. 13, 2006).

43   120 Stat. (amending 18 U.S.C.A. § 43).

Perhaps most disconcerting is the lack of leadership demonstrated by the American Civil Liberties Union (ACLU) on this matter. While groups like the National Lawyers Guild and the Center for Constitutional Rights spoke out—and continue to speak out—vehemently against the AETA,[44] the ACLU wavered between supporting and opposing the bill. Initially, the ACLU strongly urged Congress to oppose the AETA, citing numerous flaws in earlier versions of the bill.[45] Several months later, the ACLU withdrew its opposition, while simultaneously continuing to express several serious concerns.[46] Not surprisingly, the changes recommended by the ACLU were not incorporated into the final version of the bill.[47] After the House vote, but before the AETA was signed into law, the ACLU stated that it "did not and does not support the AETA [and] that expanding [the AEPA] was unnecessary."[48] Rather than formally reinstating its opposition, the ACLU merely noted that it was "disappointed" with the final version of the AETA and would monitor its application in the future.[49] Quite possibly, the ACLU's silence on this issue gave a green light for the "Green Scare,"[50] allowing an unconstitutional and unnecessary piece of legislation to be signed into federal law with the seeming endorsement of the ACLU. To date, there appears to be no mention of the AETA on the ACLU website beyond the 2006 comments referenced above.

---

44 Press Release, *supra* n. 32.

45 ACLU, "ACLU Letter to Congress Urging Opposition to the Animal Enterprise Act, S. 1926 and H.R. 4239," http://aclu.org/freespeech/gen/25620leg20060306 .html (Mar. 6, 2006).

46 Letter from Caroline Fredrickson, Director, Washington Legislative Office ACLU and Marvin J. Johnson, Legislative Counsel ACLU, to Hon. F. James Sensenbrenner, Jr., Chairman, H. Jud. Comm. and Hon. John Conyers, Jr., Ranking Member, H. Jud. Comm., "ACLU Urges Needed Minor Changes to AETA, But Does Not Oppose Bill (S. 3880, the 'Animal Enterprise Terrorism Act')," 1 (Oct. 30, 2006); www.aclu.org/images/general/asset_upload_file809_27356.pdf.

47 E-mail from ACLU, *RE: S 3880 (LTK6907566704X)* (Nov. 20, 2006, 9:32 A.M. EDT).

48 *Id.*

49 *Id.*

50 Potter, *supra* n. 41.

CASE STUDIES

After the AETA's enactment, the NABR proclaimed that "today, the AETA provides greater protection for the biomedical research community and their families against intimidation and harassment...."[51] Just over two years after the AETA's enactment, the government made its first arrest of animal activists under the AETA in the state of California. Since that time, several indictments—and subsequent convictions—have followed in Utah, Iowa, and Colorado. These cases are discussed next.

The AETA 4

In February 2009, four California activists—now known as the AETA 4—were arrested and charged with two felonies: (1) "Conspiracy" (interestingly, this count was charged under 18 U.S.C. § 371, *not* under the AETA's conspiracy provisions), and (2) "Force, violence, and threats involving animal enterprises."[52] These felonies each carry maximum penalties of five years in prison and/or a $250,000 fine with up to three years of supervised release.

The AETA 4—Joseph Buddenberg, Maryam Khajavi, Nathan Pope, and Adriana Stumpo—were alleged to have participated in protests on public sidewalks outside the homes of biomedical researchers from roughly October 2007 through July 2008. The affidavit of FBI Special Agent Lisa Shaffer states that protestors made "threats" such as ringing doorbells and chanting with a bullhorn: "1, 2, 3, 4, open up the cage door; 5, 6, 7, 8, smash the locks and liberate; 9, 10, 11, 12, vivisectors go to hell," which apparently were used to justify some vivisectors and their family members claiming "reasonable fear of death...and serious bodily injury." The AETA 4 also allegedly left a stack of about thirty flyers at Café Pergolesi in Santa Cruz entitled "Murderers and torturers alive and well in Santa Cruz, July 2008 edition." These flyers included the names and addresses of thirteen biomedical researchers, eleven of which were allegedly found online using

---

51 NABR, "Animal Enterprise Terrorism Act (AETA)," www.nabr.org/PB2Col. aspx?pageid=135.

52 Indictment at 1, *U.S. v. Joseph Buddenberg, Maryam Khajavi, Nathan Pope A/K/A Nathan Knoerl, and Adriana Stumpo*, No. CR-09-00263 (U.S. District Court for the Northern District of California, Oct. 28, 2009).

a pay-for-use Internet terminal at a Kinko's in Santa Cruz. Interestingly, since the AETA 4 did not physically cross state lines, this Internet usage appears to be the "facility of interstate commerce" hook that was necessary to pull the case under federal AETA jurisdiction.

The indictment and bill of particulars included allegations such as "threats, trespass, vandalism, harassment, and intimidation" (all of which were already crimes prior to the AETA's enactment), but neither provided any specific examples of prohibited conduct despite references to alleged Kinko's Internet research and leafleting at Café Pergolesi. This lack of detail understandably left the AETA 4—as it would any reasonable person—confused about exactly which element of their protected First Amendment speech was being labeled as illegal. Did the use of sidewalk chalk constitute criminal vandalism? Did chanting slogans or ringing doorbells constitute acts of federal terrorism, and if so, which slogans? What precisely had they done that was so terrible it could rise to that level and carry such steep penalties?

Fortunately, United States District Judge Ronald M. Whyte agreed that the government had an obligation to provide these details, and the court dismissed the indictment in July 2010 for lack of factual specificity. The court noted that "in order for an indictment to fulfill its constitutional purposes, it must allege facts that sufficiently inform each defendant of what it is that he or she is alleged to have done that constitutes a crime. This is particularly important where the species of behavior in question spans a wide spectrum from criminal conduct to constitutionally protected political protest. While 'true threats' enjoy no First Amendment protection, *picketing and political protest are at the very core of what is protected by the First Amendment.*"[53]

The good news is that each member of the AETA 4 is currently free, rather than sitting in a federal prison. However, this story does not have an entirely happy ending, because the dismissal was made without prejudice, meaning that the government could seek to reindict the AETA 4 at any time. About six weeks after the dismissal was

---

53 Order Dismissing Indictment Without Prejudice and Denying as Moot Other Pending Motions at 8, *U.S. v. Joseph Buddenberg, Maryam Khajavi, Nathan Pope A/K/A Nathan Knoerl, and Adriana Stumpo*, No. CR-09-00263 (U.S. District Court for the Northern District of California, July 12, 2010) (emphasis added).

handed down, the FBI issued a warrant for a DNA sample from Joseph Buddenberg, which could mean that the government is still attempting to gather evidence and build a case against the AETA 4. At the time of this writing, reindictment has not been sought—but the possibility still exists and the threat remains real.

The AETA 2

In March 2009, right on the heels of the AETA 4 arrest, two Utah activists—now known as the AETA 2—were indicted under the AETA for: (1) "damag[ing] and interfer[ing] with animal enterprises," and (2) "attempt[ing] to intentionally damage" an animal enterprise.[54] The first count is a felony carrying a maximum penalty of five years in prison and/or a $250,000 fine with up to three years of supervised release. The second count is a misdemeanor with a maximum penalty of one year in prison and/or a $100,000 fine.

With regard to the first count, the AETA 2—William James (BJ) Viehl and Alex Jason Hall—were alleged to have released mink from McMullin Mink Farm and destroyed breeding documents, resulting in damage and a loss of real and personal property that exceeded $10,000. The second count alleged an attempted raid of Blackridge Mink Farm. This count is particularly interesting, because the mink farmers claimed to have been terrorized and placed in fear of bodily harm; but in this case, one of the owners, Ms. Mathews, was out driving around her property alone at 4:00 A.M. when she allegedly spotted the AETA 2 driving nearby. Ms. Mathews chased them down, and when they pulled over, she got out of her car and confronted them by herself, which begs the question, how frightened could she have possibly been? It is arguable that most reasonable people, when confronted with true terrorism in the dark of night, would not be quite so bold. Far more likely is the assumption that Ms. Mathews' only true fear was a loss of profits.

In July 2009, Viehl filed a motion to dismiss for lack of federal jurisdiction, but the court maintained that the jurisdictional element was met by the use of phone lines. Similar to the AETA 4, there was no assertion that the AETA 2 had physically crossed state lines. Instead, the federal hook

54 Indictment at 1-2, *U.S. v. William James Viehl and Alex Jason Hall*, No. 2:09-CR-00119 (U.S. District Court, District of Utah, Central Division, Mar. 4, 2009).

in this case appears to have been the use of mobile phones as instruments of interstate commerce, a theory that the prosecution based on cell tower triangulation records. These records allegedly placed the AETA 2—or at least their mobile phones—in the general vicinity of the McMullin Mink Farm around the time of the release, and this was enough to pull the case under federal AETA jurisdiction and prosecute the two as terrorists.

Perhaps motivated by the fear of a politically and religiously biased jury deciding his fate, Viehl ultimately signed a plea agreement. In exchange for Viehl pleading guilty to the felony count of intentional damage to an animal enterprise, the government agreed to move for dismissal of the second misdemeanor count, recommend a $70,000 cap on restitution, and recommend that Viehl be sentenced on the low end of the guidelines (six months). The plea agreement would have no negative impact on Viehl's codefendant, Hall, who at that time was still planning to go to trial. Unfortunately, things did not exactly go as planned in court. The prosecutor did "recommend" a six-month sentence, as promised, but then proceeded to put on an elaborate performance for the court, including slide shows and speeches from crying mink farmers, which was designed to paint Viehl in the worst light possible. This villainization of the AETA 2—who were not charged with threatening or harassing anyone, or with even a suggestion of any violent act, but merely for releasing mink and destroying records—resulted in the judge deciding that six months was far too short a sentence for someone who had "terrorized" a family of law-abiding citizens. In February 2010, Viehl was sentenced to twenty-four months in federal prison—four times the recommended sentence—along with $66,753 in restitution. Hall ultimately decided against going to trial and signed a similar plea agreement to Viehl's. In June 2010, Hall was sentenced to twenty-one months in federal prison and required to split the restitution payments with Viehl.

In September 2010, Viehl was released from FCI Terminal Island in San Pedro, California, and a few months later, in January 2011, Hall was released from FCI Englewood in Littleton, Colorado. The good news is that they are now back at home with their loved ones. The bad news is that they will remain on probation for another two to two and a half years and must maintain steady restitution payments in order to remain in compliance with their probation terms. They have also been permanently branded as terrorists and served time in federal prison for felony convictions, which seems an unbelievably harsh and exaggerated penalty to pay for the entirely nonviolent crimes they allegedly committed.

Scott DeMuth

In November 2009 through April 2010, the government issued yet another round of indictments under the AETA, this time to a Minnesota-based activist named Scott Ryan DeMuth. DeMuth was charged with "conspiracy... for the purpose of causing and attempting to cause, physical disruption to the functioning of [several] animal enterprises... to intentionally damage and cause the loss of property, including, but not limited to, animals, computers, and records... and cause economic damage to the animal enterprises in an amount exceeding $10,000."[55]

DeMuth was alleged to have participated in a 2004 ALF raid of Spence Laboratories at the University of Iowa, for which he would have traveled across state lines, thus securing federal jurisdiction under the AETA. DeMuth also allegedly used "the mail and other facilities in interstate or foreign commerce, including the internet [sic] and electronic mail,"[56] which would likely be enough on its own to satisfy the interstate commerce requirement of the AETA. In addition to the 2004 raid, DeMuth was accused of releasing ferrets in 2006 from Lakeside Ferrets, Inc. in Minnesota and knowingly and intentionally conspiring against "other animal enterprises elsewhere."[57]

In September 2010, the day before his case was scheduled to go to trial, DeMuth signed a plea agreement "admit[ting] that he conspired to disrupt and damage Lakeside Ferrets, Inc."[58] In February 2011, in exchange for DeMuth "plead[ing] guilty to a lesser included offense charged in Count 1, that is, [c]onspiracy to commit animal enterprise terrorism," he was sentenced to six months in federal prison, a $5,000

---

55 Second Superseding Indictment at 1, *U.S. v. Scott Ryan Demuth*, No. 3:09-CR-117 (U.S. District Court, Southern District of Iowa, Apr. 13, 2010).

56 *Id.*

57 *Id.*

58 Plea Agreement at 1, *U.S. v. Scott Ryan Demuth*, No. 3:09-CR-117 (U.S. District Court, Southern District of Iowa, Sept. 13, 2010).

fine, and a year of supervised release.[59] DeMuth was released from prison in July 2011 and subsequently completed his supervised release.

Walter Bond (a.k.a. "Lone Wolf")

In July 2010, Utah activist Walter Bond—also known as the ALF "Lone Wolf"—was indicted in Colorado and charged with two crimes: (1) "Use of fire or explosives to damage and destroy property in interstate commerce" (this count was charged under 18 U.S.C. §844(i), *not* under the AETA), and (2) "Force, violence and threats involving animal enterprises" under the AETA.[60] Both are felonies, with the first count carrying maximum penalties of five to twenty years in prison and/or a $250,000 fine with five years of supervised release, and the second (AETA) count carrying maximum penalties of ten years in prison and/or a $250,000 fine with three years of supervised release.

Bond was accused of "maliciously damag[ing] and destroy[ing]" the Sheepskin Factory in Glendale, Colorado by burning the building to the ground in April 2010.[61] According to Bond's support website, he was turned in by his own brother in a sting operation.[62] The AETA interstate commerce hooks included "specifically travel[ing] into Colorado" and "using his phone to coordinate the logistics and communication of his purpose to damage and interfere with the operations of the Sheepskin Factory."[63] Bond also allegedly "used a stolen library card to access the internet and communicated via web sites, sending his information to a party in Florida to have it posted."[64]

The initial complaint, which predated Bond's indictment by only four days, included only the first non-AETA count of Arson of Property

---

59   Id.

60   Indictment at 1, *U.S. v. Walter Edmund Bond*, No. 1:10-CR-00389 (U.S. District Court, District of Colorado, July 27, 2010).

61   Id.

62   Walter Bond, "Final Statement to the Court (Utah)," (Oct. 13, 2011), http://supportwalter.org/SW/index.php/2011/10/13/final-statement-to-the-court-utah/.

63   Plea Agreement at 6, *U.S. v. Walter Edmund Bond*, No. 1:10-CR-00389 (U.S. District Court, District of Colorado, Nov. 18, 2010).

64   Id.

Affecting Interstate Commerce. The AETA count almost seems to have been pulled into the indictment as an afterthought. This is particularly interesting, because a press release issued by the DOJ in February 2011 includes a quote from U.S. Attorney John Walsh, stating that: "[Bond's] claimed 'cause' is mere pretext: The evidence in this case demonstrates that he has a history of committing crimes involving fire before he ever began advocating animal rights."[65] Regardless of whether there is any truth to this assertion, it begs the question—if the government truly believed the animal rights cause to be "mere pretext," why would it then choose to prosecute Bond under the AETA in addition to the arson law, which should have been sufficient to gain a conviction?

In November 2010, Bond signed a plea agreement, and he pled guilty the following day in court to counts 1 and 2 of the Colorado indictment. In exchange, he received a three-point reduction in offense level for the purpose of sentencing based on his "acceptance of responsibility."[66] Despite questioning the court's morality, denying any remorse, and referring to burning down the Sheepskin Factory as "the proudest and most powerful thing [he has] ever done" in his final statement at the February 2011 sentencing, Bond received the minimum allowable sentence: five years in prison. He was also sentenced to three years of probation and ordered to pay $1,170,253.18 in restitution.[67] Importantly, Bond's final statement to the court pointed out that he had taken specific precautions "to not harm any person or bystander," although he noted that he doubted the court was interested in hearing this.[68]

In September 2010, nearly two months after the Colorado indictment and while those proceedings were still underway, Bond was also indicted in Utah and charged with four felony counts which were essentially the

65 The United States Attorney's Office—District of Colorado, "Walter Bond Sentenced to Federal Prison for the Arson at the Sheepskin Factory in Glendale," (Feb. 11, 2011), www.justice.gov/usao/co/news/2011/February2011/2_11c_10.html.

66 Plea Agreement at 8, *U.S. v. Walter Edmund Bond*, No. 1:10-CR-00389 (U.S. District Court, District of Colorado, November 18, 2010).

67 The United States Attorney's Office—District of Colorado, "Walter Bond Sentenced to Federal Prison for the Arson at the Sheepskin Factory in Glendale," (Feb. 11, 2011), www.justice.gov/usao/co/news/2011/February2011/2_11c_10.html.

68 Walter Bond, "Final Statement to the Court (Utah)," (October 13, 2011), http://supportwalter.org/SW/index.php/2011/10/13/final-statement-to-the-court-utah/.

same as the Colorado charges: (1) "Use of fire or explosives to damage and destroy property in interstate commerce" (non-AETA), and (2) "Force, violence and threats involving animal enterprises" (AETA).[69] Each of the above counts was charged twice—once for the alleged arson of Tandy Leather Factory Store in Salt Lake City, Utah and once for the alleged arson of a foie gras restaurant called Tiburon Fine Dining in Sandy, Utah.

Bond was ultimately sentenced to eighty-seven months in prison for the Utah charges, totaling more than twelve years in prison when run consecutively with his Colorado sentencing.[70] He is currently serving his sentence at the United States Penitentiary in Marion, Illinois in a Communication Management Unit (CMU), which is believed to be one of only two such units in the U.S. penitentiary system.[71] CMUs, which were created to "[limit] the communication opportunities of inmates charged with, convicted of, or detained in relation to terrorist related activity" are designed to "severely restrict[] ... all outside communication (telephone, mail, visitation) of inmates in the unit."[72] Purportedly, "most of the inmates are Arab Muslims."[73]

UNCONSTITUTIONALITY

Drafters of the AETA have gone to great lengths to reassure Congress and the public that the statute is, in fact, constitutional.[74] However, as Will Potter, a leading voice on the AETA, has so aptly pointed out, just

69 Indictment at 1, *U.S. v. Walter Edmund Bond*, No. 2:10-CR-00844 (U.S. District Court, District of Utah, Central Division, Sept. 15, 2010).

70 http://supportwalter.org/SW/index.php/2011/12/23/walter-bonds-exclusive-post-sentencing-interview/

71 *Id.*; "United States Penitentiary, Marion," Wikipedia, http://en.wikipedia.org/wiki/United_States_Penitentiary,_Marion.

72 "Limited Communication for Terrorist Inmates," Federal Register: Apr. 3, 2006 (Vol. 71, No. 63), www.thefederalregister.com/d.p/2006-04-03-E6-4766; and "Communication Management Unit," Wikipedia, http://en.wikipedia.org/wiki/Communication_Management_Unit.

73 "United States Penitentiary, Marion," Wikipedia, http://en.wikipedia.org/wiki/United_States_Penitentiary,_Marion.

74 120 Stat. at 2654 (amending 18 U.S.C.A. § 43(e)) ("Nothing in this section shall be construed ... to prohibit any expressive conduct ... protected ... by the First Amendment ... or to preempt State or local laws.").

because the AETA states "'this law is constitutional,' doesn't make it so. If anything, it's an admission that the bill has serious flaws."[75] The AETA is unconstitutional because it is impermissibly vague, overbroad, and based entirely on content and viewpoint.

In June 2009, the AETA 4 moved to dismiss the indictment against them on the grounds that the AETA is unconstitutional on its face, because it is impermissibly overbroad and vague. In October 2009, Judge Whyte denied the motion to dismiss due to an alleged lack of standing. Whyte stated that the AETA 4 could not challenge the constitutionality of sections of the AETA under which they had not been charged, and that the sections under which they had been charged were not facially unconstitutional. The court's order denying the defendants' motion to dismiss concluded, among other things, that:

- "Since §§ 43(a)(1) and (2)(B) do not cover a substantial amount of protected speech, they are not overbroad";
- Protected activity leading to a loss of profits was not criminally sanctioned in this case, because the AETA 4 had not been charged with any "economic damage," so there was no reason to consider whether the definition of this term was unconstitutionally vague;
- The word *interfere* in the AETA's required purpose of "interfering with an animal enterprise" has "such a clear, specific and well-known meaning" that it "does not render the statute unconstitutionally overbroad" or impermissibly vague;
- Although the statutory definition of "animal enterprise" is admittedly broad, it is not unclear; and
- The AETA is not a content-based restriction, because its prohibitions "do not cut cleanly through some ideological divide (i.e., pro-choice/ pro-life) nor is the restriction specific enough to pick out any particular viewpoint for disfavor (i.e., abortion, workers' rights, animal rights)."

Despite the ruling on this motion, the bottom line is that courts sometimes get it wrong, and this decision is one of those times. It exemplifies precisely why appellate courts exist—to review the findings of lower courts to determine whether there was sufficient evidence to

---

75   Potter, *supra* n. 41.

support the determination made and whether the lower courts correctly applied the law. The following pages will discuss several of the flaws inherent in the AETA that render it unconstitutional.

Vagueness Doctrine

As a matter of constitutional due process, laws must be drafted clearly; the language used must put the public on notice as to what specific conduct will trigger prosecution.[76] The vagueness doctrine is one facet of this notice requirement. Under the vagueness doctrine, a statute is unconstitutional and must be struck down if it fails to specify a standard of conduct, such that "men of common intelligence must necessarily guess at its meaning."[77] In *Coates v. City of Cincinnati,* the United States Supreme Court found invalid an ordinance prohibiting three or more people from assembling on a sidewalk and engaging in conduct that was "annoying" to others.[78] The court held that the ordinance was vague, because what "annoys some people does not annoy others."[79] Members of the public must not be left guessing at what is prohibited, but should be given fair warning and a precise description of the prohibited conduct, so that they may act accordingly.[80]

Similar to the word *annoying* in the *Coates* ordinance, the word "interfere" in the AETA subjects people to an unascertainable standard.[81] The potential for infringement of First Amendment rights calls for greater than usual clarity; however, the AETA does not define the term *interfere* or set forth in a precise manner what would trigger prosecution. The AEPA, prior to its amendment by the AETA, criminalized the *"physical disruption"* of an animal enterprise.[82] This language was expanded by the AETA to include not only physical disruption, but seemingly any

---

76   *Connally v. Gen. Constr. Co.*, 269 U.S. 385, 391 (1926).

77   *Coates v. City of Cincinnati*, 402 U.S. 611, 614 (1971) (quoting *Connally*, 269 U.S. at 391).

78   *Id.* at 611.

79   *Id.* at 614.

80   *Grayned v. City of Rockford*, 408 U.S. 104, 108 (1972).

81   *Coates*, 402 U.S. at 614.

82   AEPA, 18 U.S.C.A. § 43(a)(1) (emphasis added).

form of interference with an animal enterprise.[83] Four and a half years and a handful of indictments later, the question remains—what sort of conduct constitutes criminal "interference"? In the absence of any limiting construction or clarification, it is unrealistic to expect a reasonable person to understand exactly what conduct is prohibited.

The term *property* is also not defined by the AETA, creating another vagueness issue. The ACLU expressed concerns that the AETA's failure to specify "real or personal property" as "tangible" property could lead to prosecution based on intangibles, such as alleged lost profits or unquantifiable loss of business good will.[84] Such losses are the very goal—and a totally legitimate goal—of peaceful activities such as boycotts, protests, demonstrations, undercover investigations, and whistle-blowing. The ACLU noted that while lawful economic disruption is exempted in the penalty provisions of the AETA, an additional and explicit exemption from "the broad prohibition on 'the loss of any real or personal property'" is necessary to avoid infringement upon legitimate activities.[85]

In addition to the danger of "trap[ping] the innocent," the AETA's vagueness creates an opportunity for arbitrary and discriminatory enforcement.[86] When explicit standards are not provided in the language of a statute, upon whose discretion do those determinations rest? Who decides what constitutes interference or whether loss of business good will is a legitimate basis for prosecution? These policy judgment calls would be delegated to law enforcement officers, judges, and jurors, but such delegation is constitutionally impermissible due to its "ad hoc and subjective" nature.[87]

Overbreadth Doctrine

Even if the AETA were not vague, it would still be unconstitutional, because the act prohibits protected conduct.[88] Under the overbreadth

83 120 Stat. at 2652 (amending 18 U.S.C.A. § 43(a)(1)) ("for the purpose of damaging or interfering with the operations of an animal enterprise").

84 Ltr., *supra* n. 45, at 1–2.

85 Ltr., *supra* n. 45, at 2.

86 *Grayned*, 408 U.S. at 108.

87 *Id.* at 108–09.

88 *Id.* at 114.

doctrine, if a statute forbids the sort of expression that may not legally be regulated—expression protected by the First and Fourteenth Amendments of the United States Constitution, such as civil disobedience—it is considered overbroad, and, thus, void. Even Representative Robert Scott (D-VA), a strong proponent of the AETA, expressed concerns during a congressional hearing on an earlier version of the bill that civil disobedience could potentially be covered under the AETA.[89] Such concerns are not to be taken lightly.

There are two main ways in which the AETA is overbroad. First, the dictionary definition of "interference" covers a substantial amount of protected speech. Second, the term *animal enterprise* could be interpreted to include unlawful animal enterprises, as well as lawful ones.

First, courts often look to the common usage or dictionary definition of a term that is not defined by a statute.[90] "Interference" is commonly defined as "the act of meddling in another's affairs; an obstruction or hindrance."[91] The definition of "interfere" cited in Judge Whyte's order denying the AETA 4's motion to dismiss is to "oppose, intervene, hinder, or prevent." These definitions clearly reach a substantial amount of constitutionally protected speech, as they provide no limiting principle to "restrict the statute's reach only to speech that rises 'far above public inconvenience, annoyance, or unrest.'"[92] The danger of overbreadth is that it might lead people to refrain from the expression of valuable and constitutionally protected speech for fear of criminal sanctions, based

---

89 H.R. Subcomm. on Crime, Terrorism, and Homeland Security of the Comm. on the Jud., Comm. Jud., *Animal Enterprise Terrorism Act: Hearing on H.R. 4239, 109th Cong* 3 (May 23, 2006) http://judiciary.house.gov/media/pdfs/printers /109th/27742.pdf.

90 *Federal Deposit Insurance Corporation v. Meyer,* 510 U.S. 471, 476 (1993); Ronald Benton Brown and Sharon Jacobs Brown, "Statutory Interpretation: The Search for Legislative Intent," 38–40 (National Institute for Trial Advocacy 2002).

91 *Black's Law Dictionary* 831 (Bryan A. Garner, ed., 8th ed., West 2004).

92 ACLU, *Brief of Amicus Curiae American Civil Liberties Union in Support of Appellant* at 7, *Cmmw. Pa. v. Haagensen* (Dec. 28, 2005) (quoting *Terminello v. Chicago,* 337 U.S. 1, 4 (1949) ("Speech is often provocative and challenging.... [But it] is nevertheless protected against censorship or punishment, unless shown likely to produce a clear and present danger of a serious substantive evil that rises far above public inconvenience, annoyance, or unrest.") [hereinafter *Amicus Brief*].

on uncertainty as to whether the AETA could reach their expression and fear of prosecution for alleged terrorism.

Second, under the AETA, an "animal enterprise" is defined to include virtually any business that uses or sells animals or animal products in any way and for any purpose.[93] This definition, coupled with the fact that remote second and third parties have now been folded into the statute,[94] effectively means that anyone with any connection to a business using animals in any way is afforded special protection. The long list of protected animal enterprises not only includes grocery stores, restaurants, clothing stores, and the usual suspects—factory farms, furriers, laboratories, rodeos, and circuses—but could also be interpreted to mandate the protection of *unlawful* animal enterprises from interference by concerned persons. The ACLU cautions that, in an earlier version of the act, a person who rescues an animal before an illegal animal fighting event could be charged as a terrorist under the AETA.[95] Despite modifications specifying the protection of *"lawful* competitive animal event[s]," the AETA remains overbroad, because it does not make clear that interference with other unlawful animal enterprises does not trigger the statute.[96]

Content and Viewpoint Basis

"If there is a bedrock principle underlying the First Amendment, it is that the government may not prohibit the expression of an idea simply because society finds the idea offensive or disagreeable."[97] The First Amendment forbids government regulation of speech when the rationale for restriction is based on the speaker's "ideology[,] opinion

---

93 *See* 120 Stat. at 2653 (amending 18 U.S.C.A. § 43(d)(1)) (including an entity that is a "commercial or academic enterprise," "zoo, aquarium, animal shelter, pet store, breeder, furrier, circus, or rodeo, or other lawful competitive animal event," and any event "intended to advance agricultural arts and sciences").

94 *Id.* at 2652 (amending § 43(a)(2)(A)).

95 Ltr., *supra* n. 47, at 2.

96 *Id.*

97 *Texas v. Johnson,* 491 U.S. 397, 414 (1989); *Hill v. Colorado,* 530 U.S. 703, 716 (2000) ("The right to free speech, of course, includes the right to attempt to persuade others to change their views, and may not be curtailed simply because the speaker's message may be offensive to his audience.").

or perspective."[98] The danger inherent in favoring one viewpoint at the expense of another is that doing so permits the government to "effectively drive certain ideas or viewpoints from the marketplace."[99] The AETA indisputably singles out animal advocates based upon their ideology and seeks to suppress a particular point of view. As such, the AETA is presumptively invalid.[100]

When contrasted with other politically motivated crimes—especially those involving actual violence against people—the singling out of animal advocates based on viewpoint becomes particularly evident. For example, it is well documented that anti-abortion activists have threatened, injured, and even *murdered* doctors for performing abortions.[101] Congress's response to these violent and sometimes deadly crimes was to enact the Freedom of Access to Clinic Entrances Act (FACE).[102] Under FACE, first-time offenders who cause no bodily injury may receive up to six months imprisonment.[103] Meanwhile, their nonviolent counterparts under the AETA are inexplicably subject to *twice* the potential imprisonment—up to one year.[104] The only difference here is the ideology behind the crimes.

Unlike animal advocates, anti-abortion activists—who have a history of violence and murder—have not been labeled by the government as "terrorists." One must wonder why a statute designed to prosecute violent activists was given such a benign name. Why was FACE not entitled the Abortion Clinic Terrorism Act? The word *terrorism* was certainly being tossed about at that time.[105] FACE was enacted two years

---

98 U.S. Constitution Amendment I; *Rosenberger v. Rector & Visitors U. Va.*, 515 U.S. 819, 829 (1995).

99 *Members City Council v. Taxpayers Vincent*, 466 U.S. 789, 804 (1984); *Amicus Brief*, supra n. 94, at 14 (quoting *Simon & Schuster, Inc. v. Members St. Crime Victims Bd.*, 502 U.S. 105, 116 (1991).

100 *R.A.V. v. City of St. Paul, Minn.*, 505 U.S. 377, 382 (1992).

101 Frederick Clarkson, "Anti-Abortion Violence: Two Decades of Arson, Bombs and Murder," Southern Poverty Law Center Intelligence Report (summer 1998), www.splcenter.org/intel/intelreport/article.jsp?aid=411.

102 Freedom of Access to Clinic Entrances Act of 1994, 18 U.S.C. § 248 (2000).

103 *Id.* at § 248(b)(1).

104 120 Stat. at 2652 (amending 18 U.S.C.A. § 43(b)(1)).

105 *See* Tamar Lewin, "Clinic Firebombed in Pennsylvania," *The New York Times*

after the original AEPA, which even then was placed in its own newly created statutory category of "Animal Enterprise Terrorism."[106]

The answer to this question is simple: the AETA was specifically designed to target and suppress the viewpoints of animal advocates. There is no better way to stifle dissent and drive a viewpoint from the marketplace than to brand its proponents as terrorists. While a person who murders an abortion doctor is not labeled a "terrorist," a person who spray-paints the word *murderer* on a fur store window without harming a single person could be convicted under a federal terrorism statute and thus placed on par with the perpetrators of such atrocities as the Oklahoma City bombing, the Atlanta Olympic Park bombing, or 9/11.

Even perpetrators of hate crimes have been protected against laws that would single them out for their beliefs. In *R.A.V. v. City of St. Paul, Minnesota,* the Supreme Court found a local hate crime ordinance facially invalid on the basis of content discrimination.[107] In *R.A.V.,* a group of teenagers accused of burning a cross in the fenced yard of an African American family was punished under the St. Paul Bias-Motivated Crime Ordinance.[108] This ordinance prohibited any act designed to arouse "anger, alarm or resentment . . . on the basis of race, color, creed, religion or gender."[109] While hate crimes are undeniably repugnant, other laws existed in this case—such as those dealing with arson and trespass—that would have been sufficient for prosecution.[110] While understanding

---

(Sept. 30, 1999) (reporting that the president of Planned Parenthood demanded that the U.S. Attorney General classify violent attacks on abortion clinics as domestic terrorism); *see also* Douglas Jehl, "Iran-Backed Terrorists Are Growing More Aggressive, U.S. Warns," *The New York Times* (Mar. 18, 1993), http://query.nytimes.com/gst/fullpage.html?res=9F0CE4D61638F93BA2575 0C0A965958260 (reporting that U.S. officials feared Iranian militant groups represented the greatest threat of a likely increase in terrorism around the world).

106 Pub. L. No. 102-346, § 2(a), 106 Stat. 928 (1992) ("IN GENERAL.--Title 18, United States Code, is amended by inserting after section 42 the following: '§ 43. Animal enterprise terrorism'"). Upon amendment by the AETA, section 43 was renamed "Force, violence, and threats involving animal enterprises," and the word *terrorism* was shifted into the very title of the act. 18 U.S.C.A. § 43.

107 *R.A.V.,* 505 U.S. at 377.

108 *Id.* at 380.

109 *Id.*

110 *Id.* at 379–80.

the city's desire to communicate that it did not condone hate crimes, the court, nonetheless, held that this desire "does not justify selectively silencing speech on the basis of its content" and struck the ordinance down as unconstitutional.[111]

Valid constitutional legislation must examine the criminality of an act, rather than the motivation behind it. "Nonverbal expressive activity can be banned because of the action it entails, but *not* because of the ideas it expresses—so that burning a flag in violation of an ordinance against outdoor fires could be punishable, whereas burning a flag in violation of an ordinance against dishonoring the flag is not."[112]

Consider, for example, an angry woman who crosses state lines or uses the Internet or her cell phone to facilitate the acts of releasing mink from her husband's fur farm, destroying breeding cards and computers, and spray-painting the word *adulterer* on the wall—all intended to cause him financial harm—after learning that her husband had been having an affair. She would likely be charged under *state* law for crimes such as trespass, property destruction, theft, and/ or vandalism. But if that same woman was driven by an ideological opposition to the unbelievably cruel methods of raising and killing innocent mink for their fur—rather than an emotional reaction to her husband's infidelity—and had spray-painted the acronym "ALF" or the phrase "No More Mink, No More Murder" on the wall instead of the word *adulterer*, she would undoubtedly be branded a terrorist and prosecuted under the *federal* AETA with amped-up penalties for committing the exact same crimes.

Every offense listed in the AETA is already an established state or federal crime. The only thing rendering the AETA unique from existing laws is its focus on the ideological motivation behind the crimes. The AETA adds nothing other than an element of special protection for animal enterprises and new criminal penalties based solely on the philosophy and beliefs of the accused. The AETA is entirely content- and viewpoint-based, and thus in direct violation of the First Amendment.

---

111   *Id.* at 378.

112   Ireland Moore, *supra* n. 24, at 267 (quoting *R.A.V.*, 505 U.S. at 385) (emphasis added).

OTHER FLAWS

In addition to being unconstitutional, the AETA contains numerous social policy flaws. First, the AETA solely regulates crimes which are already covered under existing laws and removes them from state or local jurisdiction to federal jurisdiction. Second, the act diverts limited resources and efforts that might otherwise be directed toward fighting true terrorism. Third, the AETA was designed to stigmatize animal advocacy and generate a chilling effect within the movement. Fourth, it impedes the investigation of animal enterprises that have repeatedly violated existing animal protection laws.

Crimes Covered under Existing Laws

In March 2006, the ACLU stated that the AETA is "unnecessary because federal criminal laws already provide a wide range of punishments for unlawful activities targeting animal enterprises."[113] Animal enterprises could easily invoke existing laws for protection against any of the crimes covered by the AETA, and this is true in all of the case studies cited above. The AETA encompasses such crimes as trespass, property damage, property destruction, arson, theft, vandalism, harassment, intimidation, criminal assault, and even murder—a violent crime which has never once been committed in the name of animal activism—as well as conspiring or attempting to commit any of these offenses.[114] In doing so, the AETA both improperly intrudes upon state and local government jurisdiction and imposes enhanced and disproportionate penalties based solely on the motivation behind the crime. Even Representative Scott, a staunch supporter of the AETA, has acknowledged that people who, for example, sit or lie down to block traffic into a facility already run the risk of arrest under existing laws, and thus "should not be held any more accountable for business losses...than anyone else guilty of such activities."[115]

---

113 Ltr., *supra* n. 45. (While this letter refers to earlier versions of the AETA, the ACLU's position is no less applicable, because it was directed at the bill as a whole, not individual provisions).

114 120 Stat. at 2652 (amending 18 U.S.C.A. § 43(a)(2)).

115 Comm. Jud., *supra* n. 89, at 3.

Proponents of the AETA, such as Representative Thomas Petri (R-WI), claimed that existing laws were inadequate to provide protection to animal enterprises,[116] despite the fact that the AEPA had recently been used to successfully prosecute members of SHAC for merely running a website or organizing demonstrations.[117] As a result of this prosecution, six nonviolent, aboveground animal activists—not one of whom was charged with actual trespass or property destruction, let alone harming or attempting to harm any living being—have been permanently branded as terrorists and have served federal prison sentences.[118] Disappointingly, the United States Supreme Court denied certiorari, which means that it has refused to hear the SHAC case, so the appellate court ruling stands.[119]

"Governments have a legitimate and rational basis for regulating [criminal] activity in order to protect their citizens. Regulations and prohibitions, however, should be entirely based on the offender's conduct rather than the actor's politics or moral beliefs."[120] Under no circumstances does the conduct of nonviolent activists warrant such exaggerated and disproportionate punishment. The SHAC activists, for example, were merely engaging in what many would properly consider protected speech on the Internet. Perhaps the sole exception to "regulating [criminal] activity" based on conduct rather than beliefs is that the AETA now seeks to criminalize legal activity—the First Amendment right to free speech.

True Terrorism

Rather than combating true terrorism, it is arguable that "inequitable and oppressive laws" such as the AETA may actually "propel pacifists into action, as depicted in the movie *Catch a Fire*."[121] *Catch a Fire* tells the

---

116 Potter, *supra* n. 41.

117 DOJ, "Militant Animal Rights Group, Six Members Convicted in Campaign to Terrorize Company, Employees and Others" (Mar. 2, 2006), http://newark.fbi.gov/dojpressrel/2006/nk030206usa.htm.

118 *Id.*; The SHAC 7 Support Fund, *The SHAC 7*, www.shac7.com/case.htm#ssc.

119 *Kevin Kjonaas et al. v. United States*, www.supremecourt.gov/orders/courtorders/030711zor.pdf.

120 Ireland Moore, *supra* n. 24, at 278.

121 Charlotte Laws, PhD, "AETA and the New Green Scare: Are You the Terrorist

true story of a man falsely accused of bombing an oil refinery during apartheid in 1980.[122] By falsely labeling this innocent man a terrorist, the South African government ultimately "wakes him up to injustice and ignites him into action," essentially creating a rebel fighter where none would otherwise have existed.[123]

Whether this analogy will hold true for those accused of terrorism under the AETA remains to be seen. Regardless, treating nonviolent animal advocates as terrorists does a complete disservice to the public, as it inspires unwarranted fear and imposes a misdirected burden on law enforcement agencies competing for limited resources, and thus detracting from efforts to combat true terrorism. The resources available for this purpose should not be exhausted in pursuit of nonviolent activists who pose no threat to the community.

The fact that it has become socially acceptable to draw comparisons between vegetarian advocacy groups and the Taliban is a clear indication that things have gone awry.[124] In 2005, President Barack Obama, who was at that time Senator Obama (D-IL), stated that he did "not want people to think that the threat from [animal rights] organizations is equivalent to other crimes faced by Americans every day."[125] Citing the FBI's own statistics, Obama pointed out the vast discrepancy between hate crimes (over 7,400 in 2003) and crimes motivated by animal rights ideology (approximately 60 in 2004).[126]

Next Door?" (Jan. 26, 2007), Counterpunch, http://www.counterpunch.org/laws01262007.html.

122 Id.; *Catch a Fire* (Mirage Enterprises 2006) (motion picture).

123 Laws, *supra* n. 121.

124 Ethan Carson Eddy, *Privatizing the Patriot Act: The Criminalization of Environmental and Animal Protectionists as Terrorists*, 22 Pace Envtl. L. Rev. 261, 326, n. 315 (2005) (discussing the fact that Veronika Atkins, widow of Dr. Atkins, creator of the Atkins diet, directly compared a pro-vegetarian health advocacy group to the Taliban during a Feb. 20, 2004 episode of *Dateline*).

125 Senate Committee on Environment and Public Works Hearing: Statement of Senator Barack Obama. "Oversight on Eco-terrorism Specifically Examining the Earth Liberation Front ("ELF") and the Animal Liberation Front ("ALF")," (May 18, 2005), http://epw.senate.gov/hearing_statements.cfm?id=237833.

126 Id.

The Southern Poverty Law Center (SPLC), a group that monitors hate crimes and extremist activity,[127] has stated that labeling animal rights advocates as the "No. 1 threat" to the American public is "simply ludicrous."[128] The SPLC acknowledges that no deaths have resulted from animal rights activism, and certainly "nothing on the terror scale of Oklahoma City or the 1996 Olympics has been committed."[129] All too familiar with the dangers of right-wing extremist groups known to kill police officers and hundreds, if not thousands, of innocent people, it seems as though the SPLC would prefer to see domestic anti-terrorism resources and energies focused on true terrorists, such as the Ku Klux Klan; anti-Semitic, anti-homosexual, and other hate groups; anti-government radicals; and other violent extremists who actually pose a threat to society.[130] Such a focus would undoubtedly be a better use of the FBI's time and money, and would serve to protect the public from true threats of domestic terrorism.

Scaremongering

In an era in which a Disney-like children's movie about saving endangered owls is deemed "'soft-core eco-terrorism' for kids," people are understandably on edge.[131] The AETA was designed to further this scaremongering, sending a powerful message to aboveground activists—watch your step, or you, too, might be convicted of terrorism. Due in large part to its vagueness and overbreadth, the AETA has, as predicted, already begun to "chill and deter Americans from exercising their First Amendment rights

---

127 Southern Poverty Law Center. "About the Center: Advocates for Justice and Equality," www.splcenter.org/center/about.jsp.

128 Henry Schuster, "Domestic Terror: Who's Most Dangerous? Eco-terrorists Are Now above Ultra-right Extremists on the FBI Charts," (Aug. 24, 2005), www.cnn.com/2005/US/08/24/schuster.column/; Chris Maag, "America's #1 Threat," *Mother Jones* (Jan./Feb. 2006), www.motherjones.com/news/outfront/2006/01/america_no1_threat.html.

129 *Id.*

130 *Id.*

131 Marc Morano, "New Movie Called 'Soft Core Eco-terrorism' for Kids," (May 1, 2006), http://www.cnsnews.com/ViewSpecialReports.asp?Page=/SpecialReports/archive/200605/SPE20060501a.html.

to advocate for reforms in the treatment of animals."[132] This chilling effect has been documented by Potter:[133] "Through my interviews with grass-roots animal rights activists, national organizations, and their attorneys, I have heard widespread fears that the word *terrorist* could one day be turned against them, even though they use legal tactics."[134]

In a 2006 press release, the DOJ falsely vilified SHAC activists by referring to them as transients and "thugs [who] engage in . . . violence."[135] Not one of these individuals was charged with a violent crime, but their reputations have now been permanently stained thanks to the DOJ's deceitful choice of words. Such tactics, combined with the fear inspired by the AETA itself, have certainly given activists a reason for pause and concern. No rational person wants to risk being labeled a "thug" and a "terrorist" by the United States government. Thus, the exercise of con-stitutionally protected speech has been put on hold by many, as people scramble to interpret this vague and overbroad statute and guess at what it means and how it might be applied to them. The fact that animal advocates have additionally been singled out for potential federal crimi-nal wiretapping[136] or upward departure from existing federal sentencing guidelines[137] understandably adds to the existing tension.

It has long been understood by the Supreme Court that legislation of this nature serves to deter protected speech.[138] "Many persons, rather

---

132 Ltr., *supra* n. 45.

133 Will Potter, "Bio" (Apr. 20, 2006), http://www.greenisthenewred.com/blog/bio/.

134 Comm. Jud., *supra* n. 89, at 26.

135 Press Release, *supra* n. 117.

136 Pub. L. No 109-177, 120 Stat. 192, 209 (2006) (amending 18 U.S.C. § 2516(1)(c) (2000) to authorize the "interception of wire or oral communications" by the FBI "when such interception *may provide . . . evidence* of . . . any offense which is punishable under the [AETA]") (emphasis added).

137 18 U.S.C.S. § 2B1.1 (Lexis 2007), Commentary, § 19(A)(ii) ("An upward depar-ture [from existing federal sentencing guidelines] would also be warranted, for example, in a case involving *animal enterprise terrorism* under 18 U.S.C.A. 43, if, in the course of the offense, serious bodily injury or death resulted, or substantial scientific research or information were destroyed") (emphasis added).

138 *See Grayned*, 408 U.S. at 108–09 (1972) ("Uncertain meanings inevitably lead citizens to [']steer far wider of the unlawful zone' . . . than if the boundaries of the forbidden areas were clearly marked.'" (quoting *Bagget v. Bullit*, 377 U.S. 360, 377 (1964)).

than undertake the considerable burden (and sometimes risk) of vindicating their rights through case-by-case litigation, will choose simply to abstain from protected speech, harming not only themselves but society as a whole, which is deprived of an uninhibited marketplace of ideas."[139] The "social costs caused by the withholding of protected speech" are both unacceptable and unquantifiable.[140] Moreover, people who are inclined to commit crimes such as arson, trespass, or property destruction will not likely be deterred by the AETA, as these activities were already crimes prior to its enactment.

The real targets of this legislation are aboveground activists who seek to abide by the law. In this respect, the AETA hampers the flow of ideas throughout the marketplace to the detriment of society as a whole, as activists seek to avoid the disgrace, ostracism, and potential legal ramifications that go along with being labeled a "terrorist." To be sure, a certain amount of stigma exists simply for association with someone who has been branded a terrorist. As a result, people who are sympathetic to animal rights views are encouraged to distance themselves from animal advocates for fear of guilt by association.

Obstruction of Justice

Finally, the AETA encumbers the investigation of animal enterprises that violate existing animal protection laws by making it difficult or impossible for concerned groups or individuals to lawfully obtain incriminating evidence against them. While the AETA excludes from its definition of "economic damage" disruptions resulting from "lawful public, governmental, or business reaction to the disclosure of information about an animal enterprise," it essentially criminalizes any activity that might produce such information—such as whistle-blowing and undercover investigations—by failing to provide explicit exemptions for these activities.[141]

Whistle-blowers and undercover investigators are not "terrorists," nor should they be given any reason to fear being so labeled simply for

---

139 *Virginia v. Hicks*, 539 U.S. 113, 119 (2003).

140 *Id.* at 119.

141 120 Stat. at 2654 (amending 18 U.S.C.A. § 43(d)(3)(B)).

speaking out against animal cruelty witnessed in the workplace. No other industry is afforded this sort of special protection, and there is no justification for it. Industry's profit interests should not be allowed to supersede the pursuit of justice or the First Amendment right to free speech.

Conclusion

The AETA is unconstitutional, redundant, and riddled with social policy flaws, and should be struck down by the courts in its entirety. Concerned individuals should strive to educate the public on the AETA's inherent dangers, while simultaneously lobbying federal attorneys not to prosecute under this unconstitutional law and pursuing its immediate repeal.

This article was originally published in the *Animal Law Review* 14, no. 1 (2007). It has since been substantially revised and updated, with the addition of relevant case studies. It should be noted, too, that most of the original formatting has been maintained to reflect the legalese of the law journal. This chapter is therefore formatted differently than the others.

WHO IS THE REAL "TERRORIST"?

Dara Lovitz

THE "TERRORIST" LABEL

In the decade following the 1995 Oklahoma City bombing, about sixty right-wing terrorist attacks occurred in the United States. Each year in the United States there are approximately 191,000 hate crimes, 85 percent of which involve violence. None of these has been perpetrated to further nonhuman rights. There are well over 900 active hate groups in the United States; these groups espouse anti-Semitic and white supremacist ideologies while committing violent crimes such as rapes, beatings, bombings, and execution-style murders. But it is not these violent hate groups that seem to cause primary concern for the federal government. Instead, the main focus of the federal government's anti–domestic terrorism campaign is animal rights and environmental activists.

There is no universally accepted definition of *terrorism*. Federal law alone now contains at least nineteen definitions of the term. Federal agencies such as the FBI, Department of Defense, and Department of Justice differ in their definitions of terrorism. The definition of terrorism has become even more cryptic since the events of September 11, 2001. Indeed, a new vocabulary emerged from that tragedy, including global buzzwords like "axis of evil" and "global war on terrorism."

Whether one labels another a terrorist typically depends on whether one sympathizes with or opposes the cause that the other champions. In other words, whether the speaker identifies with the victim or the actor will affect whether the speaker labels the act "terrorism," hence the saying "one man's terrorist is another man's freedom fighter." The government's efforts to combat terrorism are crafted to serve its particular political agendas. Regimes commonly label as "terrorist" those who oppose their rule. For instance, the Jewish underground in Palestine was described as a terrorist group until the 1930s and early 1940s when they gained a reputation as "Zionist freedom fighters." Meanwhile, during the Third Reich, Nazis referred to resistance groups opposing Germany's occupation of their countries as terrorists.

Menachem Begin, Israel's prime minister from 1977 to 1983 and Nobel Peace Prize winner, was labeled a "terrorist" by British authorities in the 1940s while he was protesting British policy in the country then known as Palestine. Notably, Yitzhak Shamir, the prime minister who succeeded Begin, had also been labeled a "terrorist" by the British. In Algeria in the 1950s, the National Liberation Front's terrorist attacks against the ruling French regime resulted in their independence. The assessment of the event was later called the "Battle of Algiers" and the "Algerian Revolution." During the time of the American Revolution, although the term hadn't existed yet, the acts of colonists against King George III could certainly have been considered *terrorism*, as would have the economic sabotage perpetrated by the American Patriots during the Boston Tea Party.

The relativity of the term is also an example of an us-versus-them attitude. In other words, what *we* do is valid rebellion for self-defense or independence, while what *they* do is terrorism. The United States government has certainly justified its own military offensives, such as the bombing of Hiroshima and Nagasaki, while condemning those perpetrated by other, politically hostile countries.

Animal Activists Do Not Fit the Profile of So-Called Terrorists

As philosopher and psychoanalyst Erich Fromm stated: "The successful revolutionary is a statesman, the unsuccessful one a criminal" (1994, 258). It is no surprise, then, that the groups who espouse the relatively unpopular philosophy of animal rights have been called terrorists. Examination of the standard characteristics of terrorists reveals, however, that animal activists simply do not fit the terrorist mold.

The word *terrorism* is undeniably pejorative. Although there are several long and varying definitions of the term, a consensus among scholars exists that terrorism is one or more acts of violence against innocent persons with the intent to cause fear in a particular group in order to advance a political or ideological agenda. Violence, therefore, requires the element of physical injury to innocent persons, rather than to property. As expressed by Bruce Hoffman, chair of counterterrorism and counterinsurgency at the RAND corporation, terrorists are "committed to using force" to obtain their objectives (Howard and Sawyer 2006, 20). Political scientist Cynthia Combs also considers violence a definitive component of terrorism: "The capacity and the willingness to commit a violent act *must* be present" [emphasis added] (2003, 10). In sharp contrast to terrorists, animal activists seek a nonviolent world, and to free nonhuman animals from human violence. In fact, research indicates that *opponents* of nonhuman rights are more likely than proponents to approve of interpersonal violence. As animal liberationist and environmentalist Rod Coronado has stated:

> If animal rights activists started justifying violence to supposedly *prevent* violence, we would lose our moral high ground and join the ranks of so many others on both sides of the law who also kill and maim in order to supposedly fight for peace....Targeting property was our modus operandi. Targeting people? Never. (Kuipers 2009, 279)

The animal liberationist magazine *No Compromise* has recommended that animal activists pursue the following nonviolent endeavors:

1. Work as a Humane Educator in area schools
2. Leaflet, leaflet, leaflet!
3. Wear compassion on your sleeve (or backpack or shirt)
4. Host a vegan dinner party
5. Make a library display
6. Promote animal rights on cable-access TV
7. Get involved with local community groups
8. Set up an information table
9. Write letters for the animals
10. Make requests at grocery stores and restaurants for vegan foods. (Top Ten 2005, 13)

It should be clear that such activities are in no way terrorism and that more aggressive tactics such as sit-ins and walkouts are similarly not terrorist acts.

The Animal Liberation Front (ALF), regarded by government agencies as an extremist group responsible for several "terrorist attacks," has publicly declared its completely nonviolent guiding principles:

> 1) To liberate animals from places of abuse (e.g., laboratories, factory farms, and fur farms) and place them in good homes where they may live out their natural lives, free from suffering; 2) To inflict economic damage to those who profit from the misery and exploitation of animals; 3) To reveal the horror and atrocities committed against animals behind locked doors by performing *nonviolent* direct actions and liberations; 4) *To take all necessary precautions against harming any animal, human and nonhuman* (emphases added; "ALF Guidelines" 2005, 30).

In fact, the ALF's principles are so ostensibly peaceful that enemies of the animal activist movement had no choice but to completely manufacture and misrepresent the movement's mission in its dishonest smear campaign. The American Legislative Exchange Council (ALEC), a powerful lobbying organization that represents various corporations, including tobacco companies, oil companies, agribusiness trade associations, private corrections facilities, pharmaceutical manufacturers, and the National Rifle Association, published a report titled "Animal and Ecological Terrorism in America" in 2003 which sought to incite fear about the animal rights "extremists." In citing the "terrorist" ALF guiding principles, however, the report conspicuously omitted the entire fourth principle that referenced taking all necessary precaution against harming humans. The report also listed the third principle as "To reveal the horrors and atrocities committed against animals behind locked doors" (omitting the remainder of the principle, *by performing nonviolent direct actions and liberations*).

In addition to being violent, the typical terrorist has a conspiratorial cell structure and typically influences its members through fear and intimidation. Animal activist groups, on the other hand, tend to organize around productive dialogue and positive reinforcement.

The most combative inner community interactions usually involve a difference of opinion as to what the best strategy for change is, manifesting itself in a contentious essay battle on the Internet. Fear and intimidation simply have no place in progressive animal activist leaders' handbooks.

Terrorists deliberately attack innocent civilians by way of an unannounced bombing or hostage situations. According to terrorism scholar Martha Crenshaw, terrorists take hostages because the government's greater strength and resources apparently are not an advantage when bargaining with the terrorist for the hostage's release (Howard and Sawyer 2006, 63). It is the intentional targeting of innocent civilians that distinguishes terrorism from other types of government-sanctioned warfare. As terrorism specialist at the Library of Congress Audrey Cronin has noted: "The fact that precision-guided missiles sometimes go astray and kill innocent civilians is a tragic use of force [by some state governments], but it is not terrorism" (Howard and Sawyer 2006, 69). Indeed, rules of international military behavior offer maximum protection to the innocent civilian; terrorists, on the other hand, persistently and deliberately try to harm that type of person.

In contrast, animal activists do not condone attacks on innocents. All individuals targeted for protest, property damage, or other economic damage are directly or indirectly involved in the abuse of nonhuman animals. These individuals are not random and therefore would not necessarily be considered by terrorism scholars to be "innocent" as it is they who further the cruel practices against animals. Further, such an attack on the wallet cannot reasonably be compared to an attack that threatens the personal safety of civilians who have no involvement in the terrorist's agenda other than being in the wrong place at the wrong time. Again, it is the opponents of nonhuman rights, like vivisectors, who target innocent individuals: their nonhuman victims who were bred or captured and thrown into the wrong place at the wrong time.

While terrorist attacks might involve property damage, the focus is usually on harming persons. Animal activists, on the other hand, focus on demonstrations and boycotts. Even the most extreme animal activists target property, such as destroying equipment used to torture animals. But again, the intent is to save nonhuman animals, not to harm humans. By damaging the tools of torture used by vivisectionists, nonhuman animals are given some reprieve from the suffering while the industry figures out how or whether to replace the equipment. In some instances, the particular house of animal abuse will discontinue operations when the cost to rebuild does not justify the minimal profit the business was making from the animals. Of course, this only tends to be the case with smaller, independently owned companies like fur/skin farms.

A more recent trend among terrorists in the past twenty years has been the goal of inflicting mass casualties. Former deputy chief of the Counterterrorist Center at the CIA Paul Pillar calculated that although the number of terrorist incidents from the first half of the 1990s to the second half declined 19 percent, the number of deaths resulting from such acts doubled (Howard and Sawyer 2006, 30). Terrorists achieve these widespread results using chemical, biological, radiological, or nuclear weapons (known as "CBRN terrorism"). Animal activists employ no CBRN terror methods, and, again, have no goal of injuring any persons, let alone large numbers of them.

In sum, animal activists fit neither the scholar's nor the government's definition of "terrorists," yet that label is repeatedly pasted onto animal activists. The label is a public relations ploy designed to marginalize, silence, and even imprison animal activists. Public relations campaigns against animal activists are an important investment of time and money for industries whose profit arises out of animal abuse. Such campaigns, even when they don't involve the word *terrorist*, nonetheless seek to discredit animal activists. For example, the American Medical Association's *Animal Research Action Plan* implores its readers to publicly "identify animal rights activists as anti-science and against medical progress" (Blum 1995, 145). The government and media (funded by businesses with a vested interest in maintaining nonhuman exploitation) have been exploiting the public's fear of real terrorism—especially post-9/11—to create a universal (and unfounded) fear and dislike of animal activists.

If Terrorism Is Violence-Based, Then These Are Among the Most Dangerous Terrorists

Again, according to the government's own experts, violence is a necessary component of terrorism. But violence should not be defined only by human victims. What about violence against nonhuman animals? Animal industries deliberately, methodically, and regularly use force to inflict violence against innocent nonhuman animals with no means of escape or legal protection. These industries harm and kill billions of nonhuman animals a year only to advance their own economic agendas. Thus, if terrorism is violence against innocents, then the following non-exhaustive list of industries should be the focus of any effective anti-terrorism investigation.

Agricultural Confinement Facilities or "Animal Farms"

Intensive confinement facilities have been created to enable the animal-agriculture sector of the food industry to make the most amount of money with the least amount of cost. These systems are known as "factory farms" because they operate in the same manner as other commodity-producing factories: cages are stacked one upon another, animals (the products) are stuffed into the cages with almost every square inch filled up by body mass, and conveyor belts zoom by at every turn. Every act of cruelty is ostensibly perpetrated to increase efficiency. To increase the production of eggs, for instance, hens are shocked into molting so that they all molt at the same time for the convenience and profit of the egg facility. The temperature and lighting are artificially altered and the hens are kept on an extremely low-calorie diet. To decrease the likelihood that birds peck one another, which naturally results when birds become stressed in highly crowded conditions, farmers use a hot blade to slice through sensitive tissue in order to sear off up to half of their beaks. This is so painful that immediately following the process many birds stop eating and starve to death.

The "product" has also been "improved" over time. Breeders seek to increase production numbers at low cost. Currently, more than nine billion chickens are killed for meat every year. Poultry breeders have developed a chicken, also known as a "broiler," that can grow to a market weight of five pounds in seven weeks or fewer; prior to this, a typical bird would grow to a maximum of three pounds in about fourteen weeks. Chicken farms typically subject birds to approximately twenty-three hours of artificial light per day, which is thought to make them grow more expeditiously. Egg-laying hens have been genetically modified as well: the "layer" produces twice as many eggs per year than her ancestor hen. After years of inbreeding for rapid growth, both broilers and layers suffer heart disease, organ failure, and crippling leg deformities.

Housing has been made very efficient. Up to 20,000 broilers and turkeys live crowded in a single building, standing in their own urine- and feces-saturated litter, from which they develop foot ulcers and disease. Whereas hens of the past roamed outside and eliminated waste on natural grounds, the most efficient means of egg production is to stuff the hens into wire cages. The wire structure allows manure to fall to the ground below or, as is more frequently the case, onto the heads of the hens stacked in cages below. Because housing large numbers of animals indoors is such an efficient way to raise animals, the industry enjoys this innovation of waste "removal." Wire cages and slatted floors (for hoofed animals) allow the farmers to keep the animals under strict production schedules while obviating the need for frequent manure removal.

There is waste other than manure that needs to be eliminated. Birds that are bred to lay eggs are obviously a different strain than birds bred to become chicken meat for human consumption. Male chicks that are produced as a result of the layer-breeding process are a complete waste to a factory farm: they cannot lay eggs because of their gender, but their size and flesh are not considered by industry standards to be appropriate for broiler chickens whose flesh is sold as meat. If they don't lay and they cannot be eaten, what's a facility to do with these chicks? The answer typically depends on the size of the facility: smaller hatcheries throw the live chicks into large plastic bags and suffocate, starve, or crush them; larger hatcheries tend to use either gas asphyxiation or "macerators," which pulverize them alive.

Most pigs are intensively confined and breathe high amounts of ammonia, which significantly harms their respiratory health. Typically, a breeding sow is impregnated via artificial insemination delivered with a forceful thrust of an "AI rod." They are confined in "gestation crates," which are stalls so narrow that the pigs cannot turn around or move enough to groom themselves. For their entire four-month gestation periods, sows are confined to these cramped cages in which they cannot satisfy natural urges such as socializing, foraging, or building a nest. Immediately before birth, sows are moved to "farrowing crates," which provide just enough room for them to eat, drink, and expose their teats to suckling piglets. The piglets have their teeth cut, tails chopped off, and the male piglets are castrated with a knife or razor blade. The piglets receive no painkiller for any of these procedures.

Dairy cows are typically tied to a stall on a dirt or concrete lot, which creates claw horn overgrowth, predisposing the claw to ulcers. The cows are hosed down so infrequently that manure piles up around their legs. They are repeatedly impregnated so as to supply breast milk constantly. Many cows are injected with growth hormones, which dramatically increase milk production, but which cause cows to suffer metabolic disorders, lameness, and mastitis (inflammation of the udders due to bacterial infection). The impregnation schedule of dairy cows is such that the cows give birth to a calf on a yearly basis. Whereas the average cow could live to about twenty-five years, dairy cows who are repeatedly impregnated are spent by age four or five, at which point they are sent to slaughter. The calves are taken away from their mothers immediately following their births. The males are shipped off to another facility, either to be raised as beef cattle or veal, while the females are sent to follow fates similar to their mothers, as dairy cows who will be killed after four to five years. Cows raised for beef are crowded into feedlots where they have no choice but to consume a corn derivative or other high-energy grain. This processed grain causes havoc to cows' digestive systems, which are naturally built for a greater intake of roughage. These cows are also branded, their horns are amputated, and they are castrated without anesthetic.

Animals bred for human consumption are shipped to slaughter in conditions as horrific as those in which they were raised. They are crowded into trailers with wide openings and slats and so are vulnerable to weather extremes ranging from ice storms to sweltering humidity. The ride is extremely stressful for animals, especially those who have never been transported by vehicle before. The stress is both emotional (fear) and physical (vibrations, banging, rocking back and forth). Often, the transported animals are denied any food and water, such as when they are transported across the United States between Canada and Mexico; in those instances, drivers don't stop to feed them for fear of spreading diseases to American soil.

If the animal hasn't already died in transit, the direct and torturous path to slaughter begins. Cattle, for example, experience extreme stress in the time leading up to their deaths. They are starved at least twenty-four hours prior to slaughter, which reduces the stomach content and hence bacteria. As they near the killing area, they are surrounded by the overwhelming scent of blood. They start to bellow in fear, and stop in their tracks to avoid what they fear awaits them. The cattle are driven single file—forced forward with whips, shovels, or electric shocks delivered to their anus—until they are in the restraining chutes, in which they flail and try to break away. A slaughterer then shoots steel rods into the cattle's brains using a captive-bolt pistol pressured by air in an effort to render the cow insensible. The method is often ineffective such that the cows regain their sensibility and consciously experience the process of being knifed and bled to death.

In case your local Whole Foods Market has convinced you that local, organic, or "family-owned" animal farms are any different than the abusive factory farms, be aware that many of the above referenced cruel practices (such as beak searing, male chick maceration, forced insemination, and slaughter) also take place on such animal farms. The main distinctions among animal farms—e.g. factory, organic, and family-owned—depend on the different number of animals in the facility.

Aquaculture

The horrors of factory farming are not limited to land animals. Sea animals, too, are subject to similarly cruel conditions that result from attempts to maximize profits while minimizing costs. Fish, such as tuna, are crowded into floating cages and are genetically engineered to grow larger and at much faster rates. They are subjected to large amounts of chemicals and contaminants such as mercury, flame retardant, industrial waste, sewage, and synthetic insecticides, which are also poisonous to human beings. Due to environmental stress and high stocking densities, fish, such as salmon and trout, become infested with sea lice that feast on their flesh. These marine parasites are difficult to control because their life cycles are much more complex than other aquatic life. Because of proliferating disease, any fish that escape pose a threat to wild native fish. Fish are forced to starve at least three to seven days prior to slaughter, leading to high preslaughter mortality rates. For those that survive, some are killed by being left to suffocate on bins of ice, while others are clubbed, gassed, or "brain-spiked" (to be rendered immobile) and then bled out or electrocuted.

Vivisection

Over one hundred million nonhuman animals annually are used in laboratory experiments worldwide, more than twenty-two million of them in the United States. These animals are the unwilling subjects of various experiments, whether for pharmaceutical drugs, household goods, or cosmetic products. Sometimes the experiments are not for a particular product at all, but for a surgical procedure or a study of bodily reactions to noxious stimuli. Vivisectors have performed the following experiments after developing, for instance, a hypothesis about how nonhuman animals might respond: forced rhesus monkeys to stay seated in chairs with their heads restrained and then placed them inside the inner frame of a multiaxis turntable and rotated them at varying high speeds; surgically inserted E. coli–infected clots into the peritonea of dogs; and induced alcohol addiction in cats—when the cat suffered withdrawal from the alcohol, the vivisectors lifted the cats by their tails, gave electric shocks, or injected chemicals directly into their brains.

"Entertainment" and "Sport"

There are several forms of animal use and abuse in the "entertainment" industry including zoos, circuses, rodeos, television, movies, hunting, stage performances, and pigeon shoots. Zoos are particularly noteworthy because they are a central aspect of our culture and history, so much so that schoolchildren are taken to them as part of annual field trip programs. We romanticize and legitimize these confinement facilities, but what takes place behind the stone walls and high fences is not so heartwarming.

A zoo is essentially a refugee camp for animals, many of whom were taken out of their natural, native habitats. These animals were transported great distances and confined in often barren enclosures that are both alien and often much smaller than their natural surroundings. Zoo animals cannot gather their own food, socialize with other animals, and develop the natural behaviors that their free counterparts do. Those animals who were bred in zoos and thus never lived in their natural habitat experience a different kind of deprivation. However, whether one is born into intensive confinement or forced into it later in life, it is still unsuitable.

Zoos are constructed to ensure that animals neither escape nor mix with one another. The most important consideration in the construction of a zoo, however, is that the animals are housed in a way that enables maximum visibility. While the cages and other confinement containers in which zoo animals are kept are profoundly unnatural for the animals, so is the extreme exposure that results from zoo architecture. Most of these animals lived in habitats far removed from metropolises and human-populated areas, so being in full view of humans at all times is unnerving.

Zoos simply cannot support the needs of the animals they hold captive, resulting in stress and high mortality rates. Animals held in captivity have substantially reduced life expectancies than their free counterparts. For instance, the mean life expectancy of elephants in zoos is fifteen years, while it is sixty to sixty-five years when living in the wild. A polar bear in the typical zoo is confined to an enclosure that is one-millionth the size of its natural home range (approximately 31,000 square miles); the intensive captivity results in repetitive pacing behaviors and an infant mortality rate of about 65 percent. Although zoos have claimed "improvements," the mortality rate hasn't significantly decreased in a century.

Pelt, Fur, and Skin Industry

Over forty species of animals are killed for their skin and fur. More than thirty million animals worldwide are trapped for fur each year, mostly by a steel-jaw leg-hold trap, which snaps shut when an animal steps on the trap's spring. More than eighty nations, excluding the United States, have banned the use of this trap. When the animal tries to escape, the trap cuts into the flesh of the animal, mutilating or severing a foot or limb. Trappers often fail to return to their traps promptly after setting them, leaving the animals to suffer starvation and dehydration for days before they are collected. Some animals chew their own flesh to escape; those who manage to escape typically perish soon after because of abscesses, blood loss, gangrene, hard tissue damage, or predators. Because traps cannot distinguish between those animals sought for fur and not, nontargeted animals often become ensnared.

Over forty million animals worldwide are bred, raised, and killed for their fur. Pelt industry confinement facilities (euphemistically known as "fur farms") breed chinchillas, fitches, foxes, minks, and rabbits. These animals spend their lives confined in small wire cages, which cause extreme stress and lead to repetitive, stereotypic behaviors and self-mutilation. Because facility operators don't want to ruin the animals' coats, they do not use traps. They employ less messy means, such as gassing or anal electrocution.

THE REAL TERRORISTS

It is not up for debate whether the above practices are cruel and violent. The question that should be asked is why the government is so intent on condoning, encouraging, protecting, and sponsoring these dangerous and violent industries. These nonhuman animals are the innocent ones. They are the true victims, not the industries who continuously terrorize them because of a distorted sense of economic entitlement.

Clearly, the animal activists' collective voice against nonviolence needs to be louder and more effective. We need to change the direction of the finger-pointing and show the government who the real *terrorists* are; because if terrorism is violence against innocents, then these industries are among the most dangerous terrorists.

REFERENCES

"ALF Guidelines." *No Compromise* 29 (2005): 30.

American Legislative Exchange Council. "Animal and Ecological Terrorism in America" (report). Washington, D.C.: American Legislative Exchange Council, 2003.

Blum, Deborah. *The Monkey Wars*. New York: Oxford University Press, 1995.

Combs, Cynthia. *Terrorism in the Twenty-First Century*. Charlotte: University of North Carolina Press, 2003.

Fromm, Erich. *Escape from Freedom*. New York: Henry Holt, 1994.

Howard, Russell and Reid Sawyer, eds. *Terrorism and Counterterrorism: Understanding the New Security Environment,* 2nd ed. Dubuque, Iowa: McGraw Hill Contemporary Learning Series, 2006.

Kuipers, Dean. *Operation Bite Back: Rod Coronado's War to Save American Wilderness*. New York: Bloomsbury, 2009.

"Top Ten Do-It-Yourself Animal Liberation Tips!" *No Compromise* 27 (Spring/Summer 2005): 13.

BIBLIOGRAPHY

The information cited about animal cruelty, particularly toward the end of the chapter, can be found in the following sources:

Beach, Marji, and Genevieve Sides. *The Emotional World of Farm Animals*. Vacaville, Calif.: Animal Place, 2007.

Becker, Howard C., PhD. "Animal Models of Alcohol Withdrawal." *Alcohol Research & Health* 24, no. 2 (2000): 105–13.

Cattle Network. "Milk Production and Cow Slaughter, and Near Term Effects of Sexed Semen Technology." http://www.cattlenetwork.com/Milk-Production---Cow-Slaughter----Near-Term-Effects-Of-Sexed-Semen-Technology/2009-1217/Article.aspx?oid=967981&fid=CN-MARKET_OUTLOOK-LDP&aid=760&Print=1.

Chipley, Abigail. "Furget about It." *Vegetarian Times* no. 281 (January, 2001): 17.

Clover, Charles. *The End of the Line: How Overfishing Is Changing the World and What We Eat*. Los Angeles: University of California Press, 2006.

Clubb, Ros, and Georgia Mason. "Animal Welfare: Captivity Effects on Wide-Ranging Carnivores." *Nature* 425 (2003): 473–74.

———. "A Review of the Welfare of Zoo Elephants in Europe." *A Report Commissioned by the RSPCA*. Oxford, U.K.: University of Oxford, 2003.

Cohen, Carl, and Tom Regan. *The Animal Rights Debate*. Lanham, Md.: Rowman & Littlefield, 2001.

Compassion Over Killing. "COK Investigation Exposes Farm Animal Suffering During Interstate Transport." Last updated July 15, 2005, www.cok.net/inv/interstate-transport.

Dunayer, Joan. *Animal Equality: Language and Liberation.* Derwood, Md.: Ryce Publishing, 2001.

FAO Corporate Document Repository—Agriculture and Consumer Protection. "Chapter 4: The Pig" in *A Manual for Primary Animal Health Care Worker.* Published 1994, www.fao.org/docrep/t0690e/t0690e06.htm.

FAO Corporate Document Repository—Agriculture and Consumer Protection. "Techniques and Hygiene Practices in Slaughtering and Meat Handling" in *Guidelines for Slaughtering Meat Cutting and Further Processing.* Published 1991, www.fao.org/DOCREP/004/T0279E/T0279E04.htm.

FAO Corporate Document Repository—Fisheries and Aquaculture Department. *Fishing with Traps and Pots.* Published 2001, ftp://ftp.fao.org/docrep/fao/003/x2590e/x2590e00.pdf.

FAO Corporate Document Repository—Regional Office for Asia and the Pacific. "Chapter 7: Slaughter of Livestock" in *Guidelines for Humane Handling, Transport and Slaughter of Livestock.* Published 2001, www.fao.org/DOCREP/003/X6909E/x6909e09.htm.

Garner, Robert. *Animals, Politics, and Morality.* Manchester: Manchester University Press, 1993.

Gillespie, James R., and Frank B. Flanders. *Modern Livestock and Poultry Production.* Clifton Park, N.Y.: Delmar Cengage Learning, 2009.

Girgen, Jen. "Constructing Animal Rights Activism As a Social Threat: Claims-Making in the New York Times and in Congressional Hearings" (doctoral dissertation). Tallahassee, FL: Florida State University College of Criminology and Criminal Justice. Last updated 2008, http://diginole.lib.fsu.edu/cgi/viewcontent.cgi?article=1714&context=etd.

Grandin, Temple. *Livestock Handling and Transport,* 3rd ed. Cambridge, Mass.: CABI, 2007.

———. "Return to Sensibility Problems After Penetrating Captive Bolt Stunning of Cattle in Commercial Beef Slaughter Plants. *Journal of American Veterinary Medical Association* 221 (2002): 1258–61.

Jahncke, Michael L., and Michael H. Schwarz. "Public, Animal, and Environmental Aquaculture Health Issues in Industrialized Countries." In *Public Animal and Environmental Aquaculture Health Issues,* edited by Michael Jahncke and E. Spencer Garrett, et al., 67–102. New York: John Wiley and Sons, 2002.

Jensen, Derrick, and Karen Tweedy-Holmes. *Thought to Exist in the Wild: Awakening from the Nightmare of Zoos.* Lanham, Md.: No Voice Unheard, 2007.

Mason, Jim, and Mary Finelli. "Brave New Farm?" In *In Defense of Animals: The Second Wave,* edited by Peter Singer, 104–22. Oxford, U.K.: Blackwell Publishing, 2006.

Masson, Jeffrey Moussaieff. *The Face on Your Plate: The Truth About Food.* New York: W. W. Norton & Company, 2009.

Mullan, Robert, and Garry Marvin. *Zoo Culture: The Book About Watching People Watch Animals,* 2nd ed. Champaign: University of Illinois Press, 1999.

Penn State College of Agricultural Sciences. "Effect of Flooring and Flooring Surfaces on Lameness Disorders in Dairy Cattle." Published November 13, 2008, www.extension.org/pages/Effect_of_Flooring_and_Flooring_Surfaces_on_Lameness_Disorders_in_Dairy_Cattle.

Rollin, Bernard E. *Farm Animal Welfare: Social, Bioethical, and Research Issues.* Ames: Iowa State Press, 2003.

Ryder, Richard D. "Speciesism in the Laboratory. In *In Defense of Animals: The Second Wave,* edited by Peter Singer, 87–103. Oxford, U.K.: Blackwell Publishing, 2006.

Scully, Matthew. *Dominion.* New York: St. Martin's Press, 2002.

Smith, Mark J., ed. *Thinking Through the Environment: A Reader.* New York: Routledge, 1999.

Straw, Barbara E., Jeffrey J. Zimmerman, Sylvia D'Allaire, and David J. Taylor, eds. *Diseases of Swine* (9th ed.). Oxford, U.K.: Wiley-Blackwell, 2006.

"United Egg Producers Animal Husbandry Guidelines for U.S. Egg Laying Flocks 2010 Edition." Last updated 2013, www.unitedegg.org/information/pdf/UEP_2010_Animal_Welfare_Guidelines.pdf.

United Poultry Concerns, Inc. "Debeaking." www.upc-online.org/merchandise/debeak_factsheet.html.

White, James E. *Contemporary Moral Problems.* Belmont, Calif.: Wadsworth, 2001.

KANGAROO COURT

ANALYZING THE 2006 "HEARING" ON THE AETA

Vasile Stanescu

In this chapter I provide a close rhetorical analysis of the May 23, 2006 congressional hearing that led to the passage of the Animal Enterprise Terrorism Act (AETA), signed into law on November 27, 2006 (this hearing is cited hereafter as *Animal Enterprise*, 2006). I argue that the intent of this law is to specifically criminalize acts of nonviolent civil disobedience committed by animal rights activism, including minor misdemeanors such as vandalism, whistle-blowing, and silly publicity stunts. In doing so, these activities become felony acts of "terrorism" that entail felony jail time. I also argue that while this hearing possessed the semblance of impartiality, it represented, in actuality, a "kangaroo court" that was deliberately orchestrated to construct *all* animal rights activists—even those not engaged in any criminal activity whatsoever—as "terrorists." Finally, I argue that this targeting of animal rights activists should matter even to those unconcerned with the rights or welfare of nonhuman animals since this law serves as a possible template to felonize illegal, but nonviolent, acts of civil disobedience for any group and for any reason.

FROM THE FARFPA TO THE AEPA

It is first necessary to provide some relevant background information to illustrate how this labeling of animal rights crime as "terrorism" represents such an effective, though false, rhetorical shift. The first law criminalizing specific activities by animal rights activists was originally proposed in 1989 by Representative Charles Stenholm (D-TX) in a bill neutrally entitled the Farm Animal and Research Facilities Protection Act of 1989 (FARFPA) (Guither 1998, 144). This bill possessed every legislative provision that was later added to the 1992 Animal Enterprise Protection ACT (AEPA), and it contained a majority of the provisions that would eventually become the 2006 Animal Enterprise Terrorism Act (AETA). But the 1989 bill does not use the word *terrorist*—neither in the bill itself nor in the numerous congressional hearings held on the bill (*House Report Parts 1* and *II* 1992). The bill was not even debated in a committee related to either crime or terrorism, but instead was proposed and debated solely in the Agriculture Committee of which Representative Stenholm was chair (ibid.). This seems to indicate that there was some understanding in this early bill that certain actions by animal rights activists may be illegal but do not warrant the title of "terrorism."

However, Representative Stenholm's bill *did* prove to be quite controversial for at least two reasons that led to its eventual failure: First, there was a fear of excessively federalizing crime (as opposed to leaving enforcement to the states); and second, there was a view that the bill represented only the provincial concerns of a narrow lobbying group, i.e., those companies engaged in "animal enterprises" such as factory farms or fur manufacturers. These twin bipartisan concerns managed to defeat FARFPA's passage in 1989. However, Representative Stenholm and the animal enterprise lobby were undeterred, and the next year they reintroduced a bill that was virtually identical to the one that had failed the year before. This "new" bill possessed, in essence, only one significant difference: animal rights activists and their actions were now discussed almost exclusively in terms of "terrorism" (ibid.). Indeed, there was even a separate amendment passed in the Judiciary Committee to add the word *terrorism* into the act, a change that enabled the still controversial bill to pass the committee by a single vote, and thereby allow for a new law—the 1992 Animal Enterprise Protection Act (*House Report Part II* 1992). In essence, this relabeling of animal rights activists' behavior from "criminal" to "terrorist" actually *enabled* the successful passage of the bill that could not pass, in otherwise identical form, before the terminology was added.

This relabeling was successful because it allowed the proponents to respond to all of the earlier arguments that were waged against the 1989 FARFPA bill. Proponents could now argue that "terrorism" is a national and even international problem that necessitates the federal government criminalizing such behavior. Within this rhetoric of "terrorism," each marginal and/or individual action becomes part of a global conspiracy of "animal right terrorists." Spray-painting "fur is dead," which seems, at most, a minor action of vandalism, becomes a federal issue connected to an international conspiracy of "eco-terrorism." This rhetoric of "terrorism" also allowed proponents to argue that "animal enterprises" necessitate special protections because "animal rights terrorists" were not merely attacking random targets, but instead were attacking animal enterprises as proxies of American society as a whole (ibid.).

TERRORISTS WITH AN "AL-QAEDA MINDSET"

It is this same type of rhetorical shift—of referring to predominantly nonviolent criminal actions by animal rights activist as "terrorism"— that enabled passage of the 2006 Animal Enterprise Terrorism Act (AETA). The term *terrorism* was now used in the name of the act itself; was invoked in virtually all the debate and discussion on the hearing that addressed the act; and was used in the name of the committee conducting the hearing, namely the Subcommittee on Crime, Terrorism, and Homeland Security. Representatives, lobbying groups, and conservative press outlets all invoked the word *terrorist*. In a post-9/11 America, this type of rhetoric was then used to imply that animal rights activists possessed connections to al-Qaeda, Islamic extremism, and other forms of international terrorism. The hearing on the AETA even began with Representative Coble (R-NC) implying a linkage between animal rights activists and international terrorism: "While we are still responding to the threat about international terrorism, groups of impassioned animal supporters have unfortunately employed tactics to disrupt animal research and related business by terrorizing their employees" (*Animal Enterprise* 2006, 1). This comment merely replicated the claims by the lobbying groups that favored the legislation, such as the National

Rifle Association (NRA). In a newsletter lobbying for the bill, the NRA claimed that:

> Second Amendment freedom today stands naked in the path of a marching axis of adversaries far darker and more dangerous than gun owners have ever known. Acting alone and in shadowy coalitions, these enemies of freedom are preparing for a profound and foreboding confrontation in which they will not make the mistakes of their predecessors. We'd better be ready. (National Rifle Association 2006, 1)

The same newsletter goes on to state that "this eco-terrorism movement is so dangerous, the FBI has declared it America's number one domestic terrorist threat. They've upstaged al Qaeda as the greatest terrorist threat on American soil" (ibid., 18–19).

Sound bites repeated in conservative news outlets further embellished these ideas, such as the claim that "the [animal rights] fanatics who have caused tens of millions of dollars in damages with terrorist violence to support these fringe positions don't want to debate—they want to dictate to us all. They are terrorists with an Al-Qaeda mindset" (Nichols 2002, n.p.). Such false rhetoric continues: "In the light of Sept. 11 and the need for intensified homeland security, our law enforcement agencies should investigate and prosecute environmental and animal rights terrorism with the same vigor and intensity as directed against foreign terrorists" (ibid.). This rhetorical linkage between animal rights activists and al-Qaeda terrorists continued even after passage of the AETA, with the National Fur Council sending a letter of congratulations to all the groups that supported the legislation (Fur Commission 2006). The header of this congratulations stated "Mission Accomplished!"—which was the same phrase that George W. Bush famously used when declaring victory over "terrorism" in Iraq.

As with the AEPA, the invocation of "terrorism" shifts the supposed target of animal rights activism from the animal enterprises themselves to society as a whole—i.e., society itself is under threat from "animal rights terrorists." Take, for instance, Representative Coble's claim that "eco-terrorism" is similar to international terrorism and its goal is to "destroy civilization as we know it" (*Animal Enterprise* 2006, 1).

Likewise, Brent McIntosh, the Deputy Assistant Attorney General for the U.S. Department of Justice, contended that the AETA is essential to "defeat those who would harm this country" (ibid., 2). These claims were effective in the early 1990s and even more so after 9/11. In brief, these claims are implying that such activities as illegal picketing of a fur store and liberating animals from fur producers are not just attacks on a specific store or industry, but rather attacks on America as a whole. This is similar to the wider post-9/11 logic: that the attacks on the World Trade Center and Pentagon were not merely attacks on individual buildings or businesses, but rather attacks on "America" and "Freedom." This kind of parallel, though false, logic helps garner support for the AETA, but it also insulates the AETA from the types of critiques it encountered from 1989 to 1992.

Despite these repeated invocations of "terrorism," no U.S.-based criminal animal rights activity has led to a death or serious injury (Guither 1998, 152; Best and Nocella n.d.; Potter 2011). This point is not only championed by the animal rights activists but is also actually accepted on all sides of the debate. Deputy assistant director of the FBI John Lewis even admitted during a Senate hearing that "most animal rights and eco-extremists have refrained from violence targeting human life" (Lewis 2005, n.p.). In reality, the vast majority of illegal actions committed by animal rights activists are composed of minor vandalism or the liberation or "theft" of small numbers of animals. For example, of the first three hundred direct actions committed by U.S.-based animal rights activists, the majority are the equivalent of "stealing" captive animals and damaging and vandalizing equipment and machinery (Guither 1998, 221–32).

It should also be noted that this lack of violence against people is not purely accidental. For example, the Animal Liberation Front (ALF) explicitly rejects any violence against people or animals. As Steven Best and Anthony J. Nocella document:

The ALF follows a strict code of nonviolence whereby they carefully avoid causing physical injury to animal oppressors when they attack their property. The ALF claims that in thousands of actions and over three decades of operation, they have never harmed a single human being: 'The ALF does not, in any way, condone violence

THE TERRORIZATION OF DISSENT

against any animal, human or nonhuman. Any action involving violence is by definition not an ALF action, any person involved is not
an ALF member.' (Best and Nocella n.d.)

Although many actions committed by animal rights activists may be
illegal (such as "theft" and vandalism), such actions do not meet traditional definitions of "terrorism." That is, they do not intentionally target
civilians for physical violence. (For a thorough discussion of the relation between nonviolent civil disobedience and "terrorism," see Meggle
2005). This is not to suggest that actions committed by particular animal rights activists are never controversial. Instead, I am simply arguing
that illegal activity is not synonymous with terrorism and the bombing
of the World Trade Center. As Senator Leahy (D-VT) wrote in reaction
against an earlier Senate version of this hearing:

> Today's hearing was originally noticed under the title, 'The Threat
> of Animal and Eco-Terrorism.' I can understand why that title was
> abandoned. When most Americans think of threats that currently
> face this country, we do not mean 'animal and eco-terrorism.'
> Indeed, most Americans would not consider the harassment of ani-
> mal testing facilities to be 'terrorism,' any more than they would
> consider anti-globalization protestors or anti-war protestors or
> women's health activists to be terrorists. (Leahy 2004, n.p.)

A "KANGAROO COURT"

If animal rights activists are not in fact terrorists, then how did the May
23, 2006 congressional hearing manage to make people believe otherwise? The main strategy, other than using the term *terrorism*, was to
structure the hearing in a way that excluded open and democratic debate
and that slanted the testimonies toward a preestablished bias against
animal rights activists.

The hearing had four witnesses, twelve prepared statements, four
letters addressing the issue, two studies conducted by biomedical companies, and one newspaper article for a total of twenty-three different
voices presented on the topic, in addition to the congressional representatives themselves (*Animal Enterprise* 2006). Now there can certainly be

a debate about the number of different viewpoints it takes to constitute a fair hearing—perhaps half for the bill and half against, or only a few specifically for or against the bill along with a series of experts addressing different aspects of the bill in an impartial manner, or some other combination of advocate and expert testimony. However, in this case, there was only *one* testimony against the bill—that of Will Potter, who was labeled only as "a journalist" (*Animal Enterprise* 2006). The congressional hearing did not include any testimonies from any animal rights organizations, such as People for the Ethical Treatment of Animals, Farm Sanctuary, or Earth First!, even though each of these organizations released statements against the bill and were, in fact, repeatedly referenced within the hearing itself (see the Stop AETA and Equal Justice Alliance websites for a complete list of organizations opposing the legislation). The hearing did not solicit input from any mainstream animal welfare organizations, such as The Humane Society of the United States, which also released a statement opposing the bill (Humane Society 2006). Neither did the hearing solicit input from any civil liberties organizations, such as the American Civil Liberties Union or the National Lawyers Guild, both of which opposed the legislation and sent prepared statements to the congressional subcommittee (Fredrickson and Graves 2006; Boghosian and Cohn 2006).

The witnesses testifying in support of the bill were *not* unbiased researchers or members of impartial think tanks who objectively concluded that animal rights activism is akin to terrorism. Instead, these witnesses were almost uniformly spokespersons for animal enterprise companies. The prepared statements that were not from congressional representatives were as follows: the president of the National Association for Biomedical Research, the president of the Federation of American Societies for Experimental Biology, the general counsel for Life Sciences Research and Huntingdon Life Science, Inc., the executive director for the Wisconsin Association for Biomedical Research and Education, and the executive director for the Fur Information Council of America (*Animal Enterprise* 2006). The only prepared statement that was not explicitly tied to the animal enterprise business of biomedical research, factory farming, or fur production was from Wesley J. Smith, senior fellow at the Discovery Institute. But even then, Smith's testimony was problematic in that he based his critique of animal rights activists not on empirical evidence. Instead, he rejected animal rights activism on theological grounds, arguing that animals, unlike humans, do not have "souls" (see Smith's 2010 book *A Rat is a Pig* as an example of his reasoning).

This unique convergence of animal enterprise lobbyism, political conservatism, and religious fundamentalism should not be a surprise. As the National Lawyers Guild documents:

The AETA was created by lobbyist group American Legislative Exchange Council (ALEC) in association with the U.S. Sportsmen Alliance. ALEC has the support of over 300 large corporations, including those in the tobacco, petroleum, pharmaceutical and transportation areas. It works with right-wing entities such as the NRA, the Family Research Council and the Koch, Scaife, Bradley and Heritage Foundations to influence legislation to benefit its big business members and contributors. In 1999/2000 ALEC legislators introduced over 3,100 pieces of legislation, of which over 450 were enacted, all benefiting corporations. (National Lawyers Guild 2006, n.p.)

Although the hearing maintained a rhetorical façade of impartiality, there was, in fact, no structural possibility for an actual "hearing" between two divergent viewpoints since only one viewpoint was allowed to be heard. Even if the hearing chose to have only one person properly represent a sound critique of the AETA, then the hearing could have called upon many qualified individuals. For example, famed animal rights philosopher Peter Singer would have represented a particularly nuanced choice for a witness in that he is both a seminal founder of the animal rights movement and, at the same time, one of the harshest critics of violence in the pursuit of animal rights. As he makes clear in his 1990 preface to *Animal Liberation*: "It would be a tragic mistake if even a small section of the Animal Liberation movement were to attempt to achieve its objectives by hurting people" (xix). I contend that someone like Peter Singer was not asked to testify *precisely because* of his qualifications; any comments he might have waged would have been difficult to dismiss out of hand, thus complicating the hearing's purpose of smearing animal rights activists.

Will Potter is an excellent journalist, runs a great website on issues related to the AETA and animal rights, and did well in his testimony. But it seems clear that he was only included to help support this façade of impartiality as a type of "straw man" whom the representatives could then dismiss for lack of qualifications. Potter openly admitted at the beginning of his testimony to his lack of qualifications: "It should be clear from the outset, I'm not a lawyer, I'm not a first amendment scholar, and I am not a spokesperson for the animal rights movement or underground groups. I'm here because of my freelance reporting" (*Animal Enterprise* 2006, 20). The representatives then went on to dismiss all of his testimony and, by extension, all arguments against the AETA. The following exchange between Mr. Potter and Representative Feeney (R-FL) exemplifies my point:

> Mr. Feeney: Mr. Potter, I appreciate that you don't have a legal background. In your testimony you oppose the bill because you say that it—and I quote, 'it criminalizes any activity,' that causes economic damage... In my view you're just flat out wrong. They ought to be responsible for the natural and consequential damages of their disruptive behavior. There are first amendment protections that all of us believe are very important to this country, but I would advise you not to be making statements that any activity is criminalized because it's just flat out false. And maybe next time you'll want to consult [a lawyer]—go ahead, you can answer.
>
> Mr. Potter: Well, Congressman, with all due respect, I'd like to point out that the definition given of economic damage means that replacement cost of lost or damaged property or records, the cost of repeating an interrupted—
>
> Mr. Feeney: Mr. Potter, we'll have to get you a logic course that you can understand one step to the next—
>
> Mr. Potter: If I can just finish. The easier is the loss of profits, and I think that's what would give any—
>
> Mr. Feeney: Reclaiming my time. I point out that the gentleman simply doesn't understand. You're not responsible for any of the definition you just talked about unless you have intentionally

damaged or destroyed property or threatened somebody's life or bodily injury. So all of what you're referring to is not of concern if you behave legally. I want to assure you and advise you to go talk to an attorney before you come and testify before the United States Congress about what bills do when, in fact, they do not do. (ibid.)

There are many problems with this exchange. First, Representative Feeney misconstrued Mr. Potter's argument by claiming that Mr. Potter said that the bill would "criminalize any activity." But Mr. Potter actually testified that the bill criminalized "any activity *against an animal enterprise or any company tangential to an animal enterprise that causes economic damage defined as including the loss of profits*" (emphasis added). This is exactly what the bill does and is in the text of the bill itself. Second, Representative Feeney refused to allow Mr. Potter to explain himself ("If I could just finish") and even mocked Mr. Potter ("we'll have to get you a logic course that you can understand one step to the next"). And third, and perhaps most significantly, Representative Feeney implied throughout the testimony, from the first sentence to the last, that Mr. Potter's concerns were irrelevant and ill-informed because he is not a lawyer.

The last point is quite ironic since many legal groups publicly opposed the legislation on the same grounds that Mr. Potter raised. For instance, the American Civil Liberties Union (ACLU) submitted a prepared statement to the hearing. It was neither included with the transcript nor even mentioned during the hearing. But the ACLU's statement makes clear its opposition, arguing that the AETA:

expands that class criminal behavior in 18 U.S.C. 43, by changing the term used to describe the activity 'for the purpose of causing physical disruption' to activity 'for the purpose of damaging or disrupting' an animal enterprise. The over broad class of 'disruptive' activities apply to any and all activities that result in 'losses and increased costs' in excess of 10,000. (Fredrickson and Graves 2006, n.p.)

The National Lawyers Guild makes a similar claim in its own prepared statement:

The AETA could lead to the prosecution of undercover investigators, whistle-blowers and other activists as 'terrorists.' It defines 'economic damage' as including 'the loss of profits.' Such broad language puts all activists at risk; those activists who aren't prosecuted under the AETA will still feel the chilling effect of its 'terrorist' language. (Boghosian and Cohn 2006, n.p.)

These statements demonstrate that the subcommittee could have easily summoned lawyers to testify from the ACLU, the National Lawyers Guild, or any number of other reputable organizations that publicly opposed the legislation and even provided statements to the subcommittee. Instead, the subcommittee intentionally chose a witness who was not properly qualified and then dismissed his testimony for that very reason.

The irony of that dismissal is further underscored when we consider that the House's own Judiciary Committee raised identical concerns fourteen years earlier with the 1992 AEPA. The Judiciary Committee of that time was concerned about criminalizing "physical disruptions" such as trespassing, vandalism, illegal protests, or acts of nonviolent civil disobedience. As the Judiciary Committee wrote in 1992:

> The bill as reported by the Agriculture Committee goes well beyond serious terrorism offenses, and would extend federal jurisdiction to even trivial behavior. The bill covers any intentional disruption (or attempted disruption) of an animal enterprise, regardless of terrorist intent. (*House Report Part I* 1992, 5)

The Judiciary Committee was also worried that outlawing "physical disruption" might lead to the criminalization of "whistle-blowers"—i.e., outlawing the ability of animal rights activists to expose the abuse of animals in labs, farms, and slaughterhouses might set precedence for outlawing other forms of whistle-blowing. According to the 1992 Judiciary Committee:

> Regulators, humane societies, and labor unions rely on whistle-blowing and legitimate undercover investigations to police conditions at food and fiber processing facilities and determine compliance with animal welfare and labor laws. The bill as reported by the Agriculture Committee outlaws activities which are conducted with

an intent to cause 'physical disruption' to an animal enterprise. The ambiguous term 'physical disruption' is not defined, and could be construed to make criminal whistle-blowing activity that results in a facility being shut down by regulators or protestors. At best, this would have chilled whistle-blowing; at worst, it could have resulted in actual prosecutions of whistle-blowers. (ibid.)

To clarify my general point: the 2006 AETA puts into law the *same* provisions that the House's own 1992 Judiciary Committee removed as potentially unconstitutional. If that is true, then the Animal Enterprise Terrorism Act does not itself constitute a "new bill," but rather is the successful culmination of a sustained attempt by animal enterprise lobbyists to target animal rights activists. That attempt began with the original Farm Animal and Research Facilities Protection Act of 1989 and culminated in the 2006 AETA. I also argue that the rhetoric of terrorism and turning activists' activities into felonies were not mere accidents that occurred from a Congress that may have been influenced by the post-9/11 sentiment of fear and patriotism. Instead, it was a deliberate and systematic attempt to debilitate and eliminate an animal rights movement that affects the profits of "animal enterprises."

NONVIOLENT ACTS ARE MISCONSTRUED AS VIOLENT

The ability to construe animal rights activists as "terrorists" needing special legal attention is based on rhetorical sleights of hand. For instance, the hearing argues that new laws are needed to properly deal with animal rights activists. But this is a misnomer since (1) the average animal rights activist breaks very few laws, and (2) preexisting state and federal laws are already capable of addressing more controversial activities such as vandalism, "theft," and arson. This was even admitted during the hearing by Brent McIntosh, Deputy Assistant Attorney General for the U.S. Department of Justice. As he stated, "In some cases, such as those involving arson and explosives, federal prosecutors are well equipped to prosecute and punish extremists, but not all animal rights extremists use arson and explosives" (*Animal Enterprise* 2006, 5).

This holds true for even one of the most destructive examples of animal rights activism to occur in the United States: Rodney Coronado's burning of an unoccupied medical research building (which, by the way, did *not* physically harm any person). This action was *already* "triply" illegal and prosecutable *before* the passage of the AETA: first, it could be prosecuted under state laws against arson; second, it was illegal under federal prohibitions against engaging in interstate commerce to commit arson; and third, it could be singled out for punishment under the preexisting Animal Enterprise Protection Act of 1992. A *San Francisco Weekly* article summarizes the issue well when it challenged Senator Feinstein's (D-CA) support of the AETA: "violence, threats, vandalism, and harassing assaults of the sort described by Feinstein are already illegal. Her bill criminalizes ordinary protest activities that weren't illegal before" (Smith 2006, n.p.).

Another rhetorical sleight of hand occurred when hearing testimonies grouped nonviolent actions—for example, vandalism—with other, more potentially violent actions such as "fire-bombing." This was done in a manner that implies the actions are comparable. For example, Brent McIntosh originally testified that arson and explosives were already adequately prosecuted under federal laws. But he later stated that the AETA was needed because "these violent extremists have advocated and facilitated such direct actions as vandalism—including fire-bombing homes, businesses and cars" (*Animal Enterprise* 2006, 5). Fire-bombing is an action that clearly goes beyond mere vandalism. However, the structure of the sentence, specifically the word *including*, makes it sound as though "direct action" is equivalent to fire-bombing. But this is not the case. Direct action is an extremely broad category that can include anything from spray-painting a message on an abandoned building to clogging an intersection. In many ways, fire-bombing exists in its own category of action. Moreover, the use of "these violent extremists" equates vandalism with terrorism before any of the actions are even mentioned—i.e., it negatively frames the actions that are mentioned later, which then affects people's interpretation of those actions.

It must also be noted that Brent McIntosh never stated—anywhere in his testimony—that animal rights activists had ever actually *committed* violent actions; instead, he stated only that activists had "advocated," "facilitated," or "threatened" such actions. This is an extremely important distinction since very few animal rights activists have been convicted of committing violence. Several activists have been convicted of supposedly "advocating" such actions; but none have been convicted of *doing* violent actions. This then raises serious First Amendment issues. For example, in the now famous case of the Stop Huntingdon's Animal Cruelty campaign (often referred to as "SHAC"), six activists were convicted of supposedly advocating violence by simply hosting a website that reported such actions as occurring. But there was no evidence of the convicted activists actually engaging in such actions themselves. These activists were therefore convicted for their "speech" rather than their actions. (See www.shac.net and www.shac7.com for more information.)

Perhaps the most effective mechanism for equating nonviolent civil disobedience and terrorism is by treating all illegal activities as though they are morally and criminally identical. This then creates a false dichotomy between "legal" on one side and "terrorism" on the other. Any concerns raised during the hearing about the AETA unfairly penalizing peaceful civil disobedience were met with this false dichotomy. Representatives might say, for example, that the AETA does not penalize any *legal* actions. But this does not properly respond to the concern since civil disobedience, while nonviolent, is still, by its very definition, "illegal." One of the most blatant examples of this false dichotomizing occurred when Representative Coble reassured folks that,

> [s]ince the bill has been introduced, the Committee has been approached by a couple of groups with concerns about ensuring first amendment protections that are included for lawful protests, boycotts and other activities. The legislation was not intended to infringe on these rights in any way. (*Animal Enterprise* 2006, 2)

Not only does this comment sidestep the actual concern, but it also downplays the amount of opposition. The reality is that this legislation was opposed not by "a couple of groups," but by more than 160 different organizations. Many of these groups were concerned not only with "legal protests," but with illegal ones, such as protesting a fur store without a permit, hosting a nonviolent but nonetheless illegal sit-in, or illegally though nonviolently liberating animals from research facilities. Illegal nonviolent civil disobedience is a major tool used by almost all activists and social movements. Although it may be illegal, it is commonly understood as an acceptable form of protest. The AETA sets precedence possibly eliminating this protest tactic.

CONCLUSION

Given all of the above issues, contradictions, and inconsistencies, I argue that the AETA and its accompanying "hearing" are not about preventing "animal rights terrorists" from committing "violent actions." Animal rights activists are committed to nonviolence. And even more "radical" activities—such as vandalism, "theft," and/or arson—are already illegal and prosecutable under preexisting federal and state laws. Anyone seriously analyzing the overall situation can determine that there are no equivalences between animal rights activism and the likes of al-Qaeda. The 2006 hearing was, in a nutshell, a sham, or as I have already stated, a "kangaroo court" intended to squelch open and democratic debate and to slant the outcome toward a predetermined conclusion.

I also believe that the AETA should be of concern to all activists since I cannot see why the same logic that made decreasing the profits of animal enterprise businesses illegal could not be extended to every other area of business. If these laws existed forty or fifty years ago, then perhaps Rosa Parks and Dr. Martin Luther King, Jr., would have been considered terrorists and punished as felons. They did, after all, engage in illegal civil disobedience for the purpose of decreasing profits of busing and lunch counter businesses. A 1950s version of the AETA might have stymied the civil rights movement, denied African Americans from achieving full citizenship, and maintained legalized segregation. Let's hope that the current situation does not bring about such a chilling sequence of events for animal rights or any other form of social or political justice movement.

REFERENCES

Animal Enterprise Terrorism Act: Hearing Before the Subcommittee on Crime, Terrorism, and Homeland Security of the Committee on the Judiciary House of Representatives, 109th Cong. May 23, 2006, www.gpo.gov/fdsys/pkg/CHRG-109hhrg27742/html/CHRG-109hhrg27742.htm.

Best, Steven, and Anthony J. Nocella II. "Behind the Mask: Uncovering the Animal Liberation Front." In *Terrorists or Freedom Fighters?* edited by Steven Best, PhD and Anthony J. Nocella II. New York: Lantern Books, 2004.

Boghosian, Heidi, and Marjorie Cohn. "National Lawyers Guild Opposes Animal Enterprise Terrorism Act." Published October 30, 2006, www.commondreams.org/news2006/1030-14.htm.

Equal Justice Alliance. http://noaeta.org.

Fredrickson, Caroline, and Lisa Graves. "ACLU Letter to Congress Urging Opposition to the Animal Enterprise Terrorism Act, S. 1926 and H.R. 4239." Published March 6, 2006, www.aclu.org/free-speech/aclu-letter-congress-urging-opposition-animal-enterprise-act-s-1926-and-hr-4239.

Fur Commission USA. "AETA Promises Greater Security from Eco-terror." Last revised October 7, 2007, http://old.furcommission.com/resource/Resources/AETA.pdf.

Guither, Harold D. *Animal Rights: The History of a Radical Social Movement.* Carbondale: Southern Illinois University Press, 1998.

House Report 102-498 Part I: Farm Animal and Research Facilities Protection Act of 1992, House of Representatives, 102d Cong. (April 9, 1992).

House Report 102-498 Part II: Animal Rights Terrorism Act of 1992, House of Representatives, 102d Cong. (July 27, 1992).

Humane Society of the United States. "HSUS Fact Sheet: Oppose the Animal Enterprise Terrorism Act (AETA) H.R. 4239 and S. 3880 (as amended)." September 28, 2006.

Leahy, Patrick. "Statement of Patrick Leahy on Animal Rights: Activism vs. Criminality." United States Senate Committee on the Judiciary. Published May 18, 2004, www.judiciary.senate.gov/hearings/testimony.cfm?renderforprint=1&id=4f1e0899533f7680e78d03281ff9a66d&wit_id=4f1e0899533f7680e78d03281ff9a66d-0-2.

Lewis, John. "Senate Committee on Environment and Public Works Hearing Statements." Published May 18, 2005, www.epw.senate.gov/hearing_statements.cfm?id=237817.

Meggle, Georg, ed. *Ethics of Terrorism & Counter-Terrorism.* Frankfurt, Germany: Ontos Verlag, 2005.

National Lawyers Guild. October 30, 2006 press release.

National Rifle Association. "Freedom in Peril: Guarding the 2nd Amendment in the 21st Century." Published 2006, http://boingboing.net/images/NR-F8_PERILFINAL.pdf.

Nichols, Nick. "They're Animals." *TCS Daily*, February 28, 2002, www.ideasinactiontv.com/tcs_daily/2002/02/theyre-animals.html.

Potter, Will. *Green Is the New Red: An Insider's Account of a Social Movement Under Siege.* San Francisco: City Lights Publishers, 2011.

Singer, Peter. *Animal Liberation.* New York: HarperCollins, 2002.

Smith, Matt. "Boycott Feinstein: A New Proposed Law Would Put Activists in Jail for Hurting a Company's Bottom Line." *San Francisco Weekly,* November 29, 2006, www.sfweekly.com/Issues/2006-11-29/news/smith.html.

Smith, Wesley J. *A Rat Is a Pig Is a Dog Is a Boy: The Human Cost of the Animal Rights Movement.* New York: Encounter Books, 2010.

Stop AETA. www.stopaeta.org.

Stop Huntingdon Animal Cruelty. www.shac.net.

Stop Huntingdon Animal Cruelty 7. www.shac7.com.

THE DISCONNECT BETWEEN POLITICS
AND PROSECUTION UNDER THE AETA

Lillian M. McCartin and Brad J. Thomson

The United States government has a long history of discrediting and disrupting social justice movements by using legal statutes to criminalize participants and their tactics. Often, these prosecutions have also included rhetorical attacks, demonizing the movements and the activists within them as "terrorists." These strategies have been implemented for over a century and have only increased in the years following September 11, 2001. Muslim American and Arab American communities have been primary targets of these attacks under an "anti-terror" agenda, but in recent years we have also seen the government target the animal rights movement under a similar agenda. A very clear example of this has been the Animal Enterprise Terrorism Act (AETA), passed by Congress in 2006 and used to prosecute animal rights activists for a variety of actions, including protest activities traditionally protected by the First Amendment.

The problematic nature of the AETA was apparent even before it became law, with two members of Congress, Representatives Dennis Kucinich and Steve Israel, expressing concern that it would have a chilling effect on freedom of speech and assembly by deterring individuals from participating in a vibrant and active animal rights movement. (It should be noted that Representative Kucinich, who we will discuss later, participated in debates on the House floor, but Representative Israel later provided a written statement for the record.)

The debate on the floor of the House of Representatives, just prior to the AETA's passage, provides the political framework from which to examine the countervailing viewpoints expressed during the debate. This framework provides a gauge for measuring (1) whether the AETA's enforcement has been consistent with the purposes stated during the debate, and (2) whether the AETA actually upholds its purported civil liberties protections.

House Debate on the AETA

On Monday, November 13, 2006, the Senate Bill S. 3880 for the Animal Enterprise Terrorism Act was presented to the U.S. House of Representatives for debate. The Senate had already passed its version of the bill on September 30, 2006. It was submitted under suspension of the rules, which is a procedure generally used to quickly pass noncontroversial bills. It had passed in the Senate by unanimous consent rather than by affirmative vote. It was then submitted to the House, also under suspension of the rules. The AETA would amend the Animal Enterprise Protection Act of 2002 (AEPA). The bill purported to provide "the Department of Justice the necessary authority to apprehend, prosecute and convict individuals committing animal enterprise terrorism" (152 Cong. Rec. H8590-01).

The bill in its entirety was read into the record and the House floor was opened to general debate and discussion. Those who spoke in favor of the AETA were Congressman Jim Sensenbrenner (R-WI) and Congressman Robert Scott (D-VA). Congressman Scott was the Democratic sponsor of the AETA bill, one of the leaders for civil liberties in the House. Congressman Sensenbrenner, who spoke first in support of the bill, characterized the acts of animal rights activists as "violent." Although he failed to cite any evidence of physical harm or of any significant increase in criminal acts, he insisted the changes to the statute were necessary to more fully protect those engaged in animal enterprises. He debated, in relevant part, that:

> In recent years, some animal rights activist groups have employed violence and intimidation against enterprises that use or sell animals or animal products for food, agriculture, research testing or entertainment uses.... The last several years have seen an increase

in the number and the severity of criminal acts and intimidation against those engaged in animal enterprises. These groups have attacked not only employees of companies conducting research, but also those with any remote link to such research or activities. (152 Cong. Rec. H8590-01)

Congressman Sensenbrenner explained that this new bill, which amended and updated the AEPA of 2002, was designed more effectively to protect animal enterprises by expanding the scope of the legislation to include tertiary enterprises and immediate family members, spouses, and intimate partners of individuals involved with animal enterprises. Widening the scope allowed for prosecutions to be brought for alleged acts against individuals or businesses not directly involved with animal enterprises, even tangential ties to "animal enterprises."

Congressman Scott then applauded revisions made to the bill after its introduction, which purportedly would protect civil liberties, including boycotts resulting in business loss, and would not prosecute acts of civil disobedience or protests, while prosecuting only criminal actors who would cross state lines.

> While we must protect those engaged in animal enterprises, we must also protect the right of those engaged in First Amendment freedoms of expression regarding such enterprises. It goes without saying that First Amendment freedoms of expression cannot be defeated by statute. However, to reassure anyone concerned with the intent of this legislation, we have added in the bill assurances that it is not intended as a restraint on freedoms of expression such as lawful boycotting, picketing or otherwise engaging in lawful advocacy for animals.
>
> In addition, we also wanted to recognize that there are some who conscientiously believe that it is their duty to peacefully protest the operation of animal enterprises to the extent of engaging in civil disobedience. If a group's intention were to stage a sit-in or lie-down or to block traffic to a targeted facility, they certainly run the risk of arrest for whatever traffic, trespass or other laws they may be breaking. But they should not be held more accountable for business losses due to causes such as delivery trucks being delayed any more than a boycott or protest against any other business. To

violate the provision of the bill, one must travel or otherwise engage in interstate activity with the intent to cause damage or loss to an animal enterprise. (152 Cong. Rec. H8590-01)

Toward the end of the debate, Congressman Kucinich (D-OH) raised concerns regarding the necessity of the legislation and the possible negative ramifications of enforcing the act. Then Congressmen Sensenbrenner and Kucinich debated the possible effects of the legislation.

Congressman Kucinich, who is a well-known animal rights advocate, stated that the legislation would not accomplish its goal because the legislation did nothing to address the underlying issue—the inhumane treatment of animals.

> This Congress has yet to address some fundamental ethical principles with respect to animals. How should animals be treated humanely? . . . [T]hese are really serious questions that millions and millions of Americans care about. . . . I just think that you have got to be very careful about painting everyone with the broad brush of terrorism who might have a legitimate objection to a type of research or treatment of animals that is not humane.

Congressman Kucinich also questioned the validity of the legislation, pointing out that it provides for exclusive criminal penalties and severely limits "free expression."

> So what is this all about? This bill, in effect, does provide exclusive criminal penalties for a certain type of conduct, and yet the drafting of this bill makes section −18 U.S.C.A. §43 ¶ 3 under rules of construction, totally contradictory. This says there aren't any exclusive penalties, but the whole of the bill maintains and establishes exclusive penalties. So this is why bringing up a bill like this under suspension, no matter how well intentioned it may be, is problematic.
> This bill has an inherent flaw that I am pointing out. In addition, when that flaw is held up against the constitutional mandate to protect freedom of speech, what we have done here is we have crippled free expression.
> I am not and never have been in favor of anyone using a cloak of free speech to commit violence. The Supreme Court justice said, your right to swing your fist ends at the tip of my nose. No one has

the right to yell "fire" in a crowded theater. We have heard those kinds of admonitions.

. . . .

Yet under this bill they suddenly find themselves shifting into an area of doubt, which goes back to my initial claim that this bill was written to have a chilling effect upon a specific type of protest.

Again, I am not for anyone abusing their rights by damaging another person's property or person, but I am for protecting the First Amendment and not creating a special class of violations for a specific type of protest. (152 Cong. Rec. H8590-01)

The bill was apparently passed by a voice vote of five representatives. Because five representatives voted in favor of the bill, it was reported to have been passed "unanimously," even though the full House was not present. The bill had been originally scheduled several hours later for debate and for a vote with the full House.

The primary issues for the proponents of the AETA were (1) that animal activists were "attacking" animal experimenters and others affiliated with them, (2) that the amendments to the AEPA would only apply to crossing state lines, (3) that civil disobedience would not be penalized more harshly than other forms of civil disobedience, and (4) that the First Amendment is still protected because the statute says it is.

Each of these assertions is clearly in error. The congressmen failed to present evidence of any physical attacks made by animal activists, but only made vague statements that asserted an increase in protest type activity. Further, there was no specific evidence presented that the AEPA failed to adequately protect animal enterprises, but, again, there were only assertions that loopholes in the AEPA were exploited. Most disturbingly, the proponents of the AETA assumed that the Rules of Construction provided sufficient First Amendment protections, but in fact they do not.

STOP HUNTINGDON ANIMAL CRUELTY ("SHAC")

The members of Congress who proposed and pushed for the AETA focused largely on the SHAC campaign in the United States. Actions related to the campaign were used as justification for the necessity of amending the AEPA. Congressman Sensenbrenner labeled the actions of SHAC activists as "severe" and Congressman Scott said that the tactics employed were planned "by individuals or groups skilled at exploiting gaps or weaknesses in the law" (152 Cong. Rec. H8590-01). These claims were made despite the fact that the AEPA as it was written at the time had been used to prosecute and convict activists associated with SHAC.

Historically, the SHAC campaign began in 1999 in the United Kingdom (SHAC-UK) to shut down Huntingdon Life Sciences (HLS), which is the largest animal testing facility in Europe and the second largest animal testing facility in the world. An individual posing as a lab technician at HLS videotaped the conditions inside the laboratory. The undercover video, which revealed extreme animal abuse, including the punching of beagles, was aired on television in the United Kingdom. A number of protests were initiated against HLS and gave rise to the SHAC-UK campaign with the sole mission to close down HLS (*U.S. v. Fullmer*, 2009).

The SHAC-UK campaign named and targeted individuals that were associated with HLS, including suppliers, customers, and shareholders, and targeted them for protests. British law requires companies to publish the names and addresses of all shareholders. SHAC-UK used this public information to conduct twenty-four-hour demonstrations in front of the residences of HLS shareholders. In 2002, in an attempt to protect the identity of their shareholders, HLS moved its financial base from England to New Jersey. In response, the SHAC-USA campaign began with its mission to shut down HLS in the United States.

The primary organizing tool of SHAC-USA (which we will refer to as "SHAC" for simplicity and should not be confused with SHAC-UK) was its website. That website provided information on the history of HLS, examples of HLS abuses against animals, and links to demonstration materials such as posters, petition forms, and booklets. The website listed prior protest activities as successful actions and a description of how the organizers of the website viewed their limited role in the broader campaign.

We operate within the boundaries of the law, but recognize and support those who choose to operate outside the confines of the legal system.

Big Business has shown time and time again their lack of concern for ethics, instead focusing their attention on their profits.
Often, simply targeting said business proves fruitless. However,
as aboveground activists have successfully targeted Huntingdon's
financial pillars of support, underground activists have too targeted Huntingdon's pocketbooks. Unidentified individuals as well
as underground cells of the Animal Liberation Front and the Earth
Liberation Front have engaged in economic sabotage of Huntingdon
and their associates.

They have also spent their time directly intervening and liberating the animals who are slated to die inside of Huntingdon. Animals have been liberated from breeders as well as the laboratories
themselves.

SHAC does not organize any such actions or have any knowledge of who is doing them or when they will happen, but SHAC
encourages people to support direct action when it happens and
those who may participate in it. (*U.S. v. Fullmer*, 2009)

This statement, among others, was posted on the SHAC website
and used by the U.S. government to portray the individuals who
operated the website as operating outside the First Amendment. The
individuals running the website were public about politically and
philosophically supporting illegal actions carried out by underground
activists, while their direct involvement in the campaign was largely
limited to legal actions.

The website also promoted electronic civil disobedience against
HLS and other companies associated with HLS. A particularly popular
form of electronic civil disobedience involved sending black faxes to
a phone line in order to exhaust toner of the business' fax machine or
printer. Another strategy was to direct protests not only against HLS,
but also against affiliated companies and the employees of those companies. Public information, such as the names, home addresses, and phone
numbers of affiliated company employees, were posted on SHAC's website to encourage protests against those individuals.

On May 24, 2004, seven animal rights activists were indicted by a
New Jersey grand jury for conspiring to violate the AEPA of 2002, among
other charges. The case has since been referred to as the "SHAC 7" case.

The defendants included individuals who were involved in legal, above-ground aspects of the SHAC campaign, such as operating SHAC's website, giving speeches, and organizing public protests. Notably, the prosecution neither alleged nor presented any evidence that any of the seven were personally involved in any violent, underground, illegal action.

As stated in the AETA congressional debates, the AEPA only protected animal enterprises, not any entities or individuals associated with animal enterprises, i.e., tertiary entities. The AETA extended the AEPA for that very reason—to be able to include tertiary entities. Although Congress justified the passage of the AETA by claiming that "loopholes" in the AEPA prevented prosecution of individuals for allegedly protesting tertiary targets, the SHAC 7 were convicted under the AEPA for doing just that. On March 2, 2006, a jury entered a guilty verdict on all counts—the remaining six defendants (the seventh defendant's charges were dismissed before trial) were found guilty of conspiracy to violate the AEPA and were sentenced to between one and six years in prison.

The defendants appealed their convictions, arguing that the AEPA violated the First Amendment (*U.S. v. Fullmer,* 2009). In October 2009, the Third Circuit Court of Appeals ruled that the AEPA was neither unconstitutional on its face nor unconstitutional as applied to the SHAC 7 defendants and upheld all convictions against the six activists. Lawyers for the defendants petitioned for a rehearing *en banc* to be reheard by all Third Circuit Court of Appeals judges. The petition was denied in June 2010. They then filed a petition for certiorari in an appeal to be heard by the Supreme Court. On March 7, 2011, the Supreme Court denied their petition, leaving no other recourse for appeal or option to challenge the convictions (*Kjonaas v. U.S.,* 2011).

The indictment and convictions of the SHAC 7 demonstrate that the AEPA allowed for the criminalization of association and advocacy, which are traditionally protected by the First Amendment. After the passage of the AETA, the scope of the law has been expanded and the potential penalties have increased, creating an even greater threat to civil liberties. Despite Congressman Scott's assurances that First Amendment freedoms would be protected, neither the AEPA nor the AETA have protected the First Amendment rights of animal activists.

CASES FOLLOWING THE PASSAGE OF THE AETA

The events that unfolded after the passage of the AETA show that Congressman Kucinich's premonitions were correct. He had pointed out that the AETA creates exclusive criminal penalties for certain conduct while limiting "free expression." This was apparent in the first case brought against animal activists under the AETA, which was in 2009 when a two-count indictment came down in the Northern District of California against four animal rights activists—Joseph Buddenberg, Maryam Khajavi, Nathan Pope, and Adriana Stumpo (*U.S. v. Buddenberg* Indictment 2009). This group is also known as the "AETA 4."

The indictment alleged, in language closely parroting the statute, that the four defendants "intentionally placed a person in reasonable fear of death and bodily injury" through the use of, "threats, acts of vandalism, property damage, criminal trespass, harassment and intimidation." In addition, the defendants were charged with one count of conspiracy to violate the AETA (ibid.). The charges arose from demonstrations at the residences of animal vivisectors, where the defendants participated in protests that included a variety of acts such as chanting, leafleting, and chalking on the sidewalk. Although the activists participated in public protests in the state in which they resided, the prosecutors claimed it was within federal jurisdiction because they used the Internet at a local Kinko's to conduct research. Contrary to Congressman Scott's claims during the House debate that "to violate the provision of the bill, one must travel or otherwise engage in interstate activity with the intent to cause damage or loss to an animal enterprise," the AETA has been used against activists who never crossed state lines (152 Cong. Rec. H8590-01).

All four defendants filed motions to dismiss the indictment, challenging the constitutionality of the AETA on its face, averring that it was overbroad and vague. Judge Ronald Whyte, the district court judge presiding over the case, denied the motions. The judge ruled that the subsections of the AETA with which the four defendants were charged were not unconstitutionally vague or overbroad. The ruling also stated that any vagueness in the terms, namely, "damaging...an animal enterprise," "damag[ing]...personal property" or "economic damage," did not pertain to the charges against the AETA 4, and therefore they did not have standing to challenge that subsection of the statute (*U.S. v. Buddenberg*, Or. Denying Def.'s Motion 2009).

Subsequently, the defendants filed additional motions to dismiss based on the insufficiency of the indictment. In July 2010, the judge granted their motions, finding that the indictment failed to provide adequate specificity and that it did "little more than recite the statutory language" (*U.S. v. Buddenberg*, Or. Dismissing Indictment 2010). The case was dismissed without prejudice, leaving the option to reindict the four activists with a more sufficient indictment by the U.S. Attorney. As of August 2012, none of the four had been reindicted under the AETA and it is unclear if the government intends to indict them again.

This first prosecution under the AETA of animal rights activists was a clear example of the potential for the statute to limit activists' constitutional rights. With such lack of clarity in the indictment, it is not certain what precise actions the government claimed to be illegal. This would be problematic in any criminal prosecution, but it becomes even more egregious in a situation involving First Amendment activity. In the decision dismissing the indictments, Judge Whyte wrote, "Particularly considering the protest context in which the underlying conduct has occurred and the First Amendment implications raised, it is reasonable to require the government to more specifically identify the precise conduct upon which it seeks to hold each defendant criminally liable" (*U.S. v. Buddenberg*, Or. Dismissing Indictment 2010).

The criminal complaint filed in the case listed acts of the defendants such as chanting, protesting, and distributing flyers, which clearly have First Amendment implications. The prosecution of these four activists demonstrates that the AETA can be, and has been, used against activists exercising their freedom of expression to protest animal enterprises, despite Congressman Scott's assurances during the House debate that the statute would not impinge on First Amendment rights. Practically speaking, during the year and a half the AETA 4 were under indictment, their free speech was chilled, particularly that of Joseph Buddenberg, who was held under house arrest for several months during that period. That the government did not have sufficient basis to bring the indictment points to the potential threat of prior restraint—the ultimate First Amendment prohibition. The case against the AETA 4 illustrates the way in which the U.S. government is actively attempting to repress the animal rights movement by targeting vocal and visible activists who are involved in publicly protesting animal cruelty.

In future indictments under the AETA, it is apparent that the AETA created exclusive criminal penalties for certain conduct already covered under state law—and, most troubling, for certain political beliefs. In March 2009, another indictment was brought under the AETA, this time in the Utah District Court. The case included two defendants who were animal rights activists—William ("BJ") Viehl and Alex Hall. The two were accused of participating in an animal liberation at a mink farm and attempting to liberate mink at another farm. Rather than being prosecuted as simple state common law crimes, they were indicted under two counts of violating the AETA—one for damaging and interfering with an animal enterprise and another count for attempting to do so (*U.S. v. Viehl*, Indictment 2009).

There were no challenges to the constitutionality of the statute, though a motion to dismiss was filed. The motion challenged whether the federal court had jurisdiction over the case, since the defendants and the farms were within the state of Utah, arguing the charge lacked the necessary interstate component (*U.S. v. Viehl*, Motion to Dismiss 2009). The government responded that the use of text messages and calls via cell phone met the interstate element (*U.S. v. Viehl*, Memo. in Opposition by U.S. 2009). The judge ruled in favor of the government and denied the motion (*U.S. v. Viehl*, Minute Entry Denying Motion 2009). Again, Congressman Scott's assurance that the statute would only be used to prosecute individuals who crossed state lines was proven to be incorrect.

Both Viehl and Hall each pled guilty to one count and in exchange the second count was dropped. Viehl was sentenced to two years and Hall was sentenced to twenty-one months. Both have served their sentences and have been released (*U.S. v. Viehl*, Minute Entries 2009, 2010).

Another indictment alleging "animal enterprise terrorism" was from the Southern District of Iowa filed in November 2009. The indictment charged Scott DeMuth with a single count of conspiring to commit animal enterprise terrorism and alleged that the conspiracy began in 2004 (*U.S. v. DeMuth*, Indictment 2009). Though the indictment provided few specific facts, it appeared the conspiracy was related to an action claimed by the Animal Liberation Front at the University of Iowa where property was destroyed, and according to a communiqué released after the incident, mice and rats were removed from the lab. The U.S. Attorney conjured DeMuth's anarchist politics, support of animal rights, and connection to animal liberation activists who had been imprisoned as evidence of his involvement in the conspiracy (*U.S. v. DeMuth*, Detention Hearing 2009). It ultimately became apparent that DeMuth was charged not under the AETA, but rather the AEPA, since the alleged conspiracy ended *prior to* the passing of the AETA.

Multiple motions to dismiss DeMuth's case were filed, but few were ever ruled on due to the filing of superseding indictments, rendering the motions moot. The Second Superseding Indictment filed in April 2010 alleged that the single count of conspiracy included the incident at the University of Iowa, in addition to an animal liberation at a farm in Minnesota in April 2006 (*U.S. v. DeMuth*, Second Superseding Indictment 2010). On the eve of trial, DeMuth accepted a misdemeanor plea related to the animal liberation in Minnesota, and in exchange the incident from Iowa was dropped from the charge (*U.S. v. DeMuth*, Plea Agreement 2010). In February 2011, he was given a sentence of six months, which he served and was released on July 30, 2011 (*U.S. v. DeMuth*, Sentencing 2011). This case shows how a federal terrorism statute is used in lieu of simple state misdemeanor charges, illustrating further how the AETA creates exclusive criminal charges for certain conduct. Moreover, the AETA is being used in cases like this to allow the federal government to disrupt the animal rights movement by providing increased power for prosecution and sentencing, but also by charging and convicting activists as "terrorists." This undoubtedly damages the public perception of the movement working for the humane treatment of animals.

In 2010, three arsons occurred in Colorado and Utah against businesses that were involved in the sale of animal products, including a sheepskin factory, a leather factory, and a restaurant that served foie gras. The arsons were all claimed by the "Lone Wolf" of the Animal Liberation

Front. In July 2010, Walter Bond was arrested and charged in the District Court of Colorado with arson against the Sheepskin Factory. Days later, Bond was indicted for the incident, facing one count of arson and one count of violating the AETA (*U.S. v. Bond*, 10-cr-389, Indictment 2010). There were no challenges to the statute in the case. Bond pled guilty to both counts in November 2010 and February 2011 and was given the minimum sentence of five years for each count to be served concurrently (*U.S. v. Bond*, 10-cr-389, Minute Entries 2010, 2011).

In September 2010, Bond was indicted in the Utah District Court for two arsons in Salt Lake City, one against the leather factory and the other against the restaurant. The indictment included four counts— two counts of arson and two counts of violating the AETA against the leather factory and the restaurant (*U.S. v. Bond*, 10-cr-844, Indictment 2010). On July 6, 2011, Bond pled guilty to the two counts of arson in Utah, and the two charges of violating the AETA were dropped. On October 13, 2011, Bond was sentenced to eighty-seven months (seven years, three months) to be served consecutively with his sentence for the Colorado actions (*U.S. v. Bond*, 10-cr-844, Minute Entry 2011). Although Bond was ultimately not convicted under the AETA in this case, this is yet another example of how the AETA potentially creates exclusive criminal penalties only for certain conduct *and political beliefs*. The arson charges alone would have covered Bond's alleged actions under state law, but the AETA charges were directed at his beliefs and involvement in the broader animal rights movement.

Analysis of Several AETA and AEPA Cases

It is worth noting that the cases brought under the AETA have included prosecutions of activists for both underground actions and public protests. Despite Congressmen Sensenbrenner and Scott's claims in support for the AETA, there are preexisting federal and state laws that could be used to prosecute arson, other forms of property destruction, and common law crimes. The case of the AETA 4, however, exemplifies the potential for the statute to be brought against people engaged in public forms of protest that are traditionally understood to be protected by the First Amendment.

In the House debate in November 2006, Congressman Kucinich expressed concern that the AETA was drafted with the particular purpose of having a chilling effect on animal rights protests, such that the law would seriously discourage protests targeted at animal enterprises. The potential power to cause a chilling effect on animal rights protest activity is not solely the result of the AETA's amendments—which include the label of "terrorism," the inclusion of tertiary businesses, and the increased sentences. But these elements exist in conjunction with the potential charge of conspiracy, which heightens the chilling effect. A criminal statute with a conspiracy subsection can substantially broaden the scope of the law to target a larger number of people who may intend to engage in legal protest and would be deterred by the threat of criminal prosecution.

Conspiracy charges rely heavily on associations between individuals, as they depend on agreement between parties, allowing individuals to be charged with the actions of a group, even if they themselves did not directly participate in the action. The conspiracy element of the AETA is even more likely to criminalize association as there is no requirement to show a defendant committed an "overt act" in furtherance of the conspiracy.

The SHAC 7 case is a good example of the broad finding of conspiracy absent an "overt act." The SHAC 7 were charged with conspiring to violate the AEPA and in the opinion upholding their convictions the court discussed the interplay of the First Amendment's freedom of association protection and conspiracy charges.

> The government need not introduce direct evidence to establish a conspiratorial agreement (*U.S. v. McKee*, 506 F.3d 225, 238 (3d. Cir 2007)). Rather, the government can prove the agreement with circumstantial evidence, "based upon reasonable inferences drawn from actions and statements of the conspirators or from the circumstances surrounding the scheme." Defendants in this case unquestionably agreed to advocate for animal rights as members and agents of SHAC. However, Defendants cannot be convicted solely because of their association because such a conviction would clearly run afoul of the First Amendment guarantee of freedom of association (*See e.g. N.A.A.C.P v. Clairborne Hardware* 458 U.S. 886, 918-919; *McKee*, 506 F.3d at 238). To establish a conspiracy under

these circumstances, the government must establish that the group itself possessed unlawful goals and that the individual held a specific intent to further those illegal aims.... However, the government need not show that each and every member of the conspiracy committed an unlawful act in furtherance of the conspiracy's goals. (*U.S. v. Fullmer* 2009)

The court's ruling established that an indictment could rely solely on circumstantial evidence to connect someone to a claimed conspiratorial agreement. While the opinion paid lip service to the theory that individuals cannot be convicted solely for their associations, the opinion did not say what else was necessary in order to charge the "associated" individuals. With this opinion providing such little clarity on the necessary connection of an individual to a criminal conspiracy, matched with the broad and vague text of the AETA, it would be a challenge for anyone to understand which animal rights organizations or activities could be considered criminal. It is fair to assume that, as a result of this opinion and conspiracy indictments brought against activists, individuals who would wish to lawfully advocate for animal rights would choose not to associate with animal rights groups out of fear of potential prosecution.

The Third Circuit's opinion cites *NAACP v. Claiborne Hardware* (1982), which raises many issues pertinent to the AETA. *NAACP* addressed a boycott against white-owned businesses in the late 1960s in Claiborne County, Mississippi. While many in the African American community supported the boycott and participated in it voluntarily, threats were made against African Americans who broke the boycott and in a few instances noncompliant individuals were subjected to physical attacks (*NAACP v. Claiborne* 1982).

A lawsuit was filed by the businesses against the NAACP and individuals associated with the organization for the economic losses resulting from the boycott. The suit claimed that the NAACP and Charles Evers were responsible for financial losses arising from alleged illegal actions to advance the boycott. The suit also alleged that Evers, one of the leaders of the local NAACP, had made speeches that included threats against members of the community who broke the boycott (*NAACP v. Claiborne Hardware* 1982).

The Supreme Court ruled that "for liability to be imposed by rea-son of association alone, it is necessary to establish that the group itself possessed unlawful goals and that the individuals held a specific intent to further those illegal aims," as the court's opinion in *Fullmer* stated. However, in *NAACP*, the court found that the group did not have unlaw-ful aims, as their goal of changing social and political conditions in their community was legitimate. The decision established that the First Amendment protected the freedom to associate and take collective action with others, even if other members of the group engaged in unlawful conduct. Further, in *NAACP*, the Supreme Court upheld that "highly charged political rhetoric," "advocacy of the use of force," and speech that seeks to "embarrass others or coerce them into action" is all protected by the First Amendment (*NAACP v. Claiborne Hardware* 1982).

Despite the fact that the SHAC 7's actions were for the purpose of creating social and political change through the use of political rhetoric and attempts to embarrass others into action, similar to the *NAACP* case, the Third Circuit nonetheless upheld the convictions. It did not analyze the facts to establish if each SHAC 7 defendant held the specific intent to further any illegal aims, nor did it examine the similarities or differences of facts between *NAACP* and *Fullmer* (*U.S. v. Fullmer* 2009). The Third Circuit's decision is the only appellate decision regarding the constitu-tionality of the AEPA.

The *Fullmer* decision leaves a significant lack of clarity regarding what could subject an individual to conspiracy charges under the AETA. Simply stating that it becomes criminal conspiracy when "the group itself possessed unlawful goals" is a problematic position considering that the text of the AETA lacks specificity about what is lawful or unlaw-ful advocacy.

The First Amendment of the United States Constitution states that "Congress shall make no law respecting...abridging the freedom of speech, or of the press; or the right of the people peaceably to assemble, and to petition the Government for a redress of grievances." Historically, there have been few limits to First Amendment protections. However, courts have found that incitement to violence is not protected by the First Amendment when such incitements are direct, considering the proximity and degree of the advocacy and the likelihood that violence will erupt in that moment (*Brandenburg v. Ohio* 1969).

In *Brandenburg v. Ohio* (1969) the Supreme Court upheld that the First Amendment protected the right to advocate for illegal action or the use of force, unless such advocacy was a direct incitement of imminent violence. In that case, the leader of a Ku Klux Klan group was convicted under the Ohio criminal syndicalism statute for "advocating the duty, necessity, or propriety of crime, sabotage, violence, or unlawful methods of terrorism as a means of accomplishing industrial or political reform, and for voluntarily . . . assemblage of persons formed to teach or advocate the doctrines of criminal syndicalism." The Supreme Court overturned the conviction and determined that the statute was unconstitutional because it prohibited advocacy and assembling with others to advocate for political purposes (*Brandenburg v. Ohio* 1969).

The court's ruling in *Brandenburg* is instructive. The text of the AETA prohibits "a course of conduct involving threats, acts of vandalism, property damage, criminal trespass, harassment, or intimidation" for the "purpose of damaging or interfering with an animal enterprise." This language closely resembles Ohio's unconstitutional statute in *Brandenburg* that criminalized "advocat[ing] the duty, necessity, or propriety of crime, sabotage, violence or unlawful methods of terrorism as a means of accomplishing industrial or political reform" and "voluntarily assembl[ing] with any society, group or assemblage of persons formed to teach or advocate the doctrines of criminal syndicalism." The key distinction is that the language of the AETA does not prohibit advocacy or assembly, per se. Nonetheless, advocating for illegal action, assembling, or associating with others who do so has been used as evidence of conspiracy to commit "animal enterprise terrorism."

The cases brought under the AETA and its precursor, the AEPA, can be, and have been, used to criminalize activists based on assembly and advocacy of an animal rights ideology. The Third Circuit justified upholding the SHAC 7 convictions, in part, because of speeches the court framed as advocating illegal action, their associations with each other and other animal rights activists, and significantly because a few ran a website that noted support for illegal action of others and promoted "black fax" Mondays. The court stated, "the individual defendants held up the success of the illegal campaigns as an example to other companies they targeted, in furtherance of their conspiracy to violate the AEPA" (*U.S. v. Fullmer* 2009). In addition, Scott DeMuth was charged with conspiracy, his prior expressions of support for prisoners incarcerated for animal liberation actions being presented as evidence against him (*U.S. v. DeMuth*, Detention Hearing 2009). The AETA 4 were charged for their participation in demonstrations, which is nothing more than assembling with others to advocate for a particular cause.

In December 2011, a civil lawsuit was filed by five activists challenging the constitutionality of the AETA. A significant part of the complaint was based on the way in which prosecutions under the AEPA and AETA had deterred individuals from engaging in animal rights activism. Some of the plaintiffs described observing legal animal rights actions diminish in size because individuals feared prosecution. In addition, some of the plaintiffs explained how they themselves had chosen to participate in fewer public demonstrations after seeing friends and colleagues indicted as "terrorists" (*Blum v. Holder* 2011).

One of the most dangerous aspects of the AETA is its chilling effect. Individuals who would otherwise speak freely against the cruelty and exploitation by animal industries may begin to self-censor or distance themselves from a movement for fear of prosecution. The AETA and the AEPA have been used not only in cases of animal liberations and destruction of property, but against individuals engaged in chanting, speaking on a bullhorn, distributing fliers, or promoting campaigns on websites. When actions that are some of the most traditionally accepted forms of First Amendment–protected activity become grounds for an indictment for conspiring to commit terrorism, it becomes highly unlikely that individuals will be able to navigate the balance of what is constitutionally protected and what is a federal crime. As a result, individuals are likely to opt out of participating in animal rights activism, undermining the ability of the movement to impact society.

While the ambiguity of what actions fall within the scope of the AETA creates a serious threat to civil liberties, it also establishes a significant window of opportunity. The AETA is still fairly new, it has been used in relatively few cases, and the constitutionality of the statute has yet to be fully challenged in court. The precarious nature of the statute provides us with substantial opportunities to challenge it.

CONCLUSION

Congressman Kucinich's concerns that the AETA would target First Amendment activity based on an animal rights ideology have come to fruition—not just with the AETA, but also with the earlier AEPA. The manner of the AETA's enforcement has cast aside Congressman Scott's reassurances that the AETA would not be used for such activity, for intrastate actions, or for civil disobedience. Contrary to Congressman Scott's assertion that the "First Amendment freedoms of expression cannot be defeated by statute," the AETA has done just that.

It is up to civil libertarians and animal rights activists, and the lawyers who represent them, to challenge this overreaching and unconstitutional statute in every arena possible; defenders of civil liberties should advocate for the political repeal of the act, and lawyers should bring constitutional challenges in the courts. The most critical challenge is for supporters of animal rights to refuse to be chilled by this unconstitutional statute by continuing courageously and audaciously to exercise their First Amendment protected right to freely speak and to demonstrate against industries that profit from animal exploitation. By keeping this in mind, we can proceed unimpeded by the AETA to address the issue that, as Congressman Kucinich stated, the AETA and Congress have failed to address—the inhumane treatment of animals.

REFERENCES

Animal Enterprise Protection Act of 1992, 18 U.S.C.A. § 43 (amended 1996, 2002, and 2006).
Animal Enterprise Protection Act Pub. L. No. 102-346 (Aug. 26, 1992).
Animal Enterprise Protection Act Pub. L. No. 104-294 (1996).
Animal Enterprise Protection Act Pub. L. No. 109-374 (Nov. 27, 2006).
Animal Enterprise Terrorism Act 18. U.S.C.A. § 43 (2006).

Blum v. Holder, United States District Court, District of Massachusetts, 11-cv-12229, Complaint (Dec. 15, 2011).

Brandenburg v. Ohio, 395 U.S. 444 (1969).

Congressional Record, 152 Cong. Rec. H8590-01 (Nov. 13, 2006).

Kjonaas v. U.S., 131 S.Ct 1600 (2011) No. 10-7187 (*cert. denied*).

NAACP v. Claiborne Hardware, 458 U.S. 886 (1982).

U.S. v. Bond, United States District Court, District of Colorado, 10-cr-389, Indictment (July 27, 2010).

U.S. v. Bond, United States District Court, District of Utah, 10-cr-844, Indictment (Sept. 15, 2010).

U.S. v. Bond, Minute Entry; Plea of Guilty entered by Defendant Bond (Nov. 18, 2010).

U.S. v. Bond, Minute Entry; Defendant Bond sentenced (Feb. 11, 2011).

U.S. v. Buddenberg, et al, United States District Court, Northern District of California, 09-cr-263 Indictment (2009).

U.S. v. Buddenberg, Or. Denying Def.'s Motion to Dismiss (Oct. 28, 2009).

U.S. v. Buddenberg, Or. Dismissing Indictment Without Prejudice (July 12, 2010).

U.S. v. DeMuth, United States District Court, Southern District of Iowa, 09-cr-117, Indictment (Nov. 18, 2009).

U.S. v. DeMuth, Detention Hearing (Nov. 20, 2009).

U.S. v. DeMuth, Second Superseding Indictment (Apr. 13, 2010).

U.S. v. DeMuth, Plea Agreement (Sept. 13, 2010).

U.S. v. DeMuth, Minute Entry; Sentencing (Feb. 14, 2011).

U.S. v. Fullmer, 584 F.3d 132 (3d Cir. 2009).

U.S. v. Viehl, United States District Court, District of Utah, 09-cr-119 Indictment (Mar. 3, 2009).

U.S. v. Viehl, Motion to Dismiss for Lack of Jurisdiction (July 16, 2009).

U.S. v. Viehl, Memorandum in Opposition by U.S. to Def.'s Motion to Dismiss (July 29, 2009).

U.S. v. Viehl, Minute Entry; Denying Motion to Dismiss (Aug. 10, 2009).

U.S. v. Viehl, Minute Entry; Plea of Guilty entered by Defendant Viehl (Sept. 2, 2009).

U.S. v. Viehl, Minute Entry; Defendant Viehl sentenced (Feb. 5, 2010).

U.S. v. Viehl, Minute Entry; Plea of Guilty entered by Defendant Hall (Apr. 15, 2010).

U.S. v. Viehl, Minute Entry; Defendant Hall sentenced (July 2, 2010).

PART II

POLITICAL REPRESSION
AND CORPORATE COLLUSION

THE "GREEN SCARE" AND "ECO-TERRORISM"

THE DEVELOPMENT OF U.S. "COUNTERTERRORISM" STRATEGY TARGETING DIRECT ACTION ACTIVISTS

Michael Loadenthal

OVERVIEW

Beginning in the late 1990s, the United States federal government initiated a counterterrorism campaign directed at an emerging network of domestic environmental and animal rights direct action activists targeting property (e.g. vandalism, sabotage, theft, and arson) under the monikers of the Earth Liberation Front and Animal Liberation Front. With measured pace, federally managed law enforcement agencies identified a "threat," which they perceived was growing. The State then accelerated its observation, gathered information on the environmental and animal rights movements, and began to allocate local and national resources to address the movements' surges.

Ironically, the FBI acknowledged in 2005 that the number of incidents of property damage was actually decreasing, although it attributed the drop to its Operation Backfire convictions. Nonetheless, the perceived threat of environmental and animal rights–themed property destruction was framed politically as a primary domestic threat deserving of national attention. However, the federalized investigations of these incidents represent a divergence in traditional jurisdictional limitations of U.S. law enforcement. Even court records imply that the National Security Agency (NSA), typically employed for outside military operations, might have been used to conduct wiretapping domestically on these activists.

Upon deciding to engage with these movements, the U.S. government developed laws and organizational structures for the intelligence and law enforcement community to use in their efforts to prosecute, uncover, and disrupt them. This is not dissimilar to the FBI's counterintelligence operations (COINTELPRO) of the 1960s and 1970s. However, more pervasive than COINTELPRO, the counterterrorism strategy, taken as a whole, has been able to incorporate all three branches of government. The State was able to coalesce its abilities through multidepartmental task forces built on agencies' specialized skill sets, and through information sharing and international cooperation. The FBI was able to make arrests and to use defendants' testimonies, leading to indictments, arrests, and convictions.

INTRODUCTION

In the wake of simultaneous attacks on the United States by a foreign threat, the nation's counterterrorism efforts focused on identifying and dismantling a foreign network of ideological militants with a stated declaration of war. Throughout this period, the U.S. federal government, or "the State," launched a second campaign focused on the elimination of a perceived domestic threat, the Earth Liberation Front (ELF) and Animal Liberation Front (ALF). These environmental and animal liberation direct action movements, which have no national history of violence against people, were quickly conflated within the State's rhetoric as domestic terrorists akin to al-Qaeda or the historically lethal white supremacist, antiabortion, and neo-Nazi movements. This rhetorical effort then developed from a hyperbolic discourse into a series of localized police investigations followed by coordinated, multinational, multiagency cooperative campaigns involving the combined efforts of all branches of government: executive, legislative, and judiciary.

For the executive and judicial branches of government, the task has been to identify and politically frame the "threat"—to cast it as increasingly threatening while simultaneously manageable, daunting but able to be defeated. The legislature has been tasked with the establishment of state and federal laws and the legalization of policing processes, even those used by the U.S. military, allowing the government to investigate and prosecute in new ways. For the judiciary, its task has been to be more permissive with allowing evidence, even if prejudicial, toward the defendants while using ever more stringent laws as a basis for more severe rulings. In turn, the executive is tasked to pursue individuals via police forces, prosecuting those arrested through laws enacted by the legislature. In total, domestic policing, portrayed as a counterterrorism strategy by the State, is based on a shared responsibility held by the government as a whole. This case study seeks to identify and deconstruct the counterterrorism strategy that is targeting the networks associated with the ALF/ELF, first tracing the State's perceived threat identification, and later examining the methods created to disrupt and capture those it has labeled "terrorists."

PERCEIVED THREAT AND COUNTERTHREAT STRATEGY

The counterterrorism strategy employed by the government has been termed the "Green Scare" by those activists targeted starting around 2005. Defined in the ALF support magazine *Bite Back*, the authors explain the Green Scare as:

> Legal and extralegal actions taken by the U.S. government against environmental and animal rights activists. Like the Red Scare, the Green Scare uses new laws and new arms of the State to harshly punish a few individuals in order to repress an entire movement. ("Green Scare" 2009, 8)

The reactionary development of the Green Scare label coincided with the State's own invented language—an attempt to quantify and label their enemies under one banner, "eco-terrorism," a term coined by the government in 2002. Prior to that time, such networks were discussed with labels such as "special interest extremists" (Freeh 2001). In a 2001 speech, prior to the adoption of the "eco-terrorist" label, former FBI director Louis Freeh described the ALF as "one of the most active extremist elements in the U.S." One year later, the annual terrorism report coauthored by the Department of Justice (DOJ) and FBI included a new section entitled "Trends in Animal Rights and Environmental Extremism" wherein the movement's attacks were claimed to have "increased in frequency and intensity... [with] ... violent extremist[s] on behalf of animal rights and the environment... clearly on the rise in the U.S" (FBI CTD 2002).

However, a peer-reviewed quantitative study reveals that ALF/ELF incidents during the 2001–2002 period *decreased* by nearly 50 percent (Loadenthal 2010). During this time period, these "violent extremists" injured not a single person. Throughout these 160 incidents which occurred 2001–2002, 69 percent constituted vandalism or sabotage (e.g. gluing locks, graffiti, breaking windows), 17.5 percent were arsons or attempted arsons, and 13 percent were the theft or release of captive animals (Loadenthal 2010). Throughout such incident-based, quantitative analysis, comparisons with government documents is difficult. This difficulty is due largely to the opacity of the State's dataset and resulting methods of analysis. It thus becomes impossible for an accurate comparative analysis as one attempts to compare 160 *known* incidents with an *unknown* number of incidents referenced by the FBI during that time period.

Ironic Timing of Federal Legislation

The timing of federal "eco-terrorism" legislation is mystifying when one examines the chronology of such legislation alongside the record of ALF/ELF incidents, as shown in the figure that follows. Ironically, for the years in which the Animal Enterprise Protection Act (AEPA) and the Animal Enterprise Terrorism Act (AETA) were enacted, there was already a precipitous decrease in incidents. By the AEPA 2002 enactment, there had already been a nearly five-fold decrease in incidents from 1997 (296 incidents) to 2002 (56 incidents). By the AETA's 2006 enactment, there had already been, again, a precipitous decline to 21 incidents—close to what the numbers were when the original AEPA of 1992 was enacted. Therefore, in 2006, when the AETA was enacted, as well as in 1992 and 2002 when its predecessor laws were enacted, ALF/

ELF incidents were already on a dramatic decline from the respective years preceding each enactment.

Ironically, in the year immediately following each enactment, ALF/ELF incidents increased, mostly dramatically: The year after the passage of the 1992 AEPA, incidents increased from 11 in 1992 to 67 in 1993. When the AEPA passed in 2002, incidents increased, although less dramatically, from 56 to 70 in 2003. Finally, the year after the passage of the 2006 AETA, incidents increased from 21 in 2006 to 48 in 2007.

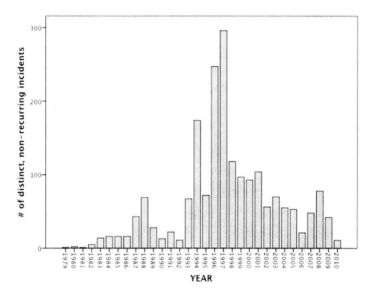

ALF, ELF, and ALF/ELF incidents in the United States,
1979–June 2010* (Loadenthal 2010).[1]

Evolution of the "Eco-Terrorism" Label

Throughout the government publications released in 2000–2001, the steady quantity of ALF/ELF incidents is simply noted without any fanfare. Not until after 9/11 does the "eco-terrorist" label emerge during a 2002 congressional speech, again ironically, since there had been a dramatic decrease in ALF/ELF incidents that year. In the speech, FBI

---

1   This figure represents only distinct, non-recurring ALF, ELF, and ALF/ELF-claimed property damage, occurring in the United States until June 2010 when data was collected.

Domestic Terrorism Chief James Jarboe uses the label twelve times, even titling the speech "The Threat of Eco-Terrorism" (2002). Among his remarks, Jarboe expounds on the FBI's new definition for "eco-terrorism" as: "The use or threatened use of violence of a criminal nature against innocent victims or property by an environmentally oriented, subnational group for environmental-political reasons, or aimed at an audience beyond the target, often of a symbolic nature" (2002). In February 2002, Dale Watson of the FBI's counterterrorism/counterintelligence division reported to the Senate that the ALF/ELF "characterize" the current domestic threat, arguing that such movements represent a "serious terrorist threat" as they are "one of the most active extremist elements in the U.S."

Then in May 2004 the threat assessment shifts remarkably as the movement begins to be described as "*the* most active criminal extremist element in the U.S" (Lewis 2004). Prior to this language shift, the ALF/ELF was listed alongside right-wing groups (e.g., neo-Nazi, militia, antiabortion) otherwise known for having a history of lethal violence. Despite this record of lethality by right-wing groups, the FBI, nonetheless, pronounced in 2004 that it had "made the prevention and investigation of animal rights extremists/eco-terrorism matters a domestic terrorism investigative *priority*" (Lewis 2004). Four years later, the FBI would report that between 1996 and 2008, small groups of clandestine ALF/ELF activists, described in State propaganda as "cells," carried out approximately 1,800 attacks against property, costing more than $110 million in damages (Ward 2008).

These "attacks," while diverse in nature, share a number of key characteristics that differentiate them from traditional "attacks" catalogued by State security forces involved in counterterrorism. "Eco-terrorist attacks" involve a non-military-styled group of clandestine individuals carrying out acts of property damage aimed at financially damaging a target seen to be harming animals or Earth. Strategically, these methods are known as "economic sabotage" and often take the form of vandalism (e.g., breaking windows, slashing tires, painting storefronts), sabotage (e.g., adding abrasives to machinery engines, gluing locks, disabling plumbing systems), theft (e.g., removing animals from vivisection facilities, stealing mink breeding records or university research materials) and, one of the least often, arson. Most of these actions are much closer to traditional notions of civil disobedience than they are to terrorism—resembling the Boston Tea Party much more than the 9/11 attacks. There are no bombings of trains, hostage sieges at office buildings, or hijackings aboard airplanes. In fact, from the first recorded U.S. ALF action in 1979, no ALF/ELF "attack" has caused a single physical injury or death. In that 1979 so-called "attack," the ALF "cell" entered vivisection facilities at New York University's Medical Center and removed one cat, two dogs, and two guinea pigs from the laboratory facilities (Young 2010c). During the time period from March 14, 1979, to June 9, 2010, the U.S. ALF/ELF claimed 3,300 incidents: 2,454 claimed by the ALF; 808 claimed by the ELF; and 38 claimed by the ALF/ELF. Most of these incidents involved low-level criminal mischief, and none resulted in any physical injuries or fatalities.

The State's Skewed Characterization

Despite this history of solely targeting property, the State continues to describe these groups as "domestic terrorists." This "eco-terrorism" characterization laid the ideological basis for the government's development of a large-scale campaign targeting the ALF/ELF and affiliated networks (Haider-Markel, Joslyn, and Al-Baghal 2006). By characterizing the movement as a growing threat, the State fulfilled a political prerequisite for the development of an aggressive counterterrorism strategy. This trend can be said to have reached its apex in 2006 when the DOJ released its terrorism report tracking incidents of domestic terrorism 2002–2005, skewed toward ALF/ELF. Within this 2006 DOJ/FBI report there is a chart labeled "Chronological Summary of Terrorist Incidents in the United States 1980–2005" (FBI CTD 2006). Here, between 2002 and 2005, the DOJ/FBI lists only twenty-four "terrorist incidents," nineteen of which are attributed to so-called "eco-terrorists"—three from the ALF, thirteen from the ELF, and three from the ALF/ELF. Of the remaining five incidents, three are linked to animal liberation activists, though all three acted *without* adopting the ALF/ELF moniker. Throughout the entire 2002–2005 chronology, only two incidents fall outside the animal liberation or environmental taxonomy: (1) July 4, 2002, Hesham Mohammed Ali Hedayat opens fire at the El Al ticket counter inside Los Angeles International Airport, killing two people; and (2) April 1, 2004, Aryan Nations corporal Sean Michael Gillespie throws a Molotov cocktail into the Temple B'nai Israel synagogue in Oklahoma City, Oklahoma.

This "chronological summary" only includes incidents that were completed, excluding arrests and plots uncovered prior to their execution. Through this process of inclusion and exclusion, the chronology is heavily laden with ALF/ELF incidents while other notable events are disregarded. For example, on August 22, 2002, Robert J. Goldstein was detained in Pinellas County, Florida, when he was found to be in possession of "numerous weapons and explosives and a 'mission statement' threatening to attack Islamic facilities in the United States" to coincide with the first anniversary of the 9/11 attacks (FBI CTD 2006). Three other individuals were later arrested for their participation in the planned bombing that was to target the local Islamic center in an act of vengeance motivated by 9/11, and attacks carried out by Palestinians in Israel. Because these individuals were arrested prior to the bombing, the planned attack is excluded from the "chronological summary." Therefore, the FBI's inclusion-exclusion methodology skews the number of recorded incidents *toward* smaller acts of low-level criminality by the ALF/ELF and *away* from conspiracies to employ lethal violence disrupted prior to execution.

This large number of ALF/ELF "attacks" documented in FBI reports may also be due to the movements' success rate (i.e., incidents which are carried out to their completion and where suspects are not arrested beforehand) and the high economic cost incurred by the targets. It is this successful campaign of economic loss that may have led the law enforcement community to focus more heavily on the ALF/ELF (FBI 2008a). In total, between 2001 and the climax of the Green Scare in 2005, at least fourteen FBI/DOJ speeches referenced the ALF/ELF as an increasing threat, deserving of the full attention of a federally managed law enforcement effort.

Operation Backfire

Despite claims that the State began to focus on the ALF/ELF around 2004, FBI affidavits demonstrate that some investigations began as early as 1996. Operation Backfire stands as the government's premier example of coordinated police efforts aimed at ALF/ELF cells with a high rate of success. The FBI has alleged in their reports that Operation Backfire defendants have been collectively responsible for "at least" twenty-five attacks, mostly arsons, costing $48–80 million (Ward 2008). The DOJ "sentencing memorandum" lists the Operation Backfire defendants as: William Christopher Rodgers, Stanislas Gregory Meyerhoff, Kevin Tubbs, Chelsea Dawn Gerlach, Daniel Gerard McGowan, Nathan Fraser Block, Joseph Dibee, Joyanna L. Zacher, Jennifer Lynn Kolar, Suzanne Savoie, Kendell Tankerley, Darren Todd Thurston, and Jonathan Mark Christopher Paul (DOJ 2007). Following a multiyear investigation, on December 7, 2005, in a series of nationally coordinated raids, seven of the abovementioned suspects were arrested in four states.

On December 20, 2005, DOJ prosecutors in the Operation Backfire investigation issued a sixty-five–count indictment including charges of arson, attempted arson, conspiracy to commit arson, and using a destructive device during a violent crime. The indictment claimed that eleven individuals were collectively responsible for seventeen incidents of property damage carried out in five states over nearly a decade. The incidents involved a variety of sites including wild horse slaughter facilities, a ski resort, police and forest ranger stations, lumber facilities, university research centers, and a tree farm. The indictment presented a legal argument that due to the nature of the cell's collective planning, *all defendants* would be charged in conspiring to commit *the entirety* of the criminal offenses. The indictment charged all defendants with conspiracy, as well as the "destructive device" offense; these charges carried a thirty-year mandatory sentence, and mandatory life sentence for multiple convictions. Thus, if the defendants chose to enter a criminal trial, and were found guilty, based on the charges levied in the indictment all would receive prison sentences of thirty years to life.

Operation Backfire utilized aggressive prosecution with the aim of producing "cooperating defendants." The strategy employed by the

DOJ, wherein defendants were indicted with felonious conspiracy and "destructive device" charges, was intended to force the accused to accept a plea agreement and cooperate with the prosecution by implicating other defendants. This strategy succeeded, and by January 2006, six of the Operation Backfire defendants (Kendall Tankersley, Suzanne Savoie, Darren Thurston, Chelsea Gerlach, Kevin Tubbs, and Stanislas Meyer-hoff) became "confidential sources" for the prosecution, providing information on other defendants, and indicting additional conspirators not named in the original indictment.

As part of their plea agreement as cooperators, additional crimes exposed in the proceedings did not carry further jail time, and all records of their cooperation were sealed to the public. Simultaneously with the DOJ's efforts, the FBI sought to locate and capture four fugitives (Joseph Dibee, Josephine Overaker, Justin Solondz, and Rebecca Rubin) who fled prosecution, listing them as "Most Wanted Domestic Terrorists" (FBI 2008b), offering $50,000 rewards for information leading to their arrest.

In other DOJ cases within the Operation Backfire prosecutions, Daniel McGowan, Nathan Block, Joyanna Zacher, and Jonathan Paul eventually negotiated plea agreements wherein they pled guilty to their crimes but were not required to provide evidence against other defendants. Briana Waters entered an independent plea of "not guilty" and was later found guilty and sentenced. William Rodgers, said to be the "leader" of the conspiracy, committed suicide while in custody prior to entering a plea.

In total, Operation Backfire is important in its disclosure of key elements of the government's counterterrorism strategy targeting of the ALF/ELF. First, it showed the utilization of multi-departmental, multi-jurisdictional investigations involving members of federal agencies including the Bureau of Alcohol, Tobacco, Firearms and Explosives (BATF), the FBI, the Bureau of Land Management, and the U.S. Forest Service (Department of Justice [DOJ], 2008). Also revealed was cooperation with Immigration and Customs Enforcement in document analysis and the pursuit of fugitives (DOJ 2006a). On the local level, Operation Backfire involved numerous jurisdictions, including police departments from Eugene, Oregon; Oregon state forces; the University of Washington; and the Lane County Sherriff's Office in Western Oregon (DOJ 2006b). This use of aggressive intelligence gathering and multi-departmental information sharing is a hallmark of the post-9/11 push to reduce redundancy and increase cooperative transparency within the various federal law enforcement bodies, as best evidenced by the creation of the Department of Homeland Security (Borja 2008).

FBI and Joint Terrorism Task Forces

The government's counterterrorism strategy utilized new methods of organizational integration, shown in the formation of 103 Joint Terrorism Task Forces (JTTF) (Lewis 2005b). In order to coalesce and coordinate investigations, the FBI established JTTFs targeting ALF/ELF networks in at least five cities: Portland, Oregon (FBI 2009), Richmond, Virginia (FBI VA 2005), Seattle, Washington (FBI SJTTF 2008), Sacramento, California (FBI CA, 2005), and San Francisco, California (Ryan, Nadel, and Becker 2003).

The FBI's development of regional JTTFs is integral to the larger federally directed counterterrorism strategy and is often touted as a sign of the agency's advancement in information sharing and intelligence gathering. Through JTTFs the FBI conducted a series of police actions including infiltrating cells and raids on high-level suspects' homes. In at least three instances, figures identified as fulfilling leadership positions had their homes raided by JTTFs that proceeded to seize movement publications, personal records, and all digital storage media. In 2000 and 2002, several years before the Operation Backfire arrests, JTTFs raided the home of former ELF spokesmen Craig Rosebraugh (Rosebraugh 2004). More recently, in 2010, FBI agents raided the home of Peter Young after he published a listing of businesses involved in the breeding of animals for the fur industry (Young 2010a).

The FBI has been exceedingly open about some of its methods utilized in investigating ALF/ELF networks, often detailing investigative programs in releases designed for external consumption. In one such document, the FBI reports they have:

disseminated 64 raw intelligence reports to our partners pertaining to animal rights extremism and eco-terrorism activity...developed an intelligence requirement set for animal rights/eco-terrorism, enabling us to better collect, analyze, and share information....Currently, 35 FBI offices have over 150 pending investigations associated with animal rights/eco-terrorist activities. (Lewis 2005b)

In yet another positive appraisal of their efforts in combating the ALF/ELF, the FBI states that their agents have "mapped our environmental and animal rights extremism cases...analyzing information from financial records, phone records, and mail...and working to increase our human source reporting...sharing intelligence...through our Joint Terrorism Task Forces" (DOJ 2008). Through these types of actions, the FBI disrupted a number of ALF/ELF cells, made a series of arrests, and provided evidence to the State for numerous successful prosecutions beyond those uncovered in Operation Backfire.

In 2005, following such victories under Operation Backfire, the FBI claimed that "serious incidents" of ALF/ELF activity had decreased due to successful law enforcement efforts creating an atmosphere of deterrence for future crimes (Mueller 2005). Despite such prosecutions by the State, the ELF and ALF networks have remained relatively resistant to discovery, infiltration, and arrest—resulting in a low number of arrests while continuing to produce regular actions.

Police and Intelligence

The use of multi-departmental teams with specialized skill sets is a strategic directive adopted by the State. Throughout the numerous investigations, a large number of agencies have participated, including the FBI; the BATF; fire departments; arson task forces; sheriff's departments; bomb squadrons; emergency response teams; and local, state, and university police (FBI 2004). These agencies were often provided with the full technical support of the FBI Academy, the FBI's Quantico, Virginia, laboratory specializing in forensic analysis, federal and state arson-explosive investigators, and the BATF databases that catalog federal intelligence involving explosives (DOJ 2009). With this cooperation, localized investigations were able to utilize the most advanced forms of human intelligence, signals intelligence, and forensic analysis available.

Multi-departmental investigative teams saw the developed capability for locally based yet federally equipped inquiries utilizing advanced methods such as DNA analysis. During one incident, DNA was taken from environmental activists affiliated with Earth First! while investigating acts of sabotage targeting a logging company (Fish 2006). In another example, while investigating an ELF-claimed sabotage and attempted arson, FBI agents collected DNA from a cigarette used in the construction of an improvised incendiary device (Mrozek 2010). This DNA sample was analyzed through the use of the Combined DNA Index System, resulting in a match with Stephen James Murphy, whose DNA records were already held by the California DOJ from a prior arrest (Eimiller 2009).

These sorts of federalized investigations represent a divergence in traditional jurisdictional limitations of U.S. law enforcement. For example, the use of FBI intelligence centers to both collect and analyze evidence is typically reserved for crimes that present a threat to American lives such as the bombing of an abortion clinic, the development of armed militia movements, or assaults by white supremacists. Such federal resources are *not* typically utilized to investigate misdemeanor-level property crimes such as the theft of minks or the burning of a milk truck.

There is even circumstantial evidence that suggests signals analysis experts at the National Security Agency (NSA) were involved in the investigation of Daniel McGowan. If NSA wiretaps were used to collect evidence on McGowan, this would constitute a breach of U.S. law, as the NSA is prohibited from investigating American citizens. When the McGowan defense filed a motion with the court compelling the State to reveal the source of its signals intelligence, prosecutors were motivated to advance plea bargain negotiations if the NSA inquiry was dropped (Goodman and González 2007). It was only through leveraging the withdrawal of the NSA motion that McGowan was able to negotiate a plea bargain while remaining a *non-cooperating* defendant. If the defense would have demonstrated that NSA wiretaps *had* been used, the entire series of Operation Backfire cases may have collapsed.

Another example of the use of advanced investigative techniques can be seen in the arrest of two individuals convicted of releasing minks from a Utah facility, uncovered in part due to tracking utilizing cell phones. According to FBI investigative documents, the "attackers" were tracked through their cell signatures as communicated to nearby relay towers and triangulated against chronological data, proving that their phones were at the target during the time the facility was attacked (Young 2010b). In a similar maneuver, according to the DOJ's memorandum, Operation Backfire defendant Josephine Overaker was reportedly tracked by comparing her phone records with roadway toll systems to determine her location and travel time (DOJ 2007). In the investigation of animal liberationist Daniel Andreas San Diego, an FBI affidavit details plans to covertly enter the property of a suspect and install "mobile tracking devices" on the suspect's car (Ryan *et al.* 2003). The affidavit explains additional FBI methods targeting the suspect, including analysis of video surveillance, cross-referencing of telephone records with known activists, and the physical surveillance of the suspect's home and those of known associates (Ryan *et al.* 2003). In addition, the document reveals the use of the Postal Inspection Service and its carriers to provide information on San Diego's movements and residential layout, as well as the use of "FBI database checks" to establish associations with other activists.

Beyond electronic and physical surveillance of suspects and associates, law enforcement agencies have expanded their cooperation to international partners. In its campaign against what the FBI has labeled as a "militant" animal rights group, Stop Huntingdon Animal Cruelty (SHAC), the FBI shared information with intelligence agencies in Canada and the U.K. (Lewis 2005a). Additionally, the FBI has helped to coordinate international conferences focusing on "eco-terrorism" with intelligence agencies from Finland, Norway, Sweden, Belgium, Germany, the Netherlands, and the U.K. (Lewis 2005a). This effort to share intelligence appears to be common. Since 1985, the U.K. has developed the Animal Rights National Index, as well as the National Extremism Tactical

Coordination Unit, which was established to provide a "national, joined up approach to single issue terrorism" (Richards 2007).

It is important to note, too, that SHAC is not the same as the ALF/ELF. SHAC is *not* a clandestine movement utilizing property destruction, but is rather an *aboveground campaign* aimed at financially isolating vivisection supplier Huntingdon Life Sciences. SHAC works to identify, map, and publicize the financial relationships between Huntingdon and its subsidiaries, suppliers, and secondary and tertiary affiliates. Individual countries have had their own SHAC campaigns, identifying potential targets, but *attacks* on such targets are the work of external actors who choose to carry out property crimes under a variety of monikers including, but not limited to, the ALF/ELF. This example of law enforcement agencies targeting SHAC amidst the ALF demonstrates the problem of conflation, where meaningful nuance and difference are flattened into the generic labeling of "militants," "eco-terrorists," and "animal rights extremists."

Not only has the U.S. developed its own domestic capabilities and shared its knowledge with foreign governments, it also informs private industry, a common target of ALF/ELF attacks on property. In one example, the Department of State, through the Overseas Security Advisory Council (OSAC), gave a presentation wherein it explained the history of the animal rights movement and its targeting and tactical tendencies and suggested preventative measures. OSAC described its role as "promot[ing] security cooperation between American business and private sector interests." OSAC's website lists numerous partner companies that have been targeted by ALF/ELF cells as well as the SHAC movement including 3M, Merrill Lynch, Monsanto, Aramark, Procter & Gamble, Raytheon, and Target.

While receiving support from the government through institutions like OSAC, private business has begun collecting and analyzing its own intelligence. In one example, prior to a conference of toxicologists, the event organizers conducted a "threat analysis and intelligence briefing" due to the observation that many of the conference participants were targets of the SHAC campaign (INA 2008). The "threat analysis" outlines local activist organizations as well as individuals known to be affiliated with such networks. The report was compiled by a private company for internal consumption but was later leaked (INA 2010). It is unclear how prevalent this type of pre-event intelligence gathering is, or how much cooperation event planners receive from the government, but in understanding the larger counterterrorism strategy, the cooperation between State and private business remains largely unexamined.

FBI Informants, Grand Juries, and Prisons

The FBI's counterterrorism strategy has relied on the use of human intelligence gained through the development of "cooperative defendants." It has also recruited contacts to infiltrate radical movements and direct action networks, and to develop informant sources. One such case is based around a government informant known under the pseudonym of "Anna." "Anna's" infiltration activities, detailed in an FBI affidavit, led to the arrest of three suspects charged with "conspiracy to damage and destroy property by fire and an explosive" (Walker 2006).

Throughout "Anna's" eighteen-month undercover investigation, she wore recording devices in conversations with defendants and at activist gatherings. Remarkably, "Anna" was responsible for purchasing materials for incendiary devices, providing instruction concerning their construction, financing the cell's travel in monitored vehicles, and arranging for the cell to carry out incendiary device construction in a cabin set up by surveillance teams (Van Bergen 2006). For her services, "Anna" was paid approximately $65,000 plus expenses by the FBI (Walsh 2007). In her infiltrator capacity, "Anna" communicated with her handler through a variety of electronic and face-to-face methods (Todd 2008). When the investigation was completed, the prosecution was able to impose heavy jail sentences and maneuver two of the three defendants (Zachary Jenson and Lauren Weiner) to act as witnesses against the third, non-cooperating defendant, Eric McDavid, who was eventually sentenced to nearly twenty years.

Such a pattern of FBI-led infiltration was also used in Operation Backfire. The use of informants or "cooperating defendants," whether working for a financial incentive or reduced jail sentences, represents a key component of the government's counterterrorism strategy. In the case of Jacob Ferguson, he served as a "cooperating defendant" who wore recording devices on his person during conversations with cell members (DOJ 2007). Both "Anna" and Ferguson were dispatched to collect evidence at activist gatherings, including an environmental law conference and Earth First! national gathering (Green Anarchy 2006).

Numerous other examples of FBI-led infiltration of ALF/ELF cells exist. Marie Mason was prosecuted through evidence collected from undercover infiltration by her ex-husband who reportedly recorded 178 conversations during a one-year period (White 2008). Like all of the previous informants (excluding "Anna"), Mason's ex-husband had previously carried out crimes, including arson, and was coerced to provide evidence in exchange for leniency in sentencing. Additional cases of State informants include Jennifer Kolar and Lacey Philabaum's testimony against Operation Backfire defendant Briana Waters, and Ian Wallace's testimony against Tony Wong and Brandon Elder (U.S. District Court Western District of Michigan 2008). A final informant is known only by her pseudonym. During her time as an FBI informant, "Sarah" attended public animal rights meetings and was known to be very inquisitive and an active notetaker (Young 2010b).

Through the post-2005 cases, the FBI has dispatched at least nine informants, while at least sixteen defendants cooperated with State prosecution, providing evidence in some form. Those individuals, routinely profiled as "informers, infiltrators, snitches, and/or agents" due to their reported cooperation with State prosecution, include: Kendall Tankersley, Suzanne Savoie, Darren Thurston, Chelsea Gerlach, Kevin Tubbs, Stanislas Meyerhoff, Jacob Ferguson, Frank Ambrose, Lauren Weiner, Jennifer Kolar, Lacey Philabaum, Ian Wallace, William Cottrell, Ryan Lewis, Zachary Jenson, and Justin Samuels.

Once the FBI's JTTFs have identified a network and arrested members, the State has attempted to gather additional testimony through the initiation of Federal Grand Juries (FGJs) held in localities with pending investigations. FGJs aid the gathering of defendant testimony by subverting traditional protections afforded to the accused within the justice system. In a traditional criminal trial, the defendant is presumed "innocent until proven guilty," with the burden of proof resting on prosecutors. In

FGJs, the indicted is coerced into providing evidence, unable to remove oneself from the process via the Fifth Amendment to the Constitution, which protects against self-incrimination. If an individual testifying before an FGJ feels that his knowledge may implicate him in a crime, he cannot choose to decline answering without risk of being charged with "contempt of court."

Beginning in 1997, with the indictment of ELF spokesman Rosebraugh, at least eighteen people were indicted in at least twenty-four FGJs. Those indicted were thought to possess relevant knowledge of ALF/ELF attacks on property. A brief history of *some* of these indictments follows:

- 1997–2000: Craig Rosebraugh indicted by eight FGJs regarding sources for receiving ALF/ELF communiqués (Rosebraugh 2004);
- 1998: Justin Samuels and Peter Young indicted by a FGJ regarding "animal enterprise terrorism" and "extortion by interfering with interstate commerce" (Story and Lincita 2009);
- 2000: Justin Samuels indicted by FGJ Wisconsin (Federal Grand Jury, Western District of Wisconsin 2000) regarding a series of mink releases;
- 2002: Marie Mason and Frank Ambrose indicted by a FGJ regarding sabotage of Ice Mountain water bottling plant (Potter 2009b);
- 2006: Camillo Stephenson indicted by FGJ Denver regarding a 1998 Vail arson (CLDC 2006a); Jeff Hogg indicted by FGJ Eugene, Oregon regarding charges stemming from the Operation Backfire investigation (CLDC 2006b); Burke Morris indicted by FGJ Denver (Lee 2006); Jim Dawson indicted by FGJ Seattle (CLDC 2006a); Nadia Winstead and Ariana Huemer indicted by FGJ San Francisco (Hermes 2006);
- 2007: Anthony Wong, Brandon Elde, and Ian Wallace indicted by FGJ Minneapolis regarding University of Minnesota 2002 arson (Potter 2007);
- 2008: Kevin Tucker indicted by FGJ Erie, Pennsylvania regarding six attacks 2002–2003 (Thompson 2008); Daniel McGowan indicted by FGJ Madison, Wisconsin regarding 2000 arson of government facility in Rhinelander (Earth Warriors Are OK! 2008);

- 2009: Scott DeMuth and Carrie Feldman subpoenaed by FGJ Davenport, Iowa regarding 2004 University of Iowa attack (U.S. District Court Southern District of Iowa 2009). Both refused to testify. Feldman was jailed for civil contempt and DeMuth was subsequently indicted for conspiracy under the AETA; Jordan Halliday indicted by FGJ Iowa regarding 2009 Utah farm attack (Support Jordan Cade Halliday 2010).

Throughout these FGJs, most of those indicted refused to appear or refused to testify. In some cases, those refusing to testify have been jailed. Jeff Hogg's refusal to answer questions to a Eugene FGJ led to a six-month "contempt of court" jail sentence (Potter 2006). Daniel McGowan's indictment occurred while he was already serving his Operation Backfire sentence. Upon his refusal to act as State's witness within Operation Backfire prosecutions, McGowan was transferred to a "communication management unit" (CMU) designated for high-security, political detainees.

The use of CMUs has been incorporated into the government's counterterrorism strategy regarding the ALF/ELF. At present, two of the convicted Green Scare defendants are either serving or have served their sentences at CMU facilities. The CMU facility at USP Marion, Illinois at one time housed Operation Backfire defendant Daniel McGowan, as well as SHAC defendant Andrew Stepanian. In 2010, McGowan was transferred from USP Marion to a second CMU located in Terre Haute, Indiana. These detention facilities were first opened in December 2006, beginning in FCI Terre Haute (Van Bergen 2007). In May 2008, several high profile inmates were transferred to a second CMU at the U.S. Penitentiary in Marion, Illinois (Potter 2009a). The CMU is designed to limit and monitor all detainee communications. All phone communication, mail, and visits are monitored by live persons and must occur in English (Hollingsworth 2008). Not only are all communications monitored, but are greatly restricted in quantity. The typical three hundred monthly minutes allotted for prisoner phone calls is reduced to fifteen minutes a week, with visiting hours reduced to two hours at a time, twice a month. These measures are key in the government counterterrorism strategy for at least two reasons. First, through monitoring the communication of political detainees the State can ensure that detainees' communications with the larger movement are known and documented, and secondly, transfer to and from such facilities can be used as punishment or incentive for defendants' cooperation with investigative efforts.

Laws and Courts

Throughout the police and judicial counterterrorism strategy of informants, FGJs, Task Forces, and CMUs is a new series of laws created at the federal and state levels to differentiate the commission of ALF/ELF crimes from those of non-politicized crimes such as common law arson, vandalism, and theft. To this end, legislation was passed that allows criminal acts targeting "animal enterprises" to be prosecuted as acts of terrorism. This legislation took the form of a series of federal initiatives with similar bills in a number of states.

The hallmark of this legislative campaign was the 1992 AEPA, its last revision being the 2006 AETA. The AEPA/AETA function in similar manners, providing enhanced sentencing guidelines for those targeting "animal enterprises," including academic institutions, businesses, and "tertiary targets," such as suppliers contracted by animal laboratories (109th Congress, 2006). Critics of the AEPA/AETA argue the laws are redundant and politically motivated, outlawing acts which are already illegal under criminal law, and function to aid and empower the larger and ill-conceived anti-ALF counterterrorism strategy (CLDC 2006c).

Not only have the ALF/ELF and other activists faced increasingly aggressive prosecution with the aid of the AEPA/AETA, but also state-level legislation has been introduced in at least sixteen states, among them Arizona (Platt 2005), California (Potter 2008a), Hawaii (State Environmental Resource Center 2004), Kansas (Berkowitz 2003), Maine (Richardson 2005), Mississippi (Game Fowl News 2004), Missouri (ibid.), New York (Animal Rights Online 2003), Ohio (Ohio Legislative Service Commission 2003), Pennsylvania (General Assembly of Pennsylvania 2005), South Carolina (South Carolina General Assembly 2009), South Dakota (South Dakota's Cattlemen's Association 2009), Tennessee (Potter 2008b), Texas (Evans 2003), Utah (Bernick 2009), and Washington (Berkowitz 2004). These bills mirror the AEPA/AETA in a number of ways, proscribing sentencing guidelines for crimes already carrying penalties. The bills carry ominous names such as Texas's Animal Rights and Ecological Terrorism bill, Tennessee's Eco-terrorism Act, and Pennsylvania's HB 213, known similarly as the Eco-terrorism bill, which is often said to be one of the most aggressive state-level AETA analogues in the country. Many of these bills were defeated in their respective houses of government, while some have become laws. Some of the state legislation attempts to mimic the grounds covered by the AEPA/AETA, namely the enhanced prosecution of those targeting "animal enterprises," whereas others seek to expand these categories to include crimes aimed at those targeting entities seen to be harming the environment.

The AEPA/AETA's focus on traditional targets of the ALF (e.g., so-called animal enterprises), rather than those of the ELF, has not gone unnoticed. In a Senate speech, FBI Counterterrorism Deputy Assistant John Lewis referenced AETA, stating:

> The statute only applies to criminal acts committed by animal rights extremists, but does not address criminal activity related to eco-terrorism....Therefore, the existing statutes may need refinements to make them more applicable to current animal rights/eco-extremist actions. (2005b)

Though Lewis's statement was made in 2005, legislation specifically targeting the ELF has not been adopted at the federal level. However, some ELF defendants have been tried under the AETA, as well as other felony-level conspiracy and extortion-related acts, such as the Racketeering Influenced Corruption Act and the Hobbs Act (Beltran 2002; Rosebraugh 2003). Such legislation is historically used to prosecute organized crime engaged in interstate extortion and racketeering. Its use for the prosecution of ALF/ELF defendants can be seen as a component of the DOJ's larger strategy wherein it is able to increase prospective jail sentences for defendants, allowing prosecutors to manipulate penalties in exchange for providing evidence.

This flexibility in prosecutorial sentencing can also be evidenced in the application of "terrorism enhancements" (TEs) during the judicial sentencing process. The selective application of TEs (sometimes referred to as terrorism *adjustments*) was utilized in the sentencing of Operation

Backfire defendants as the judge was empowered to determine whether the actions of the defendants were "intended to coerce" (Harris 2007). If he concluded that the defendants' crimes fit this categorization, the application of TEs would increase the defendants' jail sentences and can be used as evidence by the Bureau of Prisons in determining what type of facility (e.g. maximum-security or CMU) to house the convicted individual. In the government sentencing memorandum concerning the twelve Operation Backfire cases, it states: "The government's position is that the terrorism enhancement...applies to all ten defendants because each of them committed one or more federal crimes of terrorism...as well as...conspiracy" (DOJ 2007).

Despite this assertion, seven of the ten defendants received additional jail sentences due to TEs, while two of the "cooperating defendants," Kendall Tankersley and Darren Thurston, and one "non-cooperating defendant," Jonathan Paul, did not. TEs have been used in Green Scare cases unaffiliated with Operation Backfire. During the State's prosecution of Tre Arrow, convicted of two 2001 arsons, the defendant's sixty-month sentence was increased to seventy-eight months on the grounds that the crimes were "calculated to influence or affect the conduct of the victims by intimidation, coercion, and retaliation" (Immergut 2008).

CONCLUSION

The counterterrorism strategy targeting "eco-terrorists" generally, and the ALF/ELF specifically, has developed to incorporate numerous intersecting arenas of State authority, including the power of the civil police, federal intelligence services, and judiciary, all of which receive support from the legislature. Though the government's campaign contains no explicit military component due to the domestic nature of the perceived threat, nonetheless, federal law enforcement agencies do utilize methods of intelligence gathering rooted within nation-level spy initiatives typically reserved for the NSA. The use of such a spy agency against domestic activists would represent a significant shift in federal strategy—utilizing the largess of the Department of Defense to protect private property via agencies typically reserved for addressing threats to national security from foreign States. The United States's multitiered approach to fighting the ELF and ALF appears to have had some success, with police actions leading to arrests, allowing the DOJ to elicit evidence for further prosecutions. At each stage in the process—from the police's rights to gather evidence, the court's rights to coerce testimony, and the judge's prerogative to assign weighty sentences forcing plea negotiations—the legislature has assisted in empowering the State to pursue their counterterrorism strategy with increasing levels of prosecutorial ease.

The history explaining the development of this State campaign stands as a testament to measured planning and a systematic pursuit designed to destabilize, disrupt, and eliminate the perceived domestic threat. While in the 1990s the federal legislature expanded its ability to punish offenders with increasingly harsh penalties, law enforcement simultaneously began investigations utilizing newly found powers. In tandem with the pursuits of the legislature and police, the federal government embraced the emerging specter of terrorism to argue that saboteurs and a few arsonists, with no history of lethal violence, were the greatest internal threat to the country's security. The establishment of this narrative must be understood as integral to the later development of laws, policies, and police forces to address the perceived problem. The counterterrorism strategy adopted by the government exemplifies a strategically coordinated approach, wherein a perceived, yet diminishing, threat is amplified so as to politicize it, legislate against it, police it, and finally punish it with the full brunt and imprimatur of the law.

References

109th Congress. Senate and House of Representatives of the United States of America (2006). *Animal Enterprise Terrorism Act* (PUBLIC LAW 109–374—NOV. 27, 2006). Washington, D.C.: Congressional Record, Vol. 152 (2006). www.gpo.gov/fdsys/pkg/PLAW-109publ374/pdf/PLAW-109publ374.pdf.

Animal Rights Online. "Freedom of Advocacy." Animal Writes newsletter, June 15, 2003. www.all-creatures.org/aro/nl-20030608-freedom.html.

Beltran, Xavier. "Applying RICO to Eco-Activism: Fanning the Radical Flames of Eco-Terror." *Boston College Environmental Affairs Law Review* 29 no. 2 (2002): 281–310. www.bc.edu/dam/files/schools/law/lawreviews/journals/bcealr/29_2/03_FMS.htm.

Berkowitz, Bill. "(US) Anti-Factory Farm Activists Under Fire." Working for Change electronic mailing list message.. Last modified May 23, 2003. http://lists. envirolink.org/pipermail/ar-news/Week-of-Mon-20030526/001345.html.

———. "Terrorist Tree Huggers: Ron Arnold, Father of the 'Wise Use' Movement, Sets His Sights on 'Eco-terrorists.'" Working for Change, reposted on Common Dreams. Last modified July 7, 2004. www.commondreams.org/views04/0707-12. htm.

Bernick Jr., Bob. "Legislator Takes Aim at Feds and 'Eco-terrorists.'" *Deseret News* (Salt Lake City). Last modified February 6, 2009. www.deseretnews.com/ article/705283052/Legislator-takes-aim-at-feds-and-eco-terrorists.html?pg=all.

Borja, Elizabeth C. *Brief Documentary History of the Department of Homeland Security 2001–2008.* Department of Homeland Security History Office. www.dhs.gov/ xlibrary/assets/ brief_documentary_history_of_dhs_2001_2008.pdf.

Observer. "Eric McDavid Sentenced to 235 Months for Conspiracy Based on Snitch Anna." San Francisco Bay Area Independent Media Center. Published May 8, 2008. www.indybay.org/newsitems/2008/05/08/18498027.php.

Civil Liberties Defense Center (CLDC). (2006a). "Misuse of Grand Juries." http://cldc. org/wp-content/uploads/2012/07/GJ_FAQ.pdf; http://cldc.org/aboutgj.html.

———. (2006b). "Jeff Hogg." Retrieved from http://cldc.org/jhogg.html.

———. (2006c). "The Redundancy of AETA: Why Does the Animal Cruelty Industry Deserve Special Protection?" Last updated January 9, 2012. http://cldc. org/2012/01/09/aeta-the-redundancy-of-aeta/.

Department of Justice (DOJ). Bureau of Alcohol, Tobacco, Firearms and Explosives. "Prepared Remarks for Attorney General Alberto R. Gonzales at the Operation Backfire Press Conference. Washington, D.C." Published January 20, 2006 (2006a). www.atf.gov/press/releases/2006/01/012006-speech-doj-ag-gonzales-operation-backfire.html.

———. Office of the Inspector General, Audit Division. *Explosives Investigation Coordination Between the Federal Bureau of Investigation and the Bureau of Alcohol, Tobacco, Firearms and Explosives* (Audit report 10-01). Published October 2009. www.justice.gov/oig/reports/plus/a1001.pdf.

———. United States Attorney's Office, District of Oregon. "Animal Liberation Front (ALF) and Earth Liberation Front (ELF) Members Indicted by Federal Grand Jury on Conspiracy and Arson Charges" (2006b). www.justice.gov/usao/or/ PressReleases/20060120_ ALF_ELF_Members.htm..

———. United States Attorney, Western District of Washington. "Seattle Woman Sentenced to 5 Years in Prison in Connection with UW Arson: Defendant Was Active Participant in Four Arsons Including UW." Published July 18, 2008. www. justice.gov/usao/waw/press/2008/jul/kolar.html.

———. United States District Court, District of Oregon. "Government's Sentencing Memorandum: United States of America v. Dibee, Gerlach, Tankersley, Mcgowan, Meyerhoff, Overaker, Paul, Rubin, Savoie, Thurston, Tubbs, Block, and Zacher" (CR 06-60069, 06-60070, 06-60071, 06-60078, 06-60079, 06-60080, 06-60120,

06-60122, 06-60123, 06-60-124, 06-60125, 06-60126). Eugene, Oreg.: United States Attorney, District of Oregon and Assistant United States Attorneys. 2007.

Eimiller, Laura. FBI Los Angeles. "FBI Arrests Man on Federal Charges Related to 2006 Attempted Arson Linked to Domestic Terror in Pasadena, California." Published October 1, 2009. http://losangeles.fbi.gov/pressrel/2009/la100109a.htm.

Evans, G. "Texas 'Animal Rights Terrorism' Bill." Electronic mailing list message. Published February 19, 2003. www.veggieboards.com/boards/showthread.php?3536-Texas-quot-Animal-Rights-Terrorism-quot-Bill&p=65225&viewfull=1.

Earth Warriors are OK! "New Elf Indictments in Wisconsin." Published July 25, 2008. http://midwestgreenscare.wordpress.com/2008/07/25/new-elf-indictments-in-wisconsin.

Federal Bureau of Investigation (FBI). "Violence in the Name of the Environment: The Case of the Calculating Eco-Terrorist." Published May 3, 2004. www.fbi.gov/page2/may04/050304ecoterror.htm.

———. "Eco-Terror Indictments: 'Operation Backfire' Nets 11." Published January 20, 2006. www.fbi.gov/news/stories/2006/january/elf012006.

———. "Putting Intel to Work: Against ELF and ALF Terrorists." Published June 30, 2008 (2008a). www.fbi.gov/news/stories/2008/june/ecoterror_063008.

———. "Reward Increased for Operation Backfire Fugitives." Published November 19, 2008 (2008b). www.fbi.gov/news/pressrel/press-releases/reward-increased-for-operation-backfire-fugitives.

———. "Kevin Favreau Named Special Agent in Charge of the FBI's Las Vegas Division." Published December 4, 2009. www.fbi.gov/news/pressrel/press-releases/kevin-favreau-named-special-agent-in-charge-of-the-fbi2019s-las-vegas-division.

Federal Bureau of Investigation Counterterrorism Division (FBI CTD). *Terrorism 2000/2001* (FBI Publication #0308). Last accessed 2002. www.fbi.gov/stats-services/publications/terror/terror00_01.pdf.

———. *Terrorism 2002–2005.* n.d. www.fbi.gov/stats-services/publications/terrorism-2002-2005.

Federal Bureau of Investigation, Richmond Division (FBI VA). "The Richmond Division: A Brief History." Last accessed 2005. www.fbi.gov/richmond/about-us/history-1.

Federal Bureau of Investigation, Sacramento Division (FBI CA). "The Sacramento Division: A Brief History." Last accessed 2005. www.fbi.gov/sacramento/about-us/history-1.

Federal Bureau of Investigation, Seattle Joint Terrorism Task Force (FBI SJTTF). "Seattle Eco-Terrorism Investigation." Published March 4, 2008. www.fbi.gov/news/stories/2008/march/seattlearson_030408.html.

Federal Grand Jury, Western District of Wisconsin (FGJ WI). Testimony of Justin Samuel. Madison, Wisconsin: United States Federal Courthouse, Madison. 2000.

Fish, Jen. "Maine State Police Ask Environmental Activists for DNA." *Portland Press Herald.* June 9, 2006.

Freeh, Louis J. Testimony on the threat of terrorism to the United States before the United States Senate Committees on Appropriations, Armed Services, and Select Committee on Intelligence, Washington, D.C. Published May 10, 2001. www.fbi. gov/news/testimony/threat-of-terrorism-to-the-united-states.

Game Fowl News. "AR/ER Terrorism?" Last accessed August 19, 2004. www. gamefowlnews.com/archives/2004/Thurs 19 Aug 2004.htm.

General Assembly of Pennsylvania. *House Bill No. 213* Session of 2005. Last updated November 15, 2005. www.legis.state.pa.us/CFDOCS/Legis/PN/Public/btCheck. cfm?txtType =HTM&sessYr=2005&sessInd=0&billBody=H&billTyp=B&billNbr =0213&pn=3115.

Goodman, Amy, and Juan González. "Exclusive: Facing Even Years in Jail, Environmental Activist Daniel McGowan Speaks Out About the Earth Liberation Front, the Green Scare and the Government's Treatment of Activists As 'Terrorists.'" Democracy Now, June 11, 2007. www.democracynow.org/2007/6/11/exclusive_facing_seven _years_in_jail.

Green Anarchy. "Operation Backfire: The Feds Make a Monstrous Move." January 2006. www.greenanarchy.org/index.php?action=viewnewsdetail&writingId=564&wri tingTypeId=3.

"Green Scare" Defendants. *Bite Back Magazine* 14, no. 8. February 2009.

Haider-Markel, D. P., M. R. Joslyn, and M. T. Al-Baghal. "Can We Frame the Terrorist Threat? Issue Frames, the Perception of Threat, and Opinions on Counterterrorism Policies." *Terrorism and Political Violence*, 18 no. 4: 545–59. 2006.

Harris, Shane. "The Terrorism Enhancement: An Obscure Law Stretches the Definition of Terrorism, and Metes Out Severe Punishments." *National Journal*. Published July 13, 2007. http://shaneharris.com/magazinestories/terrorism-enhancement-obscure-law-stretches-the-definition-of-terrorism-and-metes-out-severe-punishments.

Hermes, Kris. "Grand Jury Resistance Project." Animal Liberation Front. Published October 4, 2006. www.animalliberationfront.com/News/2006_10/ GrandJuryResistanceProject.htm.

Hollingsworth, L. J. W. U.S. Department of Justice, Federal Bureau of Prisons. Notice to Inmate of Transfer to Communication Management Unit (Register number: 63794-053). Marion, Ill.: Federal Bureau of Prisons. 2008.

Immergut, Karin J. U.S. Department of Justice, Federal Bureau of Investigation, Portland. "Tre Arrow Sentenced to 78 Months in Federal Prison for Pair of 2001 Arsons." Published August 12, 2008. http://portland.fbi.gov/dojpressrel/pressrel08/ pd081208.htm.

INA Inc. "Threat Analysis and Intelligence Briefing." *Proceedings of the 47th Annual Meeting of the Society of Toxicology and Toxexpo 2008, March 16–20, 2008—Washington State Convention and Trade Center—Seattle, WA* (Seattle: INA, 2008): 1–12.

———. INA Investigative and Security Services homepage. Last accessed 2010. www. ina-inc.com.

Jarboe, James F. Testimony on the threat of eco-terrorism before the House Resources Committee, Subcommittee on Forests and Forest Health,

Washington, D.C. Published February 12, 2002. www.fbi.gov/news/testimony/ the-threat-of-eco-terrorism.

Katz, Basil. "Locked Up with Militants, Freed American Talks." Reuters. Published March 30, 2010. www.reuters.com/article/idUSTRE62T3MF20100330.

Lee, Jessica. "Green Scare Update: Weekend of Resistance Planned in Support of Eco-Prisoners." The Indypendent 88. June 10, 2006. www.indypendent.org/2006/06/10/ green-scare-update-weekend-resistance-planned-support-eco-prisoners.

Lewis, John E. Testimony on animal rights extremism and ecoterrorism before the Senate Judiciary Committee, Washington, D.C. Published May 18, 2004. www. fbi.gov/news/testimony/animal-rights-extremism-and-ecoterrorism.

———. Speech on the new era of global partnerships to fight crime and terrorism before the 4th Annual International Conference on Public Safety: Technology and Counterterrorism Initiative and Partnerships, San Francisco, California. Published March 14, 2005 (2005a). www.fbi.gov/news/speeches/ new-era-of-global-partnerships-to-fight-crime-and-terrorism.

———. Testimony addressing the threat of animal rights extremism and eco-terrorism before the Senate Committee on Environment and Public Works, Washington, D.C. May 18, 2005 (2005b). www.fbi.gov/news/testimony/ addressing-the-threat-of-animal-rights-extremism-and-eco-terrorism.

Loadenthal, Michael. "Nor Hostages, Assassinations, or Hijackings, but Sabotage, Vandalism & Fire: Eco-terrorism As Political Violence Challenging the State and Capital." MLitt dissertation. Centre for the Study of Terrorism and Political Violence, University of St. Andrews, Scotland, U.K. 2010.

Mrozek, Thom. "Guilty Plea in Pasadena Arson Plot Linked to Domestic Terrorist Organization." The United States Attorney's Office, Central District of California. Published January 11, 2010. www.justice.gov/usao/cac/Pressroom/pr2010/007. html.

Mueller III, Robert S. Testimony on global threats to the U.S. and the FBI's response before the Senate Committee on Intelligence of the United States Senate, Washington, D.C. February 16, 2005. www.fbi.gov/news/testimony/ global-threats-to-the-u.s.-and-the-fbis-response-1.

Ohio Legislative Service Commission (OLSC), 125th General Assembly of Ohio. Fiscal Note & Local Impact Statement: s.b. 67 (SB00671N/lb). 2003. www.lbo.state.oh.us/ fiscal/fiscalnotes/125ga/SB00671N.HTM.

Overseas Security Advisory Council (OSAC). "About OSAC." www.osac.gov/Pages/ AboutUs.aspx.

Platt, Teresa. "Heads Up! Animal 'Liberation' Elimination Bills Everywhere!" Fur Commission USA. Published May 23, 2005. http://old.furcommission.com/news/ newsF08p.htm.

Potter, Will. "Activist Resisting Grand Jury Witch Hunt Released From Jail." Green Is the New Red. Published November 18, 2006. www.greenisthenewred.com/blog/ activist-resisting-grand-jury-witch-hunt-released-from-jail/149.

———. "New Grand Jury in the Midwest: Another 'Eco-terrorist' Witch Hunt?" Green Is the New Red. Published August 24. 2007. www.greenisthenewred.com/blog/mn-grand-jury/279.

———. "Breaking News: New 'Green Scare' Legislation Pending in California." Green Is the New Red. Published April 14, 2008 (2008a). www.greenisthenewred.com/blog/california/405.

———. "Tennessee Politician: 'Eco-terrorists Are, Uh, I Guess Left-Wing Eco-Greenies.'" Green Is the New Red. Published July 24, 2008 (2008b). www.greenisthenewred.com/blog/tennessee-politician-definingeco-terrorists/484.

———. "Secretive U.S. Prison Units Used to House Muslim, Animal Rights and Environmental Activists." Green Is the New Red. April 14, 2009 (2009a). www.greenisthenewred.com/blog/communication-management-units-mcgowan/1747.

———. "Feds Hope to Set an Example with 'Eco-Terrorist' Who Refused to Snitch: Marie Mason Faces 20 years." Green Is the New Red. February 3, 2009 (2009b). www.greenisthenewred.com/blog/marie-mason-refusal-to-snitch/993.

Richards, Anthony. "The Domestic Threat: The Cases of Northern Ireland and Animal Rights Extremism." In Homeland Security in the UK: Future Preparedness for Terrorist Attack since 9/11, edited by Paul Wilkinson, 81–114. New York: Routledge, 2007.

Richardson, J. "Eco-terrorism Bill Proposes Stiffer Penalties." Morning Sentinel. Published November 23, 2005. http://findarticles.com/p/news-articles/morning-sentinel-waterville-me/mi_8150/is_20051123/eco-terrorism-bill-proposes-stiffer/ai_n50538643/

Rosebraugh, Craig. "Grand Jury Reflections with Craig Rosebraugh." No Compromise 22. Published Fall 2003. www.nocompromise.org/issues/22gj-craig.html.

———. Burning Rage of a Dying Planet: Speaking for the Earth Liberation Front. New York: Lantern Books, 2004.

Ryan, K. V., R. W. Nadel, and E. Becker. United States District Court, Northern District of California San Francisco Division. In the matter of the application of the United States of America for an order authorizing the installation and use of an electronic tracking devices on or in honda civic, California license plate 3EKT50 (No. CR 03-3113 MISC EMC). San Francisco: United States District Court. 2003.

South Carolina General Assembly (SC GA), 117th Session, 2007–2008. (2009). H. 3813 Animal Ecological Terrorism Act. Introduced in the House March 29, 2007. www.scstatehouse.gov/sess117_2007-2008/bills/3813.htm.

South Dakota Cattlemen's Association (SDCA). SDCA Legislative Update. Accessed January 20, 2009. www.sdcattlemen.org/legislativeblog.aspx. (site discontinued).

State Environmental Resource Center (SERC). "Alec's Animal and Ecological Terrorism Act." ALEC Watch. Last updated July 8, 2004. www.serconline.org/alec/alec21.html.

Story, Brendan, and Margie Lincita. "The Green Scare and Eco-prisoners: A Brief Synopsis." In Let Freedom Ring: A Collection of Documents from the Movements to Free U.S. Political Prisoners, edited by Matt Meyer, 692–713. Oakland, Calif.: PM Press, 2008.

TheThe

Support Jordan Cade Halliday. "Grand Jury." Accessed 2010. www.supportjordan.com.

Thompson, Lisa. "Eco-activist Silent on Grand Jury Appearance." GoErie. com. Last updated September 10, 2008. www.goerie.com/apps/pbcs.dll/article?AID=/20080910/NEWS02/809100365.

Todd, Andrea. "Elle Reader Investigation: The Believers." *Elle* April 2008, 266–70, 323–25.

United States District Court, Southern District of Iowa. *Subpoena to Testify Before Grand Jury (Carrie Feldman. Edina, MN)* (GJ/09-321DV). 2009. http://twincities. indymedia.org/files/GrandJurySubpoena10-13-09_0.pdf.

United States District Court. Western District of Michigan, Northern Division. *United States of America, Plaintiff, v. Ian Jacob Wallace, Defendant: Plea Agreement* (No. 2:08-CR-39). Marquette, Mich.: United States Attorney. 2008. http:// midwestgreenscare.files.wordpress.com/2008/11/wallace-plea-agreement.pdf.

Van Bergen, Jennifer. "FBI Confidential Informant Also Said To Be Provocateur." *The Raw Story.* (June 8, 2006). www.rawstory.com/news/2006/FBI_confidential_informant_also_said_to_0608.html.

———. "Documents Show New Secretive U.S. Prison Program Isolating Muslim, Middle Eastern Prisoners." *The Raw Story.* (February 16, 2007). www.rawstory. com/news/2007/Documents_show_new_secretive_new_US_0216.html.

Walker, N. United States District Court, Eastern District of California. *United States of America v. Eric McDavid, Lauren Weiner and Zachary Jenson* (Criminal Complaint case number: 2:06-MJ-0021). 2006.

Walsh, Denny. "'Anna' the Informant: Student's Path to FBI Informant." *Sacramento Bee.* Accessed September 12, 2007. http://www.sacbee.com/101/story/374324.html (site discontinued).

Ward, Michael B. Speech delivered at the Operation Backfire Press Conference Foreign Press Center, Washington, DC, on November 19, 2008. www.fbi.gov/news/ speeches/operation-backfire.

Watson, Dale L. Testimony delivered before the Senate Select Committee on Intelligence, Washington, DC on the terrorist threat confronting the United States. February 6, 2002. www.fbi.gov/news/testimony/ the-terrorist-threat-confronting-the-united-states.

White, Ed. "Feds Acknowledge Mich. Arsonist Was Key Informant." *USA Today* (October 10, 2008). http://usatoday30.usatoday.com/news/nation/2008-10-10-841975904_x.htm.

Young, Peter. "FBI Raided My House Today." Published March 15, 2010 (2010a). www. voiceofthevoiceless.org/fbi-raided-my-house-today (site discontinued).

———. "FBI Tactics—Lessons for All!" Indymedia UK. Published March 29, 2010 (2010b). www.indymedia.org.uk/en/2010/03/448305.html.

———. *Animal Liberation Front—Complete U.S. Diary of Actions: The First 30 Years.* Warcry Communications, 2010 (2010c).

TERRORIZING DISSENT AND THE CONSPIRACY AGAINST "RADICAL" MOVEMENTS

Scott DeMuth and David Naguib Pellow

In writing this chapter, our intention is to place the Animal Enterprise Terrorism Act (AETA) and its predecessor law, the Animal Enterprise Protection Act (AEPA), in a broader, historical context of State repression and criminalization of dissent in the United States. A surprisingly small number of animal rights activists view their work as part of this larger social reality. It is important to understand these links because we otherwise run the risk of isolating the animal rights movement and the government's response to it from a range of critically important histories and current relationships that connect with other activist communities and struggles.

The broader reality is that repression is a daily fact of life for countless people, populations, and communities on the wrong end of power and privilege—the working class, people of color, indigenous peoples, anarchists, immigrants, and numerous resistance movements of both past and present. Animal rights activists are far from exceptional in this regard.

While social movements are often thought of as sources of popular mobilization and direct action, they are also some of the most important loci for the creation and application of critical thinking and transformative knowledge. Ideas matter in society, and the contours and content of ideas generated by these movements have shaped the transformation of society and history. History has also shown, however, that State and corporate interests seek to control the contours and content of ideas in public circulation. Precisely because of their critical thinking and transformative knowledge, social movements are frequently the targets of State repression.

We view State repression as more than just acts of brute force; it is also a *science*. Studies of institutional repression reveal quite clearly that State and corporate institutions follow protocols of basic science in order to protect their interests against threats and competitors (Boykoff 2007). Like many forms of basic or applied science, the science of repression applies a protocol of careful, empirical observation, experimentation, data gathering, and analysis. Repression is rooted in the State's desire to develop and deploy knowledge for the advancement of particular interests (government, military, and corporate interests, for example). For those groups deemed threats to the State, the science of repression can have serious consequences. This should come as no surprise to activists and students of history.

The AETA is designed to target the animal rights movement and is only a recent example of U.S. State repression of political ideologies. Indeed, there are numerous instances of how U.S. law has been used against political ideologies, even in recent history: e.g., various immigration and alien registration laws used to exclude groups from the U.S. based on their beliefs; the FBI's infamous COINTELPRO operation that infiltrated the antiwar and civil rights movements; and federal and state versions of the USA PATRIOT Act, which infringe on constitutionally protected protest and beliefs. We consider the AETA in the context of the history of U.S. State repression directed at social movements, and then examine a number of recent indictments and cases against animal rights activists and other groups weighed against this historical backdrop.

BRIEF OVERVIEW OF THE ANIMAL ENTERPRISE TERRORISM ACT

The Animal Enterprise Terrorism Act (AETA) was passed into federal law on November 27, 2006. It is a revision of an earlier law—the Animal Enterprise Protection Act (AEPA)—passed into law in 1992 and amended in 2002. Arguments for the original AEPA had been advanced by the claim that direct actions by animal liberation activists against farming and research facilities were escalating, and that new legislation was necessary to protect those facilities. Proponents of the AEPA claimed that existing state and federal laws had failed to curtail activists' efforts and that these actions disrupted important services. The same arguments were used to support the AETA, namely, that existing laws—including the AEPA—had not provided a sufficient deterrent against animal rights activists. Aboveground, public organizers such as Stop Huntingdon Animal Cruelty (SHAC) were using bold and effective tactics to confront animal industries, while "underground" direct actions continued; animal exploitation industries and the State therefore responded with the AETA.

While the law states that it does not "prohibit any expressive conduct (including peaceful picketing or other peaceful demonstration) protected from legal prohibition by the First Amendment to the Constitution," the AETA was used in 2009 to indict four individuals for protest-related activity and chalking animal liberation messages on sidewalks. Additionally, the law does not provide explicit protection for whistle-blowing or undercover investigations. As a result of the law's passage, it is arguable that no other industry in the U.S. has ever enjoyed such legal protections against persons exercising their rights to free speech.

The AETA also addresses the "tertiary targeting" strategy used by animal rights campaigns against animal enterprises. For example, the law not only protects a vivisection lab from activist campaigns, but also any entity that does business with that lab. Supporters of the AETA bill had claimed that this was a loophole in the AEPA that needed to be closed, using SHAC campaigns as a primary example. Huntingdon Life Sciences (HLS) is one of the largest animal testing companies in the world. Some activists in the SHAC campaign ran a website that did not directly target HLS, but focused instead on those entities doing business with HLS. Those involved with the SHAC campaign were prosecuted under the AEPA and are known as the "SHAC 7." In attempting to mute this tertiary boycott strategy, the AETA creates a chilling effect on the types of otherwise lawful campaign strategies that animal rights activists can employ.

The AETA also adds new language and penalties for activism that causes "reasonable fear of serious bodily injury or death" among managers and/or employees of animal enterprises. Despite rhetoric by proponents that this law is about stopping violence and punishing "terrorism," there have not been any cases of physical violence by animal rights activists in the U.S. against individuals who participate in animal enterprises. Nonetheless, the law argues that such actions as home demonstrations, civil disobedience, vandalism, property destruction, and animal rescues "instill in another the reasonable fear of serious bodily injury" and are thus "terrorism." The AETA specifically increases imprisonment based on the amount of economic damage caused by activists and allows animal enterprises to seek restitution. This allows corporations to recoup economic losses, creates an undeniable chilling effect on aboveground and public animal rights organizers, and inappropriately labels nonviolent tactics, such as protests and civil disobedience, as "terrorism."

The AETA: Not an Anomaly, But Part of a Legal Trend

It would be naïve and historically shortsighted to view the AETA as an entirely unique legal development. The AETA is not an exception or anomaly; instead, it is part of an established trend within the history of U.S. law. When viewed in the context of other laws targeting political movements and ideologies, the AETA becomes less about animal rights activists in particular and much more about reflecting the broader trends of criminalizing dissent. It has been argued that the "Green Scare" is part of a systematic program to criminalize and further marginalize an already "fringe" component of the environmental and animal rights movements, whose ideas and tactics were beginning to gain broader support (Potter 2011). Similar scare tactics and criminalization have been applied against other movements, including anarchists, immigrants, people of color, antiwar activists, organizers against the Republican National Conventions (of 2000, 2004, and 2008), and Palestinian solidarity activists. Indeed, when viewed through the lens of history, it becomes clear that animal rights activists are only one of many groups to be targeted and criminalized for their political views.

The AETA Is Not an Anomaly

If one steps back and looks beyond the animal rights movement, there are numerous precedents that link the kind of language and power reflected in the AETA to past repression directed at other social movements. While it is true that the AEPA/AETA was the first federal U.S. law specifically designed to target the animal rights and animal liberation movements, there are numerous instances of how U.S. law has been used historically to target other political ideologies and movements, and we should make every effort to understand the ways in which these practices are linked.

One of the earliest examples of State repression in the twentieth century includes the Anarchist Exclusion Act of 1903, later expanded in the Immigration Acts of 1917 and 1918, which was used to bar entrance to the United States by immigrants who were believed to be anarchists. These acts expanded immigration law to exclude foreigners who were merely members of anarchist groups, members of groups that purportedly advocated the overthrow of the U.S. government, and individuals or groups who advocated the unlawful destruction of property. More to the point, however, the 1917 law marked the first time a federal law was used to codify the principle of guilt by association. It sought to exclude people based on membership in anarchist groups, but perhaps more chillingly, targeted people based on their beliefs.

In 1940, the Alien Registration Act, also known as the Smith Act, continued this trend. This was a federal statute that (1) required all adult foreign nationals to register with the federal government, and (2) made it a criminal offense to advocate the overthrow of the U.S. government or for anyone to become an affiliate or member of any group that embraces such ideas. The act was used as a pretext against political organizations and individuals who held a disfavored ideology, particularly that of labor organizers. Indeed, the Smith Act was sponsored and supported by an anti-labor bloc in Congress. In a law enforcement sweep enabled by this legislation, a number of political organizations and 215 Americans were indicted, and on June 27, 1941, the FBI raided Socialist Worker Party (SWP) offices in Minneapolis and St. Paul, seizing large quantities of communist literature. A federal grand jury indicted twenty-eight members of the SWP or Teamsters Local 544 for violating both the 1861 Sedition Act and the 1940 Smith Act. All defendants were found not guilty of the 1861 statute, but eighteen were convicted under the Smith Act for distributing written material encouraging insubordination in the armed services (Chang 2002). The Supreme Court, finding constitutional violations, overturned most of the convictions in 1957; however, the exonerations were bittersweet since the Smith Act has never been repealed.

In 1952, Congress passed the Immigration and Nationality Act, also known as the McCarran-Walter Act (Public Law 414). This law made it a deportable offense for any immigrant ("alien") to be affiliated with an anarchist or communist organization, or to advocate and/or teach such political beliefs. Specifically, the text of the law reads, in part:

> Any alien in the United States . . . shall, upon the order of the Attorney General, be deported who . . . is or at any time has been, after entry, a member of any of the following classes of aliens: (A) Aliens who are anarchists; (B) Aliens who advocate or teach, or who are members of or affiliated with any organization that advocates or teaches, opposition to all organized government; . . . (G) Aliens who write or publish, or cause to be written or published, or who knowingly circulate, distribute, print, or display or knowingly cause to be circulated, distributed, printed, published or displayed, or who knowingly have in their possession for the purpose of publication, circulation, distribution or display any written or printed matter advocating or teaching opposition to all organized government. . . . (McCarran-Walter Act, 1952, Title II, Chapter 5, section 241)

The McCarran-Walter Act was a McCarthy-era law used to deny visas to foreigners based on political membership and was used to exclude people such as Gabriel García Márquez and Pablo Neruda. This legislation was part of the broader context of exclusion and repression against dissidents both foreign and domestic.

Between 1956 and 1971, the FBI directed the Counterintelligence Program (often referred to as COINTELPRO), which was designed to "expose, disrupt, misdirect, discredit, or otherwise neutralize" dissident individuals and political groups in the United States. With J. Edgar

Hoover at the agency's helm, the FBI used every trick in the book from bogus mail to fabricated evidence, propaganda, infiltration and agents provocateurs, and assassinations. COINTELPRO targeted the Black Panther Party (BPP), Martin Luther King, Jr. and the civil rights movement, the American Indian Movement (AIM), Puerto Rican Independentistas (those seeking independence for Puerto Rico), labor activists, the anti–Vietnam War movement, and the New Left in general. Some vindication for these movements and for civil liberties advocates eventually occurred in 1976 when COINTELPRO was officially shut down, being denounced by congressional investigators as "a sophisticated vigilante operation."

Years later, the passage of the Immigration and Nationality Act of 1990 ushered in a repeal of the ideological exclusion provisions and the principle of guilt by association contained within the Immigration and Nationality (McCarran-Walter) Act of 1952. Thus, foreign nationals could not be excluded from the United States based on their beliefs or memberships in organizations, as long as those activities were not associated with terrorism or "material support" of terrorist groups.

Then, in December of 2003, a leaked confidential FBI memo to *The New York Times* provided details of a national program to place antiwar activists under surveillance by the FBI and by local law enforcement agencies. While the program's official focus was on "violent anarchists," it was revealed that the agencies spent most of their energy infiltrating and spying on peaceful, law-abiding organizations. The leaked FBI memo requested that local law enforcement agencies report their observations and findings to their local Joint Terrorism Task Force (JTTF) (Meeropol 2005).

JTTFs are led by the U.S. Department of Justice (DOJ) and FBI and consist of teams of local, state, and federal law enforcement officials brought together for the purpose of investigating and preventing domestic terrorism. The DOJ describes JTTFs as "small cells of highly trained, locally based . . . investigators, analysts, linguists, SWAT experts and other specialists . . ." (U.S. DOJ website). Dozens of JTTFs located throughout the United States have targeted and branded numerous groups as "terrorists." These targeted groups include, but are not necessarily limited to, the following: the Committee in Solidarity with the

People of El Salvador (often referred to as CISPES), which is a U.S.-based organization that was very active during the Reagan Administration's excursions into Central America; antinuclear activists, particularly during the 1980s; the anti-WTO activists in Seattle, 1999; organizers of the protests at the 2000, 2004, and 2008 Republican National Conventions; organizers of the 2009 anti-G20 meetings in Pittsburgh; as well as many other social justice groups, gatherings, and demonstrations.

THE BRANDING OF "TERRORISM" AND THE EROSION OF CONTEMPORARY RIGHTS

Animal rights activists are not the only contemporary social movement members branded under the "terrorism" label. Two laws have been used in the past decade to extend that label to groups that provide material support to organizations that are designated as international terrorist associations. These laws include the Antiterrorism and Effective Death Penalty Act (AEDPA) of 1996 and the United and Strengthening America by Providing Appropriate Tools Required to Intercept and Obstruct Terrorism (USA PATRIOT or PATRIOT) Act.

President Clinton signed the AEDPA into law to alleviate heightened anxieties about undocumented immigrants coming to the United States and engaging in criminal activities. The law gave U.S. Immigration and Customs Enforcement (ICE) the authority to arrest, detain, and deport noncitizens on secret evidence if they were deemed to be national security threats. The AEDPA repealed the protections provided under the Immigration and Nationality Act of 1990 around political beliefs and association. Specifically, the AEDPA reversed the ban on guilt by association, thus reviving the practice of denying visas to foreigners based on membership in various groups—this time designated as "terrorists" by the secretary of state (Cole and Dempsey 2002).

The PATRIOT Act, signed into law in 2001 by President Bush, endows government and police forces with unprecedented powers to spy on citizens, to access records and information, and to arrest and detain persons believed to be a threat to national security, no matter how little evidence to support such claims might exist. The PATRIOT

Act has serious implications for activists engaged in direct action and civil disobedience. Section 802 of the act reveals that, in addition to increased surveillance, it expands the definition of the federal crime of terrorism to include "domestic terrorism," which is defined as "acts dangerous to human life that are a violation of the criminal laws" if they "appear intended to influence the policy of a government by intimidation or coercion" and take place, primarily, in the United States.

The PATRIOT Act also limits the rights of academics and activists who wish to host speakers from other nations. Section 411 uses an ideological litmus test to determine eligibility for entry into the United States. Noncitizens who are members of groups that the secretary of state has designated as "terrorist" organizations are barred from entry into the country. This is virtually the same guilt by association provision that we saw in the McCarran-Walter Act of 1952.

Immigrants or noncitizens are generally targeted more harshly by the PATRIOT Act. For instance, the act allows for the deportation of noncitizens based on alleged participation in terrorist activity, which is defined as any crime that involves the use of a weapon or dangerous device other than for personal monetary gain. However, for the purposes of regulating immigration, other sections of the PATRIOT Act provide a broader definition of "terrorist activity." That definition includes the support of otherwise lawful and nonviolent activities of virtually any group that has used violence and any use or threat to use a weapon *against a person or property* (Cole 2005, 58). The act also expands the practice of ideological exclusion, authorizing the government to deny entry to noncitizens who "endorse or espouse terrorist activity" or who "persuade others to support terrorist activity or a terrorist organization." The PATRIOT Act expands the AEDPA's guilt by association provisions by repealing, among other things, the exceptions for providing support with medicine and religious materials. This is what is called "material support."

The material support statutes of the AEDPA and the PATRIOT Act operate under the premise of guilt by association where groups and individuals are punished not for any alleged actions, but for supporting others whose acts are viewed as illegal. Consequently, First

Amendment activities such as providing humanitarian aid and/or expert advice, and the mere act of political advocacy, are criminalized under these laws. Even more chilling, certain activities intended to promote lawful and nonviolent practices such as human rights training and participation in peace conferences fall within the "material support" doctrine (Meeropol 2005, 16). Cases include: Sami Omar Al Huassayn, an Idaho student accused of running a website where "radical" Islamists posted various materials online (he was acquitted by a jury); and John Walker Lindh, an American citizen who pled to counts of providing "material support" to terrorist organizations when the federal government lacked sufficient evidence to pursue treason or "conspiracy to murder U.S. nationals."

The Humanitarian Law Project (HLP) was a lead plaintiff in a constitutional challenge (*Holder v. Humanitarian Law Project* 2010) against the "material support" law, initiated by the Center for Constitutional Rights. The HLP is a nonprofit organization with consultative status to the United Nations and is active in advocating for the peaceful resolution of armed conflicts. As part of this work, the HLP wanted to assist the Kurdistan Workers' Party (PKK) with conflict resolution under international law, human rights monitoring in Turkey, and political advocacy on behalf of Kurds in Turkey. Included in the challenge were Tamil-American organizations, and two individuals who sought to provide medical assistance to tsunami victims and assist with health care in northeast Sri Lanka. Both of these activities would require working with the Liberation Tigers of Tamil Eelam (LTTE), which advocated for the self-determination of Kurds in Turkey and of the Tamil in Sri Lanka.

The Supreme Court's decision affirms the lower court ruling that once the secretary of state labels a group a foreign terrorist organization, everything it does is "so tainted by their criminal conduct that any contribution to such an organization facilitates that conduct." This includes everything from participating in activities of the United Nations to providing relief aid. The federal government thus concludes that giving "expert advice" on health care or providing "training" on nonviolence and/or conflict resolution constitutes "material support" to a foreign terrorist organization.

Finally, our very own state of Minnesota passed its own version of the PATRIOT Act in 2002, which was applied to the RNC 8—a group of activists in the Twin Cities who sought to coordinate protest actions at the 2008 Republican National Convention in St. Paul. These activists faced a range of charges, including "conspiracy to riot in furtherance of terrorism" (Pickering 2011). The last time similar charges were brought under a Minnesota law was in 1918, when Matt Moilen and other labor organizers for the International Workers of the World were charged with "criminal syndicalism." The Minnesota Supreme Court upheld the convictions based on allegations that workers had advocated or taught acts of violence, including acts only damaging to property.

Recent state repression directed at more "radical" factions of environmental and animal rights networks has become known as the "Green Scare." While it is not wise to judge the effectiveness of a social movement based on the level of repression meted out by the State, it can be argued that the AETA was, instead, specifically employed to marginalize a growing animal rights movement that was not only gaining public favor but also innovating new and effective protest strategies. For example, SHAC openly adopted strategies from other successful movements such as tertiary targeting, which had been employed by the anti-apartheid movement.

The AETA could easily be seen not just as a continuation of the historical trend of repression under U.S. law, but, indeed, as a precursor to future statutes that may be designed to protect still other controversial industries that may be targeted by other movements—such as the logging, mountaintop removal, tar sands extraction, hydraulic fracturing for gas, and whaling industries. It is easy to conceive of similar laws being enacted if other movements begin gaining as much ground and initiating successful strategies against industry as the animal rights movement has already done.

The Mystery of the University of Iowa Raid

On November 14, 2004, a group of individuals entered the Spence Laboratories at the University of Iowa and removed 401 animals. At least four individuals were able to gain access to secured areas in the facility, which included bypassing a four-walled security system (perimeter, elevator, corridor, and animal rooms) accessible only with keys and key cards. This was a high-profile crime even before the release of a communiqué and a fifty-minute video several days later in which the Animal Liberation Front (ALF) took credit for the animal rescue. Supporters praised the action as one of the most sophisticated and impressive animal liberations in recent memory. It was precisely because of these characteristics that the FBI indicated the crime to be a top priority. However, because investigators had little to work with other than materials provided by the liberationists, i.e., the publicly released communiqué and video, the investigation was stalled.

Five years later in November 2009, two Minneapolis activists—Carrie Feldman and Scott DeMuth—were subpoenaed to testify before a grand jury in Davenport, Iowa. Authorities tried to link DeMuth to the University of Iowa action based on data gleaned from his computer and personal journals, which had been seized in an earlier raid of his home by police attempting to neutralize protests at the 2008 Republican National Convention. Feldman and DeMuth appeared in Davenport but refused to testify before the grand jury; both were subsequently jailed for contempt of court.

In a surprising move, prosecutors in Iowa filed a conspiracy charge against DeMuth under the AEPA of 2002 relating to the University of Iowa action, despite the following facts: DeMuth was a minor at the time of the break-in; there was a general lack of evidence; and DeMuth was never informed that he was a target of the investigation when subpoenaed to the grand jury, and, in fact, was granted immunity at the time of the subpoena. Attorneys reviewing the case believed that the government could file an indictment to put a hold on the statute of limitations and then seek superseding indictments. On the issue of the statute of limitations, an appellate court judge stated:

> The district court abused its discretion when it found Ms. Feldman in contempt of court because it failed to consider a significant relevant factor, i.e., whether the statute of limitations had run on the crime for which the government seeks Ms. Feldman's testimony.... [T]he government itself cites no authority for the proposition it

can abuse the grand jury process to compel a witness to testify regarding a crime for which the statute of limitations has expired. (Appellate Order 2010)

It was only at the time of DeMuth's bond hearings that the nature of the indictments began to emerge: "Defendant's writings, literature, and conduct suggest that he is an anarchist and associated with the ALF movement. Therefore, he is a domestic terrorist" (Government's Motion 2009, 3).

DeMuth's ideas, beliefs, political activities (such as volunteering with an eco-political prisoner support group in the Twin Cities), and affiliations were sufficient for the State to brand him a "terrorist." Carrie Feldman spent four months in jail for contempt of court since she also refused to talk to the grand jury about the University of Iowa case. She was released in March 2010.

As part of its investigation (which included interviewing at least two hundred persons and subpoenaing three people), the federal government contacted David Pellow, Scott DeMuth's academic advisor, for information about DeMuth and about Pellow's research on the earth and animal liberation movements. This appeared to be a classic case of overreach by the State. From Pellow's field notes:

On Monday April 6, 2010: I arrived at my place of employment, the University of Minnesota…and went straight to my mailbox. There was…a business card with a post-it attached to it that read: 're: student, Pellow, 04/06/10, 9:15am.' The business card was for a Special Agent, Federal Bureau of Investigation, Minneapolis Division. He also left a voice message for me in my office that stated that he wanted to 'interview' me in the next day or so.… Two days later, the Special Agent called my home phone and left a message that clearly was directed toward asking questions about Scott's research and my own research. 'I'd like to ask you a couple of questions about one of your students you are the advisor for at the U—Scott DeMuth. I'd like to ask you a couple of questions about the research that you do and the research that he does for you.'

After Pellow received these notices, there was a strong belief by his research team that their communications were being monitored without their approval. In an effort to maintain confidentiality, Pellow's research team began using non-university e-mail communications in order to conduct business that was related to their research project. Primary importance was placed on protecting research participants and their privacy, as well as the privacy of colleagues, coworkers, and student employees.

Then on June 18, 2010, the DOJ contacted the University of Minnesota's Human Research Protection Program, whose purpose is to protect the confidentiality of research participants and their interviews. The DOJ asked for a copy of all human subject materials related to Pellow's research project on environmental and animal rights activists. This included Pellow's interview questionnaire, rationale for conducting research on this topic, and various university forms regarding his research participants that were otherwise designed to protect the confidentiality of his research participants. Despite the absence of any legal compulsory process or subpoena, the university, nonetheless, informed Pellow that it would comply with the DOJ's request and promptly sent out the information. U.S. Attorneys Clifford Cronk and Nicholas Klinefeldt were the authors of the letter requesting the records. It is no coincidence that they were also the prosecutors pursuing DeMuth, Pellow's advisee and research collaborator. The DOJ letter reads, in relevant part: "The information we are requesting includes, but is not limited to, the study file, the application for the research project, along with documentation to support the plan, *and the names of the participants in the project*" (emphasis added).

Those participants included students and employees working with Pellow on the project. Pellow, who solely possessed that information, had pledged to hold it in confidence, as required by his professional association's code of ethics. The university did agree to delete research participants' names to preserve their privacy. As DeMuth had been working on the project with Pellow since earlier in 2010, it appeared that this request was a continuation of the U.S. Attorneys' explorations into possible connections between DeMuth and any activists that may have been interviewed for the study.

Then in 2010, the State issued another indictment against DeMuth, this time charging him with involvement in an ALF fur farm raid in

Minnesota in 2006. In the days before trial, prosecutors approached DeMuth's lawyers stating that they would like to resolve the case. DeMuth's lawyers specifically stated that they "would not be agreeable" to any resolution that involved pleading guilty to charges related to the University of Iowa lab raid. With a recommended sentence of six months and a misdemeanor violation, DeMuth pled guilty to a lesser sentence and, in exchange, prosecutors dropped charges against him for the animal rescue at the University of Iowa.

Former ALF prisoner and outspoken activist Peter Young wrote on his *Voice of the Voiceless* blog: "For now, the story is this: The Animal Liberation Front got inside an Iowa lab, circumvented security, got 401 animals out, smashed the labs, videotaped the whole thing—and didn't get caught" (Young 2010).

The Conspiracy Against "Radical" Movements

The trend to indict individuals in "radical" movements under conspiracy charges ranges from the animal liberation and environmental movements to antiwar and other political movements. Therefore, the prosecution against DeMuth is not without context. U.S. Attorney Clifford Cronk's efforts to link the animal rights movement, anarchists, and domestic terrorism reflect a much broader strategy and priority within the FBI. On January 14, 2006, FBI spokesman David Picard stated, "One of our major domestic terrorism programs is the ALF [Animal Liberation Front], ELF [Environmental Liberation Front], and anarchist movement, and it's a national program for the FBI" (Rosenfeld 2006). The FBI employed Operation Backfire to target ALF and ELF networks that had been particularly effective at carrying out arson attacks and other property damage at a number of facilities in the Western United States. On January 20, 2006, in a press release announcing the first arrests in Operation Backfire, FBI Director Robert Mueller vowed: "We are committed to working with our partners to disrupt and dismantle these movements [the ALF and ELF]" (Department of Justice 2006). This statement is eerily similar to J. Edgar Hoover's directives of the FBI's Counterintelligence Program (COINTELPRO) to "expose, disrupt, misdirect, discredit, or otherwise neutralize" social movements.

Over the course of the past decade, the federal government has used conspiracy charges as a major tactic against "radical" movements, including aboveground, public organizers who were defendants in the cases of *U.S. v. Fullmer* (the SHAC 7) and *U.S. v. Buddenberg* (the AETA 4). In addition to the numerous indictments resulting from the SHAC 7 and the AETA 4, there have been at least fifteen cases of conspiracy targeting "radical" and anarchist movements involving around ninety individuals. Several examples follow.

On December 2, 2004, Rod Coronado was indicted on conspiracy charges related to an environmental group interfering with a mountain lion hunt. The indictment came seven days before Coronado was to stand trial for three misdemeanor charges filed after his arrest for that action. The potential penalties increased from misdemeanors to a maximum of six years in prison. Coronado was found guilty of felony conspiracy to interfere with or injure a government official, misdemeanor interference with or injury to a forest officer, and misdemeanor depredation of government property. On August 6, 2006, Coronado was sentenced to eight months in prison and three years supervised probation.

In January 2006, as part of the FBI's Operation Backfire, three earth liberation activists—Eric McDavid, Zachary Jenson, and Lauren Weiner—were indicted for conspiring to damage facilities by explosive or fire. Jenson and Weiner took cooperating plea bargains, which left McDavid to be convicted on all counts and sentenced in May 2008 to nearly twenty years in prison. This case is particularly notable, as the defendants were indicted before any action ever took place, and the conviction rested on a paid FBI informant, "Anna," who had entrapped the defendants through the use of money and flirtation.

In March 2008, earth liberation activists Marie Mason, Frank Ambrose, Aren Burthwick, and Stephanie Lynne Fultz were charged with conspiracy to commit arson. Ambrose was Mason's ex-husband and was cooperating with the FBI's investigation into "radical" environmentalist networks. Despite his cooperation with the FBI, Ambrose received a nine-year sentence—two years longer than what the prosecutor had requested. Mason, on the other hand, was facing a life sentence, but she accepted a plea bargain. On February 5, 2009, she was sentenced to almost twenty-two years.

On September 24, 2010, the FBI raided the homes of antiwar and international solidarity activists in Minneapolis, Chicago, and Grand Rapids, Michigan. The FBI served a total of fourteen subpoenas to appear before a grand jury. During the raids, agents seized documents, computers, cell phones, passports, and other "evidence" related to the "material support of terrorism" based on allegations that these activists were working in (nonviolent) solidarity with communities facing military assault by U.S. allies in the Occupied Palestinian Territories and Colombia. At the time of this writing, dozens of community organizations across the United States have publicly condemned the FBI's actions, and subpoenaed activists have refused to appear before grand juries.

The RNC 8 case involved the first use of criminal charges under the 2002 Minnesota version of the PATRIOT Act. Eight alleged organizers of protests against the 2008 Republican National Convention in St. Paul, Minnesota, were charged with "conspiracy to riot in furtherance of terrorism and conspiracy to commit criminal damage to property in furtherance of terrorism." The activists faced up to seven and a half years in prison under Minnesota's terrorism enhancement law. In April 2009, faced with increasing public pressure, Ramsey County Attorney Susan Gaertner dropped the terrorism enhancements charges. While one defendant accepted a non-cooperating plea deal to plead guilty to "conspiracy to commit property damage," prosecutors soon dismissed charges against three others and the case concluded on October 19, 2010, when the remaining defendants accepted gross misdemeanor plea deals with no jail time.

CONCLUSION

Our goal in this article was to place the AETA (and the AEPA) in a larger context of State repression and criminalization of dissent throughout U.S. history. We believe strongly that animal rights activists (as well as allies and sympathizers, such as scholars and researchers) must see themselves in this broader set of relationships and histories; otherwise, we risk making the mistake of viewing the AETA as unique and in isolation from the history and struggles that preceded it. From immigration and alien registration laws and the COINTELPRO in the twentieth century to the USA PATRIOT ACT and other forms of repressive legislation in the twenty-first century, there is a long and unbroken chain of policies and practices designed to contain, control, and destroy social movements. Both aboveground and underground movements have borne the brunt of this repression. This is especially true of activists who dared to speak, read, and even think thoughts that were out of favor with dominant practices and ideologies.

The AEPA and the AETA cannot be understood outside of this context. Fortunately, some animal rights activists are beginning to pay serious attention to the struggles and experiences of other social movements, but many are ignorant of this history and how it shapes the reality in which they exist and operate. To ignore other freedom movements and the repression thereof will ultimately undermine the animal rights movement's efficacy and relevance. The comparative/historical perspective presented here is thus vital for developing conversations—and alliances—between the animal rights movement and contemporary movements for social justice.

REFERENCES

Appellate order concerning Carrie Feldman. January 22, 2010.

Boykoff, Jules. *Beyond Bullets: The Suppression of Dissent in the United States.* Oakland, Calif.: AK Press, 2007.

Chang, Nancy. *Silencing Political Dissent: How Post-September 11 Anti-Terrorism Measures Threaten Our Civil Liberties.* New York: Seven Stories Press, 2002.

Cole, David. *Enemy Aliens: Double Standards and Constitutional Freedoms in the War on Terrorism.* New York: New Press, 2005.

Cole, David, and James X. Dempsey. *Terrorism and the Constitution: Sacrificing Civil Liberties in the Name of National Security.* New York: The First Amendment Foundation, 2002.

Department of Justice. "Eleven Defendants Indicted on Domestic Terrorism Charges." Press Release. January 20, 2006. www.justice.gov/opa/pr/2006/January/06 _crm_030.html.

Government's motion for revocation of release order concerning Scott DeMuth. November 25., 2009, p. 3.

Holder v. Humanitarian Law Project, No. 561 U.S. 1 (2010), 130 S.Ct. 2705.

Meeropol, Rachel, ed. *America's Disappeared: Secret Imprisonment, Detainees, and the "War on Terror."* New York: Seven Stories Press, 2005.

Pickering, Leslie James, ed. *Conspiracy to Riot in Furtherance of Terrorism: Collective Autobiography of the RNC 8.* Minneapolis, Minn.: Arissa Media Group/PM Press, 2011.

Potter, Will. *Green Is the New Red: An Insider's Account of a Social Movement Under Siege.* San Francisco: City Lights Publishers, 2011.

Rosenfeld, Ben. "The Great Green Scare and the Fed's 'Case' Against Rod Coronado." Counterpunch,March 10–12, 2006. www.counterpunch.org/2006/03/10/the-great -green-scare-and-the-fed-s-quot-case-quot-against-rod-coronado.

United States Department of Justice. "Joint Terrorism Task Force." www.justice.gov/jttf.

McCarran-Walter Act, Pub.L. 82-414, 66 Stat. 163 (1952).

Young, Peter. "FBI Closes Investigation into Iowa ALF Lab Raid." Animal Liberation Frontline, December 2, 2010. www.animalliberationfrontline.com/fbi-closes -investigation-into-iowa-a-l-f-lab-raid.

Interest-Group Politics, the AETA, and the Criminalization of Animal Rights Activism

Wesley Shirley

The story of the Animal Enterprise Terrorism Act (AETA) is the story of politics at work, and it has something to tell us about the way contemporary political systems operate in the United States. It is a story of two diametrically opposed groups. On one side are powerful industries and their political allies who see the use of animals as research subjects, food, clothing sources, and entertainment. On the other side is a relatively small but vocal social movement that aims to end the use and exploitation of nonhuman animals for the benefit of humans. Part of the countermovement's offensive against animal rights activists is to relabel "animal rights activism" as "terrorism," which has the effect of politically and socially marginalizing the movement. This has resulted in the labeling of the Animal Liberation Front (ALF), along with the Earth Liberation Front (ELF), as the number one domestic terrorist threats in the United States (Jarboe 2002). From the late 1980s through to the passage of the AETA in 2006, animal-using industries and their political allies have been able to pass legislation at both the state and federal levels that specifically protect animal-using enterprises against direct action and economic sabotage by animal rights activists.

In this chapter, I explore the process by which the AETA, as the latest example of animal enterprise terrorism laws, came to be. I explore how similar laws were first developed and passed at the state level, including the role of the American Legislative Exchange Council (ALEC) and the corporate interests that fund it. I examine congressional committee and subcommittee hearings that were held in relation to the AETA and on animal rights activism, with an emphasis on who had a voice and how differing opinions and attitudes were received within the hearing rooms. Finally, I examine the trend of the federalization of criminal law, and how this trend has enabled interest groups such as the pharmaceutical and biomedical industries to criminalize their political opponents' activities at the federal level, and what this means not just for animal rights activism, but for social movement activity in general.

ALEC and State Level Legislation

The federal system in the United States creates multiple layers of rule-making bodies. With states having autonomy to create laws within their borders, a system of experimentation and sharing is established between individual states and between the states and the federal government, or as Craig Volden, a professor of public policy and politics at the University of Virginia, states, "Among the potential benefits of American federalism is the ability of states to serve as policy laboratories, adopting novel policies to address their needs, abandoning unsuccessful attempts and learning from the successes of similar states" (2006, 294). It was within this framework that states began passing laws in the late 1980s aimed at protecting animal-using enterprises. By 2006, thirty-three states had laws directed specifically at various forms of animal rights activism. These laws centered on interference with animal-using enterprises, and ranged from making it illegal to release zoo animals to increasing penalties for interfering in any way with an animal enterprise—e.g., trespassing, theft, damage to property, actions that cause a loss of profits, and other similar acts (Lovitz 2010).

Who is ALEC?

The American Legislative Exchange Council (ALEC) is a nonprofit political organization that boasts of a bipartisan membership with state representatives from all fifty states (ALEC 2011b). Founded in 1973 by Paul Weyrich, a conservative activist, it has grown from a small organization to a major force at the state level in legislative processes. It claims to be the largest "nonpartisan, individual membership association of state legislators" (ALEC 2011a), with nearly 2,000 members from state legislatures, but almost 85 percent of their members are Republicans (ALEC Watch 2002). It can make a claim to bipartisanship, but it is actually a laboratory for pro-corporate, conservative policies that align with its mostly Republican membership. ALEC's political agenda tends to align most closely with business interests. As it states in its *Private Sector Membership* brochure, touting the benefits of corporate membership:

> ALEC's goal is to ensure that each of its legislative members is fully armed with the information, research, and ideas they need to be an ally of the free-market system. One of ALEC's greatest strengths is the public-private partnership. ALEC provides the private sector with an unparalleled opportunity to have its voice heard, and its perspective appreciated, by the legislative members. ALEC members benefit from this partnership of business leaders, policy experts, and legislators through networking, conferences, Task Force meetings, and Issue Briefings. (ALEC 2011a, 1)

ALEC creates model legislation that can be taken whole cloth or modified to meet individual states' needs. These bills can then be introduced in state legislatures across the country. As ALEC states in its bylaws, its aim is to:

> Assist legislators in the states by sharing research information and staff support facilities; establish a clearinghouse for bills at the state level, and provide for a bill exchange program; disseminate model legislation and promote the introduction of companion bills in Congress and state legislatures; formulate legislative action programs. (ALEC Watch 2002, 33)

ALEC consists of two distinct groups—state legislators and corporate and industry representatives. The process by which ALEC approves model legislation and legislative priorities gives equal weight to each group. A majority of each has to approve proposed resolutions, giving each group effective veto power over proposed resolutions (ALEC Watch 2002). But the importance of the private sector side extends beyond having a voice during negotiations over proposals, as "virtually all of ALEC's revenues come from corporations and their affiliate foundations, trade and professional associations, and a relative handful of ultraconservative foundations" (ALEC Watch 2002, 20). These corporate and industry contributors are a veritable who's who of large, vested interests across a vast array of industries, and include such diverse concerns as Coors, General Motors, Bank of America, Corrections Corporation of America, American Petroleum Institute, State Farm, Microsoft, GlaxoSmithKline, and RJ Reynolds, to name a few (ALEC Watch 2002).

This combination of conservative legislators and corporate interests results in model legislation that can best be described as anti-regulation and pro-business. Proposed legislation has had a direct effect on the varied corporate interests that are the financial backers of ALEC. As an example, the tobacco industry throughout the 1980s and 1990s was one of the most reliable underwriters of ALEC, and ALEC pushed a public policy agenda that aligned with the interests of the tobacco industry. These included limiting or eliminating taxation on tobacco products and creating legislation that would limit the tobacco industry's financial and legal liability in court. The Corrections Corporation of America has also used ALEC to push for state level legislation that would create more state-funded, privately run prisons, as well as legislation that would limit opportunities for parole, thereby keeping beds in their private prisons filled (ALEC Watch 2002). Bob Edgar of Common Cause, a nonprofit group that tracks political donations and spending, summarizes this process as, "Dozens of corporations are investing millions of dollars a year to write business-friendly legislation that is being made into law in statehouses coast to coast, with no regard for the public interest" (Nichols 2011). Using a nonprofit political organization, corporations are able to create legislation that directly benefits them. And through the relationships developed there, legislators will return to their home states and introduce model legislation.

ALEC and Animal Rights Legislation

It was within this framework that ALEC's Homeland Security Working Group published *Animal and Ecological Terrorism in America* in 2003, which included model legislation called the Animal and Ecological Terrorism Act. Model bills like the Animal and Ecological Terrorism Act are pushed by corporate interests with a financial stake in their passage and are moved along the legislative process by sympathetic state legislators. ALEC's Homeland Security Working Group, in keeping with its mission of giving corporate interests and public officials equal power over the development of legislative priorities, has two chairs: one elected official and one from the corporate world. In order to sit on a task force, corporations and industry pay for the privilege, giving these vested economic interests an opportunity to buy their way onto a decision-making body that has real power to push legislation at the state level. For example, it costs anywhere from $2,500 to $10,000 to sit on one of ALEC's nine task forces (ALEC 2011). The private enterprise chair of the Homeland Security Working Group at the time of the 2003 report was Kurt L. Malmgren, a representative of the industry group Pharmaceutical Research and Manufacturers of America (PhRMA) (ALEC 2003).

The pharmaceutical industry has direct concerns here, as the use of nonhuman animals as research subjects has been one of the most contentious issues for animal rights activists. Activists have made biomedical researchers and pharmacy industry executives primary targets of their direct action. Actions aimed at entities involved in animal research or their affiliates accounted for 42.5 percent of actions claimed by the underground animal rights movement between the years 2000 and 2006 (Young 2010). PhRMA is just one of the pharmaceutical and biotech entities who are major contributors to ALEC, a list that also includes the Bayer Corporation, Eli Lilly and Company, GlaxoSmithKline, Merck and Company, and Pfizer. Other animal-using industries and corporations that would benefit from legislation targeting animal rights activists also fund ALEC, including McDonald's and the National Pork Producers Association (ALEC Watch 2002).

Animal and Ecological Terrorism in America makes an explicit connection between "radical" animal rights and environmental activism and the threat of international terrorism. The introduction of the report states, "recent investigations have shown that these radical organizations operate in a similar fashion to other terrorist groups like al-Qaeda"

(ALEC 2003, 4). The conflation of international terrorism and animal rights activism is a common rhetorical device used by opponents of the animal rights movement. The report also makes connections between underground activists and aboveground nonprofit animal rights organizations, "PETA has access to ALF Support Groups, claiming to have over 10,000 members, which aid in legal defense of ALF activists charged with crimes" (ALEC 2003, 8), creating a sense that both mainstream and more radical activists are all part of the same "terrorist" network. The report briefly explains the history of both the ALF and the ELF, and the ways in which they continue to pose threats to corporate profits and to people who work in animal-using and natural resource extraction industries. It goes on to argue that states have been ineffective in prosecuting animal rights activism, largely because they have treated the cases as forms of vandalism, property destruction, and trespass. This approach, according to the report, limits states' abilities to treat the animal rights movement as a criminal venture, thereby making no distinction "between the common thug who vandalizes a public park and an organized eco-terrorist" (ALEC 2003, 12).

By the time of the report in 2003, many states had passed legislation targeting animal rights activists, as had the federal government in the form of the Animal Enterprise Protection Act (AEPA). Despite the presence of these laws, ALEC continued to push for broader legislation to be used against animal rights activists. It viewed the AEPA as a failure, stating that the act "allowed for increased penalties on an overly narrow range of acts, those dealing with specific obstructions of animal enterprises" (ALEC 2003, 15), in effect limiting the government's ability to go after networks and organizations. The report acknowledges the problems in treating activists like terrorists: "the federal definition of terrorism requires the death of or harm to people, an element not characteristic of eco-terrorists" (ALEC 2003, 15). The report also stated that the USA PATRIOT Act, despite its extensive expansion of federal police powers, was insufficient in addressing animal rights activism:

> AETA (the model legislation) allows for the definition of eco-terror as domestic terror, without reference to the USA PATRIOT Act. In other words, the penalties and identification of those who commit

eco-terror crimes are clarified without the overbearing tools provided under the USA PATRIOT Act. (ALEC 2003, 15)

The report simultaneously touts the danger to property and human life posed by the animal rights movement while acknowledging that "eco-terrorists" are actually not likely to cause harm or death to another person, or be considered terrorists under current federal law. This contradiction poses a problem for those who wish to criminalize animal rights activism, thereby necessitating the need to create a whole new category of terrorism. The report, by arguing the need to go after networks and organizations, advocates treating the animal rights movement as a criminal enterprise, allowing the federal government to treat the movement much the same as it would an illicit drug ring, the Mafia, or an international terror organization. It advocates for a definition of terrorism friendly to the corporate and industry interests that have an influence within ALEC.

The state level legislation that eventually informed the Animal Enterprise Terrorism Act can tell us much about the process by which policies travel between states and between states and Congress. Along the way, such legislation became the focus of powerful interest groups that saw this legislation as a way to beat back the gains made by the animal rights movement and as a way to politically marginalize the movement. The combination of powerful corporate interests, ideological allies in state and federal governments, and the infrastructure that brought them together created an avenue for the formation and passage of favorable legislation. The introduction and passage of the AETA provides an example of the way these relationships work at the federal level as well.

INTEREST GROUPS, CONGRESSIONAL COMMITTEES, AND THE AETA

We live in an age of interest group politics in which a federal government largely operates according to the needs and desires of the well organized, the well connected, and the well funded (Lowi 1979). The absolute number of lobbyists and the amount of money spent on lobbying has increased steadily over the last several decades. Spending on lobbying alone has increased from $1.44 billion in 1998 to $3.49 billion in 2010 (Center for Responsive Politics 2011a). Political theorists have examined the role that interest groups play in the creation of public policy, dating from 1833 to the present (Lowi 1979; Hall and Wayman 1990; Tichenor and Harris 2002; Brunell 2005).

Interest group influence in the political process is nothing new, but what is new is the sheer scope of resources spent by powerful interests in the course of getting favorable legislation passed. Political theorists, in trying to define and explain the capitalist state, find that the interests of business and of the State intersect, and even the most forgiving theorists admit that in a state with a capitalist economy, business interests have primacy over other groups in the development of public policy (Miliband 1969; Evans 2006; Smith 2006). What we can take away from this is that well-organized interest groups, especially business interests, have the opportunity to use the levers of government for their own ends. It is this atmosphere that sheds light on the passage of a law such as the Animal Enterprise Terrorism Act.

Political Spending and Influence

According to the Center for Responsive Politics (2011b), the pharmaceutical and health products industry spent significantly more money on lobbying than any other industry from 1998–2006, when the AETA was passed. In this period the pharmaceutical and health products industry spent more than $1.1 billion on lobbying alone. The insurance industry, which spent the second most of any industry during that same time period, spent just over $885 million, or about 80 percent in comparison. During this same period, pharmaceutical and health product industry political action committees (PACs) gave just over $36 million in donations to federal candidates (Center for Responsive Politics 2011c). The pharmaceutical and health products industry is a diverse and multifaceted field with a wide array of public policy interests. What this shows, though, is that resources can be brought to bear whenever these industries feel there is policy or legislation that affects them in some way.

Other industries also have a stake in seeing legislation passed that pushes back against the animal rights movement, including animal agribusiness, which includes dairy, livestock, poultry, and egg producers. Agribusiness has a significant stake in the use of animals for profit. Collectively, the livestock, dairy, poultry, and egg industries spent more than $56 million on lobbying between 1998 and 2006 (Center for Responsive Politics 2011d), while industry PACs gave more than $14.5 million in contributions to federal candidates during that same time (Center for Responsive Politics 2011e).

Political spending by animal rights and welfare groups pales by comparison. Including all the political spending recorded by the Center for Responsive Politics by animal rights and welfare groups between 1998 and 2006, it totals just under $9.54 million, or about 5 percent of what the pharmaceutical and health products industry spent on lobbying alone in 2006 (Center for Responsive Politics 2011f and 2011g).

Committee and Subcommittee Hearings

There were four prominent hearings in the years prior to the passage of the AETA, only one of which dealt directly with the AETA. Others dealt with the animal rights and environmental movements generally, with one hearing on the animal rights group Stop Huntingdon Animal Cruelty (SHAC). Within the three hearings not directly concerning the AETA, there were references made by law enforcement and industry representatives promoting wider ranging laws and jurisdiction for federal authorities in response to the "radical" animal rights movement.

The hearing that dealt directly with the AETA was held by the House Judiciary Committee's Subcommittee on Crime, Terrorism, and Homeland Security on May 23, 2006. The panel that testified was made up of Michelle Basso, a researcher from a primate lab at the University of Wisconsin-Madison, Brent McIntosh, a representative from the Department of Justice's Office of Legal Policy, William Trundley, the vice-president of corporate security for GlaxoSmithKline, and Will Potter, an independent journalist who has been critical of the government's response to the radical animal rights and environmental movements. The nature of the discussion tended to center on the need for an expansion of the Animal Enterprise Protection Act in the form of the AETA, with Potter being the only panelist to express skepticism on the expansion and constitutionality of the bill. The submitted written statements were even more overwhelmingly one-sided toward the interests of industry. Of the thirteen statements submitted by non-congresspersons, each one was associated with an animal-using entity, with a majority coming from individuals representing organizations engaged in biomedical or biotech research.

Howard Coble (R-NC), chair of the subcommittee, began the hearing with a statement and in the first substantive paragraph conflated international terrorism with animal rights activism:

> H.R. 4239 (AETA) was introduced in response to a growing threat commonly referred to as eco-terrorism. While we are still responding to the threat about international terrorism, groups of impassioned animal supporters have unfortunately employed tactics to disrupt animal research and related businesses by terrorizing their employees. (House Subcommittee 2006, 1)

In the shadow of the terrorist attacks of 9/11, Representative Coble linked the fear of international terrorism with the actions of animal rights and environmental activists. As with the ALEC report—*Animal and Ecological Terrorism in America*—he shows how both industry and political representatives have adopted the rhetoric of terrorism when referring to animal rights activists. The sentence referencing "international terrorism" does nothing to address the issue at hand in the hearing other than to conflate animal rights activists with international terrorist groups such as al-Qaeda. The ranking minority member, Bobby Scott (D-VA), expressed concern with the need to ensure First Amendment protections, but not with the bill or its overall goals. Congressman Scott has largely been seen as an advocate of civil rights and civil liberties issues, but with his support for this bill it became apparent early in the hearing that there would be no resistance from committee members to the legislation.

Mr. Potter, in his opening statement, expressed concern about the effects of this type of law on social movement activity, stating:

> Perhaps the greatest danger of this legislation, though, is that it will impact all animal activists, even those that never have to enter a courtroom. The reckless use of the word *eco-terrorism* by corporations and

the Government has already had a chilling effect, and this legislation will compound it. (House Subcommittee 2006, 21)

Potter was openly mocked for his concerns about the legislation and the way it might be implemented. The disparity between the treatment of the witnesses became apparent as Trundley, Basso, and McIntosh were asked questions and given time to reply with minimal interruption, and when interrupted it was as a way to clarify, not challenge, their statements. Potter was continually interrupted and had his intentions and intelligence questioned. The airing of dissent was continually dismissed and minimized by the representatives on the subcommittee.

There was a similar pattern of interactions during three Senate committee hearings dealing with the animal rights movement. These hearings shared witnesses, and were not convened to discuss legislation but were held as "investigations" of the animal rights movement. The first hearing, Animal Rights: Activism vs. Criminality, took place in the Judiciary Committee on May 18, 2004. Senator James Inhofe (R-OK) chaired two separate hearings in the Senate Committee on Environment and Public Works, one examining the Earth Liberation Front and Animal Liberation Front on May 18, 2005, and one examining the animal rights group Stop Huntingdon Animal Cruelty (SHAC) on October 26, 2005.

Of the fifteen witnesses who testified during these three hearings, only one could be described as being sympathetic to the animal rights movement. Dr. Jerry Vlasak, a prominent animal rights activist and spokesperson for the ALF, testified before the Senate Committee on Environment and Public Works. Ingrid Newkirk, founder and president of PETA, and Steven Best, a well-known animal rights activist and philosophy professor, were both invited to testify at one Inhofe-led committee hearing, and according to Inhofe, both declined, leaving Vlasak as the lone voice for the animal rights movement in these hearings. Later in the hearing, Inhofe stated the reason why he invited Best and Newkirk to testify: "We wanted them to defend themselves, if there is a defense" (Senate Committee on Environment and Public Works 2008, 18).

Like the House Subcommittee hearing exchanges with Potter, the exchanges between committee members and Dr. Vlasak were very confrontational, as members openly dismissed the views of animal rights activists and sympathizers. It seems from Inhofe's statement regarding Best and Newkirk that they were not invited to express their views on the animal rights movement or on legislation affecting the movement, but rather as an inquisition on their beliefs and activities.

Those advocating in the interests of industry and law enforcement were not challenged in any significant way. John Lewis, the deputy assistant director of the counterterrorism division of the FBI, acted as a witness at all three hearings. In each he advocated for an expansion of powers for the FBI to target the "radical" animal rights movement. Lewis expressed the importance that the FBI places on the "radical" animal rights movement:

> The No. 1 domestic terrorism threat is the eco-terrorism animal rights movement, if you will. As I indicated a moment ago, there is nothing else going on in this country, over the last several years, that is racking up the high number of violent crimes and terrorist actions, arsons, etc., that this particular area of domestic terrorism has caused. (Senate Committee on Environment and Public Works 2007, 18)

Lewis, as a representative of the FBI, expressed the views of the FBI and of federal law enforcement. Lewis's views were reinforced by other members of federal law enforcement as well. Carson Carroll, Deputy Assistant Director for the Bureau of Alcohol, Tobacco, Firearms and Explosives, and Barry Sabin, Chief of the Counterterrorism Section of the Criminal Division at the Department of Justice, expressed similar sentiments, placing the highest priority on the animal rights and environmental movements. Lewis, of the FBI, also stated during the SHAC hearing, "We are committed to working with our partners to disrupt and dismantle these movements" (Senate Committee on Environment and Public Works 2008, 8). Taken together, a picture begins to emerge of the importance that various agencies of federal law enforcement place on the radical animal rights movement.

Eleven of the fifteen witnesses in these three hearings used similar language in defining the "radical" animal rights movement as a terrorist movement. The additional testimony ranged from expressing the fear of being targeted by animal rights activists, to encouraging an increase in federal law enforcement activity targeting the radical animal rights movement, to advocating for investigations of mainstream animal rights advocacy groups for their purported connections to underground activists. The tenor of a large portion of the testimony can best be described as anti–animal rights movement, using the terms *terrorism* and *terrorist* to describe direct action and those who engage in it. The language of law enforcement, elected officials, and industry representatives was similar, if not identical, throughout. These hearings weren't used to examine the animal rights movement so much as to create an atmosphere—and an official government transcript—that damns and further marginalizes the movement and movement activists.

There were also statements submitted for the record for each of the Senate and House committee and subcommittee hearings. For the three Senate hearings, submitted statements by those who did not attend the hearings in person were mostly from animal rights organizations and environmental groups. Of the statements not submitted by animal rights and environmental groups, three came from representatives of biomedical corporations and industry groups, one from the Southern Poverty Law Center, which warned of the dangers of ALF and ELF actions, and two from elected representatives. A group statement was submitted on behalf of some of the largest environmental groups in the nation, including Greenpeace, the Sierra Club, the Union of Concerned Scientists, and the League of Conservation Voters, among others. Of the sixteen total statements submitted for these three Senate committee hearings, nine came from animal rights and welfare groups, with PETA and HSUS submitting six of these statements between the two of them.

The submitted statements from the animal rights and welfare groups largely defended themselves against accusations that they were collaborating with SHAC or underground groups such as the ALF, and/or reaffirmed their commitment to nonviolent, peaceful, and legal social change. During the Senate committee hearing examining the ALF and ELF, David Martosko of the Center for Consumer Freedom spent much of his testimony accusing aboveground animal rights groups like HSUS, PETA, and the Physicians Committee for Responsible Medicine (PCRM), of collaborating with and funding underground ALF and SHAC activists.

PETA, HSUS, and PCRM submitted statements claiming that these accusations were false, and that they do not condone or collaborate with activists who break the law. The only statement that mentioned federal legislation aimed at activists was the statement from the environmental groups:

> Such legislation should condemn violence regardless of the cause, helping to ensure that the threat from other kinds of terrorist groups is not ignored, or worse, unintentionally encouraged. Furthermore, some of this narrow legislation has been written in a way that potentially covers non-violent forms of protest, which could chill freedom of political expression and dissent. (Senate Committee on Environment and Public Works 2007, 138)

None of the statements by animal rights/welfare groups mentioned legislation targeting animal rights activists in their statements, even as the movement's political opponents and law enforcement representatives continually advocated for more legislation targeting the movement (Senate Committee on Environment and Public Works 2005, 2007, and 2008). It would seem that these groups didn't want to be seen fighting against legislation that targeted "terrorism" suspects, even if their own activities could ensnare them under this law. In effect, the combination of increased attention by industry, federal law enforcement, and Congress, along with the use of the term *terrorism* in a post-9/11 world, created an atmosphere where legitimate organizations couldn't speak out against legislation that might significantly impact their work.

Throughout this entire process there was little to no opposition from elected representatives to legislation targeting animal rights activists. When concerns were raised it tended to be in an effort to make sure that civil liberties and First Amendment rights were protected or to argue that other groups that posed a danger, such as white supremacists and anti-abortion activists, were being overlooked. In these committee hearings and in the official record there was no substantive challenge to the proposed legislation or to the characterization of radical animal rights activists as terrorists, with the exception of the testimony of Will Potter. There would be little opportunity to oppose this legislation in the further stages of its passage.

It was within the committee hearings that the influence of mon-eyed interests becomes most apparent. With the Republican Party, and by extension conservatives, having control of both houses of Congress and of the chairmanships of committees and subcommittees in 2006, a more hospitable atmosphere existed for the passage of pro-corporate legislation. In years prior to the passage of the AETA, the Republican Party attempted to "make the lobbying community subservient to the Republican Party…increasing interactions and ultimately creating a close relationship between the Republican Party and organized business interests" (Witko 2009, 228). Inhofe, Coble, and Hatch, the chairmen of the committees and subcommittee that held hearings on the AETA and animal rights activism, are praised as solid conservatives, with Inhofe receiving a ranking of 100 from the *National Journal* in 2010, and Coble receiving the American Conservative Union's Conservative Award in 2008. Laws like the AETA serve corporate interests by attempting to limit protests, potential disruptions, and loss of profits to business operations, and in so doing align with the pro-business values of conser-vative politicians in Congress. And with campaign contributions from corporate interests benefitting both parties, there was little incentive to take the side of the animal rights movement. The combination of the influence and resources that industry interests could bring to bear, the ideological alignment between the conservative politicians and these interests, and the absence of substantive political opposition created an atmosphere that allowed for the easy passage of the AETA out of the respective committees.

Floor Vote in the House and Senate

The AETA, introduced by Senators Inhofe (R-OK) and Feinstein (D-CA), passed the Senate on September 29, 2006 (Senate Committee on Environment and Public Works 2006). The bill was referred to the floor by the unanimous consent of the Judiciary Committee on Sep-tember 29, 2006, and passed by unanimous consent with no debate. The only discussion was an amendment introduced by Senator Leahy (D-VT) that struck a provision from the legislation that seemed to crimi-nalize peaceful protest, and which passed by unanimous consent as well

(Congressional Record 2006). The AETA was passed as part of a basket of bills, which tends to be reserved for noncontroversial legislation. The Senate bill was passed in the House of Representatives on November 13, 2006 (Office of Legislative Policy and Analysis 2011). Representative Dennis Kucinich (D-OH) spoke out against the bill, but this would be the extent of the opposition. In the House, the bill was introduced under a procedure called Suspension of the Rules. As the Congressional Research Service describes it, it allows the House to "act on relatively non-controversial legislation....Each bill gets forty minutes of debate, then an up-or-down vote, then a push out the door" (Potter 2011, 164). It was reported that few House members were present for the vote.

Despite the attention paid to the animal rights movement in committee, the act itself had little support and it was not seen as a priority by a large majority of House members. According to leaked documents from a group called the Animal Enterprise Protection Coalition—a group composed of animal-using industries and corporations organized to lobby for the passage of the AETA—only 6 percent of House members supported the legislation. Although it did not have widespread support, it also didn't have widespread resistance. No one called for a roll call vote, and it therefore passed by voice vote. It has been reported that only six members of the House of Representatives were present for the vote, but there is no congressional record to know for sure just how many people were present (Project Censored 2010). President Bush signed the Animal Enterprise Terrorism Act into law on November 27, 2006.

THE AETA AND THE FEDERALIZATION OF CRIMINAL LAW

In 1998 the American Bar Association released a report called *The Federalization of Criminal Law*. The report, prepared by the Task Force on the Federalization of Criminal Law, was chaired by former Attorney General Edwin Meese, and consisted of prosecutors, defense attorneys, judges, and legal scholars. The report argued that in the early years of the United States, federal criminal law consisted of threats national in scope—crimes such as treason, bribery on the federal level, perjury in federal court, and revenue fraud—but since then expanded to include many more crimes that are not national in scope (Strazzella 1998). In seeking a conviction, there are many benefits to a federal versus state prosecution. Lovitz states, "a federal animal enterprise statute allows prosecutors to bring defendants before a federal rather than a state court. Compared to a state court, the federal court system yields many more advantages for the prosecutor and disadvantages for the defendant" (2010, 100). These include a grand jury process more favorable to prosecutors, the lighter workload of federal law enforcement officers and prosecutors, allowing more time and attention to each case, increased likelihood of witness participation, and harsher sentencing guidelines. This trend opened space for industry groups to get legislation introduced that would label political opponents and movement activists as criminals and/or terrorists based on their political beliefs.

It was this trend of the federalization of criminal law that produced the most vocal resistance within the congressional hearings on the AETA and animal rights activism. Congressman Delahunt from Massachusetts, who argued that these types of crimes should be handled at the state level, stated, "You know, the former Attorney General under President Reagan, Ed Meese, expressed his concern about the federalization of crime in this country, and, to be candid with you, I think that this could very well serve as an example" (House Subcommittee 2006, 27). In an era where conservative lawmakers argue that federal reach has gone too far and that more power should be relegated to the states, they are expanding the role of federal power in prosecuting crimes that, according to many, should be handled at the state level.

In discussing the transformation that he sees in the United States from a nation guided by the rule of law toward a government guided by interest groups, political scientist Theodore Lowi states, "Hostility to law, expressed in the principle of broad and unguided delegation of power, is the weakest timber in the shaky structure of the new public philosophy" (1979, 93). Congress, in an age of interest group politics, passes legislation with little regard to how the law is to be implemented and enforced, as the actual implementation of legislation is delegated to any number of federal agencies. Often this legislation is pushed, if not actually written, by interest groups with a stake in its passage. Lowi was referring to the regulatory and redistribution policies of the Great Society era (i.e., domestic programs promoted by President Lyndon B. Johnson during the 1960s), but the argument can be extended to the federalization of criminal law.

Voices from across the political spectrum expressed concerns about the AETA and what it means in terms of an expansion of federal powers. In *The Wall Street Journal*, a newspaper known for its conservative and pro-business stance, Gary Fields and John Emshwiller decried the AETA as an expansion of federal power that effectively eliminates *mens rea*, or guilty mind, "a long-held protection that says a defendant must know they've done something wrong to be found guilty of it" (2011, A10). They go on to state about the AETA, "The 2006 act was cited in a joint study by the conservative Heritage Foundation and the National Association of Criminal Defense Lawyers as an example of an overly broad law, particularly the way it clashed with First Amendment free-speech protections" (ibid.). They are referring to the prong of the AETA that states if someone fears for his or her safety because of animal rights activism, that is a violation of the AETA and therefore can be prosecuted as a terrorist act. The person supposedly violating the AETA may never have intended to instill fear in another person, and therefore does not have a "guilty mind," yet may find him- or herself charged with terrorism under the AETA. The AETA fails to differentiate between legitimate threats to one's safety and First Amendment–protected activity, creating a gray area open for manipulation by federal prosecutors and law enforcement.

Extending Lowi's argument to criminal law, the expansion of the powers of the federal government and the rise of interest group politics creates opportunities to criminalize social movement activity. Larger questions of constitutional law have largely been ignored in passing the AETA in order to please a specific set of industries and to protect them from the sustained pressure of social movement activity. The AETA, based on state level laws that were written in collaboration by animal-using industries and their political allies, is written in overly broad and vague language, and its implementation is delegated to prosecutors who are left to determine if someone can be charged as a terrorist in the federal courts.

CONCLUSION

The animal rights movement challenges some of the most fundamental relationships in society, and in the process has challenged the way we view and use nonhuman animals to our own benefit. In a real sense, the animal rights movement is trying to create social change. The passage of the AETA is the story of the response of corporate interests and their political allies to this movement, but in many ways it is more than that. The animal rights movement is asking critical questions about rights, morality, and the extent that we can cause suffering in nonhuman animals for our own gain. In so doing, it is attempting to redefine social relationships, which in turn challenges the economic interests of the agribusiness, pharmaceutical, and biomedical testing industries.

The AETA may very well be a test case for future conflicts between other social justice movements and powerful economic interests. If the AETA is used successfully as a way to diminish or eliminate legitimate protest as a form of social justice movement activity, it should be expected that other industries targeted with persistent social justice movement activity would examine ways in which they, too, can diminish or eliminate their opponents. Social justice movement activity has always been met with resistance from those who have vested interests in maintaining the very relationships being challenged. The animal rights movement, in attempting to redefine the relationship between human and nonhuman animals, has met resistance that is politically powerful and well funded. It is this resistance that has attempted to redefine animal rights activism as terrorism, which may be the most politically charged and personally damning label for any activist or movement in the contemporary United States. The AETA is about the animal rights movement, but in a larger sense it is about interest group politics at work: who gets heard, who gets marginalized, and what it means for citizens attempting to create social change.

REFERENCES

ALEC. *Animal and Ecological Terrorism in America.* The American Legislative Exchange Council, 2003.

————. "Private Sector Membership." Brochure, 2011 (2011a).

————. (2011b). "ALEC State Chairmen." Last accessed 2011. www.alec.org/about-alec /state-chairmen.

ALEC Watch. *Corporate America's Trojan Horse in the States: The Untold Story of the American Legislative Exchange Council.* 2002. www.alecwatch.org/11223344.pdf.

Brunell, Thomas L. "The Relationship Between Political Parties and Interest Groups: Explaining Patterns of PAC Contributions to Candidates for Congress." *Political Research Quarterly* 58, no. 4, 2005: 681–88.

Center for Responsive Politics. "Lobbying Database." Last accessed 2011 (2011a). www .opensecrets.org/lobby/index.php.

————. "Lobbying: Top Industries." Last accessed 2011 (2011b). www.opensecrets.org /lobby/top.php?showYear=a&indexType=i.

————. "PACs: Health." Last accessed 2011 (2011c). www.opensecrets.org/pacs/sector .php?txt=H&cycle=2010.

————. "Lobbying: Agribusiness." Last accessed August 30, 2011 (2011d). www.opensecrets .org/lobby/indus.php?id=A&year=2011.

————. "PACs: Agribusiness." Last accessed 2011 (2011e). www.opensecrets.org/pacs /sector.php?txt=A01&cycle=2010.

————. "Lobbying: Misc Issues—Industry Profile, 2011." Last accessed 2011 (2011f). www.opensecrets.org/lobby/indusclient.php?id=Q10&year=2011.

————. "PACs: Citizens/Humane/Ethical Trtmt of Animals Summary." Last accessed 2011 (2011g). www.opensecrets.org/pacs/lookup2.php?strID=C00406082&cycle=2006.

————. "Lobbying: Misc Issues—Industry Profile, 2005." Last accessed 2011 (2011g). www.opensecrets.org/lobby/indusclient.php?id=Q10&year=2005.

————. "Lobbying: Humane Society of the US." Last accessed 2011 (2011g). www .opensecrets.org/lobby/clientsum.php?id=D000026546&year=2010.

————. "PACs: Humane Society Legislative Fund Summary." Last accessed 2011 (2011g). www.opensecrets.org/pacs/lookup2.php?strID=C00466813&cycle=2008.

————. "Lobbying: Intl Fund for Animal Welfare." Last accessed 2011 (2011g). www .opensecrets.org/lobby/clientsum.php?id=D000052348&year=2000.

————. "Lobbying: Soc for Animal Protective Legislation." Last accessed 2011 (2011g). www.opensecrets.org/lobby/clientsum.php?id=D000056821&year=2006.

Congressional Record. *Proceedings and Debates of the 109th Congress, Second Session,* 152 (125). Washington, D.C.: US Government Printing Office, 2006.

Evans, Mark. "Elitism." In *The State: Theories and Issues,* edited by Colin Hay, Michael Lister, and David Marsh, 39–58. New York: Palgrave-MacMillan, 2006.

Fields, Gary, and John R. Emshwiller. "The Animal Enterprise Terrorism Act Sets an Unusual Standard for Crime." *Wall Street Journal* (September 27, 2011): A10.

Hall, Richard L., and Frank W. Wayman. "Buying Time: Moneyed Interests and the Mobilization of Bias in Congressional Committees." *American Political Science Review* 84, no. 3 (1990): 797–820.

House Subcommittee. *Animal Enterprise Terrorism Act. Hearing before the Subcommittee on Crime, Terrorism and Homeland Security of the Committee on the Judiciary, House of Representatives.* One Hundred and Ninth Congress, Second Session. HR 4239: Serial Number 109-125. Washington, D.C.: US Government Printing Office, 2006.

Jarboe, James F. Testimony on the threat of eco-terrorism before the House Resources Committee, Subcommittee on Forests and Forest Health, Washington, D.C. Published February 12, 2002. www.fbi.gov/news/testimony /the-threat-of-eco-terrorism.

Lovitz, Dara. *Muzzling a Movement: The Effects of Anti-Terrorism Law, Money and Politics on Animal Activism.* New York: Lantern Books, 2010.

Lowi, Theodore J. *The End of Liberalism: The Second Republic of the United States* (2nd ed.). New York: W. W. Norton & Company, 1979.

Miliband, Ralph. *The State in Capitalist Society.* London: Weidenfield and Nicolson, 1969.

Nichols, John. "ALEC Exposed." *The Nation.* Published August 1, 2011. www.thenation .com/article/161978/alec-exposed.

Office of Legislative Policy and Analysis. Bill Tracking: S. 3880—The Animal Enterprise Terrorism Act. Accessed 2011. http://olpa.od.nih.gov/tracking/109/senate_bills /session2/s-3880.asp.

Potter, Will. *Green Is the New Red: An Insider's Account of a Social Movement Under Seige.* San Francisco: City Lights Publishers, 2011.

Project Censored. "# 20 Terror Act Against Animal Activists." Accessed 2010. www .projectcensored.org/top-stories/articles/20-terror-act-against-animal-activists.

Senate Committee on Environment and Public Works. "Inhofe Hails President Bush's Signing of the Animal Enterprise Terrorism Act." Press Release, November 27, 2006. http://epw.senate.gov/public/index.cfm?FuseAction=PressRoom.PressReleases &ContentRecord_id=86DE0E4D-CC1D-434D-B7CA-E630A7A8B678.

———. "Eco-Terrorism Specifically Examining Earth Liberation Front and Animal Liberation Front." One Hundred and Ninth Congress, Session One. Senate Hearing 109-947. Washington, D.C.: US Government Printing Office, 2007.

———. "Eco-Terrorism Specifically Examining Stop Huntingdon Animal Cruelty 'SHAC.'" One Hundred and Ninth Congress, Session One. Senate Hearing 109-1005. Washington, D.C.: US Government Printing Office, 2008.

Senate Committee on Judiciary. "Animal Rights: Activism vs. Criminality." One Hundred and Eighth Congress, Session Two. Senate Hearing 108-764. Washington, D.C.: US Government Printing Office, 2005.

Smith, Martin. "Pluralism." In *The State: Theories and Issues,* edited by Colin Hay, Michael Lister, and David Marsh, 21–38. New York: Palgrave-MacMillan, 2006.

Strazzella, James A. *The Federalization of Criminal Law*. Washington, D.C.: American Bar Association, 1998.

Tichenor, Daniel J., and Richard A. Harris. "Organized Interests and American Political Development." *Political Science Quarterly* 117, no. 4 (2002): 587–612.

Volden, Craig. "States As Policy Laboratories: Emulating Success in the Children's Health Insurance Program." *American Journal of Political Science* 50, no. 2 (2006): 294–312.

Witko, Christopher. "The Ecology of Party-Organized Interest Relationships." *Polity* 41, no. 2 (2009): 211–34.

Young, Peter Daniel, ed. *Animal Liberation Front—Complete U.S. Diary of Actions: The First 30 Years*. Voice of the Voiceless Communications, 2010.

TERRORISM, CORPORATE SHADOWS, AND THE AETA

AN OVERVIEW

John Sorenson

American philosopher John Dewey famously observed that "politics is the shadow cast on society by big business" (Westbrook 1991, 440). Some illumination can be cast onto these shadows by discussing how businesses that are based on the exploitation of nonhuman animals have constructed a myth of "animal rights terrorism" and worked to introduce legislation such as the Animal Enterprise Terrorism Act (AETA) as a means to silence their critics.

Animal rights activists raise serious but "inconvenient" questions about our use and treatment of nonhuman animals. In doing so, they not only challenge the ideology of speciesism that legitimizes our exploitation of animals, but also the profits of powerful industries based upon such exploitation. Farmers, hunters, ranchers, the pet industry, circuses, rodeos and other exploitative entertainment, the fashion industry and dealers in fur and leather, restaurants and grocery chains, and major corporations in the agribusiness, biomedical, pharmaceutical, and vivisection industries, as well as the military, all have vested interests in constructing narratives to justify their power over others, making the exploitation of other beings seem natural, normal, and acceptable, and marginalizing critics. These industries have responded to the animal rights movement by producing propaganda to mask the actual treatment of animals, presenting activists as extremists and terrorists and influencing the State to introduce legislation to repress them.

INCONSISTENT CONCEPTIONS OF "TERRORISM"

Most Americans associate "terrorism" with "the violent death of unsuspecting people" in events such as hijacked airliners crashing into the World Trade Center (Chalecki 2001, 3). Researchers note the communicative aspect of murderous violence as the central component of terrorism (Schmid 2005, 138). And government definitions emphasize these same characteristics. For example, the U.S. Department of State's Office of the Coordinator for Counterterrorism emphasizes "life-threatening attacks" in its definition of terrorism as "politically-motivated violence perpetrated against noncombatant targets by subnational groups or clandestine agents" (U.S. Department of State 2007).

State terrorism is by far the most significant, involving millions of deaths, but non-state actors also commit terrible acts involving the murder of innocent victims. Recent examples include the 2002 and 2005 Bali bombings, the 2004 Madrid train bombings, and the 2010 bombings in Kampala, all of which have been attributed to Islamist groups. Despite constant industry outcry and extensive media coverage about "animal rights terrorism," no acts have been committed by animal advocates that are remotely comparable to these violent attacks intended to kill large numbers of innocent people. "Animal rights terrorism" is the creation of industries that profit from animal exploitation, their supporters, and politicians who are rewarded for servicing them.

Most people agree that animals should not be subjected to unnecessary suffering and consider it praiseworthy to rescue them from such situations. Many feel instinctive sympathy for animals in pain and empathize with their rescuers. The likelihood that animal rights advocates would receive considerable public sympathy and support if their ethical arguments and objectives were properly understood is one reason why industries are so determined to present them in the worst possible way. Industries based on animal exploitation create propaganda characterizing compassionate people who work to protect animals as "terrorists" and "extremists" who use violence to achieve their ends. Unlike actual terrorists who deliberately kill innocent people, such as in the 2008 Mumbai attacks that killed 166 and wounded hundreds more, animal activists employ legal activities such as leafleting, demonstrations, and vegan potluck dinner events. Strategies include, but are not limited to: vegan advocacy; humane education; boycotts; media campaigns; protests; undercover investigations of factory farms, slaughterhouses, and laboratories; and open rescues in which activists do not conceal their identities while removing animals from dangerous situations and horrifying conditions. Few commit illegal actions, and most illegal actions are not "violent" at all, but consist of minor offenses such as trespassing. Even when activists engage in illegal practices, these usually consist of rescuing animals from situations where they will be harmed or killed. Some activists have damaged property, but most of this is minor, such as breaking locks or windows to gain entry to rescue animals or spray-painting slogans. In an even smaller number of cases, activists have damaged equipment that is used to harm or kill animals.

Still fewer activists have engaged in intimidation. Some of these activities are illegal and unpleasant for those targeted. However, annoying tactics, such as sending black faxes to companies involved in vivisection or even demonstrations at vivisectors' homes, cannot be equated with deliberate mass murder of innocent people or setting off car bombs in crowded markets with the intent to kill as many passersby as possible. Animal activists have not committed violence against humans. Unlike al-Qaeda or white supremacist militias, which deliberately target and kill humans, the Animal Liberation Front (considered the most extreme expression of animal advocacy) maintains the key principle that no harm should be done to animals, including humans. These principles contrast with attitudes of actual terrorists such as white supremacist Timothy McVeigh whose 1995 Oklahoma City bombing killed 168 people, including children at a daycare, and wounded hundreds more, which McVeigh dismissed as "collateral damage."

By using the term *terrorism*, industry propagandists compare those who protect animals to those who commit mass murder, attempting to delegitimize them and place them outside acceptable moral boundaries. Industry propagandists, their lobbyists, and right-wing think tanks exaggerate violence committed by activists and make outrageous claims about them, typically without evidence. For example, after the 2001 destruction of the World Trade Center, industry propagandists

consistently compared animal activists to al-Qaeda; the anti-environ-
mentalist American Policy Center even suggested that Islamists and eco-
terrorists were collaborating to destroy America. No evidence for these
claims is provided, but these serve to make the use of excessive police
force and surveillance seem necessary and justified.

BIG BUSINESS CASTS ITS SHADOW ON POLITICS

Agribusiness and pharmaceutical corporations spend millions to influence politicians (Drug Discovery and Development 2010). They hire public relations firms, lobbyists, and front groups to create and disseminate
anti–animal rights propaganda and to pressure government officials.
Corporate propagandists created the "eco-terrorism" label and used it to
demand new laws to specifically protect animal exploitation industries
and silence their critics. The American Legislative Exchange Council,
representing tobacco, oil, and pharmaceutical corporations, was a strong
proponent of new laws to repress animal rights activism and proposed
model legislation in its Animal and Ecological Terrorism Act of 2003.

One influential front group is the Center for Consumer Freedom
(CCF). The CCF worked vigorously to introduce repressive laws against
animal activists, while claiming to defend consumer choice. The CCF
began as the Guest Choice Network (GCN), established in 1985 by Richard Berman with funding from Philip Morris, to unite tobacco, food,
and restaurant industries against public health improvements. The GCN
became the CCF in 2002, with Berman claiming that more militant
efforts were needed to defeat activists. Funding increased from major
corporations, particularly those in food, alcohol, and restaurant industries, such as Anheuser-Busch, Brinker International, Cargill, Coca-Cola,
HMSHost Corp, Monsanto, Pilgrim's Pride, RTM Restaurant Group,
Smithfield Foods, Tyson Foods, and Wendy's, among others. The CCF is
a front group for these corporations, running smear campaigns against
their critics and opposing "Big Brother government," unionization, minimum wage legislation, anti–drunk driving legislation, smoking bans,
and warning labels on food, while rejecting health concerns about alcohol, antibiotic use for livestock, genetic engineering, mad cow disease,

meat, mercury levels in fish, obesity, pesticides, salmonella poisoning, and tobacco. Berman's strategy is to "shoot the messenger" and attack groups such as the United States Centers for Disease Control and Prevention, Greenpeace, The Humane Society, Mothers Against Drunk Driving, and PETA. Especially in the case of animal welfare groups, the CCF alleges that those groups support terrorism. For example, the CCF ran an outlandish campaign against PETA entitled "PETA's Fiery Links to Arsonists" featuring a large photograph of a burning building. In the ad, the CCF asserts that PETA gave $100,000 to "convicted arsonists and other violent criminals" and, thus, is "not as warm and cuddly as you thought." The CCF manipulates feelings of powerlessness and resentment, characterizing animal protection groups as "wealthy" organizations that act as "food police" to limit personal choice and delimit the personal freedom of average workers. But the CCF is no friend of ordinary workers. In fact, through its anti-union campaigns, the CCF benefits wealthy corporations like Smithfield Foods that not only kill millions of animals and destroy the environment but also exploit their labor force.

Another corporate front group is the National Animal Interest Alliance (NAIA). NAIA claims "to promote the welfare of animals, to strengthen the human-animal bond, and safeguard the rights of responsible animal owners" In reality, however, it does nothing "to promote the welfare of animals" and, indeed, actually works against this.

Board members come from animal exploitation industries that include circuses, rodeos, vivisection, dog breeding, animal racing, and agribusiness. NAIA's president, Larry S. Katz of the Animal Sciences Department at Rutgers University, is a campaigner for vivisection, as are numerous other board members. NAIA's cofounder and national director Patti Strand is a dog breeder who opposed the 2001 Puppy Protection Act and defends puppy mill operations. Another NAIA board member, Gene Gregory, is president and CEO of United Egg Producers, representing 97 percent of U.S. egg production. NAIA vice president Cindy Schonholtz is director of industry outreach for the Professional Rodeo Cowboys Association, where she blocks legislation protecting animals. Schonholtz also works for Friends of Rodeo and operates the Animal Welfare Council (AWC), both supporters of the AETA. The AWC represents the rodeo industry but also promotes ranching, the Premarin industry (which uses the urine of pregnant mares as an estrogen replacement for female humans), horse slaughter, the carriage horse industry, and circuses. Member organizations include various rodeo and cowboy associations, carriage horse operators, and circus groups such as Feld Entertainment, but also Americans for Medical Progress (AMP), a pro-vivisection lobby group. Clearly, rodeos do not further "medical progress," but AMP's willingness to join with them shows the convergence of interests in denouncing animal rights. AMP also collaborates with the Fur Council USA, another organization unlikely to advance medical progress, but one willing to embrace AMP's propaganda efforts to link animal activists with al-Qaeda (Ward 2001, fn. 1).

AMP was also a strong supporter of the AETA. AMP is a front group for the vivisection industry, with its board of directors including top executives from pharmaceutical and vivisection companies such as Abbott Laboratories, AstraZeneca, Charles River Laboratories, Glaxo-SmithKline, Pfizer, and Wyeth. These corporations have a record of violations of even the few animal welfare laws that do exist and have been the object of campaigns by animal advocates as well as various public health and consumer groups. The pharmaceutical corporations that belong to AMP have been clients of Huntingdon Life Sciences, the target of a major animal rights campaign (see, for instance, the Stop Huntingdon Animal Cruelty [SHAC] campaign). Wyeth was the subject of specific campaigns about abuse of horses in the Premarin industry. Four universities (Harvard, Oregon Health and Science University, University of North Carolina Chapel Hill, and Tulane) on the AMP board were cited by PETA as being among the "Ten Worst Laboratories." The Oregon National Primate Research Center (ONPRC) at Oregon Health and Science University was criticized by The Humane Society of the United States, In Defense of Animals, PETA, and Stop Animal Exploitation Now! for abusing primates in alcohol, nicotine, maternal deprivation, and obesity studies. Despite the fact that other primates do not develop HIV/AIDS as humans do and that animal models are widely criticized, the ONPRC continued to use animals in these studies as well. Whistle-blowers, undercover investigations, and even a 2001 report by Dr. Carol Shively of Wake Forest University Medical School, who was hired by ONPRC itself to assess the psychological condition of the center's primate prisoners, revealed ghastly abuse of these animals by poorly trained technicians.

NAIA undermines the actual welfare of animals by opposing animal rights, promoting anti-environmental messages, campaigning against spay and neuter programs, and fighting legislation against horse slaughter and the Prevention of Farm Animal Cruelty Act. In contrast, it supports hunting, vivisection, and the use of animals as entertainers by "circuses, zoos, wild animal parks, aquariums, and private entertainers and foundations." It also supports "husbandry" practices involving mutilation, such as "dehorning, . . . ear cropping, tail docking, and debarking of dogs, and removing the claws of cats" and endorses breeding animals for food, fiber, and draft, as well as the fur industry. In short, it endorses and promotes virtually every abuse of animals. Seemingly, NAIA considers "animal welfare" synonymous with "animal exploitation."

NAIA (2010) characterizes those who actually protect animals as radical extremists engaged in terrorism. It maintains an extensive list of criminal acts allegedly committed by these extremists but cites no sources. If such incidents actually occurred, they would hardly constitute "terrorism." Most actions described are nonviolent, such as releasing animals from their prisons. Other incidents involve minor vandalism: spray-painting graffiti, gluing locks, and breaking windows. Some cases even seem unlikely to be the work of animal or environmental activists.

Other corporate front groups created to combat animal advocacy are the Foundation for Biomedical Research, the National Association for Biomedical Research (NABR), and Policy Directions, Inc. All work from the same Washington, D.C. address and were created by Frankie Trull to serve the vivisection industry and to promote animal testing. Trull receives tens of thousands of dollars from individual corporations for her lobbying efforts. While claiming to promote the humane use of animals, Trull obstructs any changes that might slightly reduce their suffering. For example, she opposed even minor amendments to the Animal Welfare Act, such as a 1985 provision to allow caged laboratory dogs periodic exercise, arguing that "no scientific data" had proven the benefits of exercise (Drinkard 1986). When the Alternative Research and Development Foundation tried to amend the Animal Welfare Act to include some consideration of mice and rats in laboratories, Trull persuaded Senator Jesse Helms to amend a farm subsidy bill so that "animal" would be defined to exclude rats, mice, and birds. Trull was also a vociferous defender of Covance testing laboratories, exposed by PETA undercover investigators as a company that routinely abused animals and denied them basic veterinary care. PETA's investigation led to charges for violations of the Animal Welfare Act by the Department of Agriculture.

Trull recognizes that the corporate abuse of animals is unpopular with the general public. On its website, NABR acknowledges widespread public opposition to animal research. To undermine this public sympathy for animal protection, NABR constantly emphasizes the alleged "terrorism" committed by animal activists, citing the FBI's bizarre claim that the ALF and ELF "were responsible for the vast majority of terrorist acts committed in the United States in the 1990s" (NAIA 2007). Trull's other industry front group, the Foundation for Biomedical Research (FBR), maintains what it calls an Illegal Incident Report that provided evidence for the many acts of terrorism that, supposedly, justified the creation of the AETA. Most of the incidents listed are minor acts of vandalism or trespassing, hardly requiring new legislation. For example, NABR reports crimes such as "Goat stolen," "Circus signs spraypainted" and "Badger Snares have been removed." Citing another incident, NABR reports that activists "invaded a recruitment fair for college seniors... [and] ... handed out propaganda." Such actions are normally considered freedom of speech.

NABR created the secretive Animal Enterprise Protection Coalition (AEPC) to coordinate efforts from biomedical and pharmaceutical corporations to create the AETA. The Fur Commission, another strong advocate of harsher legislation against animal activists, said "AEPC comprises organizations supporting the AETA but whose identities have not yet been made public" Thus, in addition to opposing laws that help animals, Trull was instrumental in having repressive legislation passed to specifically target animal activists and to have them designated as terrorists. Trull (2009) boasted of her role in the passage of the Animal Enterprise Protection Act and, later, the Animal Enterprise Terrorism Act.

THE POLITICS OF THE AETA

Influential animal exploitation industries pushed for stronger legislation to stop activists. They found a willing helper in Senator James Inhofe. In 2005, Inhofe chaired the Senate Committee on Environment and Public Works hearing on "Oversight on Eco-Terrorism Specifically Examining the Earth Liberation Front ('ELF') and the Animal Liberation Front ('ALF')." Inhofe called the ALF and ELF "terrorists by definition" [who used] "intimidation, threats, acts of violence, and property destruction to force their opinions…upon society" and held them accountable for damages over $110 million in over a thousand "acts of terrorism" (Inhofe 2005, 1). Comparing them to al-Qaeda, Inhofe claimed that these "terrorist" groups were funded by "mainstream activists" including PETA. Admitting that "they have not killed anyone to date," Inhofe wildly asserted "it is only a matter of time."

Others echoed these claims. Louisiana Senator David Vitter—later notorious for his use of prostitutes, his acceptance of major financial contributions from the oil industry, and his efforts to block the Senate from forcing BP to take full responsibility for cleanup of the massive 2010 oil spill—applauded Inhofe's description of the ALF as "terrorists" and described "terrorist strikes" at Louisiana State University: In 2003, ALF activists entered a toxicology laboratory, spray-painted slogans, and damaged equipment; in 2005, activists did the same and rescued ten mice. Vitter said this caused "psychological harm" to vivisectors, and, like Inhofe, warned "it is only a matter of time" before humans were killed (Vitter 2005, 10).

John Lewis, Deputy Assistant Director of the FBI's Counterterrorism Division, told the committee that "the No. 1 domestic terrorism threat is the eco-terrorism animal rights movement"; identified the ALF, ELF, and SHAC as "today's most serious domestic threats"; stated the FBI "certainly shares your opinion that these individuals are most certainly domestic terrorists"; and identified this as one of the FBI's top priorities, calling for expanded federal laws to allow them to "dismantle these movements" (Lewis 2005, 18, 11, 13). Lewis, too, acknowledged that these "terrorists" had never harmed a human but cited an "escalation in violent rhetoric" (ibid., 12). Lewis said that, compared to anti-abortionists, the KKK, and right-wing extremists, the ALF and ELF "are way out in front in terms of the damage they are causing" (quoted in Bernton 2006).

Although Senator Frank Lautenberg challenged Lewis about more serious violence from anti-abortionists and anti-gay activists, Inhofe silenced him. Lewis denied that anti-abortionist groups could be defined as terrorists, despite the fact that they use physical violence to "force their opinions on society." Anti-abortionists had murdered at least eight people in the United States and seriously wounded at least twelve others in shootings, arsons, acid attacks, and bombings prior to the time of the 2005 hearings, and at least one other murder, along with other attacks, followed. Many "pro-life" groups endorsed these acts.

Using statistics from Department of Justice and National Abortion Federation data, Johnson (2007) compared incidents (against property and people) by animal rights and anti-abortion groups from 1977 to 1993 and found that incidents from anti-abortion groups exceeded animal rights groups at a rate of three to one—1,079 by anti-abortionists compared to only 337 by animal activists. And unlike anti-abortion activists, animal activists have *avoided committing acts against people*. Of incidents against property, the second-highest number (below "minor property damage") of actions by animal activists is in the category of "thefts" (compared to "arson" for anti-abortionists) and likely refers to rescuing animals from vivisection laboratories or fur farms where they are subjected to confinement, painful procedures, and prematurely killed.

Of incidents against people, animal activists issued only threats but committed no murders, kidnappings, acid attacks, or assaults. One incident of attempted murder is noted, but Johnson says no FBI information is included; possibly it was the case of Fran Trutt. In 1988, Trutt was charged with attempted murder after trying to place a bomb near a parking spot used by Leon Hirsch, CEO of U.S. Surgical Corporation, a producer of biomedical tools. In fact, Trutt was incited to violence by Mary Lou Sapone, an undercover agent for Perceptions International, a security firm specializing in actions against the animal rights movement. Hirsch hired Sapone and other undercover agents to infiltrate animal rights groups and prod them to commit illegal activities. The plot to entrap Trutt was discussed at a meeting that included representatives of the federal Bureau of Alcohol, Tobacco, Firearms and Explosives, the Connecticut State's Attorney's office, U.S. Surgical Corporation's security director, and Perceptions International (Berlet 1991). Sapone had relentlessly solicited numerous other activists, all of whom rejected her incitements. Perceptions International agents pretended to befriend Trutt, suggested the bombing, paid for the equipment, and drove her to the parking lot. Trutt was reluctant and called another "friend" (also a Perceptions International agent), who urged her to carry out the operation.

In stark contrast, Johnson (2007) notes that anti-abortionists committed additional murders, attempted murders, acid attacks, bombings, arsons, and death threats after 1993, but that the FBI steadfastly refused to categorize these as terrorism. Clearly, Lewis's allegations about animal activists being "way out in front" are inaccurate.

Nevertheless, the hearing was a prelude to the establishment of the AETA, passed by Congress and signed into law by President George W. Bush on November 27, 2006, replacing the 1992 Animal Enterprise Protection Act (AEPA). Crafted by the National Association for Biomedical Research (NABR), the AEPA had created the term *animal enterprise terrorism*. Other powerful AETA advocates included agribusiness and biomedical industry lobby groups such as the Animal Enterprise Protection Coalition, American Legislative Exchange Council, FBR, NABR, and the Fur Commission. However, scores of other influential animal exploitation businesses and lobby groups also endorsed the act. These industries guided the legislation through to its passage, assisted by politicians such as Inhofe, whose services they had purchased through financial contributions and who had personal investments in industries the legislation would affect. In 2006, the AETA received a warm welcome from the chair of the Committee on the Judiciary, Representative James Sensenbrenner, who owns stock in major pharmaceutical, chemical, petroleum, and defense industries. Sensenbrenner also blocked legislation to protect animals, such as the Animal Fighting Prohibition Act, which was intended to increase penalties for those engaged in such violent abuses of animals. He blocked this legislation despite the fact that it unanimously passed the Senate and had hundreds of cosponsors (it finally passed in 2007). Like Inhofe, Sensenbrenner vigorously championed the AETA, falsely claiming that existing laws were inadequate and blaming animal activists for over a thousand "terrorist" actions and millions of dollars in damages.

Animal exploitation industries cheered the new legislation they had created. NAIA (2006) "applaud[ed] the passage" of the AETA, and national director Patti Strand praised Inhofe for combating the "threat to our country posed by animal-rights extremists." However, civil rights advocates found the AETA too broad and vague, failing even to clearly define "animal enterprise" so that the law could be applied to any business involving animals. The penalties are also disproportionate, imposing longer sentences for nonviolent actions that reduce corporate profits than for those that harm people. Opponents predicted that the AETA would have a chilling effect on legal protest generally because activists would fear being charged as terrorists.

Application of the AETA seems to have borne out those fears. In 2009, four activists—Adriana Stumpo, Nathan Pope, Joseph Buddenberg, and Maryam Khajavi—were charged under the AETA for protesting at the residences of University of California vivisectors in 2007 and 2008. Police said they wore bandanas and wrote "Stop the Torture," "Bird Killer," and "Murder for Scientific Lies" on the pavement with chalk. Fortunately, in July 2010, a federal judge dismissed the indictment because it was too vague and because prosecutors could not specify how the activists had broken any laws. Nevertheless, development of the AETA clearly indicates the power and influence that business can exert over the legal system. Adequate laws already existed to penalize those who committed crimes against these industries.

CONCLUSION

The creation of the AETA illustrates at least two things: first, how powerful animal-exploitation industries invented the menace of "animal rights terrorism" in order to demonize and destroy their critics; and second, how these corporations and their hired propagandists have been able to shape the political and legal system to serve their own interests. The

AETA indeed exemplifies how "politics is the shadow cast on society by big business." This is not justice, nor is it democratic; and it surely does *not* protect the most innocent victims—the animals.

References

Berlet, Chip. "Attacks on Greenpeace and Other Ecology Groups." Political Research Associates, Published August 22, 1991. www.publiceye.org/liberty/greenspy .html.

Bernton, Hal. "Is Ecosabotage Terrorism?" *Seattle Times.* Published May 16, 2006. http://seattletimes.com/html/politics/2002977626_terrorist07.html.

Center For Consumer Freedom, The. "PETA's Fiery Links to Arsonists." www .consumerfreedom.com/advertisements_detail.cfm/ad/15.

Chalecki, Elizabeth L. "A New Vigilance: Identifying and Reducing the Risks of Environmental Terrorism. Pacific Institute for Studies in Development, Environment, and Security." September, 2001. www.pacinst.org/wp-content /uploads/2013/02/environmental_terrorism_final.pdf.

Drinkard, Jim. Untitled Associated Press report. April 6, 1986. www.primatelabs .com/archives/drinkard1986.pdf. (site discontinued).

Drug Discovery and Development. "Growing Pressure to Stop Antibiotics in Agriculture." Published January 4, 2010. www.dddmag.com/news-Growing -Pressure-to-Stop-Antibiotics-In-Agriculture-10410.aspx.

Fur Commission USA. http://old.furcommission.com/resource/pressSFbills.htm.

Inhofe, James M. Senate Committee on Environment and Public Works. Statement of Senator James M. Inhofe: Oversight on Eco-terrorism Specifically Examining the Earth Liberation Front ("ELF") and the Animal Liberation Front ("ALF"). May 18, 2005 (2005a). http://epw.senate.gov/hearing_statements.cfm?id=247266.

Johnson, Dane E. "Cages, Clinics, and Consequences: The Chilling Problems of Controlling Special-Interest Extremism." *Oregon Law Review* 86 (2007): 249–94.

Lewis, John. Senate Committee on Environment and Public Works. Statement of John Lewis: Oversight on Eco-terrorism Specifically Examining the Earth Liberation Front ("ELF") and the Animal Liberation Front ("ALF"). May 18, 2005 (2005b). www.epw.senate.gov/hearing_statements.cfm?id=237817.

National Animal Interest Alliance, The. "Mission Statement—Animal Welfare." www .naiaonline.org/about-us/mission-statements.

————. "Voices of Reason Win the Day: AETA Awaits President's Sig- nature." NAIA Newsletter. Published November 20, 2006. www .naiaonline.org/naia_newsletter_alerts/page/voices-of-reason-win-the -day-aeta-awaits-presidents-signature.

————. Animal Rights Extremism. Last accessed 2007. www.nabr.org/Activism /AnimalRightsExtremism/tabid/407/Default.aspx.

———. "Animal Rights and Environmental Extremists Use Intimidation and Violence to Achieve Their Ends." Last accessed 2010. www.naiaonline.org/body/articles /archives/arterror.htm.

Schmid, Alex P. "Terrorism As Psychological Warfare." *Democracy and Security* 1 (2005): 137–46.

Trull, Frankie. "Thirty Years…Time Flies! Ask Frankie." Blog. Published September 24, 2009. http://www.nabr.org/AboutNABR/AskFrankie/tabid/952/EntryId/10 /Thirty-years-Time-Flies.aspx (site discontinued).

U.S. Department of State. National Counterterrorism Center: Annex of Statistical Information. "Country Reports on Terrorism." Published April 13, 2007. www .state.gov/j/ct/rls/crt/2006/82739.htm.

Vitter, David. Senate Committee on Environment and Public Works. Statement of Senator David Vitter: Oversight on Eco-terrorism Specifically Examining the Earth Liberation Front ("ELF") and the Animal Liberation Front ("ALF"). May 18, 2005. www.gpo.gov/fdsys/pkg/CHRG-109shrg32209/html/CHRG -109shrg32209.htm.

Ward, Simon. "Media Link September 11 with Ecoterror." Fur Commission USA. Published October 17, 2001. http://old.furcommission.com/news/newsF03p .htm.

Westbrook, Robert B. *John Dewey and American Democracy.* Ithaca, N.Y.: Cornell University Press, 1991.

PART III

THEORIZING THE AETA

A Green Criminologist Perspective on Eco-Terrorism

Anthony J. Nocella II

Green Criminology

Green criminology, first coined in 1990 by Michael J. Lynch, argues that crimes can be committed against the natural world. "At its most abstract level, 'green criminology' refers to the study of those harms against humanity, against the environment (including space), and against nonhuman animals committed both by powerful institutions (e.g., governments, transnational corporations, military apparatuses) and also by ordinary people" (Beirne and South 2007, xiii). Therefore, green criminology proposes that nonhuman animals, plants, and other elements of nature demand respect and possess legal rights allowing for lawsuits against individuals, governments, and private firms. Some criminologists use the terms *green criminology* and *conservation criminology* interchangeably (Herbig and Joubert 2006). Others will even interchange *environmental criminology* with *green criminology* (Clifford 1998), but the problem with this comparison is that environmental criminology is a highly developed subfield of criminology that specifically looks at the urban terrain and examines and maps crime scenes (Lynch and Michalowski 2006; White 2008).

Analysts argue over the title of this recent concept of green criminology. Nigel South (1998) and Rob White (2008) suggest that it has yet to emerge as a developed theory. Instead, it is a perspective. White (2008, 15) identifies three important principles of green criminology that must not be violated:

1. Ecological citizenship and ecological justice based on humans as part of the natural world rather than the assumed human domination over nature.
2. Environmental rights and environmental justice based on the protection of the natural world for its own sake and for the enhancement of human life.
3. Animal rights and species justice based on protecting non-humans from humans, including protection from any and all exploitative practices associated with entertainment, research, food, and/or labor.

Within the guise of green criminology, people, governments, and corporations are to be held accountable for environmental damage. Corporations are of particular concern because of their large-scale, world-wide activities that alter environments and commonly use animals for research and production (Beirne and South 2007; Bruns, Lynch, and Stretesky 2008; Clifford 1998; Lynch and Michalowski 2006; White 2008; South 1998). Green criminologists believe corporations need to be accountable for the massive global destruction caused by the quest for economic profit, and green criminology emphasizes that industrial capitalism not only kills birds, people, plants, and other elements in the ecosystem, but, ironically, it also destroys the natural environment that all corporations depend upon for survival.

Still in its adolescence, there is much new and diverse ground to examine in this field of criminology. To advance green criminology, classical terms in the field of criminology must be used and adapted as needed. Green criminology, while interested in recognizing offenses and pursuing paths to justice, looks to identify the harms that are committed, with particular interest in the global ecological system. There already exists an environmental sociology, environmental politics, environmental anthropology, and environmental literature, so it is appropriate that today there is an environmental or "green" criminology. Within green criminology, classic criminological terms such as *deviance, control,* and *terrorism* are revamped with new definitions and a new prefix of "eco," i.e., *eco-deviance, eco-control,* and *eco-terrorism.*

Eco-deviance: Division of Nature by Humans

Similar to classic criminal deviance, corporations recklessly destroy the environment in pursuit of selfish interest. In doing this, people intellectually and physically *divide* themselves from a family that they are part of—the environment. The environment is then ideologically and economically converted into a "natural resource" to be bought and sold. This socially constructed binary of human versus nature, which is often associated with the rise of "civilization," developed long before corporations emerged. But green criminology critiques corporations for their reinforcement of this socioeconomic binary. A corporation that fails to recognize the need for environmental protection (whether for its own survival or the survival of others) violates White's first principle of *ecological citizenship and ecological justice*.

Eco-control: Domination of Nature by Humans

Corporations have developed the global-industrial complex, which may be subdivided into specialized-industrial complexes such as the agricultural-industrial complex, the animal-industrial complex, the military-industrial complex, the academic-industrial complex, the prison-industrial complex, and the medical-industrial complex. These complexes act as domesticating institutions, which control, police, and observe. Green criminology portrays the global-industrial complex not only as a means to control nature, but to conquer it. Because it assumes human domination over nature, eco-control violates White's second principle of *environmental rights and environmental justice*.

Eco-terrorism: Destruction of Nature by Humans

Many law enforcement officials use the label of "eco-terrorist" to describe those who destroy a McDonald's or free nonhuman animals from places of exploitation. But I argue, from a green criminologist perspective, that governments and corporations can, by definition, also be identified as terrorists for committing such actions as clear-cutting forests, slaughtering nonhuman animals, and polluting the water, air, and land. Stressing that the term *terrorism* has no clear definition, the FBI writes:

There is no single, universally accepted, definition of terrorism. Terrorism is defined in the Code of Federal Regulations as 'the unlawful use of force and violence against persons or property to intimidate or coerce a government, the civilian population, or any segment thereof, in furtherance of political or social objectives' (28 C.F.R. Section 0.85). (Federal Bureau of Investigation 2005, iv)

The debate between green criminologists and the law centers on one term in this definition: *unlawful.* What is lawful, who gets to determine the law, and by what criteria do we create laws? Much land and many nonhumans are considered property under the law. But again, who gets to claim ownership? Furthermore, if we do not want to claim that non-humans, land, air, and water are "property," then these can be placed under "any segment thereof" in the above definition. Finally, vivisection, factory farming, animals in entertainment, clear-cutting forests for malls and universities, and dumping toxins into lakes and rivers are often if not always motivated by social and/or political gain. For example, when the owner of a mall destroys a forest to make way for economic growth in a particular community, he or she has been influenced by "social or political objectives," which are the political and community investors.

The first green criminologist to argue that the government could be identified as terrorists was Nigel South. In "Corporate and State Crimes Against the Environment: Foundations for a Green Perspective in Euro-pean Criminology," South wrote:

States condemn "terrorism," but of course have always been per-fectly capable of resorting to terrorist-type methods when in conflict with oppositional groups. A notorious example is the 1985 sinking of the Greenpeace flagship, *Rainbow Warrior*, in Auckland Harbour, New Zealand. This was a crime of terrorist violence carried out by Commandos from the French Secret Service. (1998, 447)

South goes on to write:

In his book *Eco-Wars*, Day (1991) charts a variety of state-sponsored acts of violence and intimidation against environmental activists or groups. His comments on these and the *Rainbow Warrior* affairs are highly relevant to the idea of criminology which takes environmental issues and politics seriously. (ibid.)

In the context of green criminology, terrorism committed by corporations is eco-terrorism. Currently, "eco-terrorism" is the label attached to environmental and animal advocates whose activities cause economic loss to governments, individuals, and corporations (Arnold 1997; Liddick 2006; Long 2004; Miller and Miller 2000). This particular use of "eco-terrorism" is most dramatically illustrated by the 1992 passage of the Animal Enterprise Protection Act (AEPA) and the 2006 passage of the Animal Enterprise Terrorism Act (AETA). These will be further discussed later in the chapter, but for now it is important to recognize that this use of "eco-terrorism" is a form of political repression. The AEPA and AETA systematically deploy the term *eco-terrorism* in order to silence dissent and instill fear, thereby quarantining and even erasing radical animal and environmental activism. As Jason Del Gandio writes:

> Anyone tagged with the terrorist label is automatically deemed evil. It is becoming common, for instance, to label (and legally charge) radical environmentalists as eco-terrorists. This is quite puzzling since over-consumption, fossil fuels and corporate polluters are the ones actually terrorizing the environment. (2008, 119)

In contradistinction to this law enforcement tactic, I propose that "eco-terrorism" be defined as the "systematic or premeditated killing, torturing, kidnapping, or threatening destruction of the environment and nonhuman animals for social, political, and economic purposes." Within this definition, "eco-terrorism" can include clear-cutting over half the Earth's forests; removing monkeys from the wild to use in painful vivisection experiments; destroying our drinking water by factory farm runoff or dumping of chemicals; systematically killing over 10 billion nonhuman animals a year; and/or any other of the hundreds of terrifying corporate-sponsored violent acts to the environment and nonhuman animals. Therefore, corporations that destroy the environment to gain profit or power are not only criminals but actually eco-terrorists. Because the act of eco-terrorism (so defined) does not recognize the intrinsic rights and value of the environment or the protection of nonhuman animals, it violates White's third principle of *animal rights and species justice.*

Transformative Justice and Healing

In today's world, governments and societies tend to be competitive, violent, and oppressive. We must therefore resist the urge to fight back with similar tools. As Audre Lorde (1984) said, "the master's tools will never dismantle the master's house." Rather than fighting violence with violence, we must work together in a collaborative, creative, and inclusive manner that heals rather than hurts. This type of orientation to social change falls under the broad rubric of "transformative justice," which is a system of thought and practice that blends restorative justice and social justice. Restorative justice focuses on the needs of both the victims and offenders; it tries to address the wants and needs of all who are affected by a "criminal" action. However, restorative justice has traditionally ignored such issues as the privileges and oppressions of identity politics. Social justice does address such issues, but it can be insufficient for bringing people together through dialogue and mediation.

Transformative justice adopts the best of both paradigms, fills in where each lacks, and approaches problems, crimes, and issues as systemic in nature. Rather than blaming a single individual, transformative justice seeks to address the various systems that motivate individual choices and actions. From this perspective, then, the answer is not necessarily to lock up those who harm nonhumans or destroy the ecosystem. Such an approach would simply contribute to the prison-industrial complex. Instead, we must address the wider systemic conditions that motivate such destruction and figure out alternative methods for holding people accountable. It is unlikely that isolated individuals are capable of generating such alternative methods of justice. Instead, such alternatives must be collectively generated through discussion, debate, collaborative projects, conferencing, speaking and writing for the public, and by creating organizations dedicated to transformative approaches.

The remainder of this chapter addresses a variety of issues—the current state of the world, the nature of the corporate-State complex, and so-called eco-terrorism—from the perspectives outlined above. The hope is to foster a different kind of thinking, which then compels action and justice.

State of Nature

> The world is experiencing very troubled times. Global warm-
> ing, for instance, is altering patterns of temperature and
> precipitation, raising sea levels through polar ice melting,
> increasing vulnerability to flooding and land loss, and chang-
> ing ecosystems worldwide ("Coastal Zones and Sea Level
> Rise" n.d.; Pollack 2010). NASA defines global warming as:
> an increase in the average temperature of Earth's surface. Since the
> late 1800s, the global average temperature has increased about 0.7
> to 1.4 degrees F (0.4 to 0.8 degrees C). Many experts estimate that
> the average temperature will rise an additional 2.5 to 10.4 degrees
> F (1.4 to 5.8 degrees C) by 2100. That rate of increase would be
> much larger than most past rates of increase. (Mastrandrea and
> Schneider 2005, 1)

This rapid growth in global temperature has caused terrible and lasting effects, threatening humans and other species if actions are not taken immediately. In 2005, *The Washington Post* reported on a study that claimed global warming increased the frequency of "destructive hurricanes," such as Hurricane Katrina, which destroyed much of New Orleans in 2005 (Eilperin 2005, 1). In addition, a 2006 study by Dr. Camille Parmesan, a biologist at the University of Texas at Austin, stated that global warming is causing species extinction specifically within sensitive habitats, such as in the Antarctic and Arctic. This situation was also noted by former Vice President Al Gore in his award-winning docu-mentary *An Inconvenient Truth: A Global Warning*. Gore's documentary claimed that global warming causes rapid melting of glaciers worldwide. Gore goes on to say that "forty percent of all the people in the world get their drinking water from rivers and streams that are fed more than half by the melted water coming off the glaciers and in this next half century those forty percent of the people on Earth are going to face a very serious shortage because of this melting" (ibid.). Further, species within forests are also greatly at risk because of global warming, which causes forests to be drier and hence more vulnerable to longer and more extreme forest

fires. It was noted by researchers at the Scripps Institution of Ocean-
ography and the University of Arizona that "four times as many large
wildfires occurred in Western forests between 1987 and 2003 compared
to the previous 16 years" (West 2007).

In the documentary *The 11th Hour*, narrated by Leonardo DiCaprio,
Nathan Gardels, editor of *New Perspectives Quarterly*, explains the divide
between economy and nature that occurred with the industrial revolution. He states that, "nature was converted into a resource"; it was thought
of as limitless and thus free to be exploited with no consequences; it was
all done in the name of progress and growth of human society. These
assumptions about a world consisting of limitless resources for human
consumption have served as the ideological driver for widespread environmental havoc and destruction. Richard Kahn (2010) writes in *Critical
Pedagogy, Ecoliteracy, and Planetary Crisis: The Ecopedagogy Movement*:

> In 2005, the UN-funded Millennium Ecosystem Assessment (MEA)
> released the most encompassing study to date about the state of the
> planet's ecology. The study found that during the last fifty years
> humanity altered and mainly degraded the earth's ecosystems "more
> rapidly and extensively than in any comparable time in human his-
> tory."' (MEA 2005, 2)

Thus, the increased scope, magnitude, and frequency of flooding,
species extinction, hurricanes, glacier melting, ecosystem destruction,
environmentally related health ailments, forest fires, deforestation, and
rising sea levels have one significant similarity: these environmental
problems are rapidly reaching a level of global disaster that cannot be
managed or ignored, resulting in possible massive ecocide (Bodley 2005;
Churchill 2002). Global warming threatens all life on this planet, creating "global environmental or ecological crisis (or crises)" (Kahn 2010,
4). Global warming is not only an environmental and social issue, but a
highly charged political one as well.

The corporate-dominated mass media, reflecting the interests of its
owners, has given credence to those who see global warming as either
a hoax or an exaggerated threat. Many scientists and politicians avoid
openly stating that global warming exists and that the current global
economic system causes climate change, as these claims may be viewed

as leftist propaganda (Gore 2006; Halpern 2010). President Obama's failure to mention climate change in his 2011 State of the Union speech reveals the degree to which this issue is viewed as unpopular with corporate interests in America (Goldenberg 2011). From the perspective of some analysts (including myself), global capitalism is the prime force behind climate change.

Grounded in competition, domination, and inequality, capitalism is a cultural system that directs technical and economic processes toward the goal of supporting primarily the interests of political elites (Bodley 2005). In doing so, capitalism essentially perverts human capacity for knowledge and morality, while motivating human beings to destroy themselves and the life-nurturing processes of the planet for a false value of wealth driven by greed and destruction (Best and Nocella 2006; Kahn 2010; Tokar 1997). Capitalism as a way of life flourished under the industrial revolution, with corporations emerging as key economic actors in the establishment of a global market and political system that transcends borders. Today, capitalism is the most adopted and popular economic system in the world, with powerful global institutions, such as the World Bank and International Monetary Fund, as well as national governments and business interests, all promoting private property and production for profit (Yuen, Burton-Rose, and Katsiaficas 2004).

The United States is the biggest supporter of global capitalism. With the end of the Second World War in 1945, the United States emerged as the Earth's largest and most powerful industrial capitalist country. The collapse of the Soviet Union in 1991 and the end of the Cold War, along with the embracing of neoliberalism ("neo laissez-faire economics") by governments worldwide, confirmed the political and ideological predominance of America. For decades, the country has disproportionately consumed the world's energy supply and other resources (Harvey 2006). "In 2000, Americans made up less than five percent of the world's population but consumed nearly twenty-five percent of the world's commercial energy" (Bodley 2005, 380). Even with the rise of China in recent decades, the United States has the largest and most technologically powerful economy in the world, and it is the major apostle of the culture of consumption and materialism (Klein 2002). Once again, climate scientists contend that unchecked production and private consumption are the greatest causes of global warming and other ecological crises.

Capitalism has, for the most part, trumped religious and other ethical value systems on this planet, and corporations have been picked repeatedly in line-ups with thousands of other possible causes. Identified by U.S. courts as individuals, corporations are never arrested; CEOs are merely fired or asked to respectfully retire to avoid negative media. It is even common for CEOs to be safeguarded from losing their jobs; corporations simply rename themselves. As John Bodley explains:

> Giant commercial corporations now dominate American life. Corporations are given the same rights as individuals, but unlike individuals and sole-proprietorship businesses, corporations can live forever and grow ever more powerful. Corporations also are not limited to particular places, and they can project their commercial power throughout the world. Furthermore, corporations' structure and limited liability makes it difficult to hold corporations responsible for the total cost of their activities, even when they are criminal. (2005, 408)

While inanimate corporations are considered individuals with rights under the laws, actual creatures—living, breathing, sentient nonhuman animals—are considered property without rights under our laws. Critics feel that with all of these firms' rights and limited liability for their actions, something has to give or else corporations will do what they want without impunity. Although legally corporations and individuals are treated the same, they are in fact very different entities. An individual has a heart, mind, and soul. A person possesses a moral conscience based on a set of values. Corporations are a social technology that people have created to pursue the particular economic and political interests of their owners. Therefore,

> Both the corporate structure and the surrounding regulatory system need to be changed: we should do away with limited liabilities and "personhood" under the Constitution and demand an increase in corporate accountability, stronger antitrust laws and international liability, the extraction of corporations out of the political process, extended producer responsibility, internalized (versus externalized)

costs, and total stakeholder responsibility (and it should be recognized that stakeholders include workers, fence-line communities, consumers, and vendors, etc. (Leonard 2010, xxxi).

According to critical theorists, corporate interests have become firmly entrenched in government in contemporary America through multiple means, including campaign financing, lobbying, and the shuffling of individuals between corporate and government roles. This political power enhances the ability of corporations to act globally with very little accountability and limitations (Korten 2001; Bakan 2004).

Corporations are designed not to benefit others or have long-term human sustainability, but rather for making the most money as quickly as possible. Kenny Ausubel, founder of Bionners, said in *The 11th Hour*, "Probably the greatest weapon of mass destruction is corporate economic globalization. And there has always been a greed factor in human civilization. What has happened in corporations which are the dominant institution of our age, is that they perfected that as a system, and what we literally face today is that we will kill our host, the planet" (*11th Hour* 2010). From the BP Gulf Coast oil spill to McDonald's clear-cutting of the Brazilian rainforest, multinational corporations are reshaping the world into commodified resources. KFC kills more than one *billion* chickens a year ("Kentucky Fried Cruelty"), and Lockheed Martin, the largest corporation that contracts with militaries around the world, profits from war ("Lockheed Martin"). Lockheed Martin claims to have "increased their dividend payments by more than 10 percent for the seventh consecutive year—perfectly in line with the increase in war spending by the United States. Its chairman, Robert Stevens, received over $72 million in compensation over the past three years" (Quigley 2010, para. 16).

It must be stressed that the concept and the structure of a corporation is not the problem, as "corporations are not inherently good or evil. A corporation is just a legal entity. It's how the corporation is run that makes it an asset or a detriment to the broader society" (Leonard 2010, xxx). The problem is the mission of the corporation that was created by the founders and supported by the shareholders. Consequently, "When corporations control such a huge percentage of global resources, it's pretty hard to rein them in when they start trashing the planet, as far too many do. In 2007, 60,000-plus multinational corporations controlled half the world's oil, gas, and coal and generated half the gases responsible for global warming. Corporations are designed to make money for their shareholders at any cost, even if that means putting billions of dollars into lobbying for war, prisons, or environmentally risky offshore oil drilling. These corporations often enter into large contracts with government agencies such as local, state, and federal law enforcement and corrections, which aid in the development of the prison-industrial complex (Davis 2003); similarly, corporate dealings with the military have formed the military-industrial complex.

I believe, as do many activists who are highly critical of global capitalism, that we are living in the most destructive era on this planet since the arrival of humans as a species (for an extension of this argument, see Best and Nocella 2006, 8–30). While five great extinction crises have already transpired on this planet, the last one occurring 65 million years ago in the age of the dinosaurs, we are now living amidst the sixth extinction crisis, caused by humans rather than natural phenomena. Human devastation of local and even regional environments is not a new occurrence, but the altering of climate is unprecedented. The closer humans come to total domination, the closer we come to self-destruction. The Earth has been domesticated, colonized, commodified, bred and cross-bred, genetically engineered, cloned, and transformed into forces of mass destruction, refuting the myths and fallacies of progress, development, science, technology, the free market, and neoliberalism (Harvey 2005; Giroux 2008). Overall, our current global crises demonstrate the inherent *contradiction* between capitalism and ecology (Kovel 2002).

The human species' existence can be easily marked at a period in the Earth's history of mass destruction promoted by the Five Cs of human domination of the planet: civilization, colonization, capitalism, corporatization, and commodification. Civilization is the development of hierarchical, urbanized human societies that are not locally self-dependent, but reliant on external resources from distant lands. The demand for accumulation propelled the exploration and expansion, referred to as colonization (Ashcroft, Griffiths, and Tiffin 2006). By the 1500s, European nations participated in colonization, heightening competition for goods and services in the marketplace, creating the economic system referred to today as capitalism. This system involves commodification, transforming all aspects of nature and humanity into goods that can be bought and sold. In the logic of capitalism, all species are commodified, serving only as a "resource" to provide profit (Best and Nocella 2004). The processes of capitalist and colonial expansion were facilitated by the establishment of companies that have evolved into today's global corporations. Corporate management is responsible only to the shareholders who seek to maximize their profit. For some animal rights activists, corporations are new modern-day slave owners, buying and selling their "property" at the New York Stock Exchange (NYSE), much like other stockyards.

Civilization is inherently hierarchical at multiple levels (Bodley 2005). It involves social, political, and economic inequalities that are based on and reinforced by cultural categories. The elite separate themselves from commoners, i.e., those who are seen as different and/or those who fall outside direct social or economic control. The elite also seek to define a divide between nature and humans (Best and Nocella 2006; Jensen 2006a; Jensen 2006b; Kovel 2002). The natural world is portrayed as inferior to civilization; and terms such as "savage," "primitive," or "illiterate" are applied to people seen as not fulfilling the norms of elite culture. European colonization extended this political economy and cultural system across the world.

Today, we live in a world marked by profound differences between the haves and the have-nots where classism and inequality are rampant. A particular cultural system seeks to impose a worldview where nature is converted into resources and owned goods. The highly unequal industrial world is reinforced by institutions such as the medical-industrial complex that supposedly cares for the common good while it actually keeps the public safe and orderly for the benefit of elite economic and political interests. And science, supposedly serving progressive and universal goals, largely contributes to the strengthening of capitalist interests and goals.

Nature of the State

The current global political climate is steeped in fear and rhetoric about terrorism and security (Chomsky 2002; Chomsky 2003; Kellner 2005; Klein 2007). The twenty-first century began with drastic shifts in U.S. policies in the name of national security, which has been used to justify the repression of nonviolent dissent and the violation of civil liberties. We have entered a neo-McCarthyite period rooted in witch hunts against activists and critics of the ruling elites (Best and Nocella 2004 and 2006). The terms and players have changed, but the situation is similar to the 1950s (albeit, without government-aided assassinations or physical torture and with very few extreme prison sentences carried out). The terrorist threat supplants communism; Attorney Generals John Ashcroft and Alberto Gonzalez donned the garb of Senator Joseph McCarthy, and the Congressional Meetings on Eco-Terrorism stand in for the House Un-American Activities Committee (Best and Nocella 2004). As in the past, the government informs the public that the nation is in a permanent state of danger, such that security, not freedom, must become our overriding concern. Officials conjure up dangerous enemies everywhere, not only outside our country, but, more menacingly, ensconced within our borders, lurking in radical cells.

The alleged dangers posed by foreign terrorists are used to justify the attack on "domestic terrorists," and in a panic-stricken climate, the domestic terrorist is apparently any citizen who expresses dissent. Within this environment, the former Bush administration unleashed— and the Obama administration has maintained—an unprecedented surveillance machinery to monitor the communications of all Americans post-9/11.

With so much tension between those who are fighting to protect the natural world and those who are destroying the world, it is important to expose and unpack the political repression that occurs through labeling and stigmatization. For instance, it has become common practice to label activists who defend the planet against human-based ecological destruction as "eco-terrorists." Even more historically common is the use of the word *property* to label and to *justify* the exploitation of nonhuman animals, plants, and natural elements. Such labels and stigmatizations minimize the contributions that activists actually make to the world, deter people from becoming activists, perpetuate the perceived divide between nature and civilization, and reinforce various oppressions and ills.

These labels and stigmas are used by corporations—and the State—to silence voices that speak truth to power. What is beginning to unfold is a mass political-repressive environment whereby the corporate-State is targeting earth and animal liberationists (Best and Nocella 2006; Lovitz 2010). Similar to the Red Scare of the 1950s, in which the U.S. government attacked communists, anarchists, and other political activists, there is currently a Green Scare, characterized by similar State tactics against those defending nonhuman animals and the Earth from attack (Potter 2011). History is repeating itself, such that one ideological scare is replaced by another in an attempt to protect capitalism from its critics and challengers.

It cannot be stressed enough that the Green Scare is being led not only by law enforcement agencies such as the FBI, but ultimately by corporations such as Huntingdon Life Sciences, Bristol-Myers Squibb, Proctor and Gamble, SC Johnson, Scott Paper Co., and Kleenex (to name just a few). These corporations are fearful of what activists will convey to the public about corporations' destruction of the Earth and the torture of nonhuman animals. If the public finds out, then the company image is damaged, the customer trust is broken, and the company profit is ultimately decreased. The earth and animal liberationists are not necessarily going after people or even the government; but rather, they are targeting the superpowerful global corporations. They are conducting both legal protests and illegal economic sabotage, and engaging in tactics ranging from boycotting The Gap to breaking windows of McDonald's franchises. It is here that the FBI is carrying out the job assigned to them by the United States Congress, which has been strongly lobbied by corporations.

Clearly, one of the most significant events within the recent history of the animal liberation movement was the arrest and conviction of the SHAC 7 (Best and Kahn 2004). In May 2004, police rounded up non-violent activists Kevin Kjonaas, Lauren Gazzola, Jacob Conroy, Darius Fullmer, John McGee, Andrew Stepanian, and Joshua Harper. The government issued a five-count federal indictment that charged each activist, and SHAC USA, the nonprofit 501(c)3 corporation, with violations of the 1992 Animal Enterprise Protection Act (AEPA). Then, in March 2006, the SHAC 7 defendants (minus John McGee, who was dropped from the case) were found guilty of multiple federal felonies for advocating the closure of Huntingdon Life Sciences. All had to serve prison time (see www.shac.com for more information about the SHAC trial and convictions). The AEPA was later expanded in September 2006 to the Animal Enterprise Terrorism Act (AETA). In brief, the AEPA and AETA are intended to shield animal-exploiting corporations from public dissent and criticism.

Many corporate industry proponents hope that convictions under the AETA will clear the way for the government to develop similar laws capable of targeting other activists who conduct successful campaigns against big business (Lovitz 2010). This may be unjust and unconscionable, but it is not uncommon. The repression of political dissent and the targeting of political dissidents are long-standing aspects of American politics (Lynd and Lynd 1995; Schultz and Schultz 2001; Zinn 1995). In the 1960s and 1970s, the FBI hunted down radical social groups such as the Black Panther Party, the American Indian Movement, and anti-war activists (Abu-Jamal 2000; Churchill and Vander Wall 2002a and 2002b; Jones 1998; Peltier 1999; Shakur 1987). For the past decade or so, the FBI has begun targeting the animal liberation and environmental movements, particularly anyone suspected of participating in or even supporting the Animal Liberation Front (ALF) and the Earth Liberation Front (ELF). The FBI has gone so far as designating these two the top "domestic [terrorist] threat in the United States" (Lovitz 2010, 106).

With so much time and effort dedicated to these groups, one might think that the ALF and ELF have no sound or logical arguments. But this is not the case. The ALF and ELF and their supporters act upon a philosophy that privileges the natural world and nonhuman animals; this philosophy argues for the uniqueness—and thus for the protected rights—of plants, rivers, oceans, forests, animals, insects, and so on. These living beings and entities should not be viewed as inferior commodities to be bought and sold, but rather as free and equal and, therefore, protected as important members of the bio community. Each element and being is interdependent and interconnected in a complex and interwoven diversity of life. And *all* life should be respected and valued, *equally*.

Animal Advocacy

The basic mission of the animal liberation movement is to stop the abuse, torture, and killing of nonhuman animals for food, science, entertainment, pets, and profit (Best and Nocella 2004; Regan 1983; Singer 1985). Animal liberationists argue against the notion that nonhuman animals are property. These activists see the notion of "property" as developing through an economic system of exploitation.

It is common for a social elite class to use science or religion to establish a "less-than status" of "others." The elite class also uses economics to define these "others" as property—e.g., slaves, indentured servants, labor, and natural resources. This was done to women, people of color, people with disabilities, nature, and nonhuman animals. I contend that much of the backlash against animal advocates and environmentalists is rooted in the iconoclastic nature of their political beliefs: they are challenging accepted ideas and practices that are ingrained within the very fabric of American society and culture. The ALF, for example, is an anarchist-based organization challenging the notion of property. The ALF liberates nonhuman animals that are being exploited and killed; it destroys materials that aid in this exploitation and killing; and it strives to never harm a living creature (*including humans*).

Today, the global animal advocacy movement (broadly conceived) is made up of tens of millions of people. Like many social movements, animal advocacy does attract its share of "extremists"—i.e., those people who are perceived as committing extreme forms of nonviolent civil disobedience or extreme underground tactics. From the perspective of some animal advocates, such "extremists" invite the stigma of "eco-terrorism," and thus harm the overall movement. However, others stress that these particular activists play an important role in showing the public *the extreme abuses* that are inflicted upon nonhuman animals.

Established in 1976 in Britain, the ALF is an international, decentralized, underground organization with no leaders. It operates with an open membership to all, and with members of unknown culture, race, class, physicality, spirituality, sexuality, gender, ability, and mental identity. Activities range from burning down research laboratories at universities to freeing thousands of minks from fur farms. The Animal Liberation Front Guidelines, which serve as the ALF's foundational doctrine, are as follows:

1. To liberate animals from places of abuse, i.e., laboratories, factory farms, fur farms, etc., and place them in good homes where they may live out their natural lives, free from suffering.
2. To inflict economic damage to those who profit from the misery and exploitation of animals.
3. To reveal the horror and atrocities committed against animals behind locked doors, by performing nonviolent direct actions and liberations.
4. To take all necessary precautions against harming any animal, human and nonhuman. (Best and Nocella 2004)

The ALF seeks to create a compelling critique of corporate capitalist society by taking up *action*: e.g., by destroying property and causing economic sabotage in the name of animal liberation (Best and Nocella 2004). The ALF's critique of capitalism is rooted in anarchist and politically progressive literature and ideas, and is supported by the field of critical animal studies (Best and Nocella 2004; Best, Nocella, Kahn, Gigliotti, and Kemmerer 2007; Best 2009a and 2009b). Because it is a clandestine group, the ALF communicates its message to the public solely through communiqués.

The Rise of State-Defined Eco-Terrorism

The post-9/11 U.S. political climate is built on the fear and rhetoric of terrorism and security (Brasch 2005; Chang 2002; Chomsky 2007; Del Gandio 2008; Griffin and Scott 2007; Johnson 2004a, 2004b, and 2006; Katovsky 2006; Klein 2007). This climate is created, in part, by propaganda. Such propaganda is powerful because it "provides a false sense of fulfillment by telling people what they want to hear. We all want to feel good about ourselves, we all want to believe in what we are doing and we all want to feel proud of our country, culture and government. Propagandists know this and thus use language that fulfills our unmet desires" (Del Gandio 2008, 120). People have a common and even natural fear of terrorism—i.e., a fear of unwarranted and unpredictable attack and violence. The use of "terrorism" thus fulfills a certain psychological desire: "terrorists" are inherently perceived as the bad guys, and thus by default the rest of us become elevated to the status of the "good guys"; we attain a positive status by stigmatizing others, and are thus made to feel better about ourselves (ibid.).

Intense controversy still brews over who is a terrorist and the actual definition of terrorism. But it is important to keep in mind that such designations and definitions are more than likely ruled not by the government, but instead by wealthy corporate interests that are rooted in the financial-industrial complex, the military-industrial complex, and the gas- and petroleum-industrial complex (Chomsky 2004). The question thus arises: Who and what are "terrorists"? And, conversely, who and what are "freedom fighters"? What is "violence," and who are the main perpetuators of violence? It is imperative for critically reflective analysts, activists, and everyday citizens to resist corporate, State, and mass media definitions and propaganda in order to distinguish between nonviolent civil disobedience and "domestic terrorism," or between ethically justified destruction of property and wanton violence toward life (Chang 2007; Chomsky 2005). As Douglas Long writes:

> The FBI categorizes ELF/ALF attacks as acts of "eco-terrorism," which it defines as "the use or threatened use of violence of a criminal nature against innocent victims or property by an environmentally-oriented, subnational group for environmental-political reasons, or aimed at an audience beyond the target, often of a symbolic nature." (2004, 3–4)

I argue that the greatest reason the ALF and ELF are identified as eco-terrorists is because of their ideological difference (Del Gandio 2008, 119)—i.e., they challenge capitalism by conducting economic sabotage toward corporations. The acts these groups commit may be crimes, but they are nonviolent crimes that do not harm actual people. Such crimes might include trespassing, vandalism, and arson. With hate groups throughout America wanting to harm people, an important question must be asked: How is it possible that right-wing hate groups are not perceived as more of a national threat? The answer for many in the animal advocacy movement is that these right-wing hate groups are conservative and are not trying to create new change, but rather return to how things were in the past (oppressive race relations, traditional gender roles, patriarchal households, etc.). Meanwhile, the ELF and ALF are left-wing groups that want to create new social change—they want to break the current norms and promote more ethical and inclusive norms. It is important to realize that the change these groups want (ending the exploitation of nature and nonhuman animals) would affect the entire nation and even the world. Thus, their goal is to end, or at least alter the very nature of, the corporate-industrial complex.

Since the events of September 11, 2001, the U.S. government has initiated a strategic campaign to eliminate animal and earth liberationists. Donald Liddick writes, "In labeling environmental and animal rights radicalism the most dangerous domestic terror threat in the United States, the U.S. government . . . has set the stage for the application of the Patriot Act to the prosecution of so-called eco-terrorists" (2006, 99). The USA PATRIOT Act, signed into law by President George W. Bush on October 26, 2001, broadened the definition of terrorism, allowed the detaining of people on suspicion alone, greatly reduced the protection of privacy by law enforcement, and decreased the oversight by courts (Brasch 2005).

John E. Lewis, the deputy assistant director of the FBI's Counterterrorism Division, remarked that, "Investigating and preventing animal rights extremism and eco-terrorism is one of the FBI's highest domestic terrorism priorities" (Lewis 2005). In its efforts, the government has brought the whole animal advocacy movement under fire with regular investigations, grand juries, home raids, infiltration of organizations, congressional hearings, and arrests. Douglas Long writes, "The Federal Bureau of Investigation (FBI) estimates that between 1996 and 2002, the ELF and affiliated organization, the Animal Liberation Front (ALF), committed more than 600 criminal acts in the United States, resulting in damages in excess of $43 million" (2004, 3). It must be stressed that the ELF and ALF have never committed an action that harmed a human or nonhuman animal; much of the reported damages are property destruction and the loss of animal research. Furthermore, the ALF has never represented a direct or overt threat to the U.S. government or the American people.

If there is any doubt that the U.S. government defends the animal-industrial complex, then the AEPA and AETA make that explicitly clear, and such legislation does so at the expense of basic constitutional rights. As the Center for Constitutional Rights states:

> The AETA covers many First Amendment activities, such as picketing, boycotts and undercover investigations if they "interfere" with an animal enterprise by causing a loss of profits. So in effect, the AETA silences the peaceful and lawful protest activities of animal and environmental advocates (Center for Constitutional Rights).

While the AEPA has criminalized First Amendment activities, the AETA has made way for the "terrorization" of civil disobedience. *Terrorization*, a new concept within the academic field of "label theory," is the act of stigmatizing one's adversaries as terrorists. This labeling demonizes dissidents and marginalizes their causes and goals while, conversely, legitimizing the beliefs and actions of the accuser. The terrorization enacted by the AETA may have been officially passed by Congress, but it was lobbied into law "by wealthy biomedical and agri-business industry groups such as the Animal Enterprise Protection Coalition (AEPC), the American Legislative Exchange Council (ALEC), and the Center for Consumer Freedom (CCF), with bipartisan support from legislators like Senator Dianne Feinstein and Representative James Sensenbrenner" (Center for Constitutional Rights, n.d.).

The AETA uses overly broad definitions of what constitutes "animal enterprise," "criminal activity," and "interference" with animal enterprises. Such legislation can easily end *all* social movements since there is no cause or issue that does not relate in some way to nonhuman animal enterprises. For instance, the prison abolition movement affects any company that sells meat, eggs, and dairy to prisons. Likewise, activists concerned with particular university operations could be affected. Universities contract out to companies for food and clothes, which obviously use nonhuman animals. The same could be said for antiwar activists who target military contractors; anti-consumer activists who target advertising companies; feminists, LGBT advocates, and racial justice workers who fight for more inclusive work environments (within "animal enterprise" companies). Nearly every institution depends upon an animal-exploiting industry in some way—grocery stores, car dealerships, oil companies, shoe and clothing companies, computer companies, and so on. Consequently, there is nearly no social movement that does not directly or indirectly "interfere" with an "animal enterprise."

This is, therefore, a call to all activists and movements: expose and resist the AETA.

REFERENCES

Abu-Jamal, Mumia. *All Things Censored.* New York: Seven Stories Press, 2000.

Arnold, Ron. *EcoTerror: The Violent Agenda to Save Nature: The World of the Unabomber.* Bellevue, Wash.: Free Enterprise Press, 1997.

Ashcroft, Bill, Gareth Griffiths, and Helen Tiffin, eds. *The Post-Colonial Studies Reader,* 2nd edition. New York: Routledge, 2006.

Bakan, Joel. *The Corporation: The Pathological Pursuit of Profit and Power.* New York: Free Press, 2004.

Beirne, Piers, and Nigel South. *Issues in Green Criminology: Confronting Harms Against Environments, Humanity, and Other Animals.* Portland, Oreg.: Willan Publishing, 2007.

Best, Steven. "Rethinking Revolution: Total Liberation, Alliance Politics, and a Prolegomena to Resistance Movements in the Twenty-First Century." In *Contemporary Anarchist Studies: An Introductory Anthology of Anarchy in the Academy,* edited by Randall Amster, Abraham DeLeon, Luis A. Fernandez, Anthony J. Nocella II, and Deric Shannon, 189–99. New York: Routledge, 2009 (2009a).

———. "The Rise of Critical Animal Studies: Putting Theory into Action and Animal Liberation into Higher Education." *Journal for Critical Animal Studies* VII, Issue I 2009 (2009b): 9–52.

Best, Steven, and Richard Kahn. "Trial by Fire: The Shac7 and the Future of Democracy," Journal for Critical Animal Studies, 2(2), 2004, 1–36.

Best, Steven, and Anthony J. Nocella II. *Igniting a Revolution: Voices in Defense of the Earth.* Oakland, Calif.: AK Press, 2006.

———. *Terrorists or Freedom Fighters? Reflections on the Liberation of Animals.* New York: Lantern Books, 2004.

Best, Steven, Anthony J. Nocella II, Richard Kahn, Carol Gigliotti, and Lisa Kemmerer. "Introducing Critical Animal Studies." *Journal of Critical Animal Studies* 5 (1), 2007: 1–2.

Bodley, John H. *Cultural Anthropology: Tribes, States, and the Global System*. New York: McGraw Hill, 2005.

Brasch, Walter M. *America's Unpatriotic Acts: The Federal Government's Violation of Constitutional and Civil Rights*. New York: Peter Lang, 2005.

Bruns, Ronald G., Michael J. Lynch, and Paul Stretesky. *Environmental Law, Crime, and Justice*. El Paso, Tex.: LFB Scholarly Publishing, 2008.

Center for Constitutional Rights. *The Animal Enterprise Terrorism Act (AETA)*. http://ccrjustice.org/learn-more/faqs/factsheet%3A-animal-enterprise-terrorism-act-%28aeta%29.

Chang, Nancy. *Silencing Political Dissent*. New York: Seven Stories Press, 2002.

Chomsky, Noam. *Hegemony or Survival: America's Quest for Global Dominance*. New York: Metropolitan Books, 2004.

———. *Imperial Ambitions: Conversations on the Post-9/11 World*. New York: Metropolitan Books, 2005.

———. *Media Control: The Spectacular Achievements of Propaganda*. New York: Seven Stories Press, 2002.

———. *Power and Terror: Post-9/11 Talks and Interviews*. New York: Seven Stories Press, 2003.

———. *What We Say Goes: Conversations on U.S. Power in a Changing World*. New York: Metropolitan Books, 2007.

Churchill, Ward. *Struggle for the Land: Indigenous Resistance to Genocide, Ecocide and Expropriation in Contemporary North America*. Monroe, Me.: Common Courage Press, 2002.

Churchill, Ward, and Jim Vander Wall. *Agents of Repression: The FBI's Secret War Against the Black Panther Party and the American Indian Movement*. Boston: South End Press, 2002 (2002a).

———. *The COINTELPRO Papers: Documents from the FBI's Secret Wars Against Dissent in the United States*. Boston: South End Press, 2002 (2002b).

Clifford, Mary. *Environmental Crime: Enforcement, Policy, and Social Responsibility*. Gaithersburg, Md.: Aspen Publishers, 1998.

Davis, Angela Y. *Are Prisons Obsolete?* New York: Seven Stories Press, 2003.

Del Gandio, Jason. *Rhetoric for Radicals: A Handbook for 21st Century Activists*. Gabriola, B.C.: New Society Publishers, 2008.

Eilperin, Juliet. "Severe Hurricanes Increasing, Study Finds." *The Washington Post*. Published September 16, 2005. www.washingtonpost.com/wp-dyn/content/article/2005/09/15/AR2005091502234.html.

Federal Bureau of Investigation, *Terrorism 2002–2005*, Reports and Publications. http://www.fbi.gov/stats-services/publications/terrorism-2002-2005.

Giroux, Henry. "The Militarization of U.S. Higher Education after 9/11." *Theory, Culture, & Society*, 25(5), 2008, 58–82.

Goldenberg, Suzanne. "Climate change, Barack Obama less interested than Bush, analysis reveals," *Guardian*, January 26, 2011.

Gore, Al. *An Inconvenient Truth: A Global Warning* DVD. Directed by Davis Guggenheim. Hollywood, Calif.: Paramount, 2006.

Griffin, David R., and Peter Dale Scott. *9/11 and American Empire: Intellectuals Speak Out*. Northampton, Mass.: Olive Branch Press, 2007.

Halpern, Michael. "The Costs of a Climate of Fear." American Association of University Professors, 2010. http://www.aaup.org/article/costs-climate-fear#.U5slLqiM7oo.

Harvey, David. Spaces for Global Capitalism: Towards a Theory of Uneven Geographical Development. New York: Verso Press, 2006.

Herbig, F. J. W., and S. J. Joubert. "Criminological Semantics: Conservation Criminology—Vision or Vagary?" *Acta Criminologica* 19, no. 3, 2006: 88–103.

Jensen, Derrick. *Endgame: Volume 1—The Problem of Civilization*. New York: Seven Stories Press, 2006 (2006a).

———. *Endgame: Volume II—Resistance*. New York: Seven Stories Press, 2006 (2006b).

Johnson, Chalmers. *Blowback: The Costs and Consequences of American Empire*. New York: Metropolitan Books, 2004 (2004a).

———. *The Sorrows of Empire: Militarism, Secrecy, and the End of the Republic*. New York: Owl Books, 2004 (2004b).

———. *Nemesis: The Last Days of the American Republic*. New York: Metropolitan Books, 2006.

Jones, Charles E. *The Black Panther Party Reconsidered*. Baltimore: Black Classic Press, 1998.

———. "Political Repression of the Black Panther Party 1966–1971: The Case of Oakland Bay Area." *Journal of Black Studies* 18, no. 4, 1988: 415–35.

Kahn, Richard. *Critical Pedagogy, Ecoliteracy, and Planetary Crisis: The Ecopedagogy Movement*. New York: Peter Lang Publisher, 2010.

Katovsky, Bill. *Patriots Act: Voices of Dissent and the Risk of Speaking Out*. Guilford, Conn.: The Lyons Press, 2006.

Kellner, Douglas. *Media Spectacle and the Crisis of Democracy: Terrorism, War, and Election Battles*. Boulder, Colo.: Paradigm Publishers, 2005.

"Kentucky Fried Cruelty" (n.d.) PETA. http://www.kentuckyfriedcruelty.com/w-whykfc. asp.

Klein, Naomi. *No Logo*. New York: Picador, 2002.

———. *The Shock Doctrine*. New York: Metropolitan Books, 2007.

Korten, David C. *When Corporations Rule the World*. West Hartford, Conn.: Berrett-Koehler, 1995.

Kovel, Joel. *The Enemy of the Nature: The End of Capitalism or the End of the World?* New York:.Zed Books, 2002.

Leonard, Annie. *The Story of Stuff: How Our Obsession with Stuff Is Trashing the Planet, Our Communities, and Our Health—and a Vision for Change.* New York: Free Press, 2010.

Liddick, Donald R. *Eco-Terrorism: Radical Environmental and Animal Liberation Movements.* Westport, Conn.: Praeger Publishers, 2006.

"Lockheed Martin". "10 companies profiting the most from war," by Samuel Weighley. *USA Today,* March 10, 2013.

Long, Douglas. *Ecoterrorism.* New York: Facts on File, 2004.

Lorde, Audre. *Sister Outsider: Essays and Speeches.* Freedom, Calif.: Crossing Press, 1984.

Lovitz, Dara. *Muzzling a Movement: The Effects of Anti-Terrorism Law, Money & Politics on Animal Activism.* New York: Lantern Books, 2010.

Lynch, Michael J., and Raymond Michalowski. *Primer in Radical Criminology: Critical Perspectives on Crime, Power & Identity.* Monsey, N.Y.: Criminal Justice Press, 2006.

Lynd, Staughton, and Alice Lynd. *Nonviolence in America: A Documentary History.* Maryknoll, N.Y.: Orbis Books, 1995.

Mastrandrea, Michael, and Stephen Schneider. "Global warming." *World Book Online Reference Center.* Last accessed 2005. www.worldbookonline.com/wb /Article?id=ar226310 (site discontinued).

Miller, Joseph A., and R. M. Miller. *Eco-Terrorism and Eco-Extremism Against Agriculture.* Arlington, Va.: Joseph A. Miller, 2000.

Peltier, Leonard. *Prison Writings: My Life Is My Sun Dance.* New York: St. Martin's Press, 1999.

Potter, Will. *Green Is the New Red: An Insider's Account of a Social Movement Under Siege.* San Francisco: City Lights Publishers, 2011.

Quigley, Bill. "Corporations Profit from Permanent War: Memorial Day 2010. Center for Constitutional Rights. Published May 24, 2010. http://ccrjustice.org /corporations-profit-permanent-war-memorial-day-2010-bill-quigley.

Regan, Tom. *The Case for Animal Rights.* Los Angeles: University of California Press, 1983.

Schultz, Bud, and Ruth Schultz, eds. *Testimonies to Political Repression in America: The Price of Dissent.* Los Angeles: University of California Press, 2001.

Shakur, Assata. *Assata: An Autobiography.* Chicago: Lawrence Hill Books, 1987.

Singer, Peter. *Animal Liberation.* New York: Avon Books, 1985.

South, Nigel. "Corporate and State Crimes Against the Environment: Foundations for a Green Perspective in Europe." In *The New European Criminology: Crime and Social Order in Europe,* edited by Vincenzo Ruggiero, Nigel South, and Ian Taylor, 443–61. New York: Routledge, 1998.

The 11th Hour. DVD. Directed by Leila Conners and Nadia Conners. Hollywood, Calif.: Warner Bros, 2010.

Tokar, Brian. *Earth for Sale: Reclaiming Ecology in the Age of Corporate Greenwash.* Boston: South End Press, 1997.

West, Larry. "What Causes Global Warming?" 2007. Retrieved July 17, 2011 from http://environment.about.com/od/faqglobalwarming/f/globalwarming.htm.

White, Rob. *Crimes Against Nature: Environmental Criminology and Ecological Justice.* Portland, Oreg.: Willan Publishing, 2008.

Yuen, Eddie, Daniel Burton-Rose, and George Katsiaficas. *Confronting Capitalism: Dispatches from a Global Movement.* Brooklyn, N.Y.: Soft Skull Press, 2004.

Zinn, Howard. *A People's History of the United States 1492–Present.* New York: HarperCollins, 1995.

THE RHETORIC OF TERRORISM

Jason Del Gandio

If society used non-speciesist definitions of violence and terrorism, ones that respect both human and nonhuman beings as subjects of a life, then the outcry against terrorism would shift from the activists trying to prevent injury, loss of life, and environmental degradation to the industries and individuals profiting from bloodshed, torture, and destruction (Best and Nocella 2004, 31–32).

Terrorism as Rhetorical Construction

As the saying goes, one person's terrorist is another person's freedom fighter. Such distinctions often depend upon whether or not you are persuaded to agree with the person's goals and philosophies. If you agree, then you see an act of liberation to be celebrated and applauded. If you disagree, then you see an act of terrorism to be condemned and admonished. For example, the Boston Tea Party of 1773 involved American colonists deliberately damaging British property. This act of defiance has been generally framed as a necessary step for American freedom and independence, and thus has been celebrated in children's history books. But activists who destroy solely property nowadays are labeled as "criminals" and "terrorists." This point is easily demonstrated by the criticisms directed against anti-WTO protesters of 1999, the Black Bloc tactics used during the Occupy movement, and of course the animal and earth liberationists' use of sabotage. Mass media and political pundits demonize these actions while simultaneously celebrating, for instance, the bravery of early American revolutionaries who not only destroyed property, but also took up arms. It should be noted, too, that the current Tea Party, which gets its name from the Boston Tea Party, is rarely accused of violence or terrorism even though it has engaged in property damage and death threats (Rucker 2010; Potter 2010). Tea Partiers also celebrate a hypermasculinized gun culture, espouse anti-government slogans ("don't tread on me"), and often display a militancy in defending "individual liberty and freedom." The Tea Party's particular use of militant rhetoric goes unnoticed because, for the most part, it is part and parcel of the American psyche—most Americans presume that violence is justified in the defense of freedom and democracy. But of course that freedom and democracy are only for particular people (usually Americans) and a particular species (humans).

Numerous other examples highlight the nuances of the "terrorist" label. For instance, South African leader Nelson Mandela was once hated and imprisoned as an anti-apartheid terrorist for taking up arms against a segregationist government. After serving twenty-seven years in prison, he went on to become president of South Africa, and honored and revered around the world. Former Iraqi dictator Saddam Hussein was once a strategic ally to the United States. The Reagan and Bush Sr. administrations equipped him with money, weapons, and verbal accolades. Then, sometime in the late 1980s and early 1990s, Hussein became an enemy and Iraq was bombed, sanctioned, and dubbed a "rogue nation." The Bush Jr. administration eventually accused Hussein of *potentially* aiding and abetting al-Qaeda terrorists with weapons of mass destruction, which was used as the justification for the 2003 U.S. invasion and occupation of Iraq. Osama bin Laden, the most infamous terrorist of all, emerged from the Mujahideen, a jihadist group during the 1980s. Ronald Reagan once hailed the Mujahideen as freedom fighters and kept them as a close ally in the U.S. fight against the Soviet Union. And, of course, there is the conflict between Israel and Palestine. Both sides are engaged in an ongoing military conflict. But only the Palestinians, who are besieged by poverty and are forced to use primitive forms of weaponry and attacks, are considered terrorists. Meanwhile the Israelis, backed by the United States and equipped with some of the most sophisticated weapons in the world, are considered to be acting in "self-defense." As longtime animal liberationist Paul Watson succinctly states:

One common definition of terrorism is the utilization of low-tech or no-tech weapons in the hands of civilians against high-tech weapons systems under the control of a government. Throw a Molotov cocktail onto a tank and you're a terrorist. Drop a napalm bomb on a school bus from a $100 million aircraft and you're striking a military target. It's all about the price of the hardware (2004, 280).

The political classifications of terrorists, criminals, and enemies, as well as heroes, allies, and freedom fighters, are rhetorical constructions. That is not to say that all rhetorical constructions are completely relative and interchangeable; a certain level of accuracy and fairness must be accounted for. Al-Qaeda *did* murder thousands of people on 9/11, and Saddam Hussein *was* a horrid, oppressive dictator who killed and tortured his own people. But the myth of absolute objectivity died long ago, and we are awash in a sea of divergent political discourse. If this is the case, then social and political transformation is an ideological battle, and activists and liberationists must continually define, explain, argue, debate, decipher, and critique various viewpoints and political designations. Power relations play a key role within this discursive battle. For example, who has the authority to determine what constitutes terrorism? What people, institutions, and/or systems benefit from that determination? How might the profit motive and/or the desire to hold political office contribute to these definitions? Are particular groups being targeted for political repression? If so, why? And what kind of values, practices, and worldviews are created, maintained, and/or demonized by these definitions and determinations?

The AETA as Rhetorical Construction

Such questions undoubtedly apply to the Animal Enterprise Terrorism Act (AETA). At the surface level, the AETA is intended to "provide the Department of Justice the necessary authority to apprehend, prosecute, and convict individuals committing animal enterprise terror" (U.S. Congress 2006, opening line). But "animal enterprise" is a euphemism for the corporate exploitation of nonhuman animals; and "terror," as it is *loosely* defined in the legislation, can mean anything from physical violence to public harassment to property damage to lost revenue. When reading the

AETA through a critical lens, it is beyond obvious that this piece of legislation is about persecuting and prosecuting *anyone* who inhibits corporations from earning a profit—*period*. This protection of corporate profit has been accomplished by deploying a "rhetoric of terrorism."

At its base, the AETA follows the same protocol as every other piece of legislation—it is a collection of words printed on a page bounded by authority and enforced by the threat of State-sanctioned violence. Legislation begins with small groups of people using language to articulate a vision. Their language then moves through various stages of approval, amendment, debate, and discussion. Eventually, that language is either signed into law or vetoed. The language of these legislators is the "law of the land" because these individuals are able to access, mobilize, and direct engines of force. If you disobey the law and challenge its force, you may be arrested, fined, imprisoned, and, depending upon the law and the offense, even executed. Even the most basic violations are subject to this force. For example, refusing to exit your vehicle when pulled over for a traffic violation warrants physical force. The police officer has the legal right to *physically* remove you from the vehicle. You will concede one way or another; any resistance on your part will be met with force until you finally submit. This is a blatant exercise of violence that is legitimized by social and cultural infrastructures—e.g., educational, political, and economic systems; police departments, court systems, the military, and intelligence agencies; mass media, popular culture, and historical narratives; and discourses, anecdotes, and everyday assumptions about obeying and respecting authority. Since these are the basic parameters of the average person's experience, most people are not motivated to question or challenge legislation and its world-making effects. This is a vicious cycle—the more people obey the law, the more it becomes naturalized and accepted as "that's just the way it is." But of course not every law is morally correct or politically just. For example, it was once *legal* to own slaves in America, and it is currently *legal* in most states to deny equal rights to same-sex couples. Both are an affront to a free, democratic society. The public at large therefore has an obligation to question and challenge not only individual laws, but the entire sociopolitical infrastructure that enables such laws.

This is exactly why radical animal liberationists are perceived by legislators and corporate industries as such a threat. Animal liberationists demonstrate in no uncertain terms that the current power structure *can* be challenged. Releasing mink into the wild, sabotaging research facilities, and publicly shaming animal exploiters undermines the mystique of the all-powerful monolith. Many onlookers will find such actions unsettling. But these very same actions pique curiosities and evoke critical questions. Why would someone take such a risk in saving animals? Should I learn more about animal-abusing industries? Can other systems of exploitation be challenged and undermined? Are alternative economic systems possible? Can we live differently?

The Stop Huntingdon Animal Cruelty campaign—also known as SHAC—is an example of what I am arguing. SHAC has brought international attention to Huntingdon Life Sciences (HLS), which is the largest contract animal laboratory in Europe. HLS contains approximately 70,000 animals on site and conducts experiments for pharmaceuticals, pesticides, herbicides, household cleaners, food additives, and genetically modified organisms. Its testing animals include, but are not limited to, rats, cats, rabbits, dogs, monkeys, and birds. While SHAC has not achieved its goal of shutting down HLS, it has seriously damaged HLS's reputation, profits, share prices, and ability to secure and maintain stockholders. SHAC's campaign has also acted as a form of public education, bringing necessary attention to the cruelties of HLS's operations. HLS is by no means a household name, but it has become a common reference point for many radical communities, with various activists studying and debating SHAC's campaign strategies (see, for instance, the SHAC Model [2009] cited in the reference list). If this is true, then SHAC demonstrates a direct threat to the wider system of corporate profit and animal exploitation.

SHAC has obviously attracted the attention of corporate industries and law enforcement agencies. SHAC activists have been harassed, arrested, fined, and imprisoned. However, the larger campaign goes on, demonstrating the vulnerability of the animal-industrial complex. That vulnerability is a driving force behind the AETA. Rhetorically constructing animal liberationists as "terrorists" allows corporate industries to (a) quarantine challenges to its power, (b) persuade average citizens that corporations are "victims," and (c) divert public attention away from the abuse and exploitation of nonhuman animals.

The AETA: A Brief History

The AETA has been nearly thirty years in the making. Public defense attorney Rebecca K. Smith (2008) provides the details of this history in her analysis of the term *eco-terrorism*. Here is a partial overview of her findings:

1983: The term *eco-terrorism* is first used by Ron Arnold in *Reason* magazine. Arnold is executive vice president of the Center for Defense of Free Enterprise (CDFE), and, according to the Smith article, seeks to "destroy environmentalists by taking their money and their members" (545).

1988: Arnold and the CDFE organize a conference that attracts private industries whose profits are threatened by environmental activism. Broad, powerful private industry coalitions are formed within three years of the conference.

1988: While testifying about the completely unrelated issue of the Anti–Drug Abuse Act, Senator James McClure of Idaho refers to Earth First! as an *eco-terrorist* organization, thus setting legal precedent for the term.

1992: Congress passes the Animal Enterprise Protection Act (AEPA), a basic precursor to the AETA.

1995: The *Houston Law Review* publishes an article that draws an analogy between acts of vandalism committed by "environmental *terrorists*" and acts of murder committed by "abortion *protesters*."

1998: There is a congressional hearing on "Acts of Eco-terrorism by Radical Environmental Organizations." Some of those testifying ask that the AEPA be amended (i.e., expanded). Ron Arnold is the final witness to testify and defines eco-terrorism as "a crime committed to save nature." He claims, remarkably, that such crimes include everything from trespass to murder.

2001: The September 11th terrorist attacks occur. The Bush administration goes into hyperattack mode and famously declares that "you are either with us or with the terrorists." The entire country is transformed into a mobilizing anti-terrorism unit, which includes but is not limited to: the USA PATRIOT Act, the Department of Homeland Security, airport security checks, color-coded alert systems, the invasion and bombing of Afghanistan (and later, Iraq), paramilitary police guarding subway and bus terminals, tip hotlines, FBI watch lists, yellow ribbons and American Pride bumper stickers, domestic surveillance, Guantanamo Bay, and compulsive comments about "these colors don't run!" Fear, defensiveness, and patriotism are pervasive and compulsory.

2002: Five months after 9/11, the FBI testifies before Congress that the Earth Liberation Front (ELF) and Animal Liberation Front (ALF) have caused more than $43 million in property damage since 1996. These two groups are thus declared the top priority in domestic terrorism. The FBI defines eco-terrorism as "the use or threatened use of violence of a criminal nature against innocent victims or property by an environmentally-oriented subnational group for environmental-political reasons, or aimed at an audience beyond the target often of a symbolic nature" (Smith 2008, 553). With this definition, an action can now be construed as terrorism if that action is "environmentally motivated" and involves the *mere* threat of violence against *inanimate objects*, even if no property damage actually occurs.

2002: The AEPA is amended with the possibility of increased prison sentencing.

2003: The private industry group operating under the deceptive name of the American Legislative Exchange Council publishes model legislation (i.e., a highly suggestive mock legislation that Congress might adopt) entitled the Animal and Ecological Terrorism Act. It is another precursor to the AETA.

2005–2006: There are a series of congressional hearings addressing the ELF, ALF, and other environmental and animal rights activists, including the Stop Huntingdon Animal Cruelty campaign.

2006: The AEPA is amended and renamed the Animal Enterprise Terrorism Act.

This history is underwritten by the collusion of private industry coalitions, right-wing think tanks, lawmakers, court systems, and the FBI. All of this is held together by America's cultural predisposition of obeying authority and demonizing activists who challenge the status quo. Demonizing real terrorism is understandable—we all have a natural inclination to protect ourselves from unwarranted attack and abuse. But the inclination to obey authority can and should be challenged. Is liberating animals from abusive and even torturous conditions really terrorism? And are corporate industries that profit from that torture really victims?

Corporate Industry: Victim versus Terrorist

Radical animal liberationists no doubt engage in debatable tactics—e.g., property damage, sabotage, vandalism, firebombing, arson, public harassment, and smear campaigns. However, animal liberationists have not and would not physically harm another human being. The Animal Liberation Front (ALF), which sits at the top of the FBI's most wanted list, blatantly denounces physical violence toward both humans and nonhumans. And as far as I know, the ALF has never been found guilty of such violence. Animal liberationists seek to save the lives of nonhuman animals, and as a consequence, improve the human condition—since human and nonhumans share an interspecies existence, improving the living conditions of one improves the living conditions of the other.

If this is true, then the real terrorists in this scenario are the proponents of animal-exploiting corporate industries. Below is a brief list of corporate offenses toward nonhuman animals.

- The fur industry kills more than fifty million animals per year. The furs of those animals are not used for the necessity of warmth and survival (technological advances have long outdated such "necessity"), but for superficial style and fashion (Humane Society, n.d.).
- Twenty-five million animals are used every year for the researching and testing of cosmetic and household products. Such tests are conducted not only on mice, which are often perceived as nothing more than pesky, disposable rodents, but also on dogs, rabbits, and chimpanzees (ibid.).

- Millions of other animals—including cats, pigs, turtles, and frogs—are used for vivisection. Such "educational dissection" often occurs in the seemingly benign context of high school biology class. This early enculturation no doubt perpetuates the belief that animals exist for human use and consumption (ibid.).

- Scientists, medical students, veterinarian students, and military personnel conduct medical experiments on goats, sheep, and numerous other animals. Such experiments involve the shooting of animals; the withholding of pain medication in order to test stress levels; and medical operations not only on deceased but also living animals (ibid.).

- Every 24 hours, 90,000 cows and calves are killed in the United States for food consumption. Another 14,000 chickens are killed *every minute*. All told, approximately 10 billion food animals (not counting fish and other aquatic creatures) are killed each year in the United States (Center for Food Safety).

- Much of this food production revolves around factory farming, which is utterly inhumane and unsustainable. Factory farms neglect and abuse animals, force animals into undersized cages that severely restrict natural and necessary movement, and allow animals to live in their own excrement, often producing agonizing illness. The unsanitary conditions of factory farms also expose humans to increased risk of disease and illness. An estimated 89 percent of U.S. beef patties contain traces of E. coli; approximately 650,000 Americans are sickened by salmonella-tainted eggs each year, with about 600 dying; and more than 5,000 people become sick with Campylobacter (food poisoning), the primary source of which is contaminated chicken flesh. Factory farms also devastate the environment. According to the Food and Agriculture Organization of the United Nations (FAO), animal agriculture is responsible for 18 percent of human-induced greenhouse gas emissions. This occurs because the production of eggs, milk, and meat involve producing grain to feed the animals; producing fertilizer to maintain the soil; and expending water, gas, and electricity to run operations and transport animals and goods (ibid.).

These statistics obviously focus on animal-exploiting industries. But the corporate industry *as a whole* is even more damaging. For example, in 1979, the top 1 percent of Americans owned 20.5 percent of the nation's wealth while the bottom 99 percent owned 79.5 percent. By 2007, the top 1 percent increased its share to 34.6 percent while the bottom 99 percent declined to 65.4 percent (Domhoff 2013). In 1980, the pay ratio between the average American CEO and average American worker was 40 to 1. As of 2009, the ratio was 263 to 1 (Anderson, Collins, Pizzigati, and Shih 2010). That ratio actually peaked in 2000, when it was 500 to 1. Worldwide, approximately 1.2 billion people live on less than $1 per day and approximately 2.8 billion people live on less than $2 per day (Kerbo 2006). There are about 6.8 billion people in the world, which means that more than 40 percent of the world's population lives on $2 per day or less. These statistics do not even touch upon war profiteering, the prison-industrial complex, the corporatizing of higher education, labor exploitation, political corruption, media monopolies, pollution and environmental degradation, and the enclosure of the commons (such as water, land, and food). Given this evidence, it is hard to believe that animal liberationists are terrorists. Instead, it is the profit motive of corporations that terrorize our social and natural worlds. Private industry and capitalism bring harm to people, animals, and the environment every day. Rather than quarantining animal liberation, we need legislation that quarantines corporate greed and private profit.

Rhetoric and the Creation of Reality

People often think that rhetoric is analogous to deception, dishonesty, coercion, or manipulation. But these negative understandings are misnomers. Rhetoric can be deceptive *or* honest, negative *or* positive, oppressive *or* liberating. It depends on who is engaging in the rhetoric, how and why they are doing it, and for what purposes. Animal-exploiting industries use rhetoric, but so do animal liberationists. Press releases, communiqués, websites, manifestos, speeches, books, spray-painted messages, and even property damage are rhetorical acts.

At the most basic level, rhetoric is well-crafted communication that allows you to achieve your personal, social, and/or political goals. If that is true, then we all engage in rhetoric all the time. A five-year-old child will address a particular parent using particular words when asking for another hour of television or a second bowl of ice cream. Teenagers know what details to highlight or downplay when requesting permission to use the car. College students display just the right balance of defiance and deference when disputing a grade with a professor. And romantic partners decide on the right time, situation, emotions, and poetries when expressing their love to one another. Everyone strategically crafts and delivers messages for particular purposes. That is the basis of rhetoric.

But at a more complex level, rhetoric is also the process by which human beings materialize their realities through the immaterial means of communication (Del Gandio 2008, 14–23; Del Gandio 2011, 129–34). Reality does not fall from the sky or hide beneath a rock. Instead, we create our realities through communicative processes. There are the basic facts and raw materials of the world. For instance, the tree sitting outside my window is over one hundred years old. I did not plant that tree, and I do not "create" that tree in any direct, physical sense. But that is not the totality of reality. Instead, reality is co-constituted through (1) the "facts of the world" and (2) what we bring to those facts. Our signs, symbols, words, languages, narratives, discourses, and what we say and how we say it evoke and manifest ways of perceiving, understanding, experiencing, and orienting to the world; i.e., our immaterial communication about the material facts provokes the creation of reality.

Why is any of this relevant to animal liberationists and the AETA? Because animal liberationists and the creators of the AETA are engaged in a battle of reality creation. The latter seeks a reality of corporate dominance and political repression, while the former seeks a reality of radical social change driven by interspecies respect and harmony.

This insight about the political nature of reality creation is not necessarily new. For example, the 1960s counterculturalist Abbie Hoffman often talked about communication and the creation of reality. During his testimony at the Chicago 7 trial, Abbie argued that hippies constituted a unique culture held hostage within American society. Hippies did not necessarily constitute a physical or geographical boundary with national standing and binding legislation. Instead, hippies constituted a way of life that existed within their minds, hearts, and bodies. When asked for his place of residence, Abbie replied, "Woodstock Nation." He was then asked to explain.

> It is a nation of alienated young people. We carry it around with us as a state of mind in the same way the Sioux Indians carried the Sioux nation around with them. It is a nation dedicated to coopera-tion versus competition, to the idea that people should have better means of exchange than property or money, that there should be some other basis for human interaction. It is a *nation*... (emphasis added; Levin, McNamee, and Greenberg 1970, 140–41)

Abbie is basically arguing that the communicative acts of his fellow coun-terculturalists gave rise to an alternative "hippie reality." That reality is as real and legitimate as any other reality, including that of "America."

The Zapatistas of Chiapas, Mexico, have also evoked an alterna-tive reality, one that is unapologetically anti-capitalist and anti-author-itarian. They have done so by organizing international conferences, assemblies, and delegations, and releasing press packets, communiqués, photographs, stories, poems, books, manifestos, and websites of black-masked indigenous revolutionaries declaring, "All for everyone, nothing for ourselves." Although imagistic and captivating, they are not a shal-low, one-dimensional spectacle. Instead, the Zapatistas have created a unique reality that is tangible to themselves and others. In the words of Subcomandante Marcos:

> Zapatismo is not an ideology, it is not a bought and paid for doc-trine. It is... an intuition. Something so open and flexible that it really occurs in all places. Zapatismo poses the question: "What is it that has excluded me?" "What is it that has isolated me?"... In each place the response is different. Zapatismo simply states the ques-tion and stipulates that the response is plural, that the response is inclusive... (quoted in Carrigan 2001, 440).

Zapatismo, then, is a set of values, outlooks, understandings, orien-tations, and beginning points. It is *a way of seeing and living*. Zapatismo is not reducible to an ideology or a ten-point program. It lives within us as we live it, and it is passed on through our languages, utterances, and actions. It is manifested and carried on by our communicative/rhetorical efforts. Zapatismo is the participatory creation of a twenty-first century revolutionary reality.

We can look to rhetorical scholars to help flesh out the nature of these political movements. For example, rhetorical theorist Ronald Greene (2004; 2006; 2007) argues that basic, everyday communication is by its very nature a laborious process—it takes a lot of work, effort, and exertion. A simple conversation between two friends involves listening, processing, responding, paraphrasing, misinterpretations, nonverbal cues and adjustments, empathy, and emotional support. But Greene also argues that communication is a form of, and might even be the basis of, *living labor* (in the basic Marxian sense). Human beings are communicative beings, and without that communication no labor exists—i.e., labor *is* communication. Greene uses this framework to reconceptualize the nature of rhetorical agency. The classic political *rhetor* (think of Dr. King, for instance) is often understood as intervening into social affairs by means of persuasion, argumentation, deliberation, advocacy, or even sit-ins, strikes, and boycotts. But the political *rhetor*—as a communicative laborer—does not simply intervene, negotiate, mediate, or express; instead, the political *rhetor* creates and communicatively calls into existence new ideas, words, perceptions, emotions, feelings, and imaginary terrains.

Another scholar of rhetoric, Robert E. Terrill, makes a similar point when discussing the political significance of Malcolm X. Terrill acknowledges that Malcolm is a historically transformative figure. But, strangely enough, Malcolm never directly orchestrated any traditional political action. According to Terrill, Malcolm:

> [N]ever led his followers in large-scale collective action, never organized a mass protest march, and never was associated with the passage of any piece of legislation designed to improve the condition of African Americans....What Malcolm did do was talk, and his talk often was criticized as taking the place of real political action. The hundreds of speeches and statements and interviews and newspaper columns that Malcolm produced, a flood of words augmented

by his radio and television appearances that has few rivals in either its vehemence or in its sheer volume, often was—and is—dismissed as mere verbal swagger. (2004, 1–2)

But how can this be true? How can Malcolm be so historically impactful without directly engaging concrete political processes? Terrill argues that Malcolm's public address was social change; his words are his deeds. It is through his public discourse that members of his audiences are made to see the limits imposed upon them by the dominant white culture and are shown attitudes and strategies that invite them to transgress against those limits (6).

According to Terrill, Malcolm's rhetoric and politics cannot be separated; each helps to inform and constitute the other. Malcolm's speeches did not lead to liberation, but instead *were* liberation. His rhetorical labors evoked and manifested the reality of black defiance and resistance. Malcolm's rhetorical work *was* the insurrection, and *that* is why he is so historically significant.

And as one last explanation, scholar of rhetoric Kevin Deluca (1999a; 1999b) argues that rhetoric is not reducible to linguistic communication or public address. Instead, our *embodied activities* are also rhetorical acts that mobilize "signs, images, and discourses for the articulation of identities, ideologies, consciousnesses, communities, publics, and cultures" (1999a, 10). We do not simply speak or write reality into existence, but we also, and more fundamentally, *enact* reality into existence. If this is true, then activists' bodies are fundamentally important for challenging the status quo and for proposing alternative ideas, values, and practices. In reference to Earth First! actions such as blockading roads and occupying tree tops, Deluca states that:

> These images of bodies at risk are encapsulated arguments challenging the anthropocentric position granting humans dominion over all living creatures and implicitly advocating ecocentrism as an alternative. By arguing against reducing trees and ecosystems (old growth forests) to economic resources and instead proposing that they have intrinsic value and inalienable rights, Earth First! contests the linking of economic progress with nature as a storehouse

of resources, thus deconstructing the discourse of industrialism that warrants the use of technology to exploit nature in the name of progress.

The bodies of Earth First!, then, question the possibility of property and the definition of the land as a resource and, instead, suggest that biodiversity has value in itself…(1999a, 14).

If Deluca is correct, then the protests, direct actions, sabotage, public shamings, and property destruction of animal liberationists are also rhetorical acts of political importance: animal liberationists embody and enact anti-speciesist values and practices that directly challenge fundamental pillars of Western society. As Steven Best and Anthony Nocella (2004) argue:

Animal liberation is the next logical development in moral evolution. Animal liberation builds on the most progressive ethical and political advances human beings have made in the last 200 years and carries them to their logical conclusions. Animal liberation demands that human beings give up their sense of superiority over other animals and tear down the Berlin Wall between species. It challenges people to realize that power demands responsibility, that might is not right, and that an enlarged neocortex is no excuse to rape and plunder the natural world. Animal liberation requires that people transcend the comfortable boundaries of humanism in order to make a qualitative leap in ethical consideration, thereby moving the moral bar from reason and language to sentience and subjectivity (14).

In other words, animal liberationists embody and evoke a reality that is radically different from the current world of corporate profit, animal exploitation, environmental degradation, and unreflective speciesism.

Final Remarks and a Call to Action

In brief, the AETA (1) legitimizes private industry, corporate control, and the profit-making system; (2) demonizes anyone who questions and challenges that legitimacy; (3) draws our attention away from corporate terror while simultaneously shaping a negative perception and understanding of animal liberation; (4) enables, perpetuates, and even deepens such injustices as animal abuse and exploitation, economic inequality, environmental damage, overconsumption, political corruption, and the incarceration of political activists; and (5) diminishes if not eradicates the connection between human and nonhuman animals.

Such a rhetorical construction affects not just animal liberationists, but all activists and politically conscientious individuals. If the corporate-State complex can orchestrate the AETA, what else can it do? What other forms of activism will be attacked? What other acts of justice will be demonized? What other political movements will be targeted, quarantined, and legally undermined? Regardless of one's relationship to animal liberation, the AETA must be exposed, critiqued, and overturned. Opposing the AETA is not simply an issue of animal liberation, but the moral duty of all politically minded people.

References

Anderson, Sarah, Chuck Collins, Sam Pizzigati, and Kevin Shih. "Executive Excess 2010: CEO Pay and the Great Recession." Institute for Policy Studies. Published September 1, 2010. www.ips-dc.org/reports/executive_excess_2010.

Best, Steven, and Anthony J. Nocella II. "Introduction." In *Terrorists or Freedom Fighters: Reflections on the Liberation of Animals,* edited by Steven Best and Anthony J. Nocella II, New York: Lantern Books, 2004: 9–63.

Carrigan, Ana. "Afterword: Chiapas, the First Postmodern Revolution." In *Our Word is Our Weapon,* edited by Juana Ponce de León, New York: Seven Stories Press, 2001: 417–43.

Center for Food Safety. "What's Wrong with Factory Farming?" Published April 7, 2004. www.centerforfoodsafety.org/files/factoryfarmingfactsheet.pdf.

Del Gandio, Jason. *Rhetoric for Radicals: A Handbook for 21st Century Activists.* Gabriola, B.C.: New Society Publishers, 2008.

———. "Rethinking Immaterial Labor: Communication, Reality, and Neo-radicalism." *Radical Philosophy Review* 14, no. 2 (2011): 121–38.

Deluca, Kevin Michael. "Unruly Arguments: The Body Rhetoric of Earth First!, ACT UP, and Queer Nation." *Argumentation and Advocacy* 36, Summer 1999 (1999a): 9–21.

———. *Image Politics: The New Rhetoric of Environmental Activism.* New York: The Guilford Press, 1999 (1999b).

Domhoff, G. William. "Wealth, Income, and Power." Who Rules America? Last updated February 2013. http://sociology.ucsc.edu/whorulesamerica/power/wealth.html.

Greene, Ronald Walter. "Rhetoric and Capitalism: Rhetorical Agency as Communicative Labor." *Philosophy and Rhetoric* 37 no. 3 (2004): 188–206.

———. "Communist Orator." *Philosophy and Rhetoric* 39, no. 1 (2006): 85–95.

———. "Rhetorical Capital: Communicative Labor, Money/Speech, and Neo-liberal Governance." *Communication and Critical/Cultural Studies* 4, no. 3 (2007): 327–31.

Humane Society of the United States, The. "Issues." www.humanesociety.org/issues.

Kerbo, Harold R. *World Poverty. Global Inequality and the Modern World System.* New York: McGraw-Hill, 2006.

Levin, Mark L., George C. McNamee, and Daniel Greenberg. *The Tales of Hoffman.* New York: Bantam Books, 1970.

"New Feature: The SHAC Model." CrimethInc. Ex-Workers' Collective. Published March 28, 2009. www.crimethinc.com/blog/2009/03/28/new-feature-the-shac-model.

Potter, Will. "When Are Militias and Tea Party Members 'Terrorists'?" Green Is the New Red. Published April 7, 2010. www.greenisthenewred.com/blog/tea-party-terrorist/2616.

Rucker, Philip. "Former Militiaman Unapologetic for Calls to Vandalize Offices Over Health Care." *The Washington Post.* March 25, 2010. www.washingtonpost.com/wp-dyn/content/article/2010/03/25/AR2010032501722.html.

Smith, Rebecca K. "'Eco-terrorism'? A Critical Analysis of the Vilification of Radical Environmental Activists as Terrorists." *Environmental Law* 38, no. 2 (2008): 537–76.

Stop Huntingdon Animal Cruelty. www.shac.net.

Terrill, Robert E. *Malcolm X: Inventing Radical Judgment.* East Lansing: Michigan State University Press, 2004.

United States Cong. *Animal Enterprise Terrorism Act.* 109th Cong. (Public Law 109-374—NOV. 27, 2006). Washington, D.C.: Congressional Record. www.gpo.gov/fdsys/pkg/PLAW-109publ374/pdf/PLAW-109publ374.pdf.

Watson, Paul. "AFL and ELF—Terrorism Is As Terrorism Does." In *Terrorists or Freedom Fighters: Reflections on the Liberation of Animals,* edited by Steven Best and Anthony J. Nocella II, New York: Lantern Books, 2004: 279–87.

CRITIQUING THE AETA

A FOUCAULDIAN READING

Sarat Colling, Eric Jonas, and Stephanie Jenkins

When George W. Bush signed the Animal Enterprise Terrorism Act (AETA) into United States federal law in late 2006, it signaled a turning point in political discourse: a group of people ideologically opposed to violence against all sentient life came to be regarded as "terrorists." Backed by industry groups such as pharmaceutical companies and agribusiness, the AETA purports to "provide the Department of Justice the necessary authority to apprehend, prosecute, and convict individuals committing animal enterprise terror" (U.S. Cong. 2006, 1).

This chapter provides a theoretical reading of the AETA, relying heavily on the work of French philosopher Michel Foucault. In the first section, we examine how the AETA functions as an artifact of a particular system, what Foucault refers to as a "discursive formation." We are particularly interested in understanding how the AETA functions as a discursive formation within the U.S. corporate-State complex. Then, in the second section, we examine Foucault's concept of the panopticon in order to analyze how the AETA and the "anti-terrorism" rhetoric underpinning it have helped to make animal rights and animal welfare activists docile and self-policing. Analyzing the AETA as an instance of panopticism helps demonstrate how this law discredits all animal rights and animal welfare activism, and how this indiscriminate delegitimizing of animal activism is intrinsic to the functioning of this law. Taken together, these two Foucauldian approaches to the AETA demonstrate how this law functions as a discourse: it casts those who struggle to protect animals as violent terrorists while, conversely, aligning those who harm animals for profit, sport, and/or entertainment as victims in need of special protection.

THE AETA AS DISCOURSE

A discourse is a network, system, or ground of thought that encompasses perception, values, practices, and languages that belong to a community, society, and/or particular historical period. Discourses shape social practices, and social practices shape discourses; the two are mutually constitutive. Together, these two provide a "lens" by which we come to understand, think about, and act within, the world. Foucault believed that to understand the intrinsic qualities of how a particular discourse is formed—how it emerges and becomes accepted by a community or society—one must identify the rules that govern it; rules that determine why particular statements will appear in the formation. It is important to understand that these "rules" are not set forth by people or institutions. Instead, these rules are different factors and conditions that enable a discourse to emerge and be recognized. It's more of a diffuse and implicit, rather than overt and explicit, phenomenon.

We can understand how the AETA functions as a discourse in today's political climate by examining two of the governing rules as set out by Foucault. First, what can be shared and what is considered a viable form of discourse? And second, who is allowed to speak, write, or, more generally, communicate (Foss, Foss, and Trapp 2003, 348–50)? As Foucault states: "We know perfectly well that we are not free to say just anything, that we cannot simply speak of anything, when we like or where we like; not just anyone, finally, may speak of just anything." And that is because "in every society the production of discourse is at once controlled, selected, organized and redistributed according to a certain number of procedures, whose role is to avert its powers and its dangers, to cope with chance events, to evade its ponderous, awesome materiality" (Foucault 1972, 216). These "rules" then lead to the formation of a particular discourse, which in effect reflects "a world-view, a slice of history ... [and] a certain structure of thought" (ibid., 191). A particular worldview comes to fruition *at the expense* of some other worldview.

The AETA, along with the emergence of the term *eco-terrorism*, exemplifies Foucault's discursive formation. Who is allowed to speak about these issues? Who is considered knowledgeable about these issues? What issues and topics are introduced and deemed worthy of discussion and acknowledgment? What topics are ignored? Who and what controls this discourse? The AETA emerges in a long history of silencing dissent in the United States, whether it be of anarchists of yesterday and today, socialists and communists during the Red Scare, social justice activists during COINTELPRO, indigenous peoples, or more recently those of Middle Eastern descent. Today radical animal rights and environmental activists—particularly the Animal Liberation Front (ALF) and Earth Liberation Front (ELF), which are international, decentralized, and underground movements composed of small groups and individuals who use illegal direct action (primarily liberatory practices) to pursue their aims—are of special interest to United States law officials (Best and Nocella 2006; Potter 2011).

As early as 1983, the term *eco-terrorism* was applied to radical environmental activists by Ron Arnold of the Center for the Defense of Free Enterprise (Potter 2011). This initial labeling set in motion a particular discourse. At the time, Arnold defined "eco-terrorism" as "a crime committed to save nature" (ibid., 55). Arnold later reworded the statement to emphasize the criminality of activist crimes against corporations. Indeed, this discourse began dispersing attention away from, and in stark contrast to, corporate crimes against the Earth. In Foucauldian terminology, this exemplifies discontinuity of truth—i.e., what is considered to be "the truth" changes with times and conditions. For Foucault, such discontinuity is another characteristic of discursive formation. In other words, this discontinuity undergirds the emergence of different and even competing discourses; if no discontinuity existed, then there would be only one continuous discourse that never changes or encounters opposition.

This is helpful for activists to understand because it means social change is not only possible but inevitable. But most people do not recognize the contingency of a discursive formation; people commonly understand each new discourse as a truth that is absolute and eternal.

In this case, then, we can argue that the discourse of "eco-terrorism" is mistakenly taken as a truth when in fact it is a socially constructed— and in our opinion, an unfounded and highly inaccurate—depiction of activists.

The government's uses of "eco-terrorism" (and its variants) have drastically contributed to this discursive formation. For example, a 1988 congressional hearing was entitled "Acts of Eco-terrorism by Radical Environmental Organizations," and the FBI refers to the crimes committed by animal rights activists as "domestic terrorism" (Potter 2011, 56). After September 11th, 2001, "eco-terrorism" was used at an unprecedented rate by corporate media and government officials, essentially stigmatizing animal and environmental activists. On September 12th, 2011, Representative Greg Walden participated in this discursive formation by stating that the Earth Liberation Front posed a threat "no less heinous than what we saw occur yesterday here in Washington and New York" (ibid., 58). One year later, the 2002 amendment to the 1992 Animal Enterprise Protection Act (AEPA) was passed, to be amended just a few years later in 2006 with the AETA. While the AEPA already included "animal enterprise terror" in its text, the AETA brought the deviant label to the forefront in the bill's title, expanded on what actions constitute terrorism, and used vague language suggesting that activists who target corporate profit can (and should) be labeled as "terrorists."

There are a number of institutions and entities imbued with authority to determine what can be discussed and shared and what is a viable form of discourse under the AETA. Passed by Congress, backed by the FBI, and drafted by corporations, including the American Legislative Exchange Council, the AETA determines an otherwise "acceptable" and "legitimate" discourse on the purported rights and protections of animal-exploiting industries and the prosecution and penalization of activists' actions. This discussion begins under the title "Force, violence or threats involving animal enterprises" (U.S. Cong. 2006, 1), starting with a minor penalty and leading to a maximum twenty-year prison sentence for economic damage exceeding $1 million and serious bodily injury, and life imprisonment if the act involves human death (ibid., 2). But these are strange penalties given the fact that even the most "notorious" activists—the ALF and ELF—have never injured anyone through their actions, and this is basic to their philosophy. Even the opposition, the Foundation for Biomedical Research, which claims to be the only group that tracks eco-terrorist crimes, did not report a single human injury resulting from these groups from 1996–2006, which the foundation considers to be the most active period of these movements (Potter 2011, 48). Associating activists with such destruction, harm, and violence does at least three things: (1) it diverts attention away from animal-exploiting industries, (2) it marginalizes activists, and (3) it deters activists not just from destroying property, but from targeting for protest the main object of the scrutiny—mega-corporations that exploit and abuse animals.

Laying out such disciplinary measures is recognized as a viable form of discourse under the AETA. The law formulates "rules that silence certain dimensions of experience simply by not recognizing them as objects of discourse" (Foss, Foss, and Trapp 2002, 349). In fact, leafleting, protesting, and chanting are seemingly discouraged under the law lest they "interfere with" the operations of an animal enterprise. Even the definition of an "animal enterprise" expands which entities are allowed to speak: An "animal enterprise" can range from "a commercial or academic enterprise that uses or sells animals or animal products..." to a "zoo, aquarium, animal shelter, pet store, breeder, furrier, circus, or rodeo, or other lawful competitive animal event" (U.S. Cong. 2006, 2). Meanwhile, the AETA fails to address concerns of safety or humane treatment of these animals; the AETA does not recognize those concerns as viable forms of discourse. The dimension of the animals' experience in captivity is not acknowledged, and the activists' attempt to alleviate that experience is neglected. Dismissing the experience of animals and activists constitutes a discourse in which property and profit are privileged at the expense of all else—i.e., the animals' best interests and activists' attempts to call attention to those interests are excluded and silenced.

Another category of Foucault's governing rules involves who is allowed or qualified to actually speak, write, or communicate (Foss, Foss, and Trapp 2002, 349). Here, it is not so much about *what* can be said, but rather *who* can say it. In the AETA, this is "the Senate and House of

Representatives of the United States of America in Congress Assembled" (Cong. 2006, 1). The bill was passed unanimously in Congress (although many were not in attendance) with Dennis Kucinich as the sole voice of opposition on the House floor. Kucinich challenged why the special legislation was needed when the crimes listed in the bill—theft, harassment, and trespassing—were already treated as crimes (Potter 2011, 169). When Kucinich brought up issues of animal cruelty, his attempts to garner consideration for his concerns appeared futile. It is obvious, then, that not all congressional representatives can speak and be heard, although those who apparently represent corporate interests and animal-exploiting industries may speak through this law (Best 2007, 4). That the AETA was written into U.S. federal law shows that corporations with the support of Congress are deemed qualified authorities to speak.

For Foucault, that which is considered truth is always dependent on the discourse formation in which it resides. Those who are allowed to speak are "meaning-makers" in society in that they imbue the discourse with their own significances. These meaning-makers also create their own protection, thus enabling them to maintain their control over the discourse. Take, for instance, the repeated references to "serious bodily injury" and "substantial bodily injury" (Cong. 2006, 2) of someone who is associated with an animal enterprise. These references serve to (1) invent penalties for extreme physical violence where no such evidence exists historically, and (2) deflect attention away from protected entities in the AETA discourse—animal enterprises—who inflict extreme physical violence on nonhuman animals on a mass scale.

The fact that animal rights and environmental activists have come to be identified as terrorists in this particular society and at this particular historical juncture demonstrates that corporate profit and inanimate property guide the formation of discourse. Yet, these groups, at their core, question society's pervasive dependence on the use of nonhuman animals. They ask that the billions of animals in factory farms, vivisection laboratories, and places of "entertainment" be recognized as sentient beings in need of protection. But the AETA, as a discourse, ignores this worldview and only acknowledges activists as those who threaten property and profit. Certainly, any texts, ideas, or actions that encourage protest are not seen as valid in this discourse. That is because the reasons for which someone would undertake such protests are considered illegitimate (or simply not considered at all). This is due, at least in part, to the logic of our contemporary economy: animals are property; property is money; and money is, or *should be*, at the center of our lives. Many animal and environmental activists challenge this logic, and therefore they are silenced and even condemned within the discourse of the AETA.

Foucault's concept of governmentality, as developed in his lecture series *Security, Territory, Population* (2007), can help us understand what is at stake in delegitimizing the discourse of animal rights activists, including those who engage in or defend direct action for animals. As he develops this concept in his February 8, 1978, lecture, Foucault argues that government refers to something more than the mere imposition of negative or prohibitive law under threat of punishment by a sovereign. Rather, it refers to control over "movement in space, material subsistence.... It refers to the control one may exercise over oneself and others, over someone's body, soul and behavior" (Foucault 2007, 122). To be clear, Foucault's use of "government" and "governmentality" does not refer to an actual institution like a congress or administration. Instead, he is referring to how discourse affects and influences our thoughts, actions, and decision-making processes. In this sense, then, discourse "governs" our lives.

Foucault holds that governmentality has its roots in the ability of Christian pastoral power to manage its flock of believers (ibid., 123). Unlike sovereign majesty, pastoral government is "a power of care. It looks after the flock, it looks after the individuals of the flock, it sees to it that the sheep do not suffer, it goes in search of those that have strayed off course, and it treats those that are injured" (ibid., 127). As good as this may sound, it is important to note that, for Foucault, the flock that is governed is always comprised of people (ibid., 122). Furthermore, the pastor, while showing great concern for members of his flock, "is someone who keeps watch. He 'keeps watch' in the sense, of course, of keeping an eye out for possible evils...and avoid[ing] the misfortune that may threaten the least of its members" (ibid., 127).

As the governing of souls and the managing of social intercourse within the flock, governmentality first separates those who will be recognized as persons from those who will be seen as things, objects, or nonpersons. Governmentality then manages the interaction and relationships among the members of the flock in a way that the pastor thinks is maximally beneficial. Viewed in this light, we could say that animal rights activists who support or engage in direct action to protect animals transgress the contemporary discourses that govern our lives. Animal rights activists seek to expand the range of those who are recognized as persons and members of the flock, and consequently, of those who are to be cared for rather than exploited. When understood in this way, it is obvious that the AETA is an attempt to recognize and enforce certain kinds of relationships and interactions: only humans are valued; animals are property and objects of profit; anyone violating this code of interaction is a criminal.

The knowledge created in this discursive formation cannot be separated from the power relations that exist between activists, corporations, and the U.S. government. In the face of "the growing influence of the animal liberation movement" (Best 2007, 2), the U.S. government and animal industries have used the AETA to exert their power by constructing a discourse that marginalizes activists in the public eye, restrains their bodies, and obstructs their potential. By applying the term *animal rights terrorist* to those who were previously thought to engage simply in gluing locks or rescuing animals, the system has exploited the public's fear of terrorism. Such labeling is even more detrimental than one might think since it pathologizes activists: activists become viewed as deviant by society, and to the degree that activists internalize that label, they might begin to monitor and curb their activities.

However, it is important to realize that activists can also affect discourse. And they appear to do be doing this quite effectively considering the emergence of the AETA. Such legislation would not exist if activists were not effective in countering the corporate-State complex. As Foucault says, "all individuals exercise power ... and all are subjected to it" (Foss, Foss, and Trapp 2002, 352). Each action, as seen by Foucault, is a practice of power relations, and those relations can be altered in numerous ways. Foucault discusses the "specific intellectual" as one example of this alteration and resistance. Specific intellectuals are:

> Ordinary people who have knowledge of their circumstances and are able to express themselves independently of the universal theorizing intellectual. Because Foucault objects to the idea of a knowledge of a truth outside of networks of power relations, specific intellectuals must work "not in the modality of the 'universal,' the 'exemplary,' the 'just-and-true-for-all,' but within specific sectors, at the precise points where their own conditions of life and work situate them (housing, the hospital, the asylum, the laboratory, the university, family and sexual relations)" (ibid., 356).

Confronted by the adversary of "the multinational corporations, the judicial and police apparatuses, the property speculators, etc.," the specific intellectual is mindful of social struggles and engages in both theory and action (Foucault, 1984). Thus, the specific intellectual may be the consumer who boycotts animal products or a laboratory worker who decides to break into the testing facility at night and steal videotapes to expose the conditions of animals. It is only by "exposing lines of power and control [that] individuals can envision new ways of thought" (Schnurer 2004, 117). By sharing their knowledge and educating people about animal abuse and exploitation, activists exert *their* productive power.

Given all that we have addressed so far—the governing rules of what can be spoken of in discourse, what issues or worldviews are acceptable, and who is allowed to speak, write, and communicate, and the power dynamics that constitute the AETA—it is obvious that the current discursive formation of the corporate-State complex constructs a dichotomy between those who comply with the animal-exploiting agenda and those who reject this agenda. The latter are criminalized and identified as terrorists who threaten the capitalist way of life in which animals are property and activists are deviants. It is an overall system that depends on docile bodies mechanically consuming the products of the multi-billion-dollar industries that pushed for the AETA. People in the system may be unaware of the subtle ways that power affects their lives, but as the AETA shows, we are subject to the disciplinary practices and governing relations of the AETA's discursive formation.

THE AETA AS PANOPTICON

We now examine in greater detail how the AETA—as a governing, discursive formation—operates to police activists and to motivate activists to police themselves. Many of Foucault's later works deal with the ways in which expert discourses normalize and legitimize the interrogation, surveillance, and scrutiny of thoughts and actions. According to Foucault, the ubiquity of surveillance aimed at normalizing the population leads to a state of universal *abnormality*. That is, because everyone is scrutinized over their conformity with norms, everyone is revealed to be in some way and to some extent abnormal (Foucault 2003, 109–10, 132). As Foucault describes in his 1974–1975 lecture series *Abnormal* (2003), the integration of psychiatry into the roles of policing criminal behavior led to a situation in which psychiatrists and the police came to investigate not just overt criminal behavior, but also "little abnormalities," analyzing and investigating the criminal potential behind everyone's "bad habits, little perversities, and childish naughtiness" (ibid., 110). That is, every small misdeed becomes, if not itself criminalized, at least an object of investigation for criminal psychiatry, since it may indicate some past, present, or future criminal proclivity. At its limit, everyone is inscribed within the logic of potential criminality and is therefore subject to potentially endless, minute scrutiny.

The internalization of these processes of surveillance and normalization is described in Foucault's famous discussion in *Discipline and Punish* (1995) of Jeremy Bentham's panopticon. The panopticon is a prison that has a guard located in a central tower, surrounded by cells whose openings face the central guard. The prison is constructed in such a way that the guard can observe any prisoner at any time without the prisoner knowing whether or when the guard is observing him or her. As Foucault describes the panopticon, each prisoner

Is seen, but he does not see; he is the object of information, never a subject in communication. . . . Hence the major effect of the

Panopticon: to induce in the inmate a state of conscious and permanent visibility that assures the automatic functioning of power. So to arrange things that the surveillance is permanent in its effects, even if it is discontinuous in its action; that the perfection of power should tend to render its actual exercise unnecessary; that this architectural apparatus should be a machine for creating and sustaining a power relation independent of the person who exercises it; in short, that the inmates should be caught up in a power situation of which they are themselves the bearers (Foucault 1995, 200–01).

There are two features of the panopticized subject worth highlighting for our present purposes. First, prisoners in the panopticon do not know when or how often they are being scrutinized, and they do not know how closely they are being watched. The panopticon works by subjecting prisoners to potential surveillance at all times and to any degree of closeness and invasiveness. They are merely passive recipients of surveillance. Second, because prisoners in the panopticon know that they can be watched at any time with any degree of scrutiny, they adjust their behavior such that they act as though they are always being watched with minute detail. The fear brought on by the indefinite scope and duration of the prison guard's gaze leads prisoners to internalize the guard. In other words, the prisoners become their own guards, watching over themselves in order to enforce the rules of the guards on themselves.

Regarding the first feature of panopticism, the AETA instantiates a widespread "anti-terrorism" discourse. It is predicated on the State's use of generalized fear and suspicion of terrorism to legitimize State surveillance. The demand for constant vigilance against the threat of terrorism, domestic or foreign, promulgated in the wake of September 11th, has produced expert "anti-terrorism" discourses that have led to a presumption of terrorist intent among many broad groups of people, including Muslims, immigrants, environmentalists, antiwar activists, and, pertinent to our present inquiry, animal rights activists. Within the discursive context of generalized fear and suspicion of terrorist intent, the AETA signals a special scrutiny placed on animal rights activism. That special scrutiny has been formalized by the State's creation of a new juridical category of behavior called "animal enterprise terror."

This scrutiny is not saved for only the most "radical" or "illegal" activities. For example, in 2005, the American Civil Liberties Union (ACLU) exposed the fact that the FBI covertly infiltrated People for the Ethical Treatment of Animals (PETA) (ACLU 2005). The ACLU revealed that the FBI had sent operatives to investigate the activities of PETA (along with other nonprofit organizations, notably Greenpeace and the American-Arab Anti-Discrimination Committee) by infiltrating PETA's internship program. The FBI's justification for their infiltration and surveillance was the presumption that PETA is or is likely to be involved in or lend support to "terrorist activities." As the ACLU reports, the FBI, in its efforts to discover evidence of terrorist activity in PETA's ranks, saw fit to monitor (a) the organization's distribution of informational booklets on plant-based diets known as "Vegetarian Starter Kits," (b) the organization's participation in a public conference on animal rights, and (c) a fur protest (ibid.). Monitoring outreach activities as apparently benign as these sends a clear signal that experts in charge of "anti-terrorism" cast an overarching (and highly misinformed) glance at animal rights and animal protection activities. As anyone who has participated in animal rights activism at the grassroots level knows, it is not only large, national organizations such as PETA that have been subjected to scrutiny, suspicion, and infiltration. Small grassroots organizations are frequently treated as potential criminals by local authorities. Support for and participation in animal rights and animal protection activities appears to be sufficient justification to be subjected to intrusive government investigation. This "anti-terrorism" expert discourse does not merely sort out terrorists from non-terrorists; it also places *everyone* on a *continuum* of terrorism. Everyone, seen by the State as a relatively undifferentiated mass, more or less partakes of terrorism—whether it be actual, potential or imagined—and everyone must, therefore, be subjected to constant surveillance.

As outlined in Section One, the institutional system supporting and benefiting from the AETA is motivated primarily by the pursuit of profit gained through the exploitation of animals, specifically, and of the Earth, more generally. It is hardly surprising, then, that activism that challenges these industries would be discredited on the basis of a contrived link to "eco-terrorism." The blanket suspicion of animal rights and animal protection activism, which obviously contributes to the phenomenon of panopticism, is highly advantageous to these corporate interests.

Regarding the second feature of panopticism, animal rights activists are not simply passive recipients of State suspicion and surveillance. Many activists and activist organizations have begun *policing themselves*. Likewise, segments of the animal rights movement have begun criticizing, disavowing, and distancing themselves from illegal actions for animals and chastising activists who promote illegal actions. This has been particularly true since the passage of the AETA, and often in response to it. For instance, Lee Hall of the animal rights group Friends of Animals states that, "Animal advocates who seem unpredictable and dangerous are disengaging themselves from the movement's ethical platform, and from any moral framework that most people recognize, allowing an oddly effective sort of anti-activism to emerge" (Hall 2006). Hall raises a legitimate concern, and such issues should be discussed and debated among animal rights activists. But it is hard not to also see Hall's concern as a result of the panopticon—i.e., an internal monitoring that is worried about broad, undefined "illegal activities." That harkens, in many ways, the discourse of the AETA.

In a similar vein, Wayne Pacelle and J. P. Goodwin of The Humane Society of the United States have chastised illegal activism, writing that:

> Experienced campaigners know that winning reforms is tough, even when the stars are aligned in our favor. When people within our movement pursue tactics that are viewed as far outside what is generally acceptable, and in fact deploy behaviors that conflict with the basic tenets of respect and compassion that animate our movement, it hurts us all; effecting change becomes even more complicated and difficult. (Pacelle and Goodwin 2004)

Animal rights philosopher Tom Regan argues that there is room for reasonable disagreement regarding the justifiability of direct action for animals, even going so far as to state that "members of the ALF are courageous in their acts and sincere in their commitment" (Regan 2004, 191). But nevertheless, he takes the position that such actions are both unjustified and dangerously counterproductive for the animal rights movement:

> Without a doubt, many people are turned off when they read about ARAs [animal rights activists] breaking a furrier's window or trashing a vivisector's office. . . . It is also a tactical disaster. Even when animals are rescued, the story the media tells is about the "terroristic" acts of ARAs, not the terrible things that were being done to animals. The one thing ARA violence never fails to produce is more grist for the mills run by spokespersons for the major animal user industries. . . . [V]iolence done by ARAs, in my judgment, is wrong; it does not help, it hurts the animal rights movement. (Regan 2004, 188–91)

Whether explicitly responsive to the AETA or not, these types of sentiments call on animal rights activists to accede to the threat of being labeled "terrorists." This discourse of "accepting responsibility" for denouncing or distancing oneself from forms of activism reliant upon direct action can be understood in Foucauldian terms as a panoptic scene of reform. As institutions of power survey and investigate activist behavior with ever greater suspicion, activists become aware of the constant threat of being labeled "terrorists" or "terrorist sympathizers." As in Bentham's panopticon, it is not sufficient for prisoners to modify their behavior in response to the observation of guards; prisoners must internalize the guard's critical gaze and thereby become guards of themselves. We can see this kind of internalized policing within the animal rights movement, e.g., activists calling on other activists to be vigilant about the inescapable threat of juridical or public castigation. Such behavior emerges from one's own internalized condemnation of "anti-terrorism" discourses.

CONCLUSION

The strategic question provoked by this Foucauldian analysis is how to deal with a discourse that places animal rights activists under close scrutiny and surveillance, and imbricates animal rights activists with a self-disciplining, self-monitoring power. The "anti-terrorist" discourse

THE TERRORIZATION OF DISSENT

instantiated by the AETA is a delegitimizing operation that places animal rights activists—and potentially *all* activists—in an undifferentiated mass along a continuum of terrorism, whether contrived or imagined. We do not believe that the animal rights movement should strive for a legitimacy that cannot be attained. That is a losing battle. Instead, we must (1) challenge the very institutions, authorities, industries, and laws that promulgate and enforce the process of panopticism; (2) find ways to correct the very set of meanings and understandings promulgated by the "anti-terror" discourse; and (3) unmask the rhetoric of the AETA and "eco-terrorism." Only by dismantling these discursive rules and practices can animal rights activism be properly understood as a nonviolent movement opposed to abuse and exploitation of *all* kinds.

REFERENCES

American Civil Liberties Union. "New Documents Show FBI Targeting Environmental and Animal Rights Groups Activities as 'Domestic Terrorism.'" Published December 20, 2005. www.aclu.org/national-security/new-documents-show-fbi-targeting-environmental-and-animal-rights-groups-activities.

Best, Steven. "The Animal Enterprise Terrorism Act: New, Improved, and ACLU Approved." *Journal for Critical Animal Studies* 5, no. 1 (2007): 1–17.

Best, Steven, and Anthony J. Nocella II. "Introduction." In *Igniting a Revolution: Voices in Defense of the Earth*, edited by Steven Best and Anthony J. Nocella II. Oakland, Calif.: AK Press (2006): 8–30.

Foss, Sonja K., Karen A. Foss, and Robert Trapp. "Michel Foucault." In *Contemporary Perspectives on Rhetoric*, 3rd edition. Long Grove, Ill.: Waveland Press, 2002 (339–78).

Foucault, Michel. *Abnormal: Lectures at the Collège de France 1974–1975*. Translated by Graham Burchell. Edited by Valerio Marchetti and Antonella Salomoni. New York: Picador, 2003.

———. *The Archaeology of Knowledge*. Translated by A. M. Sheridan Smith. New York: Pantheon Books, 1972.

———. "Truth and Power." In *The Foucault Reader*. Edited by Paul Rabinow. New York: Pantheon Books, 1984: (51–75).

———. *Discipline and Punish: The Birth of the Prison*. Translated by Alan Sheridan. New York: Vintage Books, 1995.

———. *Security, Territory, Population: Lectures at the Collège de France 1977–1978*. Translated by Graham Burchell. Edited by Michel Senellart, Francois Ewald, Alessandro Fontana, and Arnold I. Davidson. New York: Palgrave MacMillan, 2007.

Hall, Lee. "Working for the Clampdown: How the Animal Enterprise Terrorism Act Became Law." *Satya*. Published December 2006/January 2007. www.satyamag .com/dec06/hall.html.

Nocella, Anthony J. II. "Understanding the ALF: From Critical Analysis to Critical Pedagogy." In *Terrorists or Freedom Fighters? Reflection on the Liberation of Animals*, edited by Steven Best and Anthony J. Nocella II. New York: Lantern Books, 2004: 195–201.

Pacelle, Wayne, and J. P. Goodwin. "Looking at the Bigger Picture: Violence, Change and Public Opinion." *Satya*. March 2004. www.satyamag.com/ mar04/pacelle .html (site discontinued).

Potter, Will. *Green Is the New Red*. San Francisco: City Lights Publishers, 2011.

Regan, Tom. *Empty Cages: Facing the Challenge of Animal Rights*. Lanham, Md.: Rowman and Littlefield Publishers, 2004.

Schnurer, Maxwell. "At the Gates of Hell: The ALF and the Legacy of Holocaust Resistance." *Terrorists or Freedom Fighters? Reflection on the Liberation of Animals*, edited by Steven Best and Anthony J. Nocella II. New York: Lantern Books, 2004: 106–27.

United States Cong. *Animal Enterprise Terrorism Act*. 109th Cong. (Public Law 109 -374—NOV. 27, 2006). Washington, D.C.: Congressional Record. www.gpo.gov /fdsys/pkg/PLAW-109publ374/pdf/PLAW-109publ374.pdf.

United States Cong. *Animal Enterprise Protection Act*. 102nd Congress (Public Law 102- 346—AUG. 26, 1992). Washington, D.C.: Congressional Record. www.nal.usda .gov/awic/legislat/pl102346.htm.

STOP HUNTINGDON ANIMAL CRUELTY

A QUEER CRITIQUE OF THE AETA

Jennifer D. Grubbs

When taken separately... [they] all seem to represent a queer edge in a larger cultural phenomenon. When considered together, they add up to a fierce and lively queer subculture that needs to be reckoned with on its own terms. —**Judith Halberstam**

The rhetorical potential of direct action poses a threat to the industries that are most profitable for the federal government. The boundaries of accepted means of protest are blurred through direct action, such as those articulated by the international campaign Stop Huntingdon Animal Cruelty (SHAC). The SHAC campaign utilizes a method of naming, shaming, and blaming individuals who hold top positions with secondary and tertiary corporations connected to the international vivisection and breeding lab Huntingdon Life Sciences (HLS). The tactics used by the international SHAC campaign span a continuum of legality, and range from street protests, leafleting, and home demonstrations to aggressive forms of sabotage including arson in the United Kingdom. SHAC was formed in 1999 by three British activists in response to an undercover investigation by People for the Ethical Treatment of Animals (PETA). PETA released a video that captured hours of violent vivisection conducted inside HLS. The direct action campaign uses public forums—such as public sidewalks or the Internet—to reveal the violence that takes place out of public view. The direct action campaign utilizes the model of secondary and tertiary targeting, which targets not only HLS employees but also customers, shareholders, connected financial institutions, and anyone else fiscally linked to HLS.

SHAC's tactical approach not only challenges animal and eco-industries but also "queers" various social and political discourses that sustain animal abuse and ecological exploitation. This queering effect refers to SHAC's ability to expose, alter, and/or invert taken-for-granted understandings and practices. For example, SHAC's use of public performance *as* direct action calls into question and challenges a slew of otherwise accepted "truisms": that human animals are more valuable than nonhuman animals; that "doing one's job" absolves one from political and/or ethical responsibility; that government and corporate interests are distinct and separate; that legislation is passed for the public good rather than private profit; and, on a different kind of note, that average, everyday people are powerless to change various structures, laws, and customs. In this sense, then, SHAC *is* a queer performance that plays with and transgresses the normative boundaries of society. And that is one of the major reasons why the SHAC campaign is so feared: because it poses an effective, convincing, and powerful critique that *queers* social/political normativity.

In this chapter, I adopt a model of engaged anthropology that emphasizes participant-observation ethnography. I am not writing from a detached perspective, but rather as someone who has attended protests, rallies, and demonstrations. Within a trajectory of critical scholarly work, activist ethnography and engaged research hold a *queer* potential to challenge the "academic versus activist" divide. Anthropologists such as Wendy Brown and Barbara Nelson have examined the relationship between capitalism and the State. David Graeber, Nancy Scheper-Hughes, and Philippe Bourgois have immersed themselves in liberationist struggles in order to create theory that emerges from action. Feminist anthropologists challenge the patriarchal structures that naturalize oppressions associated with gender, race, class, age, ethnicity, and so on. These scholars include Melissa Wright, Chandra Mohanty, Nancy Naples, and Michele Tracy Berger. Environmental anthropologists, like Patrick Huff and Carla Hadden, have studied the ways in which consumption and production practices exploit not only humans but also animals and the "natural" world. These activist anthropologists adopt theoretical methodologies such as ethnography to facilitate participatory research that is reciprocal for both the researcher and the community. I may write about animal liberation and the SHAC campaign as a doctoral candidate in anthropology, but I am also a vegan animal liberationist. In other words, as an academic, I am capable of using my privileged position to turn political work into theory and to turn the details of late night demonstrating into anecdotal material for pedagogical and scholarly purposes.

This chapter focuses on SHAC's use of direct action as public performance, and, more specifically, SHAC's use of protest as spectacle. The chapter begins with an overview of the Animal Enterprise Terrorism Act and its relation to the SHAC campaign. The chapter then provides a brief explanation of direct action as a protest strategy, followed by a discussion of SHAC's queering of the protest as spectacle. The chapter concludes with a discussion of how SHAC uses *playfulness* during home demonstrations as a queer mode of protest.

Animal Enterprise Terrorism Act (AETA)

The federal government has had a difficult time dealing with the tactics undertaken by SHAC-affiliated activists. Everything from hyperbolic news stories to television shows like the 2001 episode of *Law & Order* titled "Whose Monkey Is It Anyway?" demonstrate the public's uneasiness with direct action animal liberationists. The confrontational SHAC campaign and its allies pose moral dilemmas that are often overlooked when it comes to vivisection. The campaign holds individuals accountable for their tacit involvement through employment with secondary and tertiary companies connected to HLS. Rather than simply name, shame, and blame the "scientist" conducting the experiment, or target the facilities holding the animals in captivity, the SHAC model is expansive. The model exposes an international web of corporate connection to HLS. Consequently, anyone connected to HLS in any way is considered a potential protest target. This has meant that even FedEx has been a target for its contractual relationship with HLS (SHAC 2011a). As the SHAC campaign's net grows wider, the financial hit against HLS grows bigger. Thus, the federal government faced a great deal of pressure to diffuse the campaign in the United States.

Many of the tactics used in the SHAC campaign fit within existing legislation and carry minimal penalties and sentencing. For example, each state has misdemeanor laws regarding public demonstrations, ranging from noise ordinances to restrictions on time of day and laws banning the wearing of masks. The SHAC model implements the strategy of secondary and tertiary targeting by identifying a singular entity tied to HLS and pressuring individuals employed by this entity to cease ties to HLS. Thus, the campaign that focused on AstraZeneca (a global research-based pharmaceutical company) involved publicly identifying key employees and publishing their otherwise publicly accessible personal addresses and phone numbers on the website. The financial and shareholder loss to HLS since the inception of the SHAC campaign demonstrates its highly effective nature. The federal government thus needed to find a way to discourage activists from joining the campaign efforts. The threat of a noise violation or trespassing charge was not enough to discourage animal liberation activists from joining the cause.

The AETA of 2006 was federal legislation that amended the 1992 Animal Enterprise Protection Act (AEPA) and gave the Department of Justice a heightened form of power to respond to so-called "threats" posed by animal rights activists. A much wider array of nonviolent forms of dissent can now be considered as both federal crime and "terrorism." The act's use of broad and general language *does not definitively explain* the nature of "animal enterprise" or what is meant by "interfering with" such an enterprise—for example, it fails to differentiate a classic sit-in from arson, where both might be considered "interference" and thus "terrorism." Such loose language specifically enhances the government's power and greatly denies the civil exercise of the First Amendment.

The act redefined already State-recognized crimes as federal offenses, and redefined them within the realm of "domestic terrorism." It also increased the existing penalties, including fines that are based on the amount of financial damage caused, and it allowed animal enterprises to seek monetary restitution. The language used to defend the legislation argued that the AETA offers necessary power to the Department of

Justice to arrest, prosecute, and convict activists without much juridical struggle. In other words, the government is able to apprehend and arrest social actors without much due process, denying the accused access to a fair trial.

Combined with the passage of the USA PATRIOT Act in 2001, governments can use surveillance and infiltrate organizations recognized under the AETA. The federal government is able to overstep states to prosecute people not only for *what they do* but also *what they thought when they did it*. The SHAC campaign experienced multiple levels of government surveillance prior to the arrest and prosecution of six activists in the SHAC 7 trial (one of the accused was eventually dropped from the case, hence the original seven became six). Dara Lovitz (2010) has detailed the government's stalking, infiltration of social networks, and phone recording that was used to build a case against the individuals in this case. The rhetoric of *conspiracy*, a word used throughout U.S. history to fragment activists, became a loose basis for many of the charges in the SHAC 7 case. This element of the AETA is one of the central and most revealing aspects of the law.

Within the logic of the AETA, corporations—and the laboratories that house, maim, and disfigure animals and inflict physical and psychological violence on them—are rearticulated as "helpless victims." Meanwhile, animal liberationists attempting to remove animals from laboratories and using their First Amendment freedom of speech to pressure shareholders are "criminals" and even "terrorists." Scholar Adrian Parr recounts a similar act of rearticulation with the use of terrorist enhancement charges in the 2007 trial of political prisoner Daniel McGowan (Parr 2009, 87). McGowan was arrested along with five other activists as part of the U.S. investigation called "Operation Backfire." The six activists collectively faced a sixty-five–count indictment. McGowan was charged with arson and conspiracy to commit arson for the 2001 Earth Liberation Front actions against Superior Lumber and Jefferson Poplar Farms in Oregon. McGowan received a "terrorist enhancement" with his sentence and was placed in highly restrictive Communications Management Unit prisons in Illinois and Indiana. Parr argues that the public trial and sentencing of McGowan was an act of *discursive rearticulation*:

what was once perceived as activism, or perhaps at the most, a basic criminal act, was rearticulated as "terrorism." Likewise, with the AETA, the public is misled to believe that protest, rather than vivisection, is violence and terrorism.

Direct Action as Strategy

The SHAC campaign relies heavily upon direct action rather than, say, more traditional efforts of political lobbying. This is because direct action provides an effective use of time and effort. For instance, SHAC campaigns identify corporations and individuals and then aggressively (and very publicly) confronts them. These tactics require little time compared to the bureaucratic processes involved with legal analyses, drafting regulatory policies and reforms, and schmoozing people behind closed doors. *Direct action*, as the term implies, directly challenges those in power through time-efficient, cost-effective tactics that rely on activist energy and creativity. Direct action, as defined by anthropologist and activist David Graeber, represents a particularly advanced vision for the remaking of social relations.

> Direct action represents a certain ideal.... It is a form of action in which means and ends become, effectively, indistinguishable; a way of actively engaging with the world to bring about change, in which the form of the action—or at least, the organization of the action— is itself a model for the change one wishes to bring about. At its most basic, it reflects a very simple anarchist insight: that one cannot create a free society through military discipline, a democratic society by giving orders, or a happy one through joyless self-sacrifice. At its most elaborate, the structure of one's own act becomes a kind of micro-utopia, a concrete model for one's vision of a free society. (Graeber 2009, 210)

Direct action is not defined by the physical act, but by the ideological underpinnings and symbolic meanings that the act represents. Within this logic, direct action is not a label of tactic demarcation (act A = direct = good, versus act B = indirect = bad), but rather it is an inclusive framework to conceptualize activism. Although all actions taken in defense of animals are important, direct action implies there is no intermediary.

Direct action creates a queer space—i.e., an open space in which people are invited and even encouraged to play with and transgress normative boundaries. Such a space enables politically repressed and marginalized peoples to reclaim power. Rather than relying on someone else to make social change, the participants push for that change themselves. This type of action is a transgressive experience that empowers individuals to politically engage the movement while initiating themselves into a global struggle for animal liberation.

This occurs even more so with the use of new technologies in which activists solidify their commitment through social networks. Public access to global media and social forums has provided the platform for a global solidarity movement. The political terrain is effectively remade through the "technorevolution." Communiqués are posted to the Internet moments after an action has taken place. Photographs and videos can be accessed on the Internet from across the world. Also, support systems for political prisoners expand far beyond physical boundaries of geography.

The SHAC campaign not only challenges the notion of accountability by targeting secondary and tertiary companies, but the campaign also queers the realm of tactical approaches. For example, the SHAC campaign has used tactics that include black faxing (the looped sending of completely black fax pages to drain ink and occupy the line), website defacement and data theft, denial-of-service attack, unsolicited subscription for mailings, services, and goods, and publicizing targets' personal information (although otherwise publicly accessible). These tactics queer the spectrum of protest within the realm of animal advocacy by crossing accepted boundaries—by playing with the lines of acceptability and introducing ideas, practices, and forms of dissent and resistance. In many ways, then, the SHAC campaign sits at the cutting edge of direct action and radical social change.

Queer Challenges to Speciesism and the Profit Motive

The SHAC campaign has had a significant influence on HLS in the United States and United Kingdom. The significant economic loss inflicted by the SHAC campaign would indicate that the model is working. The SHAC model adheres to a strict policy advocating non-violence (SHAC 2012), and is based on a three-tiered approach that includes campaigning against (i) "customers who provide HLS with an income and profits"; (ii) "suppliers who provide HLS with vital tools to carry out research"; and (iii) "financial links such as shareholders, market makers and banking facilities" (SHAC 2011b). The SHAC campaign is cited globally as the impetus behind smaller grassroots animal liberation campaigns that utilize secondary and tertiary targeting, although historically that is nothing new. The withdrawal of financial contributors to HLS has severely impacted the financial support of the corporation. Companies have realized that it is easier to revoke funding or cease ties with HLS than to deal with the targeted campaigns of SHAC. Ultimately, HLS relies on capitalism to survive. Without the corporate contracts, shareholders, and government protection through the AETA, HLS would crumble in the face of the SHAC campaign. In the past, when any of these elements of support have been jeopardized, HLS has begun to unravel.

This particular mode of activism—direct action that targets HLS's profit motive—provides an effective critique of speciesism. The campaigns against HLS point to how capitalism facilitates the systematic domination and exploitation of *other-than-human* animals. The rhetoric of pharmacapitalism has successfully indoctrinated the public to believe they can "cure" ailments and illnesses if only they could get even more money and more animals to vivisect. People who have lost someone to illness know the powerlessness that comes with waiting for "science" to have a medical breakthrough. Whether someone wants to sparkle in their hot pink attire and walk a few miles for breast cancer or fundraise by washing cars outside of the grocery store, it is apparent that people are affected by disease and death. But the notion that animal "science" has led to medical breakthroughs has been increasingly discredited while the profit motive of animal "science" has been revealed—the animal model apparently perpetuating the very disease that it purports to be "curing" (Greek and Greek 2000).

In light of these facts, it becomes increasingly apparent that the notion that *human* life warrants *animal* death is predicated on the constructed hierarchy that divides and privileges human over animal. SHAC, however, places footage and photographs in the public eye that capture the conditions in which these animals live—the violent handling and grotesque maiming at the hands of vivisectors. The public is confronted with the realities veiled behind the corporate walls of "science." The pseudo-utilitarian rationale is confronted with what that actually means to excuse the violent vivisection of *some* to *possibly* aid others, or so the rhetoric goes. The speciesist hypocrisy embedded in the vivisection logic—that through *animal* death we save *human* lives—is exposed through the violent laboratory reality.

The dichotomizing and privileging of humans over animals is presented by SHAC as inherently violent. Within the artificial confines of the laboratory, the beagles and rabbits stuffed into wire cages and forced to endure exploitation are far removed from "scientific rigor." The emphasis in the SHAC campaign has consistently exposed the systematic oppression of animals at the hands of humans. The bunnies that live in school classrooms, the frog dissected in seventh grade biology, and the pig fetus used in undergraduate human reproduction courses are all a part of a larger discourse on species relations. The SHAC campaign publicizes the violent treatment of animals within HLS and creates a queer counterpublic to understand human–animal relations.

Protest as Spectacle

Graeber (2009) encourages activists to utilize the political and social imaginary in order to challenge the "neoliberal moment." Neoliberalism refers to a new form of "neo laissez faire economics." As scholar-activist Jason Del Gandio succinctly states:

[Neoliberalism is] based on the deregulation of free markets and the privatization of wealth. It subordinates government control to the interests of private profit. The government—rather than regulating the market to assure a level playing field—becomes an extension of market activity, the servant of the industries to which it is captive. Neoliberalism provides tax breaks for the rich, reduces spending on social programs and welfare, expands corporate control and eradicates labor rights, environmental protections, drug and food regulations and even national law. The basic purpose is to allow private interests to own and control every aspect of the human, social and natural world. (2010, n.p.)

In reference to a key topic of this chapter, the animal industry privatizes and profits from the suffering and murder of nonhuman animals. Challenging this hegemonic cruelty must involve imagining a post-capitalist and post-speciesist reality. Such imagining is facilitated by "disidentification"—i.e., to get people to disidentify with the current conditions and practices of neoliberalism, the animal industry, and speciesism. SHAC's use of direct action—conceived here as a form of political theater—is one way to facilitate an alternative political imaginary.

The home demonstrations conducted by SHAC-affiliated activists often rely upon the use of "spectacle." By spectacle, I am referring to the construction of reality through public theater. For instance, SHAC often conducts home demonstrations—i.e., protests at the residences of HLS employees and affiliated constituents. The performativity of such home demonstrations creates a scene—similar to a theatrical play—in which the grim and hidden realities of vivisection are publicly staged for all to see. In other words, HLS's violence (which is often masked behind corporate walls) is brought to the forefront by the garishness of the publicly performed *spectacle*.

It should be noted that Guy Debord of the Situationist International famously critiques "the spectacle." In *Society of the Spectacle* (1970), Debord argues that authentic social life has been replaced by mediated representation. We no longer relate as humans, but as commodities that are filtered—or mediated—through the confluence of capitalism, advanced technologies, and mass media. As Debord states, "the tangible world is replaced by a selection of images which exist above it, and which simultaneously impose themselves as the tangible *par excellence*"; the spectacle "is not a collection of images, but a social relationship among people, mediated by images" (original emphasis; Debord 1970, 36 and 74).

It is not a stretch to apply Debord's critique to the human-over-animal hierarchy that animal liberationists fight against. How many movies, songs, commercials, billboards, political metaphors, and everyday sayings and practices maintain and perpetuate both the idea and practice of exploiting animals for human use? In this sense, then, many humans relate to nonhuman animals as commodities—as mere representations of actual sentient creatures that have lives and existences of their own.

However, despite Debord's persuasive critique of mediated society, the spectacle can be appropriated for positive and profound social change. According to social theorist Stephen Duncombe (2007), media technologies are here to stay. Rather than shunning such technologies, activists must learn to critically appropriate those technologies in the service of progressive causes and liberatory practices. Duncombe agrees that the overarching, dehumanizing spectacle—as described by Debord—must be critiqued and overturned. However, he also agrees that there are liberatory elements within the spectacle. Learning to tease out those elements can enable activists to create an *alternative* spectacle—one that teaches people to be reflective, ethical, conscientious, and active creators rather than passive consumers. It is within Duncombe's framework that SHAC activists employ direct action strategies.

For example, the SHAC home demonstrations are an attempt to amplify the problem (animal exploitation) and the motivation (profit) by creating an alternative spectacle (one based on truth-telling and the adoption of an ethical relation to nonhuman animals). Demonstrators do this by creating a public performance. The demonstrators use their bullhorns to amplify their message and turn a public sidewalk into a public theatre. The power of the spectacle lies in its ability to demand attention and render abstract concepts into accessible courses of action. The method is both confrontational and invaluable. As Jean Baudrillard states, "This is our theatre of cruelty, the only one left to us—extraordinary because it unites the most spectacular to the most provocative" (2001).

The demonstrators begin their performance by ringing the doorbell or buzzing an apartment complex intercom. "Hi, John/Jane [Doe]. We spoke several days ago, but you refused to meet with me in person. I wanted to meet with you and talk about your client, Huntingdon Life Sciences." Once activists confirm that the "target" is home, and the performance takes off, usually beginning with a series of chants. "One, two three, four. Open up the cage door! Five, six, seven, eight. Smash the locks and liberate! Nine, ten, eleven, twelve. John/Jane can go to hell!" These chants solidify the activists' solidarity and remind onlookers that the demonstration was all about targeting John/Jane. In between chants, a few of the organizers might give speeches or proclamations that address the target loudly enough for all to hear. For example, "We tried to meet with you, John/Jane. We are sure you would not want to be affiliated with the grotesque cruelty that Huntingdon Life Sciences is conducting on your behalf." The demonstrators then make sure to recount the horrific vivisection, the thousands of animals ordered from the breeding facility, and the discredited research that results. It is important during such demonstrations for the activists to appear rational and eager to resolve the issue. The demonstrations are intended to make it all look simple: cease relations with HLS and the campaign against *you* will cease.

This spectacle invites the audience (onlookers and passersby) to witness the exchange as it exposes HLS, challenges the violent archetypal portrayals of animal advocates, and mocks many of the taken-for-granted truisms of global capitalism (for example, that our lives should be based on profit and/or that "the market" equals freedom). The proclamations ensure that the audience clearly understands how many animals are being exploited through HLS contracted vivisection. The demonstrators do not break from their theatrical characters during the performance— they playfully engage "the audience" and politely but markedly turn off their bullhorns when a leashed animal is walked past. All of this accentuates the heightened sense of spectacle that is being enacted.

Lastly, the demonstrators consistently use the first name of the person targeted while repeatedly asking the target to come outside and discuss the situation. Those in the "audience" might think that the demonstrators are shortsighted by their faith in such an invitation to talk and discuss. A passerby might stop and say, for instance, "Don't you guys realize this person can't do anything about it? He works for some larger company that doesn't care what one person has to say. He has the job to pay his bills, and if he stands up to company practice then he will just be fired." But the demonstrators are not so naïve; they know full well that the target is unlikely to come outside and even less likely to change his or her company's practice of animal exploitation. Instead, this kind

of demonstration—as a queer performance rather than a literal political plea—exaggerates the agency of the target, and therefore highlights
powerlessness common to the average person living within capitalism.
As an additional queering effect, this demonstration also highlights the
passerby's implicit understanding of this powerlessness. Everyone gets
the insight that we are, for the most part, powerless to effect change, but
no one calls it out. And that is a significant aspect of this spectacle—to
call attention to what we all already know, impelling people to confront
the issues and problems of the current system and thereby become more
empowered to actually enact social change.

SHAC's Use of Play

The use of "play" is a big part of SHAC's direct action strategy. According to activist and performance theorist Benjamin Shepard, play creates
"open spaces where new sets of rules and social relations take shape.
Play refers to the jest infused with satirical performance that brings joy
and lightheartedness to otherwise serious and enraged activism. Here
social actors feel compelled to participate in a broader social change
drama" (2008, 53). Shepard argues that these types of direct actions
serve to empower individuals that are systematically excluded from
bureaucratic decision-making processes; rather than passively accepting the laws, rules, and regulations made by detached decision makers,
people *directly participate* in the reconstruction of alternative reality. That
reality may not be wholesale or long term, but it is, at the very least, the
creation of a new *now* that challenges a targeted grievance. The ability to
create and recreate shared realities during a direct action relies on playfulness exemplified by a series of sarcastic and satirical rituals, such as
collective chants. The spectacle of the protest queers—in other words,
it reimagines and rearticulates—the ways in which dissent is performed
and understood.

The SHAC campaign is obviously not the first to use play and political
theater. Suffice it to say that play and political performance are part and
parcel of most if not all contemporary social movements—the Occupy
movement, the Quebec student strikes, the anti–Iraq War movement, the
global justice movement, ACT UP and the AIDS awareness movement,

Abbie Hoffman and the Yippies, and so on. Playful demonstrations and theatrical protests create a public space to challenge oppressive systems such as homophobia, globalization, economic inequality, and health disparities. Public direct action brings marginalized issues to such centers of daily life as shopping districts and residential neighborhoods. Social movements use play to creatively fuse critiques of social structures with such joyful activities as drum circles, dance, and song (Shepard, Bogad, and Duncombe 2008, 6).

SHAC's use of play is quite telling in the face of its topic/target—animal abuse and exploitation. Activists utilize the empowering nature of play as an attempt to counter the overwhelming sense of loss of animal lives. Continually thinking about the overwhelming sense of animal cruelty and repeatedly protesting outside a lobster restaurant or university laboratory is emotionally exhausting. Constantly reminding oneself of the millions of animals that are killed dominates the work of an animal liberationist. The power structure is so blatantly controlled by animal oppressors that even the most strident campaign can appear minuscule compared to multi–billion-dollar agri-vivisection industries. Play is therefore a way to combat these negative emotions—it is a cathartic release and a creative rechanneling of one's emotional life. Play enables animal activists to laugh even while confronting some of the worst atrocities committed by fellow humans.

While recounting the animal abuses through a megaphone, activists may intersperse a call-and-return chant to lighten the tense atmosphere. For instance, activists in Niagara Falls, Canada, had gathered outside the home of John Holer, founder of the Marineland amusement park. Holer and Marineland were targeted because the amusement park's animal exhibits are not only exploitative, but also negligent and cruel, keeping animals in unsanitary and unsafe conditions. The demonstration concluded with a remix of Carly Rae Jepsen's dreadful (but catchy) radio hit "Call Me Maybe." The activists' playful remix was directed at the Niagara Regional Police (NRP) who had been present the entire time. One demonstrator shared a video and commented that, "five hours with the NRP. We ended it off with a dance party blasting 'Call Me Maybe' into their cars. Don't call me. Ever." (This quote was found on a 2012

Facebook post.) The song and dance party were obviously done in jest, which helped create an uplifting and "spectacular" moment for the activists engaged in a long campaign against Marineland.

The creativity and playfulness of such direct action queers the ways in which marginalized peoples can confront systems of power. SHAC activists, for instance, commonly infuse their chants, proclamations, and printed materials with humor and sarcasm. But this humor and sarcasm are also aggressive, seeking to effect serious social change. As SHAC 7 defendant Josh Harper (2012) states:

> This was the threat of Stop Huntingdon Animal Cruelty; we saw through all of the social conditioning that tells us that we are too weak to effect change. We went straight to the homes of those in power, challenged them on their golf courses, [and] screamed at them while they vacationed at summer homes. We were the barbarians at the gate, an alliance of the kind of people who did not usually get heard by the mega-rich of the world. Tooth and nail we went after their profits, and along the way refused to divide and fracture over broken windows or graffiti. Everyone was welcome if they would fight, and I smile so big [that] it hurts when I think of the grandmothers, the punks, the students, and all the other unlikely comrades who marched together in defiance of the false hierarchy that tells us to keep separate and leave the rich to their own devices. We didn't stay in our place. In fact, we recognized that our place was wherever the hell we chose, and the world of finance and animal abuse was rocked as a result. (SHAC Revisited, n.p.).

This statement helps to illustrate how SHAC's home demonstrators blend both humor and creative aggression into an effective campaign. The strategic use of humor, in combination with physical performance, infuses *power* into play. A playful chant, for instance, can help to interrupt activists' aggressive proclamations and heated interactions with neighbors. That humor then places people at ease, which can actually aid the persuasiveness of the direct action. The fact that any activist can (more or less) spontaneously create and lead a chant at any point during the demonstration also establishes a more open space. In this way, then, the playfulness of chants reflects a wider goal and vision: to create a more inclusive, bottom-up social order in which everyone—both humans *and* animals—are able to live freely and joyously.

Conclusion

The SHAC campaign encourages activists to publicly disrupt exploitive structures through creative means. SHAC's use of performance, direct action, and spectacle queers the act of protest that is aimed at secondary and tertiary targets. Activists creatively engage in playful and satirical direct action while aggressively targeting corporations. The successes of the SHAC campaign demonstrate the power in playful protest, and the importance of direct action in the animal liberation movement.

In the spirit of playfulness and creativity, I conclude by inviting readers to imagine themselves standing collectively with one another. Imagine yourself singing and shouting jovial tunes, dancing on sidewalks, and protesting outside the residences of executives from AstraZeneca, Bristol-Myers Squibb, Pfizer, GlaxoSmithKline, and the like. What songs would you compose, what performances would you embody, what chants would you shout? What cultural assumptions would you challenge, and what discourses would you undermine? And then, more importantly, imagine that the world you are fighting for is actually becoming a reality—a post-capitalist, anti-authoritarian world that is free for both humans *and* nonhumans.

REFERENCES

Baudrillard, Jean. "The Spirit of Terrorism." Translated by Dr. Rachel Bloul. *Le Monde* November 2, 2001. www.egs.edu/faculty/jean-baudrillard/articles/the-spirit-of-terrorism.

Debord, Guy. *The Society of the Spectacle*. Detroit: Black & Red, 1970.

Del Gandio, Jason. "Neoliberalism and the Academic-Industrial Complex." *Truthout*. Published August 12, 2010. www.truth-out.org/archive/item/91200:neoliberalism-and-the-academicindustrial-complex.

Donovan, Josephine, and Carol Adams, eds. *The Feminist Care Tradition in Animal Ethics: A Reader*. New York: Columbia University Press, 2007.

Duncombe, Stephen. *Dream: Re-imagining Progressive Politics in an Age of Fantasy*. New York: New Press, 2007.

Greek, C. Ray, and Jean Swingle Greek. *Sacred Cows and Golden Geese: The Human Costs of Experiments on Animals*. New York: Continuum, 2000.

Graeber, David. *Direct Action: An Ethnography*. Oakland, Calif.: AK Press, 2009.

Dunayer, Joan. *Speciesism*. Derwood, Md.: Ryce Publishing, 2004.

Halberstam, Judith. *In a Queer Time and Place: Transgender Bodies, Subcultural Lives*. New York: New York University Press, 2005.

Harper, Josh. "SHAC Revisited" (2012, July 2). http://angry-hippo.tumblr.com/post/26342116108/this-was-the-threat-of-stop-huntingdon-animal.

Parr, Adrian. *Hijacking Sustainability*. Cambridge, Mass.: MIT University Press, 2009.

SHAC. "AstraZeneca shareholder, AXA & HLS suppliers have protests." Published May 20, 2011 (2011a). www.shac.net/news/2011/may/20.html.

———. "Introduction to SHAC." Last accessed 2011 (2011b). www.shac.net/SHAC/shac_intro.html.

———. "SHAC FAQ's." Last accessed 2012. www.shac.net/SHAC/faq.html.

Shepard, Benjamin. *Queer Political Performance and Protest: Play, Pleasure, and Social Movement*. New York: Routledge, 2008.

Shepard, Benjamin, L. M. Bogad, and Stephen Duncombe. "Performing vs. the Insurmountable: Theatrics, Activism, and Social Movements." *Liminalities: A Journal of Performance Studies* 4, no. (3) (2008): 2–30.

PART IV

INTERVIEWS AND PERSONAL REFLECTIONS

Interview with Joseph Buddenberg
of the AETA 4

Dylan Powell

Joseph Buddenberg grew up in Virginia, where he became active in social justice causes as a teenager. He fed the hungry with his local chapter of Food Not Bombs, and he participated in protests against the policies of the World Bank and International Monetary Fund and against the U.S. invasion of Iraq. He campaigned against Huntingdon Life Sciences (HLS) and became active in animal liberation campaigns just after the SHAC 7 convictions (*U.S. v. Fullmer* 2009). He was one of the first to be indicted under the Animal Enterprise Terrorism Act (AETA) in *U.S. v. Buddenberg* (2009), and was held under house arrest for several months during the pendency of the indictment (the indictment was later dismissed). Joseph currently resides in Oakland, California, where he continues his activism with vegan outreach, companion animal rescue, and political prisoner support work. He has been vegan for ten years.

When did you become interested in animal activism? What compelled you?

The vegan straight edge band Earth Crisis first exposed me to the idea of animal liberation as a teenager. I just happened upon one of their records at a local record store. They were very outspoken about animal rights and "eco" issues. They introduced me to the brutality of animal exploitation and the ethic of veganism. Their songs, imagery, and liner notes challenged me to think about my own complicity in animal suffering. I had never even heard the word *vivisection* before listening to their song "Deliverance." The song described in detail the violence that nonhuman animals endure in vivisection laboratories, as well as the individuals who break down laboratory doors to bring liberation to the animals.

Other bands from that era like One King Down and Raid were very vocal about their support for animal liberation. The vegan straight edge scene tended to focus on militant direct action, and a philosophical support for groups like the Animal Liberation Front. There was definitely, at times, a macho glorification. But I know that I wouldn't have made personal change if those bands and individuals hadn't pushed the envelope by endorsing ecotage and "illegal" direct action. The early Victory Records catalog helped me to frame veganism as, quite literally, the least I could do.

Around the same time, I became involved in other activist causes [that were] introduced to me through the hardcore, punk community. I participated in antipoverty and anti-globalization campaigns. I also experienced state repression and police violence for my early activism. I didn't get heavily involved in animal liberation campaigns until moving to the San Francisco Bay Area around five years ago.

When did you first hear of the Animal Enterprise Terrorism Act? What was your reaction?

I heard about the AETA soon after it was signed into law from an activist working on the campaign against HLS. I wasn't surprised. Our movement is up against some of the most powerful and callous industries on the planet. Though none of the animal exploitation industries are hurting financially, I'm mainly speaking of the pharmaceutical industry. Every year, corporate AETA lobbyists like Pfizer and Wyeth report net revenues in the tens of billions of dollars. I campaigned against the University of California, which has experimented on animals with the funding of Phillip Morris and the Department of Defense. Of course, the wealthy are going to strike back against our movement's momentum and campaign victories utilizing their police forces that have always done their bidding.

It would take a tremendous amount of privilege to expect benevolence or even fairness from law enforcement. Every progressive movement in the United States has faced brutality and repression from the State. Unfortunately, our movement is no exception. My words can't do their work justice, so everyone should read Ward Churchill and Brian Glick's work, learn about COINTELPRO, and understand the role of the State in a capitalist society. Only by understanding the tactics and strategies of the State can we begin to work around them and continue our vital activism.

What do you think got you targeted by law enforcement?

There was an amazing amount of activism aimed at the University of California (UC) for the two-year period in question. From the discovery provided in our case, our attorneys were able to note 162 police reports concerning UC Berkeley vivisection in an eighteen-month period. They simply couldn't catch the anonymous people trying to pressure the vivisectors using a diversity of tactics.

All of the targeted vivisectors at UC Berkeley were visited with illegal direct action. They had their windows broken, received phone calls at home and at work, had their mail illegally forwarded, and received hundreds of e-mail threats. The fight against vivisection had a great deal of energy and momentum at the time and the vivisectors and university officials were in fear of their pocketbooks being further threatened. Clearly, the University of California, a lobbyist for the AETA, met with their friends in law enforcement and pushed them to arrest someone—anyone—to try and stem the tide.

The four of us served as convenient scapegoats precisely because we were so public. For example, one Berkeley vivisector had his home windows broken on several occasions, red paint thrown on his home, and his mail illegally forwarded. His hearsay to the FBI that I was "probably responsible" for all of the sabotage showed up in discovery. I'm sure these kinds of statements made the FBI look at me with even more suspicion. Our arrests were a public relations move for law enforcement to save face—and, as they had hoped, a deterrent against those acting against vivisection in any capacity.

I was very outspoken and was often the only unmasked demonstrator at protests. In their hierarchical minds, and in the minds of the vivisectors who provide written notes which showed up in discovery, I was a leader. The repression would often start small and move up the ladder. The police would cite or arrest me for petty local charges—disturbing the peace, illegal posting of flyers, trespassing, and so forth. When this didn't work, they went federal.

What was the specific charge against you?

I was arrested February 20, 2009, along with three others, on a criminal complaint charging an AETA violation. When I read the complaint and my alleged crimes, I was astounded that a judge would ever give this the go-ahead. My charges were superseded by a two-count indictment around three weeks later. In the end, I was charged under AETA, but not for any alleged economic damage. Instead, I was charged under the specific subsection of the statute that alleged placing individuals in "reasonable fear of death or serious bodily injury." I was also charged under 18 US Code 371—Conspiracy. This is a customary charge for cases with multiple defendants. The charges carried a maximum of five years in prison, had we been convicted.

Strangely enough, the criminal complaint offered more details than the indictment. The complaint contained allegations of chalking "defamatory slogans on the public sidewalk," wearing bandanas and black clothing, chanting slogans, and leaving flyers with the names and home addresses of University of California vivisectors at a Santa Cruz coffee shop. The indictment just offered dates and a recitation of the language in the statute. I believe this was a strategic move for the government. They wanted to be able to arrest anyone where there's a climate of political activity which troubles them, and put it before a jury without any pretrial judicial scrutiny. This failed, and the presiding judge dismissed the indictment for being too vague. Even Judge Whyte, a conservative judge, knew that it wouldn't hold up before the court of appeals in the event of a conviction. His dismissal was without prejudice, meaning the prosecutor can refile charges at any time consistent with the statute of limitations.

How did media identify you? How did you feel about the media representation of the trial?

The local print and TV news coverage was terrible for us. The *San Jose Mercury News* and *Santa Cruz Sentinel* did everything in their power to bias a potential jury pool in the FBI's favor. They called the demonstrations "attacks" and took the FBI's word as gospel. Local FBI spokesperson Joseph Schadler solicited media and appeared on TV and radio broadcasts in a concerted effort to convict us in the court of public opinion. This is atypical because the media usually solicits both sides of the story. The only counter to the press assault against us was one fair piece from a San Francisco weekly, as well as Will Potter's work.

We need to figure out ways to handle corporate press campaigns that come with movement arrests. We need to have folks who can handle the media in a cohesive and professional way.

What was the physical and emotional toll of this case? How has this affected you?

It was an incredibly stressful ordeal. We experienced traumas that most activists will fortunately never have to endure. Homes were raided multiple times. Our cars were searched and impounded. There were physical surveillance operations. There were bogus arrests by local police that continued even after the case was dismissed. There were two court-ordered visits to the local FBI office; one to provide DNA to match bandanas and bullhorns that were seized, and another to provide the FBI two days' worth of handwriting samples, which failed to match fraudulent U.S. Postal Service mail forwarding requests in the names of several UC Berkeley vivisectors.

I was labeled a "terrorist" and smeared in the media. I received death threats on the Internet, which no doubt the FBI would never investigate. Despite having absolutely no criminal record, every time I'm stopped by a police officer, they are informed on their computer database that I'm a member of a terrorist organization. They are instructed to approach with caution and report all contact to the FBI immediately. This sort of insanity will likely follow me for the rest of my life.

Subsequent to my arrest on the AETA charge, I was taken before federal Judge Nandor Vadas, a UC Santa Cruz graduate, for my initial hearing. He stated in court that the complaint was one of the most chilling documents he'd ever read. He, and the later magistrates, gave the prosecutors everything they requested with regard to bail. As a result, I spent the bulk of 2009 on house arrest and was forbidden contact with my codefendants. At the same hearing, Vadas scolded me that the charges "aren't something to laugh about." I guess this was in response to me smiling at my crying friend and codefendant. Comically, he yelled at me to not mess with Genentech, a vivisecting biotech company that I assume he has stock in.

That said, I didn't get involved in this movement for any perceived benefit to myself. Not for money or popularity. We didn't have the support of any large organization or access to many resources. I knew at the start of this campaign that I risked facing severe repression, and I was aware of the government's capability. The campaign was done on a shoestring budget, with a small number of young people and a lot of determination. Yes, we made mistakes and lacked strategy at times. But I believe my heart was always in the right place.

I got involved in this movement because the reality of animal imprisonment brought me to tears, and I strive to be selfless for their benefit. I persevered and faced down a great deal of state repression, and I now know that I can endure any amount of persecution that they throw at me.

As a result of our indictment, there was definitely a decline in activism and direct action in the area, and that is unfortunate. One of the hardest things to deal with was feeling like I was about to go to prison for several years and no one was going to pick up the slack. Campaigns aimed at such wealthy corporations and institutions may take years to see a victory or considerable impact. We can't succumb to the chilling effect that has already scared so many great activists away from our movement. At the end of the day, we're not as disempowered as we may think. The campaign against UC Berkeley shows a multitude of actions across the tactical spectrum, only four arrests, and not a single conviction.

What advice do you have for other activists who are targeted by such repression, or who feel they may be targeted by such repression?

Be effective. Think strategically and make your actions count. We have a tremendous gift and an ability to move beyond the symbolic and save lives with our actions.

I don't buy into the AETA horror stories. While it is troubling that our movement is labeled the "number one domestic terrorist threat" and the State has increased resources and funding to fight us, I don't think this legislation is as groundbreaking as we're making it out to be. If you're at risk of being prosecuted under the AETA, I believe that you'll know it. You're either doing underground direct action, or you're active on a pressure campaign that pushes the envelope and is sending shockwaves through the animal exploitation and murder industries. I made plenty of mistakes with my activism. Let us not make those mistakes again. But let us continue to put the enslaved animals, not our own safety, first.

The SHAC 7 case is still the most troubling case to me, with regard to repression of our movement. It seems they were just very unlucky. They were tried in a conservative district and had an unprepared legal team. The courts have nothing to do with right or wrong, truth or justice. If that were the case, people like Leonard Peltier and Ed Poindexter would not still be languishing in prison after decades for crimes they did not commit. If that were the case, violations of the Animal Welfare Act would not be met with a measly fine while violating the AETA can land you in prison for several years. Solid, experienced attorneys will mean the difference between an acquittal and imprisonment.

Obviously I can't speak to those indicted and accused of sabotage or liberation. But if you are part of this movement and charged with free speech activity, my experience shows that the support will be beyond anything you could imagine. When I was placed in a halfway house following my arrest, dozens of people called the facility and successfully demanded that I be provided vegan meals. Hundreds of people donated funds, organized and attended benefits, and showed their support at every one of our court dates. The support from those I'd never even met really did lift my spirits. If you do find yourself one of the infinitesimally few arrested or imprisoned for aboveground campaigning, you will be taken care of. I would hope that the same is true for those few arrested and imprisoned for underground action.

How do you think legislation like the AETA can be challenged effectively?

I'm not holding my breath that we can overturn a statute designed to protect the profits of the incredibly wealthy pharmaceutical industry. It is, however, worth a shot.

But I think the best way is to focus on material support for individual cases. Let's be prepared for the government's punches before they come. Let's have a general AETA legal fund set up to fight these cases even before another indictment is handed down.

We can show support and build coalitions with other progressive movements so that they have our backs when we are facing repression. And we should have theirs as well. In the AETA 4 (*U.S. v. Buddenberg*) case, the government did not anticipate that experienced radical movement attorneys like Tony Serra and Robert Bloom would represent us. Linking our movement to other anti-oppression movements and unifying with them could make the government reluctant to convene grand juries over basic protest activity. The government wants easy victories. They simply aren't looking to bring cases with questionable outcomes.

We should also make a strong push to seek political prisoner designation for eco and animal liberation prisoners. We have individuals in the United States serving two decades for property crimes only because they are connected to earth and animal liberation movements.

The police and federal agents are protectors of the status quo. We can create a movement and climate that means never talking to state agents, never cooperating with the State, and resisting grand juries. This means rejecting the false "good activist/bad activist" dichotomy and never publicly condemning others' activism or choice of tactics.

Interview with Scott DeMuth, Former ALF Political Prisoner

Brad J. Thomson

Scott DeMuth is a doctoral candidate in sociology at the University of Minnesota, Twin Cities. He is a grand jury resistor and has been indicted for conspiracy under the AETA. He has been actively involved in several prisoner support projects in the Twin Cities, including the Anarchist Black Cross and EWOK! (Earth Warriors are OK!). Scott is currently a member of the nonprofit Oyate Nipi Kte, which focuses on Dakota language and land recovery. He is a member of the Anpao Duta editorial collective, which publishes Dakota language materials and a community journal under the same name.

When did you first get interested and active in social and political issues, and how did animal rights issues fit into that?

The first thing I really did that was kind of a social issue was growing up with my family—my grandmother was active with an organization called Sharing and Caring Hands, which was a homeless shelter. My grandma and my uncle worked there, and all my uncles were involved in different charity work in Haiti and/or homeless shelters. Having family members involved with that meant I grew up volunteering at the shelter and things like that.

It was probably around the age of thirteen that I started really identifying politically in any sort of way. It was actually because of a social studies class where we were talking about different forms of government. One of the first things our teacher covered was anarchism, and she was talking about the idea that there are no authoritative leaders and that decisions are made by consensus. She actually made a really good, accurate representation of what anarchism is, and I was like, "Huh, why aren't we doing that? That makes a lot of sense." I think it was at that point, in seventh grade, when I was like, "Yeah, this is what I'm going to be. I'm going to be an anarchist." It was at the same time that a lot of my friends were getting into punk music, so there were a lot of influences at the same time, and it just kind of congealed and I decided I would be an anarchist. That was the first time I identified politically in any sort of way.

The first project I did was the Anarchist Black Cross (ABC). At the time, I went to Catholic grade school and was very influenced by Catholic teaching, and I was thinking about things that needed to be done that weren't being done. Groups and organizations were feeding people and there were a lot of ways that people could plug in. One thing that I thought was being overlooked was prisoner support. So I started working on that and the Anarchist Black Cross just sort of fit. So prisoner support has been a big part of what I've done politically for the last, well, eleven years now.

That's actually what got me more into animal rights and animal liberation movements. I was sixteen when I joined ABC, and around then there wasn't a whole lot going on to support animal liberation prisoners. We were mostly writing to Black Panthers; there was some stuff going on with Critical Resistance; and there were a few prisoners like Jeffrey Luers.

It was actually when I learned about the University of Iowa raid that I got interested and excited about animal liberation. I was charged with it, but I really had no connection to the action and didn't know anything about it until I read about it online a few months after it happened. After reading about it, I thought, "This is cool, I could support this politically."

I had friends that were vegan and I was dating a girl that was vegan. We did a trade where I would go vegetarian and she would stop drinking and that's what we each did. After that, I kept going with it. So it was really prisoner support work that got me interested, and the University of Iowa thing happened and I just remember being really excited. Even at the time it happened I wasn't vegetarian, but I just remember seeing it and thinking, "This is something I could ideologically support, going in and freeing animals."

It was really when the Green Scare stuff started happening too and Peter Young was arrested in spring of 2005. I remember there being a lot of energy around his case. Following the Green Scare, there was work going on around that and it was a year later I started working with the Twin Cities Eco-Prisoners Support Committee, which became Earth Warriors are OK! (EWOK!).

I know you've been really active around indigenous and decolonization issues. Can you describe how you became involved in that struggle?

I always had an interest in doing indigenous support work. I really got involved when I went up to a land occupation by Sixth Nation, near Caledonia, Ontario, in the summer of 2006. I had known some people who had been involved up there who said they needed support. I went up there with the mindset that I would be an ally in solidarity. It was definitely a turning point in my life, and when I was up there, something clicked and a lot of things came in line together. There were a lot of experiences and relationships that were built there that have been really important in my life.

I went up again in summer of 2006, then again in the winter of 2007, and was spending a lot of time with people there. At one point, I was faced with a decision of, "Is this where I'm going to be and put my energy?" I had an adopted mom up there and I spent a lot of time talking with her about what I needed to be doing. I was in school at the time, but I had this idea that I would drop out and this is where I would be. Right around when I was making that decision, she said, "No, you need to go home and take this work to your own community. You need to take what's going on up *here* back *there*."

It was kind of a challenge, and it was tough at the time because all this work had been laid out and it was easy to jump into a support role. It was daunting on a couple of different levels to be told, "We love you, we want you to be here, but you need to go home." That was definitely a challenge for me.

I ended up coming back home and it was then that I got involved with a group of Dakota people organizing around treaty rights. One thing that kept coming up was that the Minnesota Historical Society was doing a 150th anniversary sesquicentennial of Minnesota statehood. They were really ignoring indigenous voices as part of that. I started getting involved with a group of folks around that, and we started organizing protests around the events that were going on.

One thing included in that was that they were taking covered wagons across Minnesota to Fort Snelling, which is the site of a Dakota concentration camp and one of the first forts in the area. So it was really problematic on lots of levels, and on top of that it was a myth; there was no covered wagon trail which came through the area. A lot of people were upset and felt that their voices weren't being heard, so they thought, "Well, let's make our voices heard."

What happened was we blockaded the fort so the wagons couldn't get through. A lot of young folks were arrested at that time. I think for a lot of us, we didn't think anything we were doing was all that big. It was just that, when your voice is being pushed down and ignored, you feel like you have to do something. We kept going with it, and any time there was a centennial event, we would protest it or try to disrupt it through different means.

For me, having been involved in other protests, it changed my perspective. Just seeing the State's response to these things, it was on such a different level than I was used to. If you go to a vigil or antiwar protest, you see a police presence, but you don't see the same thing that I saw here—state troopers walking around with shotguns and flak jackets. It was definitely within my realm of what I *thought* they were capable of, but it was a different thing to actually see it.

There was one protest at a state park where maybe ten to fifteen folks from the community came to disrupt it—actually, not even really to disrupt it . . . but just came out with a megaphone to tell the truth of what had happened during the War of 1862 and the Dakota removal. And you had officers openly brandishing weapons and intimidating people, which was an entirely different response than I was used to at antiwar protests, for example. I think for me and some other folks, it triggered something to say that the State deals with these communities differently.

They weren't really big events, and we didn't think they would be really big events, but personally they became really meaningful. Having people come together with similar ideas about truth and visions of this land-base and what it could look like. It came together at an important time, and a lot of things have come from that. On a personal level, I came out of that with a relationship with my current partner. There have also been other things—the people that got together there are mainly the people doing a Dakota community journal called *Anpao Duta*, for which I am part of the editorial collective.

Moving on to the issues of your case, you were initially subpoenaed to testify before a grand jury. Can you describe how you reacted to that and what you chose to do?

With the subpoena for the grand jury, Carrie [Feldman] had been subpoenaed first, and I think that kind of came as a shock. A lot of us had been doing different kinds of legal support work, and seeing one of our friends subpoenaed, we were like, "Oh shit." None of us really expected that. After that happened, people were a little more on their toes because usually when one subpoena comes, more are likely to come. So I guess it wasn't totally surprising that I got one a month later, because Carrie and I had previously been in a relationship.

There were a lot of different reasons and things going into play in resisting the grand jury. At the forefront of that was quite simply seeing the institution of the grand jury, for lack of a more eloquent response, as a really fucked-up process. You basically aren't allowed a lot of rights that people believe they have during a trial or even in general. For example, the right not to be questioned, the right to plead the Fifth, the right to have an attorney present, those don't apply in a grand jury. Then looking historically at how grand juries have been used against liberation movements and social movements. Looking at how those two play together—for me it was just an easy decision to decide not to participate in that.

Did you feel supported by the different communities you were organizing within?

Yeah, definitely. That was kind of an interesting thing—just seeing a lot of different communities and scenes, being involved locally in
the anarchist community, the Dakota community in Minnesota and the
native community in the Twin Cities, being a graduate student at the
university. I was a part of a lot of different communities and had a lot of
different areas of support as part of that. I had a great legal support team
and a lot of different support in different areas.

*Native American tribes often have a different philosophy regarding animals
than the typical animal rights movement member. Working with the Dakota
community, were there any issues with you having a charge related to animal
liberation actions, or did it come up in any way?*

It came up in a couple of different ways. Personally, I hunt; I'm a bow
hunter, and that came up in some ways. One way to look at it is that this
is one of the things I would have done differently about my case. You
know, it's hard to think of how to frame things when you're basically
looking at prison time. People put their own spin on things. One thing
that came up as a defense was, "Well, he's a bow hunter, so how could he
possibly be involved in an animal liberation action?" At the time I guess
I appreciated being defended, but on an ideological level there are a lot
of animal liberation actions I totally support. So looking back, that's one
thing I wish I could have done differently. Why couldn't a person who
bow hunts also support an animal liberation action?

I had a lot of discussions with other hunters—even while I was facing
these charges—about food and where food comes from. A lot of interesting things were talked about. Hunters will see traps and trap lines along
the freeway and think that it's not right. It was interesting hearing these
kinds of things come up during conversations. I don't think they consider themselves to be animal rights activists, and animal rights activists
would oppose the fact that they hunt, but there's something else at play
here—there is a consciousness about where our food comes from.

My analysis is definitely not from a single stance on animal rights
or animal liberation, but more from a stance on anti-capitalism. From
an anti-capitalist perspective, I look at some of these animal rights
arguments that factory farms are terrible for animals, but people still

consume soy products that come from factory farms with horrible work conditions.

I think there are a lot of people who support things that the ALF and other animal liberation groups do. Looking at my case, I was charged with the University of Iowa action. But there were a number of people who are not animal rights activists who would say things like, "I don't know if you did this, but I think it's pretty awesome." Some people have sympathy toward these actions and ideologically support them when they happen. I think there's a big disservice done when the issue is framed as a diet choice of eating or not eating meat, rather than looking at our larger economic system and where food comes from. Also looking at all the issues involved in the process, whether it's the pigs and turkeys being slaughtered, or the workers in the fields, or the animals who are displaced because forests are being destroyed for huge factory farming fields. I think the issue is a lot more complicated than just dietary choice. It's easier to make it black and white than to engage in these much more complex ideas and complex struggles.

I would be at a feast and we would be eating deer soup or whatever and I'd have all these people coming up to me, basically saying that they were supporting the actions I was being charged with. It's something I constantly heard throughout my case, and it left me thinking, "How many people are there out there who aren't vegans or vegetarians who support these things?"

After you refused to testify, you were being held in contempt for a few days, and that's when you were charged criminally. What was your reaction when you first found out you were indicted?

My literal reaction was, "What the fuck?" Of all the things I thought might happen, I figured I might get contempt of court for refusing to testify, and I was prepared for that. But to get hit with conspiracy charges for the actual University of Iowa action? Initially, it was very surprising. But when I had a few minutes to think about it, it really wasn't so shocking given the use of conspiracy charges against other political folks—not just in the last few years, like the RNC 8, but over the last few centuries. "Conspiracy" is this vague legal term that's been used to get at different movements.

When I saw the first initial indictment, I just kind of laughed. I didn't think it was actually going to be held up in court; I didn't think the judges in Iowa would go along with it. It was literally, "Mr. DeMuth is being charged with this statute for conspiracy to commit this crime on these dates," and that was it. I was used to seeing someone indicted for having a bag of weed and getting an indictment five pages long. It was ridiculous, and I thought it wouldn't go anywhere. I was more shocked to see a federal judge go for it. In consulting with the legal team and consulting with other lawyers, people were definitely surprised to see what could pass.

Can you talk more about what that was like, with the vagueness of that charge, and what it was like to defend yourself when you didn't know what exactly you were being accused of?

Working on the legal team, I'm sure you understand the frustration of not really knowing. Because it's a conspiracy, my thoughts initially were, "Am I being charged with actually going in and liberating these animals and rescuing them? Am I being charged with being a driver? Or am I being charged with possibly receiving some of these animals?" There were so many different ways it could go, and I don't think the prosecution even knew what they were charging me with. This is really a lot of speculation, but to me it was, "This kid didn't testify in the grand jury, let's throw this conspiracy charge at him and see if he's going to cooperate. We're going to up the stakes a little bit and see if he'll cooperate and give information on other people." Obviously, they thought I had some sort of information because I got subpoenaed to a grand jury.

It seems kind of unclear, too, because looking at the arguments that prosecutor [Clifford] Cronk made throughout the course of the case, it seemed he was trying to avoid ever taking a position about what I may have actually done. Any time he was pushed on that he would evade it, and it seemed like if he knew or had any evidence of me actually being involved with the action in Iowa in any way, he would have come out and said, "We're charging him with this specific thing." Either breaking in, or being involved with receiving the animals and being involved in a conspiracy that way, or we're charging him for being very vocal about the ALF and supporting their actions.

That was really legally frustrating. How do I defend myself without knowing what specifically they're claiming I did? There's no way to fight that. We could have easily shown that I wasn't in Iowa. But if they're trying to make another claim, how do you defend yourself against that?

On the eve of trial, you chose to plead guilty. At this point, the charge was broader and included another incident in Minnesota. If you're comfortable speaking about it, can you discuss that decision?

It was definitely interesting to see what was able to fly in the courts dealing with Iowa with Judges [John] Jarvey and [Thomas] Shields. They brought this charge that came when the statute of limitations should have been up, and it was really a vague indictment and they were allowed to run with it. Then, when contested about the statute of limitations, the prosecutor first alleges that the ALF is one big conspiracy, so the statute couldn't run when actions keep happening.

Then the Second Superseding Indictment included an animal release in Minnesota. The argument was that since the charge was for both incidents, then it was one giant conspiracy to do both of these things. It didn't really seem to hold a lot of weight and it was a really hard argument to be able to connect these two things in any way, beyond being the ALF. But anyone who knows anything about the ALF knows that these are small groups of individuals or autonomous groups that go out and do these actions. It's not one group going out and doing all these actions.

Preparing legally for trial, we were prepared to go ahead and fight these charges. We hadn't really asked for a plea agreement or really shown any interest in one, and it was actually the prosecutor who came to us and asked us if we would be interested. We definitely set some strict limits about what we'd be willing to plea to, and one of those was not pleading to the case in Iowa.

Personally, the idea of doing prison time wasn't as influential, as it was going to court when other people were being subpoenaed to testify.

If they had refused to testify, they could have possibly been facing greater amounts of time than I was offered in the plea agreement. What it came down to for me was a matter of how much time everyone would have to do overall. If I took a misdemeanor for six months, then that would be the least amount of time. If I went to trial and I won, but other people were doing time for contempt of court for longer, then it [accepting the plea bargain] seemed like the best decision.

It may not have been the best decision on a political level to say that this is a valid charge or that this is "animal enterprise terrorism." Politically, these were things I wasn't totally comfortable with. But on a simple level, it was looking at how much everyone had to do, not just me personally.

It's something I think back on a lot; something that I reflected on while I was in prison; and I think about it even now. There's always some level of, "How could things have been different?" I think me doing time wasn't so much the issue. It was more a question of, "Was this the best decision, or could I have made a better decision?" That's what I reflect on more than anything else. There were a couple of layers involved. If I had been charged with conspiracy with a group of other people, it seems easier to fight conspiracy charges as a group. When you're being charged collectively, it's easier to rally together.

Can you describe your experience while you were in prison?

I guess it's not very typical for federal prison. Going to federal prison for six months isn't something you hear about very often. Even being there, when I would be getting processed, guards would be confused. Having a charge like "animal enterprise terrorism" got interesting reactions from people. A lot of people, especially guards, thought I was in for raising animals like dogs or chickens for fighting. Some people thought I was involved in animal abuse somehow or people would ask if I killed an eagle or something. People's perceptions about "animal enterprise terrorism" were interesting, and people were surprised when I said, "No, it's this law that protects these industries." So it was a funny interaction that I had to deal with each time I got to a new place.

In terms of the actual experience, I was in jail in Iowa for about a month, and it wasn't too difficult there. I had done some time in Iowa jail for the contempt, so it was what I expected it to be. As a federal prisoner in county jail, you have an easier time. A lot of people transfer in and out, so people who were in longer had more of a say about certain things—like what's on TV—and people give you stuff when you leave. I met some good folks there, too.

Leavenworth was interesting because it was a private institution and it was just terrible. They give you the cheapest food they possibly can, which basically consists of potatoes at every meal and some sort of mystery meat and maybe if you're lucky you get some sort of vegetables. I think I only saw fruit two or three times while I was there.

I came in at a time when an inspection was coming through to make sure that everything was up to code. The unit I had been placed with was originally being housed in three-man cells and those were not up to code. So they moved everyone out of those units and we were all moved to the segregation unit. Before the inspectors came in, they moved all the third beds to make everything look up to code. That's what's going on in these private facilities. They operate to run as cheaply as possible and to basically get as much money as possible for each inmate.

You saw guards sometimes when they brought people in or came around doing checks during lockdowns. But mostly it was just people hanging out in their units, which can be good in some ways—you don't actually have to interact with guards. But then there are also a lot of cases of sexual assault happening and rapes happening in those private institutions. I don't know what the statistics are compared to the federal institutions, but in my experience I heard of sexual assault and rape happening a lot more frequently in that private institution than the rest of my stay in federal institutions.

After that, I got moved to Oklahoma and I was in county jail there for a week. Then I got moved eventually to Milan, Michigan, to the federal institution. I did about two and a half months there. By that point, I was so sick of being moved around that I was just excited to be in one place and finish my time. While I was at Oklahoma, I met a lot of people who had been transferred from Milan, so I was doing a bit of networking and trying to find out what Milan was like and who I should know about. One thing I did was get the names of the people I was meeting in Oklahoma and ask if there was anyone they wanted me to say *hi* to. That was pretty useful, because when I got to Michigan, as soon as I got to the compound, I made sure to meet a couple of people and work out a chance to say, "This one guy said to say *hey*; he's on his way to Texas." So that way, the first couple of days, I had already built up a network of people.

One of the easiest things about that compound was that there are a lot of people checking your papers to make sure you're not a snitch or sex offender or something like that. Having the grand jury resistance in my paperwork, I could show it with a little bit of pride. Once people found out about that, I think I had an easier time for the rest of my stay there. I would come back to my cell, and I would find things on my bed, like vegetables from the garden, protein bars, shoes, shorts, a radio, things that would help me get set up. It was nice. The time I did there went pretty quick, all things considered. I had an easier time there than at any of the other institutions.

How were you treated by the guards and staff or other prison officials?

It was interesting. Some of them didn't say anything, but a lot of them were like, "Why are you even here?" That's more of the response I got from guards—"Why did they even bother?" Especially when they saw what I pled to, that it was some $500 animal release and it was a misdemeanor. Most of the guards would just roll their eyes when I was being processed. Some of the guards were even shocked about sending a kid to federal prison for six months for a misdemeanor.

Another response was interesting, which I got a couple different times from guards. One time, one of them pulled me aside and said, "I heard your charge and one of my friends did the same thing with a chicken farm and went to county jail with a misdemeanor." She was confused about why I would end up in federal prison, and I told her, "Well, there's this thing called the Animal Enterprise Terrorism Act, and it makes it an act of terrorism to do these things."

I only had a hard time with one officer. He would do the special group assessments to assess the gangs in prison. He pulled me aside and I was put in the Special Threat Assessment group for being part of the

ALF, and he was questioning and harassing me. He wasn't too bad—just kind of an asshole.

As you mentioned, you've done prisoner support work for years. After spending time in prison, would that change your approach to doing prison work in the future, or has it taught you anything specific about prison solidarity?

One of the things I've always done is write letters to prisoners. It was always one of those things that didn't seem as concrete as fundraising. If you raise $300 or $500 for a prisoner's commissary or defense fund, there's a concrete attachment to that and the contribution you're making. I always wrote letters, but I wasn't sure about the actual impact.

But that was the biggest thing I thought about while I was in there—realizing the importance of letter writing. I had letters coming in every day, and it was really reaffirming and empowering. Being in touch with the outside world and knowing that I had a lot of support had a big impact, even just getting one letter. There were times when I was being moved and it was hard to get in touch with me. Oklahoma was one of those places where I was only there for a week, but after a few days I started getting letters.

You feel isolated and alone—especially when you're in transit, because the relationships you develop on the inside and the spot you've settled into are suddenly ripped away. You're transplanted to a new spot. You're sort of in shock and thinking, "Now I'm in this whole new place and I have to build these new relationships." Getting letters during transit was one of the most meaningful times—I didn't feel totally alone and I felt like I could have some connection. For me now, I think about people being transferred, and that will be a time when I put more intention into reaching out to prisoners.

Throughout this process—which isn't completely over, since you're still on probation—what has been the most challenging time? What about the most inspiring?

The most challenging definitely would have been the period of time after I took the plea but before I went to prison. I was basically in this limbo phase. Originally my sentencing date was going to be in December, so I was preparing myself to go to prison at that time. Then it got

pushed back, and I was like, "Okay, I can't really take on any relationships right now and I need to prepare myself for this next stage." On
an emotional level, it was one of the most difficult. Then having it get
pushed back again, it was like starting the process all over. That was one
of the hardest parts, more so than preparing for trial or even [being in]
prison. One of the hardest things was waiting to go to prison; having
that hang over my head, having that weight on my shoulders.

As for the most inspiring, that's kind of a hard one. There were a lot
of different ways I was inspired through the process. One of the most
prominent ones was the amount of support, especially for me and Carrie
when we were subpoenaed to the grand jury. In the Twin Cities, an awesome support group stepped up, even more than I would have expected.
Knowing that in the Twin Cities it was possible to build that kind of
network was really inspiring. Doing support work over the years and
seeing the different kinds of support groups, it was definitely a blessing
to have the one I did. It was definitely a solid crew of folks.

There were a lot of other elements, too. Even while being in prison,
there were a lot of different moments—having conversations with people through letters or conversations with people in prison. There were
different moments that were really impactful.

Interview with Walter Bond, Current ALF Political Prisoner

Carol L. Glasser

Walter Bond, born April 16, 1976, has been an activist in the vegan, animal liberation, and straight edge communities for over fifteen years. ("Straight edge" refers to a subculture, typically surrounding hardcore punk music, that rejects the consumption of any form of drugs or narcotics. It may also refer to refraining from promiscuous sex, prescription drugs, and/or caffeine.) He has spent much of his adult life working toward animal liberation with a focus on sanctuary work and vegan outreach. He was arrested in 2010 for arsons that were attributed to the "ALF Lone Wolf." Walter was convicted of three arsons in Colorado and Utah—at a sheepskin factory, a leather factory, and a restaurant that served foie gras—for which he was sentenced to over twelve years in prison. Though currently imprisoned, Walter refuses to be silenced and continues his fight for animal liberation through his prolific writings.

Note: The following interview was conducted in the summer of 2011, several months prior to Walter Bond's final sentencing for arsons in Utah.

According to your support page, you have been dedicated to the work of animal liberation and anti-capitalism for over fifteen years. Can you please describe how and when you became involved in activism, in particular activism geared toward animal liberation?

In the winter of 1996, when I was nineteen years old, I got a job with a company named Dakota Mechanical. Its home office was in Jefferson,

South Dakota; however, most of its work crews were scattered around the Midwest and Iowa in particular. I was hired as a forklift operator and apprentice plumber. I worked building two separate slaughterhouses, one in Logansport, Indiana—which was a brand new facility—and one in Perry, Iowa, where we built an extension to an already running "kill floor." Both slaughterhouses were IBP (Iowa Beef Producers), which have over twenty death camps in the state of Iowa for pigs alone.

During the six months that I was employed at the Perry, Iowa, facility, I saw every single area of production and confinement. I witnessed daily the profound cruelty that is simply industry standard in "pork production," culminating in viewing a 500-pound pig being beat to death with blunt force by IBP workers. This particular individual animal had escaped his leg hold shackle and went running off the kill floor bleeding from the throat. As he was beaten to death I also witnessed my work crew cheering and high-fiving each other, as if it were a sporting event. This event had a very profound effect on me—a very internal effect.

Before that day I had always viewed the carnage as a necessary evil, but after that day I began to question all of it. Within twenty-four hours of that nameless hog's death I went vegetarian; within two weeks I quit my job; and within ten months I was a vegan and studying any book or information I could find about animal rights. Ironically, at this exact time in my life I came across a CD at a local record store. The band was called Earth Crisis and the CD was titled *Destroy the Machines*. On the back was a dedication to the vegan straight edge. After listening to the music and reading the lyrics, I decided that the movement for total liberation would be my life's work. From then through the last fifteen years I have been an activist.

My main focus for most of those years was vegan outreach and education of the public and also working directly with animals at sanctuaries and rescues. As time went on I began to feel disempowered, always picking up the pieces of human cruelty. It seems I was constantly viewing or helping animals that had suffered so terribly at the hands of speciesist human oppressors. I finally got sick of it. Talking with people was simply not direct enough in the context of how animals suffer and die. I believed then, as I do now, that the enormity of this oppression and murder deserved a severe response. To that end, I became an illegal direct activist, employing arson as a tactic to not only shut down businesses that make money from animals' dead bodies, but also to bring these issues to light in the media.

I became an operative under the banner of, and according to, the guidelines of the Animal Liberation Front. I authored two communiqués under the name "ALF Lone Wolf" and passed them anonymously to the media, giving a brief explanation of why the arsons were committed. Today, as a prisoner for those actions, my activism consists of writing. I mainly try to explain the philosophy, tactics, and ideology of abolition and animal liberation activism. I do this through provocative articles written primarily in the manifesto "this is how it is" style.

For what reasons were you targeted by law enforcement?

I was targeted by law enforcement because my brother called the FBI crime tips hotline after he learned there was a reward for information leading to the arrest and conviction of the person or persons involved in the arson at the Sheepskin Factory in Denver. After reviewing the discovery documents in my case, it's clear no government agency had any clue it was me until my brother called them out of the blue. It's also clear that his motivation was reward money, which, incidentally, he never got paid. In order to collect he would have to testify at my trail, and since I pled guilty and waived my right to trial, he got nothing. In any event, after the arson at the Tiburon Restaurant, the stress of living homeless, and my ALF campaigns, [it all] had caught up with me. I was worn out both mentally and physically. I had recently contacted my brother, and he was curious as to why I was seemingly homeless, unemployed, and wandering around the United States. In a moment of weakness and against my better judgment I told him to Google the Sheepskin Factory in Denver and that's what I'd been up to. The first website that came up on the search engine was an animal rights website. After he saw that he began reading about the Sheepskin Factory arson in the mainstream media online, where he found out about the reward. Within forty-eight hours of our phone conversation he was working with the ATF [Alcohol, Tobacco, Firearms and Explosives] and FBI.

For the next four weeks our phone conversations and my wanderings around Salt Lake City were monitored. He lured me back to Colorado with promises of money and a place to stay and rest—even going so far as to send me pictures of my nieces and nephews I have never met. I went to Denver to meet with my brother who had traveled to Colorado from Iowa under the false pretense of helping our half-brother move. He got a hotel room, which I found out later was being audio and video monitored by the Feds.

Tired from my travels and happy to see my brother after many years, we began to talk. He began telling me about crimes he had committed, and soon we were talking away. It was then that I gave him a rather detailed account about my arsons, after which he drove me up to the northern suburbs to talk to an old employer about some construction work. I was under the illusion that I would see my brother later that evening. Instead, I was arrested by the FBI in the front yard of the house my brother had dropped me off at. Once under arrest I was interrogated and told by the cops that if I did not speak with them they would charge my bother with my crimes. They told me that anything I would say could only help me. I refused to say anything, not one word. My interrogation lasted maybe ten minutes, after which time no recognizable federal agent has ever asked me about anything again.

Of course, now, in my prison cell, as I reflect back on that meeting with my brother, it is the biggest regret of my life. However, by working alone in my illegal animal liberation campaign, I was able to keep that mistake limited to only me having to deal with the repercussions. And already I've begun making peace with my regret. While it is true that I will always hate my brother absolutely and vociferously, I also know that it was an honest mistake on my part. I had taken on more stresses in my life than ever before and was in a vulnerable and compromised position, and the FBI and my brother had perfect timing in exploiting that.

Can you please describe the legal charges against you? Do any of them include charges under the Animal Enterprise Terrorism Act (AETA)?

In Colorado I was charged with one count of federal arson. It's considered federal because the business itself is involved in interstate commerce, meaning they ship and receive items across state lines just as nearly every business does. [I was also charged with] one count of "threats, acts, and violence against an animal enterprise" under the AETA. I received a five-year prison sentence for the arson and also five years concurrent for the AETA charge, meaning I did not get any additional time for my AETA charge. But I do now have the label of "domestic terrorist," which may affect my security rating within the prison system and definitely does whenever I am moved from one facility to another.

Currently, at the time of this interview, I am in Utah and have just pled guilty to my two remaining arson charges, which are also federal cases. In exchange for my pleading guilty the government agreed to drop my two AETA enhancements. Since I already have one on my record from Colorado, and the enhancements do not affect my time regardless, it is literally no help to me. Which is of course why they allowed it.

The ridiculous thing about the AETA in my cases is that it's an enhancement that alleges my arsons are made worse because of them being animal rights related. What is the logic here? Had I been burning things down at random because of compulsion or pyromania, that would be better? Surely I would not have faced domestic terrorism enhancements even if those fires would have resulted in death! But since I had an animal liberation message it's worse...only to the government. I might add at this point also that it's not an accident that no one was harmed. I took many security precautions to ensure that all I was engaging in was property damage.

It's a strange type of terrorism that harms no life. I try not to let buzzwords bother me, but equating me or the Animal Liberation Front with organizations that behead people on live video streams is ludicrous! [Beheadings were occurring in the U.S.–Iraq war during the mid-2000s.] The true terrorists are those industries that perpetuate the animal and Earth holocaust that is raging around the world. Wherever mechanized society exists, *there* you will find billions of victims of true terrorism— mainly our Mother Earth, her animal nations, and many people deemed "expendable humanity" by the power elite.

The media reported on some of the actions for which you were charged before they were tied to you. How did the media initially portray these actions? Is it any different from how they portray you or these actions now?

It's true that the "Lone Wolf" arsons caught the eye of local media in Denver and Salt Lake City. But I feel that outside of the animal lib community the mainstream media did not want to pay it too much attention. The tone of much of the television coverage was very matter-of-fact, but they did read communiqués in their entirety and give a fair amount of attention to what the Animal Liberation Front is and some brief history of past actions.

During the time I was first arrested I was an easy target for criticism, being as I am somewhat of a spectacle with half my face tattooed and "vegan" tattooed across my throat. The media at once set out to vilify me and make me look like a hypocrite or lunatic. That did not at all shock me. What did, however, was the initial response from the animal rights community. The first letter I ever received in jail was from some anonymous person accusing me of eating burgers at a BBQ and being nothing but a joke to most "real animal rights advocates."

The first interview I ever granted was with some animal welfarist creep that scolded me about someone burning down his mother's house and then generally poking fun at me and my tattoos. It was only after I debated him into a corner three or four times in a row that his tone began to change and he admitted I actually may have some brains after all.

It was shortly thereafter that I decided to start writing statements and articles. I figured the only way to combat the negative media about me and the militant struggle for animal liberation was to show everyone that I have thought deeply about the issues and spent years verifiably fighting for this cause. Later on, I kept writing because I love to, and it's very important for me to stay as active as I can. In this way I am able to reach more people now than I ever was able to with arson. Still, I will never forget how so many reactive, so-called animal rights activists and anarchists were incredibly quick to try and assassinate my character without ever knowing me.

My first major hurdle was not the mainstream media—their response was predictable. My first hardships were immediate and internal. I also will never forget a finite few people that I had never before met in my life that have given me support that put my mind at ease. The good doctor Jerry Vlasak, Nicoal Sheen, and Greg Kelly come to mind here.

After those first few months, it became obvious that the tide had turned and that many of those who thought I was a crackpot now think everything I have to say is very valid. The mainstream media seems to take me and my message of animal liberation, whatever it may take, more seriously as well. Of course, their vilification of me never stops. But I'm fine with that so long as there is talk about the animals' plight. At any rate, I made a conscious decision from the outset of my arrest not to be reactive. When I speak out I say what I mean and what I feel, regardless of what the media thinks, or my supporters, or even courts of law. I'm constantly reevaluating my writings and statements to make sure I am not being provocative simply for shock value or holding back to appeal to more people. I think the countless billions of animals we cannot save at least deserve to have a few people keep it real and speak clear truths and also an underground army to secure their lives and freedom.

The experience of activism and of incarceration can be extremely traumatic. What were the hardest emotional, mental, and physical experiences you have had?

Within activism the hardest part for me is never feeling like I'm doing enough. The burden of compassion is such that the more you care, the more you act, [and] the more of yourself you give away. You give until there is nothing left and then you realize you cannot single-handedly change institutionalized cruelty. That's the point when many activists burn out and stop trying. They fail to recognize that perpetual struggle against these atrocities and oppressions is the victory! And that the relentless feeling of not doing enough is par for the course. But still, it is difficult and at times depressing.

As far as incarceration is concerned, I'm still wrapping my mind around the fact that I will most likely spend several years of my life in a cage. My parents are old, and I wonder if I will see them again as a free man. I worry about what kind of hellhole the prison system will find for me since they seem to hate my defiance and outspokenness so much. All of these things I am still digesting.

There is no way for me to accurately portray the life I now lead. If it were just jail, that's not such a big deal—several million people have gone to prison for long periods of time. Being able to cope with that is not at all insurmountable. But add to that dealing with your own brother snitching you off, the media, my own activism which never stops, courts, plea agreements, struggling with an inadequate vegan diet, and continually trying to motivate a movement of lazy, whiny Americans to liberate animals and get passionately active, mentally and emotionally. It's too much for my brain. It's like if you were set down in a room that was full of enough food to feed a banquet hall and you had to try to eat everything all at once; it's too much to digest! So I just focus on whatever is on my plate for the day.

And ultimately, nothing that I'm going through will ever compare to what animals suffer at the hands of speciesist human oppressors. For entertainment, food, vivisection, clothing, and hundreds of other novel and unnecessary reasons animals live and die in conditions of filth and squalor, sadism and pain that we cannot even truly comprehend. Actually, empathizing with their plight never ceases to lessen my own.

I know that activism has its rewards, and incarceration may even have some positive aspects. What have your most rewarding experiences been?

In activism my rewarding experiences have been profound. I have had my face licked by baby llamas, which, by the way, are some of the cutest little critters I have ever seen! I have learned how to gobble at just the right octave to get turkeys to gobble back in unison. I have felt a liberated rooster purr in my lap and then three weeks later try to peck my ankles off! I've gotten a neck massage by a python. I made friends with a goat named Jeffrey who was just as cantankerous as myself. One time a goose protected me from a pig that was bullying me, and that same pig, Lucas, used to demand that I give him a good ear scratch. I have educated people about animal liberation and veganism and am proud to say that more than a few people in Colorado and the Midwest went vegan because of me. I've argued with animal abusers that were quite confused about how to intimidate a 6-foot 2-inch, 220-pound vegan straight edger covered in tattoos! In the underground I experienced the true freedom and effectiveness that can only be known with a bandana and cover of darkness. I've gone to sleep still smelling like gasoline and with a big smile on my face. These are just a few of my amazing experiences as an animal liberationist and direct activist.

It seems that the more I have given of myself the more I have gained in return. Interconnectedness is like that. Despite the hardships I am absolutely honored to speak, act, and defend all innocent life, and I will never forget that it is a privilege and my duty to do so.

And prison, just like all things, has its good and bad. On the positive side, it's a far simpler life. I prefer real experiences and interactions. There is a certain honesty to prison and a lot less pretense. Modern civilization has become a fear-based culture of subjectivity and fakery. In prison you know who is friend or foe. You know who the oppressor is. They come here every day and we call them correctional officers. They even know they're here to oppress us. At least, everyone is not busy trying to look like a good person but not actually being a good person.

I'm able to read and write as much as I want, undisturbed. I am able to have the time to focus on exercise and sport. And I plan on learning Spanish fluently, writing a couple books, and earning a degree while incarcerated. Time in prison is only a detriment if you don't use it.

What advice do you have for other activists regarding political repression and challenging the AETA?

As far as challenging the AETA, I don't have much practical advice since that falls very much into a realm of activism that I have no experience in—mainly, the political. I definitely will say that in a court of law, in my experience, the AETA is more about attaching a label to you. If I were facing the AETA charge alone I would fight it until the end. Legally, the only way to challenge any statute and put it on trial is to plead not guilty and make the government define it. That's one of the main problems with the AETA—it's too fluid and elusive. But as I said, in my case, it was just a splinter in the two-by-four.

Regarding the political repression of the Earth and animal liberation movements, my advice is never give in to it. One must understand that when a government seeks to dismantle a social justice cause it does so through intimidation and often violence. It also seeks to scare many by punishing one. We must think in terms bigger than just ourselves.

Ours is and must always remain a selfless movement. This is the price of admission for any revolutionary cause. And this is a revolutionary cause because we seek a change in human society diametrically opposed to the status quo.

Everything has been built thus far from the standpoint that our Mother Earth and her animal nations are ours to use in any way we wish. Historically, these types of drastic changes have and do occur, but not without a multifaceted fight on all fronts. These changes don't occur without sacrifices, passion, single-pointed focus, correct tactics in action, and defiance in the face of adversity!

Our movement has come nowhere close to paying its dues; we are nowhere near earning our right to change the institutionalized brutality. Will we? No one can honestly answer that, not right now. But the true beginning of that process starts with you and with me. It begins with a resolve to never lose hope, to never lose heart! The path of action that that resolve leads each individual to is tailor-made for each person's individual nature, talents, and abilities. The answer to repression is revolutionary progression! In other words, the way is through it. Inevitably, we answer to those voiceless animals that have no viable representation in the human world, and what they would want us to do is the same thing you would want another to do if you were in their predicament. You would want freedom from fear, torture, murder, rape, and objectification by any means necessary, whatever it may take!

INTERVIEW WITH JOSH HARPER
OF THE SHAC 7

Dylan Powell

Josh Harper was raised in the Pacific Northwest and has been an activist for over fifteen years, struggling for animal liberation and wilderness defense. This has included campaigns against whale hunting, deforestation, vivisection, and fur. Josh has also dedicated time and efforts to creating and archiving alternative radical media, with the *Breaking Free* video magazine (late 1990s) and most recently with the radical earth and animal liberation archive project, The Talon Conspiracy (formerly Conflict Gypsy). In 2000 and again in 2001, Josh defied grand jury subpoenas investigating the Animal Liberation Front and Earth Liberation Front. Josh was later part of the Stop Huntingdon Animal Cruelty (SHAC) campaign against Huntingdon Life Sciences (HLS) and in 2006 was sentenced to three years in prison as part of the SHAC 7 trial. He is currently out of prison, off probation, and living in Portland. He is also working on a book that will chronicle the history of the radical animal liberation in North America from 1977 to the present.

Josh can you please tell me how, when, and why you got involved in political activism?

My initial activism was inspired by my mom. She was always a very compassionate person and was concerned with the popular human rights causes of the '80s, including the rights of farm workers to not be sprayed with cancer-causing pesticides, to have fair wages, and to be treated with dignity and respect. In the '90s, she took me to some protests against the Gulf War and that [was] when I started to develop my own politics as I met young activists for the first time.

When did you specifically get involved with animal liberation, how old were you, and can you tell me the story?

Since I was very young I had always had an affinity with animals and didn't like human treatment of nonhumans. Like so many other people in this culture, I was made to feel numb towards animals after having my concerns about them ridiculed, but in my mid-teens I went vegetarian, and in my early twenties I met a vegan feminist named Davida Douglas who helped me change my sexist and speciesist attitudes and behaviors. She started taking me to the People for Animal Rights office in Portland where I met Craig Rosebraugh, Elaine Close, and other animal liberationists. It all sort of unfolded rapidly from there.

When you got involved with the SHAC campaign in the U.S., did you think it was going to be as large and effective as it was?

I didn't know what would happen with the campaign against HLS; I just knew that the militant grassroots in the U.S. wasn't seeing the kind of successful campaigning happening in Europe at the time. When a chance to do something more strategic came along, I jumped at the chance and encouraged others to do the same. For all of the wonderful potential of our movement, we fall short too often, and I saw HLS as a target that the grassroots could unite behind.

Did you think you were going to receive that much repression from what you were doing?

I knew that I was going to do some time [given the nature of the movement and the political context], but I thought it would be a few months on some misdemeanor charges. I didn't expect to serve three years for a couple of public speeches.

Would you call yourself nonviolent? And if so, how do you follow that throughout your life on a daily basis?

I am nonviolent to the degree that most people are nonviolent. I have very little cause for physical or verbal aggression in my day-to-day interactions with other people. In general, I think that violence is counterproductive.

When you were arrested in 2004, what were you charged with? Were any charges dropped or changed, and if so, why?

I was initially charged with one conspiracy count for violations of the Animal Enterprise Protection Act, but a superseding indictment added a telecommunications conspiracy charge for describing how to send black faxes.

What was your first reaction to being arrested? What did your friends and family think or do? How did your relationships and your job, if you had one, change? Were you fired?

I know that there is a macho political line in the animal rights world where we are supposed to bravely face arrest and not care about consequences, but when the Department of Homeland Security knocks at your door, of course you feel some fear. I didn't know what was going to happen to me, or what charges were ultimately going to be brought. I was out on signature bond by that night, though, and managed to keep my job. My mother and sister were very supportive of me, but my grandmother was concerned that I was a terrorist, and most of my other family members treated me as though I was a dangerous lunatic as well.

During your arrest, what would you have done differently, if anything?

There is only one way to handle yourself during an arrest—keep your mouth shut, keep your head up, and demand to see your lawyer. I did those things and I wouldn't change anything about that.

During your trial, working with your lawyer, your fellow SHAC 7 (U.S. v. Fullmer, 2009) defendants, and your support committee, what did you think went well? What would you have done differently?

This is a difficult question because nothing went very well for us. We had terrible legal advice, almost no funding, and supposed allies who helped the prosecution more than they helped us. I wish I had been more vocal about how people like Jerry Vlasak and Pam Ferdin used our trial to promote their own agenda, I wish that I had fired my lawyer, and

I wish that I had been kinder to my codefendants in some of our more stressful moments.

How has prison changed you? What did you learn about being in prison?

Prison taught me some valuable lessons about my ability to cope with duress and repression, and in some ways I feel stronger. But I also learned that there is nothing romantic about the prison experience, and that the threat of imprisonment is something we need to take seriously. I am still dealing with the trauma of what I saw and endured behind bars.

Can you speak to the emotional, mental, and physical trauma that you went through?

Prison is one of those things that cannot really be described; you can only know what it is like by passing through it. Even though I was at a relatively safe prison, I went through some terrible difficulties, including spending ninety-six days in the hole, during which time I was locked down twenty-four hours a day with two other men in a cell designed to house one person. One of my cellmates was a guy who was doing time for torturing people to make them pay their drug debts. He was remarkably violent and was in the hole for raping another prisoner. At night, I slept with improvised weapons that I bought from the orderlies when we would get taken to the showers. Living with that sort of fear wears you down, especially when you cannot speak about it. Friends of mine from the outside world would visit, and I could tell that it was taxing for them just to go through the intake process, so I didn't want to scare them away by sharing everything that was happening.

That whole thing was really just the tip of the iceberg, though. My father died while I was in prison, and I found out about it in the visiting room. In that hypermasculine environment, I couldn't show any emotion, so I just had to keep it all inside. I missed his funeral, just like I missed my grandmother's funeral. My girlfriend of six years left me while I was in prison, and I just had to eat all of that despair.

The worst thing for me, though, was that I was a big-city environmentalist in a small-town prison in Oregon. The surrounding towns were full of idle timber mills and other extraction industries that had been slowed through the rise of the Northwest's wilderness defense movement. The guards hated me, and as I wouldn't play along with the race politics in prison, no one had my back. The staff knew that they could fuck with me and get away with it, so for a period of several months I endured humiliating pat-down searches from one officer. It started out as uncomfortable and before long moved to outright sexual assault.

I am still dealing with the things that happened to me behind bars, and I am sure that I will be dealing with them for the rest of my life. I can't even bring myself to speak about all of it, yet. There is one bright side, though—I swore that the prison system would not be able to take from me the things that I loved most about myself, and I am proud to say that I kept that promise. I am still vegan, still active, and still maintain that mix of deep love and passionate anger that made me a fighter to begin with.

How do you think the movement has changed from the "no compromise" radical grassroots animal liberation movement of the 1990s to today?

I could fill several books with all the differences between now and the '90s. The important thing is that we are still a movement, and despite the best efforts of some very powerful groups and individuals, we are still fighting. I'd like to see a return to some of the regional networks that we had back then, but other than that there is little I would emulate from that period. For all of our sacrifice and bluster in those years we really accomplished very little. If we could combine the fighting spirit of those years with some new strategies and better infrastructure we could go very far!

I guess one difference worth noting is that in the '90s, you were judged by what you put into the movement and how hard you fought. In the age of Facebook, you can pretend to be an activist by posting tough-sounding blogs and no one seems to notice that the posturing loudmouths aren't the ones actually putting up a resistance to speciesism. That is sad, and I hope it changes soon.

If you were going to give advice based on experience, what would you put forward as "effective"?

Well, before I can answer this I would like to first say that experience has taught me that our opponents will react to protect their financial interests and power, so our strategies must take into account likely back-lash and have a plan for continuity of action. Without that, our efforts are futile. That being said, "effective" is always a matter of scale, and our goal must always be to increase that scale.

For example, liberating animals from a factory farm is effective in saving those lives, but that same action can be even more effective if a well-written statement is issued defending the action; and that statement is even more effective if a reputable, popular group supports it; and their support can be even more effective if they were to suggest other people replicate such actions, and so on. The same thing goes for anything we do. Whether you are involved in vegan education, or building sustain-able, compassionate food networks for the poor, or giving sanctuary to animals, or increasing their habitat through wilderness offensives, always aim higher and try to push your area of influence as far as you possibly can.

Why do you think the AETA was passed just months after your trial?

I think it was because the rich want to continue being rich, and ani-mals are the raw materials that many of them turn into money. Money controls politics in this country, so it goes without saying that animal abusers have more legislative pull than we do, especially given the fact that they can prop up or take down the tax base of entire regions. When we were convicted and it became clear that the prosecution was not going to get the kind of sentencing they had hoped for, the industry acted to protect its own interests. It wasn't hard for them to do—they were armed with some of the ugliest rhetoric you can imagine from peo-ple who never in a million years would have acted upon their fantasies of "shooting vivisectors on their doorsteps." The industry just repeated over and over that someone was going to be killed, and then they used the testimony of certain posturing do-nothings to confirm the paranoid nonsense that they were feeding Congress.

What advice do you have for activists who are facing political repression or who want to challenge the AETA?

As far as practical advice goes, plan for repression before it occurs. Be in touch with good attorneys and try to build bridges with even better attorneys! Learn about and practice security culture, and don't help our enemies by giving them prosecutable evidence on yourself or your friends. Never, ever, ever talk to law enforcement.

Also, be kind to others in and outside of the movement, even when you disagree with them, because those are the people you might need to ask for solidarity later on. If you aren't in love with cupcake-pushing, potluck-planning slacktivists, simply do what you do and encourage like-minded folks to join you. When you need bail money or a job while you are on probation those "lifestyle vegans" that you abhor are the ones you might need to approach—so don't burn bridges.

Next, work to build an atmosphere of support and resistance, and contribute to the defense of others already facing repression—*especially* those folks outside of our own movement. When the SHAC 7 were indicted, no one came to our aid, and part of the reason for that was that we had shown so little solidarity across movement lines when other folks needed it. Animal activists in San Francisco, however, attended demonstrations against grand juries targeting other political movements, and when they began receiving subpoenas they had numbers and resources that weren't available to SHAC.

Finally, fight bravely. No struggle in history ever succeeded without experiencing some degree of brutality. If you are sincere in your desire to make a better world for the oppressed, chances are good that at some point you will suffer for your efforts. If you only choose the path of comfort, though, you will never see progress. So find your courage, and when you run out of it, borrow some from your friends. And when they run out, try to remember all of those beautiful people throughout history who spit in the faces of tyrants and laughed on the gallows. We may not have their courage, but we can do our best to honor their memories by forging ahead for one more day, and then another. And then another...

A Personal Story
and a Plea to Other Activists

Aaron Zellhoefer

First they came for the socialists,
and I didn't speak out because I wasn't a socialist.
Then they came for the trade unionists,
and I didn't speak out because I wasn't a trade unionist.
Then they came for the Jews,
and I didn't speak out because I wasn't a Jew.
Then they came for me,
and there was no one left to speak for me.
> **—Martin Niemöller**

The major problem with the Animal Enterprise Terrorism Act is that it criminalizes one's politics rather than one's political activity. This federal law, passed in 2006, is directed at activists that target "enterprises" (companies, corporations, and, presumably, individual profit-seekers) that use animals. I believe this law sets a dangerous precedent, and if it goes unchallenged it could lead to other copycat federal laws—for example, an arms manufacturing enterprise protection act, an old-growth logging enterprise protection act, a sweatshop enterprise protection act, and so on.

If this is true, then other activists have a direct investment in challenging and overturning the AETA. But, from my own experience, this seems like an uphill battle. That's because there seems to be a complete lack of awareness about the AETA from participants in other social justice movements. I am an activist who works at the intersection of many different issues: gay rights, environmentalism, labor struggles, anti-militarism, etc. Unfortunately, I have seen first-hand the apathy, and at times blatant disregard, for the government's assault on animal rights activism. I have stood on picket lines and have provoked many conversations with other demonstrators about this threat. The reactions have ranged from ignorance to dismissal. Such responses are often rooted in a deep interest in *not* legitimizing the anti-speciesist cause because doing so means challenging significant parts of people's diets, wardrobes, entertainment, cultural traditions, and even religious heritages. Simply put, embracing an animal rights ethic—no matter how philosophically, ethically, ecologically, and scientifically sound—is too much; it makes life "too uncomfortable," and is thus selfishly trivialized. I hate this attitude, but I can understand it. But what I really find incomprehensible is the failure to acknowledge the root problems of the AETA. In my opinion, the AETA should be seen as a test run for other possible laws; a law that has been created for and applied to a small and marginalized niche movement, but in the future could be broadened out to a much grander corporate-sponsored and government-colluded assault on all kinds of activists and causes.

From my experience, the best way to pierce this naïveté is to inform other activists about the seemingly far-fetched, but unfortunately very true, story from my own life. The AETA doesn't just challenge or frustrate noble attempts to save and protect nonhuman animals; it also ruins the lives of those who dare to speak out. My story starts with what seems like a silly, heavy-handed presence of federal law enforcement. Since the late 1990s, I have seen countless demonstrations surveilled by the FBI. These demonstrations have been typically small, permitted, and law-abiding events. The presence of the FBI has often taken the form of agents in their signature windbreakers videotaping every activist and placard within sight. The FBI's presence, and what it forebodes—e.g., grand jury subpoenas, visits from agents to the workplaces of activists, being named in civil litigation, possible indictments for Kafkaesque conspiracy charges—intimidates and therefore chills future expressions of civil dissent. This, of course, leads to a trend: One or two visits from the FBI often leads to a precipitous drop off in the number of people participating in future events.

Law enforcement intimidation is obviously not unique to animal rights activism, and there is a long, sordid history in this country of disgracing the constitutional protections to speak and protest. Take, for instance, the famous case of Charles Schenck. Schenck was the secretary of the Socialist Party of America during the early twentieth century. As a protest against World War I, he sent out leaflets to potential draftees asking them to oppose the war. That seems reasonable enough, especially in the United States, where we supposedly have the right to free speech and the right to petition the government for a redress of grievances. But Schenck was charged and convicted under the Espionage Act of 1917. The Supreme Court heard his case and ruled that his conviction was constitutional. According to the Court, the First Amendment did not protect the behavior of handing out leaflets that encouraged insubordination. The Court's summary basically argued that wartime circumstances permit the government to restrict First Amendment rights. In his famous written opinion, Oliver Wendell Holmes, an associate justice of the Supreme Court during the *Schenck v. United States* case of 1919, set precedence for the "clear and present danger" test:

> The most stringent protection of free speech would not protect a man in falsely shouting fire in a theatre and causing a panic.... The question in every case is whether the words used are used in such circumstances and are of such a nature as to create a clear and present danger that they will bring about the substantive evils that Congress has a right to prevent.

In other words, if you were an antiwar activist in the earlier part of the twentieth century, you could not hand out leaflets in opposition to the draft because the United States was at war. Such behavior was considered equivalent to yelling fire in a crowded theater, thus placing people in unnecessary danger. This is not only illogical, but also unconstitutional.

This brings us back to the current problems with the AETA and the misplaced attention given to animal rights activism. Throughout the course of just one grassroots animal rights campaign from 2002–2004, literally hundreds of law enforcement agents participated in a coordinated crackdown on an all-volunteer, nonprofessional effort dedicated to closing the notorious animal testing lab Huntingdon Life Sciences (HLS). It is not an overstatement to say that these law agencies used Orwellian methods: for instance, wiretapping the phones of the campaign headquarters and the personal lines of the volunteers; listening to the most intimate conversations and even mocking them, as later revealed in court transcriptions; raiding the homes of key organizers and seizing all computers, files, campaign paraphernalia, and personal items; paying confidential informants and planting plainclothes agents at events to gather silly gossip and/or to provoke illegal activity; showing up unexpected to embarrass or threaten the employers, relatives, and loved ones of key organizers; and ultimately, prosecuting and imprisoning several activists for no actual criminal wrongdoing aside from their public statements. This is where my story personally begins.

We received a phone call around 5:00 A.M. one morning in May of 2004. I was living in Northern California with my partner Kevin and two others involved in a campaign to close the aforementioned lab (HLS). The caller was a friend whom had just been alerted that at 6:00 A.M. EST a couple of prominent activists had been arrested by federal authorities for violations of the Animal Enterprise Protection Act. We were told there were other names on the indictment.

Kevin got up, showered, and dressed in appropriate court clothing. He had been anticipating this moment ever since he found out that a grand jury had been impaneled over a year earlier to investigate the campaign of which he was the president. The rest of us nervously tried to go back to sleep, hoping that he was wrong. But at 6:00 A.M. PST, Kevin stood at the picture window of our rented hillside home and watched as an army of masked, shielded, and heavily armed agents ran at the house complete with a battering ram. I remember Kevin yelling to the rest of the house, "here we go, here we go!"

Within those first few chaotic minutes our home filled with agents representing the FBI, the Secret Service, the ATF, and U.S. Marshals Service. Their guns were drawn and pointed at our heads. The two companion dogs Kevin and I cared for—a gentle and fat beagle and an eager and playful Labrador retriever—were threatened with death if they did not "shut the fuck up." Kevin and our two housemates were all cuffed and carried out to awaiting unmarked cars, and I was chained to a chair, half naked, while the agents conducted a "search" of our home.

Kevin and six others, who would become known as the SHAC 7, were all indicted for conspiracy to violate the Animal Enterprise Protection Act (AEPA, although at the time this was already being called the Animal Enterprise Terrorism Act, AETA) and related charges. The indictment laid out no specific allegations of surreptitious illegal activity against any of them. Hundreds of agents spent thousands of hours, and the operation must have cost millions of dollars. But strangely, the entire case rested on what was taken from public sources of information: the campaign website, recorded speeches given at demonstrations, and comments on radio interviews and printed in comical newsletters. The indictment was brought down in New Jersey by Chris Christie. Christie, now the governor of the state, was at the time the U.S. Attorney for the District of New Jersey. He was appointed by George W. Bush, and at the time of appointment he had never tried a criminal case.

Over the course of 2004 and 2005, I struggled to watch Kevin and the others reject plea bargains. Despite the fact that all odds were against them and that they were looking at possible twenty-year sentences, they maintained their innocence and took their case to trial not once but twice. After an initial mistrial, they proceeded to a second trial in February of 2006 in New Jersey. From the very start, the deck was stacked against them. All but two of the codefendants were represented by overwhelmed and underfunded federal defenders. The judge, an aged and feeble appointee from the 1970s, struggled with the thorny technological issues and could barely stay physically attentive. For the first time outside of a mafia trial in New Jersey, the jury would remain anonymous and was told so during the voir dire (the time of the jury selection). It is not a stretch to believe that such a decision created an immediate bias in the jury against the defense.

After two weeks of the prosecution giving testimony of legal protest activity with innuendo-laden hearsay, the defense mounted a pathetic one-day rebuttal before sending the case to the jury. This jury, which was *not* of the defendants' peers, returned guilty verdicts against all of them.

Aside from the Center for Constitutional Rights, many from social justice and free speech communities ignored the ramifications of this assault on activism. I felt more disillusioned than disappointed. As a student of political history I understood that social movements lived and died by the coalitions they could build and maintain. This was also personal for me. It wasn't as if people were just ignoring a cause that I champion; they were also ignoring the love of my life, my partner whom I would be losing to several years of incarceration.

For me, the AETA is manifested in those five years that Kevin spent locked up in a federal correctional institution. During that time I worried about his physical safety, about the harassment he received from a discriminatory staff, about his isolation and emotional health, about his lack of vegan food that the judge ordered but that the prison refused to give to him, and about how I would extend my care to his shell-shocked family. I spent those years alone, separated from the person I loved because the United States government would rather protect corporate interests than the rights of its citizens.

Kevin and I came out of this ordeal okay and learned some very valuable lessons. We no longer romanticize and envy those epic movements of the past. Instead, we appreciate the gravity of their sacrifices. We also don't take for granted our time together or the small achievements in animal rights that we have metaphorically bled for. I try as often as possible to tell this tale to those progressives and social justice activists who are unaware of the scourge that is the AETA. People need to start paying attention, because the AETA's practices will not end with this story. If the AETA is successful in silencing the animal rights community, then it will not be long before the federal government and its corporate sponsors set their sights on others. If that happens, then I warn all of my activist compatriots that they should not look to me for solidarity; I won't be there. But I will keep them company once they themselves get locked up.

BLUM V. HOLDER

*Sarahjane Blum, Jay Johnson,
and Ryan Shapiro*

In December 2011, five longtime grassroots animal rights activists and the New York City–based Center for Constitutional Rights filed a lawsuit in federal court. The suit, named *Blum v. Holder*, challenges the Animal Enterprise Terrorism Act (AETA) as an unconstitutional infringement on free speech. Coinciding with the filing of the suit, the brief pieces included below were written to explain the lawsuit, and three of the plaintiffs' involvement in it, to the general public.

The pieces illustrate that by criminalizing basic protest tactics, the AETA has created a constantly shifting ground beneath us as we work to defend animals. And though our personal fears and confusions are a running theme, we did not voice our anxieties to frighten our fellow activists or discourage protest. Rather, we sought to make clear to the public at large how the AETA is corrosive to civil liberties.

On March 12, 2013, the District Court granted the defendant's motion to dismiss, ruling that plaintiffs did not have standing to bring the case. The case is currently on appeal to the First Circuit. No matter the final outcome, the act of filing suit against the Justice Department and this unjust law has already struck a blow against the AETA's underlying purpose of chilling animal activists into silence. Government repression is real, but so is the suffering we fight to end. We might be scared, but we can't be stopped.

SARAHJANE BLUM

Once upon a time, I had a moment of reality TV renown. As a graduate student at Georgetown University and a teaching assistant for one of those intro courses where the students will do anything to avoid talking about the readings they didn't do, I became a source of intrigue and conversation during discussion sessions due to my appearance as the warm and fuzzy heroine of an episode of *Pet Story*. Duck Girl, they called me, when they heard the story about the rehabilitation of two sick and injured ducks that I rescued from that life of suffering. I had named the ducks Harry and Penhall, after two characters on *21 Jump Street*, my favorite TV show growing up. Before their rescue, Harry and Penhall were living in small cages barely bigger than their bodies, being force-fed to the brink of death to fatten their livers. They had lost the ability to eat or walk on their own. I took them to vet visits and helped them learn to eat again on their own, and to regain muscles in their legs through physical therapy. While caring for the pair, I was contacted by a television producer who thought their return to health made for a sweet, unusual story. At the time, my biggest concerns about turning my tale of rescue into a TV episode were that the "quirky" angle used by the narrator made me look beyond square, that someone would find out I was talking about basic cable rather than *Abelard and Heloise*, and that naming my companions after near-forgotten 1980s TV characters made me look old. Those fears are quaint to me today. Now when I show that footage, I look over my shoulder for the FBI. Just hitting PLAY could have me arrested for terrorism.

In 2003, along with my coplaintiff Ryan Shapiro and others, I founded GourmetCruelty.com, a coalition dedicated to exposing the cruelty of the foie gras industry through undercover video footage and open rescue. For over a year we investigated what happens behind the closed doors of these farms and made a documentary of what we saw. Excerpts from that documentary were featured on network and cable news, and I did extensive interviews surrounding the release of the footage. I, my colleagues, and the journalists we spoke with all understood our work to be part of a proud history of civil disobedience and whistle-blowing in this country, and to build upon the heritage of Upton Sinclair and

Martin Luther King, Jr. Though foie gras farming has been outlawed in California due to our work, and moves to further protect animals from the sort of cruelty I witnessed are being put before state and national legislators every year, this law criminalizes me for speaking out about these very issues.

I live in Minnesota, home to one of the few foie gras farms in the United States. I want to educate my fellow Minnesotans about this issue so that they can choose not to support animal cruelty. But the more people I convince to forgo foie gras, or even to bypass McDonald's for a more ethical dining option, the more I impact the profits of animal enterprises, and the more likely it is that I will be prosecuted as a terrorist.

The Animal Enterprise Terrorism Act—steamrolled through Congress by the heavy lobbying of corporate interests from factory farming, animal research, and the fur industry—has as of yet attracted little notice throughout the country. For many of us who have chosen to work to oppose animal abuse, however, it has created a perilous climate where free speech is ever more dangerous. By evoking national fears of "terrorism," big business was able to push through a law that makes criminal any work found to have caused the loss of property or profits to a business or other institution that uses or sells animals (or animal products) or to "a person or entity having a connection to, relationship with, or transactions with an animal enterprise." But no protest against injustice can change anything unless it hurts the bottom line of the powerful.

We have seen, during this recession, the impact of unfettered corporate power on the American landscape. The AETA is but one example of what happens when corporations start making America's laws. Striking down this unconstitutional legislation will be one step toward ensuring that individuals remain free to speak their minds without fear of arrest.

When I left the foie gras farm, carrying Penhall in my arms, I made a promise to the countless ducks I left behind that I would do what I could to help them, too. Still the duck girl, I want to tell their story, to show the suffering that goes on behind the closed doors of factory farms. But how can I speak with conviction when I know that the more convincing my words are, the more criminal they become?

Without question the Animal Enterprise Terrorism Act is a concerted assault on free speech. Which is why four fellow activists and I have filed a lawsuit asking the federal court to strike down the law as a violation of the First Amendment. Compassion is not terrorism, and the Animal Enterprise Terrorism Act cannot be allowed to silence us.

Jay Johnson

I became involved in the animal rights movement in the fall of 1999. I worked on a variety of campaigns over my first two years of activism, but my main organizing work began in the summer of 2001 when I helped start the Chicago chapter of Stop Huntingdon Animal Cruelty (SHAC). Over the course of that campaign, I saw the formation of a vibrant and active social justice movement not just in Chicago, but also around the country and the world. Lots of people were coming out to demonstrate against the mistreatment of animals, and it really did feel like an exciting time to be an animal rights activist.

Then in 2006, six activists were convicted under the Animal Enterprise Protection Act for their free speech–related activities in the SHAC campaign. Shortly thereafter, the Animal Enterprise Terrorism Act was signed into law. Those two events completely changed the community I had become a part of. Organizers I had worked with in Chicago for years stopped coming to demonstrations. When I asked them why, they told me that it simply wasn't worth the risk to protest anymore with the threat of being labeled a "terrorist" looming over them. A friend of mine, whom I have organized with for seven years, told me that he wanted to buy a house someday and have a family and he was worried that if he kept going to protests, he might be put on a terrorist watch list that would make getting a mortgage impossible. There was a general fear in the community that engaging in First Amendment–protected speech was simply too dangerous to be worth it with the AETA in place.

I did all I could to keep organizing, but the chill that had rushed through my once passionate community was so strong that I simply couldn't get most people to come to demonstrations anymore. Even Fur Free Friday, an international annual day of action that has been a tradition since the 1980s, became controversial to certain members of the animal rights community within Chicago.

Before the passage of the AETA, Fur Free Friday was a day where animal rights activists from all sects of the movement came together to protest the fur industry. Now activists, for fear of being labeled as "violent" because the march included chanting, have argued that the event should be canceled or drastically altered away from the protest march it had traditionally been. The argument that chanting was too militant was never articulated, and was quite frankly unthinkable, before the passage of the AETA.

When I moved to New York to go to school, I had hoped that I would be able to plug into existing activist networks here and get back to campaigning for animal rights, which had become more or less impossible in Chicago. Unfortunately, it seems the chill I had seen take its toll on the animal rights community in Chicago had had similar effects in New York as well. When I ask people about what groups are active in the city, there simply don't appear to be any. The most I have been able to find is a protest here and there, but it is a far cry from the powerful movement that existed before the passage of the AETA. The community simply seems scared to engage in sustained, demonstration-based campaigning with the threat of being labeled as a "terrorist" hanging over their heads.

Honestly, I fully understand that trepidation. It's incredibly difficult to ignore that fear in the back of your mind with the AETA casting its shadow over the animal rights movement. That shadow has made any effective exercising of our First Amendment rights incredibly challenging, if not utterly impossible. That is why I chose to be a plaintiff in this lawsuit. Striking down the AETA would remove the shadow of fear that the movement currently exists under. It would remove the ability of the government to label nonviolent activists as terrorists for nothing more than their views on the treatment of animals. Perhaps most importantly, it would make activists once again feel safe in sustained public demonstration, the bedrock of any social justice movement, without the fear of government reprisal if a company's profits fall as a result.

RYAN SHAPIRO

It's only by chance that I'm writing this from behind a desk in Cambridge, Massachusetts, rather than from behind bars in a federal prison. While earning a master's degree in American history in 2003, I co-coordinated an undercover investigation of notoriously cruel foie gras factory farms. In the course of this investigation, and as an act of civil disobedience, we openly rescued a number of ducks from the appalling cruelty we encountered. Putting my undergraduate film degree to use, we also made a short documentary film to educate the public about the systemic suffering hidden behind the closed doors of these factory farms. The images we captured played a crucial role in sparking national and international campaigns against foie gras, and in the successful 2004 ballot initiative to ban the production of foie gras in the state of California.

From the Boston Tea Party to the suffragettes to the civil rights movement, civil disobedience has a long and proud history in American political discourse. In this tradition, we did everything openly and took full responsibility for our actions. Fellow investigator Sarahjane Blum and I were eventually convicted of misdemeanor trespass and sentenced to community service. This was a reasonable and acceptable price to pay for bringing to light the sad realities of life on factory farms. However, even as we performed our community service, a series of legislative and law enforcement shifts began to make future activism of this sort exceedingly dangerous.

In 2005, the FBI designated the animal rights and environmental movements the leading domestic terror threats in the United States. This is despite the fact that neither of these movements has ever physically injured a single person in their decades of existence. Then, in 2006, under heavy lobbying from the pharmaceutical, animal agriculture, and fur industries, the United States passed the Animal Enterprise Terrorism Act (AETA). The AETA seeks to criminalize as terrorism political dissent that targets any business that uses or sells animals or animal products. One especially pernicious element of the AETA is that the statute is written so broadly that merely affecting the profits of these businesses can qualify as a terrorist offense. So, if someone chooses not to purchase foie gras after viewing footage of its production, whoever produced or screened that footage could now be prosecuted as a terrorist. Indeed, a distressingly high number of my closest friends and associates have since been convicted as terrorists for engaging in free speech and civil disobedience advocacy on behalf of animals.

As I watched my friends, classmates, and roommates hauled off to federal prison, I shifted to a greater emphasis on academics. I am now a PhD candidate in the Department of Science, Technology & Society at MIT. In part trying to make sense of the current situation, my research focuses on disputes over animals and national security from the late nineteenth century to the present. Sadly, the AETA actually stands on the shoulders of a century of similar efforts to marginalize animal protectionists as threats to American security. From spurious allegations of animal protectionist collusion with the Kaiser, Hitler, and Stalin, my research demonstrates that politicians, industry, and law enforcement have long employed the rhetoric and apparatus of national security to counter effective animal advocacy.

As intended, the AETA has cast a chill over the animal rights community. Many animal advocates, myself included, began to censor themselves and refrain from speech that is protected by the First Amendment, or from nonviolent civil disobedience in the tradition of some of America's greatest voices.

The fear behind this self-silencing is well grounded. Through the Freedom of Information Act, I've uncovered documents revealing explicit FBI consideration of AETA charges against those who expose factory farming cruelty. To fight back, I have become a plaintiff in a lawsuit that asks the court to strike down the Animal Enterprise Terrorism Act as an unconstitutional infringement on free speech. Though I am now a scholar behind a desk, I just as easily could have found myself a "terrorist" behind bars. Corporate power should not dictate the limits of political dissent. It's time to do away with the undemocratic and un-American AETA.

AFTERWORD

Heidi Boghosian

An informed woman with a conscience, a will of steel, and a picket sign is more threatening to some corporations than is risk of industrial sabotage. Corporations and government allies know that a vibrant people's movement can engage the public's conscience in ways that slick advertising campaigns can never do, representing the single most powerful way to expose unethical corporate practices and hope that moral intervention will supplant personal greed. The First Amendment to the U.S. Constitution affords activists a direct artery to the masses through protected activities such as sharing images of human exploitation of animals, tabling outside of puppy mills, engaging in Internet-based organizing, and distributing leaflets. These are the most precious commodities in advancing social justice causes.

Animal rights and animal welfare activists have been highly effective in their advocacy, helping raise awareness among the general public of animal-related issues. For that they have been deemed enemies of the State and labeled "terrorists," subject to the multifarious abuses attendant with a perpetual war on terror that pours profits into the pockets of corporations and contractors.

How does one continue to advocate for animal rights and welfare given the risk of being charged with terrorism? It's useful to visualize the desired results—no more LD-50 tests, no more foie gras, no more slaughtering of horses, no more genetic engineering, no more animals in sport or entertainment, to name just a few—and to chart a roadmap to attain such results. Below are a few pointers that may be useful during the process of working toward larger goals.

1. Derive inspiration from history. Every significant social, legal, and political gain, every right and benefit, has been secured by individuals who demanded it. At great personal expense, and often at the hands of violence from state officials, principled individuals have stood up to powerful political and economic forces. Hard-fought victories have been made by ordinary people with extraordinary commitment to challenging power dynamics.

Native Americans occupied the island of Alcatraz from 1969 to 1971 to draw attention to many social problems they faced, from racism to unemployment to lack of educational opportunities. Along with the occupation of Wounded Knee, these protests resulted in Congress passing legislation allowing them more power to govern themselves on reservations. For years, black civil rights and/or liberation activists put their lives on the line at enormous personal sacrifice. The Civil Rights Act and Voting Rights Act represent some of the major legislative accomplishments of that era.

Persistent actions on a nationally coordinated level to oppose the Vietnam War drew attention to peaceful protest and acts of civil disobedience about United States military intervention abroad and led to the end of military conscription. Despite these activists and others being subject to the usual arsenal of government tools to suppress free speech (grand jury abuses, pretextual and mass arrests, spying, infiltration, and disruption), their protests served to inspire many other movements.

Gay rights activists, and later LGBTQ activists, have picketed government agencies in Washington, DC to fight discriminatory employment policies. After the raid on the Stonewall Inn in New York in 1969, a gay rights movement gained power, leading to hard-fought reforms in decriminalizing homosexuality, and reducing police and institutional harassment. Sexual orientation was added to civil rights statutes. ACT UP and other community-based groups educated the public and fought discrimination, cutting through bureaucratic red tape and demanding resources for education and health care programs.

2. Be persistent, and patient. Individual as well as mass victories remind us that challenges to injustice may take years, but we should never concede. An international movement to free five Puerto Rican

Nationalist prisoners who fought for Puerto Rican independence—Rafael Cancel Miranda, Irvin Flores, Oscar Collazo, Lolita Lebrón, and Andrés Figueroa Cordero—won a victory in 1979 when the sentences of the four who remained in prison (Andrés Figueroa Cordero was released in 1978 with terminal cancer) were unconditionally commuted and they were released. Approximately 3,000 people greeted the freed patriots in Chicago, 10,000 in New York, and 25,000 jammed the San Juan airport in anticipation of their return.

World-renowned writer Mumia Abu-Jamal was released to general population in 2012 after spending twenty-nine years on death row. And in 2013, Russell Maroon Shoatz was also transferred from over two decades in solitary confinement to a medium security facility. Both had patient, committed defense committees working for decades to draw attention to their cases.

3. Keep sight of the end goals when challenges arise. Social activists have always worked against enormous odds. Modern day coalitions facing similar daunting prospects share a common imperative: putting a human face (or images of animals) to injustices to show how authorities perpetuate disinformation and fear to rein in public movements. It was ordinary individuals in the 1970s who exposed J. Edgar Hoover's counterintelligence programs that aimed to "neutralize" activist leaders and groups working for positive change. And it's up to ordinary individuals to expose how corporations and government agencies work to discredit and disrupt individuals and grassroots movements who have been successful in raising awareness of unjust and inhumane policies.

4. Find safety in numbers. Join one of the many animal rights and animal welfare organizations doing work near you or focusing on the specific area of interest to you. Talk to your friends, families, and new people that you meet about projects you're working on. Share a photo or story of a particular injustice. Use every opportunity to share a short anecdote or fact that might prompt someone else to think about the issue from a new angle, whether on a train ride or in a cab or waiting in line at a movie theater. Learn about national and local advocacy efforts; write a letter and forward it to a friend. Arm yourself with facts, and use creativity, humor, and compassion to speak up on behalf of our nonhuman friends.

5. Know the law and your basic rights. Become familiar with federal and local anti-terrorism laws and consequences. This book's in-depth examination of the Animal Enterprise Terrorism Act, and the book's many knowledgeable contributors, are an excellent resource. **Identify local legal resources and hotlines** that provide assistance to individuals who are targeted for political and free speech activities. Know whom to call if you need legal assistance, and carry that person's number on your person. **Know your basic rights.** Avail yourself of the many Know Your Rights information sheets and booklets available on the web. Pay special attention to what you should do if an agent or law enforcement representative visits you at your place of employment or home.

6. Practice safe security. Government intelligence and law enforcement agencies have invested enormous resources—financial, personnel, and public relations—into monitoring individuals, nonprofit organizations, and local associations and groups working on behalf of animal rights and animal welfare issues. Exercise prudence and common sense when planning and communicating about protests or direct actions, and do not share information on the telephone or put in writing anything that you would not feel comfortable making public. Assume that all your communication is being monitored.

7. Know your personal limits, and don't compromise once you've decided on a course of action. Don't let anyone pressure you into engaging in an action that you do not feel 100 percent comfortable about participating in. Decide before you participate whether you are willing to risk arrest, and act accordingly. Government agencies, multinational corporations with their own intelligence units, and private security firms use infiltrators and agents provocateurs to encourage, entrap, and provide money and materials for activists to engage in certain actions that they might not otherwise engage in. This is often accomplished by instigating intimate relationships with naïve or trusting social welfare activists. Don't be swayed into doing something because you want to please or impress someone else.

8. Try not to be intimidated by anti-terrorism legislation and fear mongering in the media. When you know your personal limits and have a basic command of the laws in your jurisdiction, proceed with confidence. Do not be afraid to speak out and to take part in protests or mass mobilizations. The creators of the AETA want you to be afraid. The American Legislative Exchange Council and allied legislators and corporations are banking on the fact that confusion and trepidation about the AETA and equivalent state laws will stifle participation in robust political speech and First Amendment–protected activities. Each time you are confronted with a decision about what to do, about whether to join in a particular action or a growing animal welfare movement, take a moment and listen to your conscience. Picture the millions of monkeys, dogs, cats, rabbits, and other animals subjected daily to scientific experimentation and tortured at the hands of humans. What would you do if you were standing in the laboratory witnessing acts of obscene cruelty?

Some otherwise enlightened individuals may still ask, with all the social problems confronting modern society, what value does animal rights welfare advocacy hold? The answer lies in the manner in which a civilization treats those unable to advocate on their own behalf; it is a measure of its morality. Countries such as the United Kingdom have found that animals are sentient beings and not commodities, and they have changed their laws accordingly.

Animals are big business in the United States, so it's no wonder that the industries want to silence animal rights groups. When Mercy for Animals produced videos of a daily dairy farm operation in New York showing how the tails of cows are cut off without anesthesia (tail docking), or how a staff member hit a cow on the head with a wrench when it would not move, it helped prompt a debate on the need for laws regulating dairy cows.

The power of the animal industry is seen every day. When Oprah Winfrey commented on a mad cow disease outbreak in Europe on national television in 1996, she landed in court fighting the powerful cattle industry. In 1998 cattle producers sued Winfrey under the Texas version of a food libel law, the False Disparagement of Perishable Food

Products Act of 1995. Cattle producers claimed that Winfrey and her guests' remarks caused cattle prices to plummet by $12 million, even though, as Winfrey's attorney claimed in his opening remarks, one of the cattle producers actually made $140,000 in the aftermath of the show by betting in the cattle futures market that prices would go down. Although the jury found that Winfrey's comments did not constitute libel, the woman ranked as one of Fortune's 50 most powerful women in business never again spoke publicly about the issue.

The animal rights and animal welfare movements, and progressive movements generally, face a dual threat of spying and infiltration by the government and by corporate targets of protest. Spying by corporations such as Goldman Sachs or JP Morgan introduces new fears that undermine First Amendment freedoms. Infiltration provides the government and the private sector with an unfair advantage in the face of legitimate and important political grievances. It splinters people's movements as undercover agents divide members and erode the trust between movement participants. The corporate and government's response reflected growing animosity toward animal rights activists. In sharp contrast, the creative forms of protest that they engage in help foster a sense of caring that has long been missing in this country.

As the world's superpower, this nation wields major influence on other countries. By punishing animal rights and animal welfare activism, the United States sends a signal to others that we are willing to violate our own constitution and that we sanction outright cruelty to animals.

Animal rights and animal welfare activists must continue to ignite anger in the hearts and minds of Americans; we must not let them slip into complacency as our government wages flagrant abuses on animals, who are victimized daily by corporate interests and human selfishness. If we allow the Animal Enterprise Terrorism Act to stand unchallenged we are complicit in deliberate horrors. We owe a debt of gratitude to the thousands of individuals who have gone undercover in animal enterprises to expose illegal actions. They serve as a wake-up call for the rest of the country, and indeed, for the world, about the gross inhumanities that animals suffer at the hands of profit-oriented corporations. And we owe a debt of gratitude to the editors and contributors of *The Terrorization of Dissent* for sharing with others the tactics of a government afraid of the power of its people.

ACKNOWLEDGMENTS

We, Jason and Anthony, would like to thank our families and friends for their lifetime of support even when they did not agree with us. It was that value that laid the groundwork for us to believe in defending the First Amendment and the voices in this book.

We would like to also thank Lantern Books for supporting this project—Wendy Lee, who worked directly with us throughout the editing process, as well as Martin Rowe, Kara Davis, and Gene Gollogly. We thank Tucker Culbertson and Odette Wilkens, who were there at the beginning of this project, for providing support and editorial direction.

We would like to express gratitude to the many people who wrote kind and very supportive reviews of this book, reinforcing that this project is an important tool for dismantling the Animal Enterprise Terrorism Act—A. Breeze Harper, Heidi Boghosian, Ronnie Lee, Kim Socha, Richard Kahn, Ingrid Newkirk, the *Journal for Critical Animal Studies*, Daniel White Hodge, Peter McLaren, Samuel Fassbinder, and Leslie James Pickering.

This book would not have been possible without the many contributors who provided committed and passionate essays and interviews—Piers Beirne, Will Potter, Kim McCoy, Dara Lovitz, Vasile Stanescu, Lillian M. McCartin, Michael Loadenthal, Scott DeMuth, David Naguib Pellow, Wesley Shirley, John Sorenson, Sarat Colling, Eric Jonas, Stephanie Jenkins, Jennifer D. Grubbs, Brad J. Thomson, Carol L. Glasser, Dylan Powell, Aaron Zellhoefer, Sarahjane Blum, Jay Johnson, Ryan Shapiro, Heidi Boghosian, Joseph Buddenberg, Walter Bond, and Josh Harper.

And lastly, we would like to thank all of the activists, organizers, advocates, liberationists, and social movements, both past and present. These courageous individuals have granted us the intellectual strength, moral consciousness, and political fortitude to challenge the corporate repression and legal corruption of the Animal Enterprise Terrorism Act.

ABOUT THE CONTRIBUTORS

Piers Beirne is a professor of sociology and legal studies in the Department of Criminology at the University of Southern Maine. The founding coeditor of the journal *Theoretical Criminology*, his books include *Law, Criminology and Animal Abuse* and *Criminology: A Critical Approach* (with James W. Messerschmidt). His current research interests include the development of concepts of cruelty, green criminology, and agrarian outrage in nineteenth-century Ireland.

Sarahjane Blum, active in the animal rights movement since the mid-1990s, is one of five plaintiffs in an ongoing lawsuit seeking to overturn the Animal Enterprise Terrorism Act. In 2003, Sarahjane cofounded GourmetCruelty.com, a grassroots coalition dedicated to exposing the abuse of ducks and geese raised for foie gras. Sarahjane serves on the board of directors of Support Vegans in the Prison System and is the coeditor of *Confronting Animal Exploitation: Grassroots Essays on Liberation and Veganism*. A small business owner and author, she lives in Minneapolis, Minnesota, and holds a master's degree in history from Georgetown University.

Heidi Boghosian is the executive director of the National Lawyers Guild. She cohosts *Law and Disorder*, the weekly civil liberties radio show on Pacifica's WBAI in New York and over fifty national affiliates. She is the author of *Spying on Democracy: Government Surveillance, Corporate Power, and Public Resistance*. She lives in New York's East Village.

Sarat Colling has a degree in writing, rhetoric, and discourse and is pursuing a master's in critical sociology at Brock University. Her research interests include critical animal studies, animal geography, anarchism, and transnational feminism. Sarat grew up on Hornby Island, British Columbia, and has volunteered for environmental, animal, and social justice organizations in British Columbia and Southern Ontario. She is the founder of *Political Media Review* and coauthor of *Love and Liberation: An Animal Liberation Front Story.*

Jason Del Gandio, PhD, is an assistant professor of Rhetoric and Public Advocacy at Temple University (Philadelphia). His areas of scholarly expertise include the philosophy of communication, social and political theory, rhetoric, and critical analysis with a focus on social movements and radical social change. Jason has participated in the Global Justice Movement, the antiwar movement, the anti-RNC demonstrations of 2004, fair trade campaigns, Latin American solidarity work, and the Occupy movement. He has appeared on television and radio, and regularly speaks on college campuses and at public venues. Jason has written on such topics as autonomy, immaterial labor, corporate control, the rhetoric of Barack Obama, performance art, the Occupy movement, and the relationship between neoliberalism and the university. In 2008 he published his first book, *Rhetoric for Radicals: A Handbook for 21st Century Activists.* More information can be found at www.jasondelgandio.net.

Scott DeMuth is a doctoral candidate in sociology at the University of Minnesota, Twin Cities. He is a grand jury resistor and has been indicted for conspiracy under the AETA. He has been actively involved in several prisoner support projects in the Twin Cities, including the Anarchist Black Cross and EWOK! (Earth Warriors are OK!). Scott is currently a member of the nonprofit Oyate Nipi Kte, which focuses on Dakota language and land recovery. He is a member of the Anpao Duta editorial collective, which publishes Dakota language materials and a community journal under the same name.

Carol L. Glasser received her BA from Tulane University and her PhD from the Department of Sociology at the University of California, Irvine, where she is currently a research fellow. Carol has been involved in the animal liberation movement as an academic and an activist. She formerly served as the research director at the Humane Research Council and has organized and participated in various grassroots campaigns in Southern California. Her current research focuses on gender, the intersections of gender and species oppression, and social movements, including the animal rights movement.

Jennifer D. Grubbs is an anarchist anthropologist and doctoral candidate at American University. She received an MA in communication and in women's, gender, and sexuality studies at the University of Cincinnati. Her research examines the intersections of privilege and exploitation with species relations, the neoliberal corporatization of academia, and the political repression of animal and earth liberationists. Despite that jargon-filled research summary, she remains committed to creating theory that also matters to those outside of university walls.

Josh Harper was raised in the Pacific Northwest and has been an activist for over fifteen years, struggling for animal liberation and wilderness defense. This has included campaigns against whale hunting, deforestation, vivisection, and fur. Josh has also dedicated time and efforts to creating and archiving alternative radical media, with the *Breaking Free* video magazine (late 1990s), and most recently with the radical earth and animal liberation archive project The Talon Conspiracy (formerly Conflict Gypsy). In 2000 and again in 2001, Josh defied grand jury subpoenas investigating the Animal Liberation Front and Earth Liberation Front. Josh was later part of the Stop Huntingdon Animal Cruelty campaign against Huntingdon Life Sciences and in 2006 was sentenced to three years in prison as part of the SHAC 7 trial. He is currently out of prison, off probation, and living in Portland. He is also working on a book that will chronicle the history of the radical animal liberation in North America from 1977 to the present.

Stephanie Jenkins is an assistant professor in Oregon State University's School of History, Philosophy, and Religion. She received her BA in philosophy at Emory University in 2003, her MA in philosophy from Pennsylvania State University in 2007, and her dual PhD in philosophy and women's studies from Pennsylvania State University in 2012. Her dissertation, "Disabling Ethics: A Genealogy of Ability," argues for a genealogy-based ethics that departs from traditional bioethical approaches to disability. Her research and teaching interests include twentieth-century continental philosophy (especially French), feminist philosophy, disability studies, critical animal studies, and ethics. In her spare time, she enjoys spending time outdoors hiking, biking, and running, baking, and listening to live music.

Jay Johnson is a longtime animal rights activist from Chicago. Jay first became involved in animal rights activism in the fall of 1999 after viewing undercover footage that exposed the horrors of animal agriculture. Within a month of viewing the footage, Jay had gone vegan and became one of the key organizers with the Chicago chapter of the Animal Defense League, working primarily on anti-fur activism. In the summer of 2001, Jay began organizing with the Stop Huntingdon Animal Cruelty campaign (SHAC) and eventually became the legal representative for SHAC Chicago. In addition to his years on the front lines of animal rights activism, Jay has been active in prisoner support work, most notably by heading SHAC 7 prisoner Lauren Gazzola's support committee for her four-year and four-month incarceration. Currently, Jay is attending school in New York City and is one of the plaintiffs on the Center for Constitutional Rights' facial challenge to the Animal Enterprise Terrorism Act (AETA).

Eric Jonas is a student in Northwestern's doctoral program in philosophy, where he works at the intersection of theories of alterity, contemporary continental philosophy, feminist and gender theory, and critical animal studies. His current work uses the theory of alterity put forward by Jacques Derrida as a theoretical framework to examine the potential shortcomings of existing discourses on human–animal relations. Eric has presented his work at conferences across the country. Prior to attending Northwestern, he was involved in the animal rights movement, both as a volunteer for numerous small grassroots organizations and as an employee of two national organizations.

Michael Loadenthal is a proud father, anarchist organizer, clandestine conspirator, and Washington, D.C.-based academic insurgent. Over the past fifteen years he has been involved in a number of anti-capitalist and anti-authoritarian projects around the world, and at present he focuses his energies on developing challenges to the State's criminalization of dissent. In 2010, he completed a master's degree in terrorism studies at the Centre for the Study of Terrorism and Political Violence at the

University of St. Andrews, Scotland, focusing on a data-driven defense of direct action and economic sabotage. In 2011, Michael began teaching Terrorism and Political Violence at Georgetown University, and completed a doctoral fellowship at the School for Conflict Analysis and Resolution at George Mason University. Currently, he splits his time among raising a vegan daughter, researching statecraft, teaching theory, writing constantly, and agitating for a better world. He regularly publishes propaganda and political theory under a variety of pseudonyms.

Dara Lovitz is the author of *Muzzling a Movement: The Effects of Anti-Terrorism Law, Money, and Politics on Animal Activism.* She is an adjunct professor of animal law at Temple University's Beasley School of Law and the Earle Mack School of Law at Drexel University. She was selected by *Super Lawyers* magazine as a Rising Star. Ms. Lovitz earned her BA *magna cum laude* from the University of Pennsylvania and her JD from Temple University Beasley School of Law, where she was selected by her classmates to be the graduation ceremony speaker. Ms. Lovitz was appointed special prosecutor to try the pivotal case *Commonwealth v. Esbenshade,* in which the district court determined the criminal liability of a battery-cage egg facility owner under Pennsylvania's animal cruelty statute. She is a board member of Four Feet Forward, the Peace Advocacy Network, and the Equal Justice Alliance.

Lillian M. McCartin is a criminal defense attorney working in Chicago. She obtained her JD from Chicago-Kent College of Law, with a certificate in public interest law. In her practice, she represents individuals charged with a variety of offenses, including misdemeanors and felonies. Her clients have included activists and radicals who have committed civil disobedience or have otherwise faced criminal charges resulting from their political actions and associations. She has been active in the National Lawyers Guild, acting as president of the Chicago-Kent chapter while she was a student there, and she currently acts as cocoordinator of the Next Gen Committee of the Chicago chapter. She also volunteers with First Defense Legal Aid and fosters rescued animals.

Kim McCoy is a passionate animal and environmental advocate with a BS in business administration from the University of Tennessee and a JD with honors from Lewis & Clark Law School. During law school, she served as editor-in-chief of the *Animal Law Review* and interned with the National Center for Animal Law and the International Environmental Law Project. Kim is currently executive director of the One World One Ocean Foundation. She is a member of MENSA and the proud mother of a healthy, thriving toddler who has been vegan since conception. Having previously worked for Sea Shepherd Conservation Society in a variety of roles, including executive director and director of legal affairs, Kim remains deeply committed to the defense of animals worldwide and believes firmly in the merits of aggressive, nonviolent, direct action as an effective and necessary means to accomplish this goal.

Anthony J. Nocella II, award-winning teacher, author, and community organizer, is a visiting professor in the School of Education at Hamline University and a senior fellow of the Dispute Resolution Institute at the Hamline School of Law. He received his doctorate in social science at the Maxwell School at Syracuse University. His areas of interest include disability studies, critical animal studies, critical/green criminology, critical pedagogy, and urban education. He is a cofounder of more than fifteen active political organizations including the Institute for Critical Animal Studies (ICAS) and four scholarly journals including the *Transformative Justice Journal*. Nocella has published more than fifty-five scholarly articles/chapters and fifteen books including co-editing: *Contemporary Anarchist Studies: An Introductory Anthology of Anarchy in the Academy*, *Academic Repression: Reflections from the Academic Industrial Complex*, *Terrorists or Freedom Fighters? Reflections on the Liberation of Animals*, and *Igniting a Revolution: Voices in Defense of the Earth*. Visit him at www.anthonynocella.org.

David Naguib Pellow, PhD, is a professor and Don A. Martindale Endowed Chair of Sociology at the University of Minnesota. His teaching and research focus on environmental justice issues in communities of color in the United States and globally. His books include: *The Slums of Aspen: Immigrants vs. the Environment in America's Eden* (with Lisa Sun-Hee Park); *Resisting Global Toxics: Transnational Movements for Environmental Justice*; *Power, Justice, and the Environment: A Critical Appraisal* *of the Environmental Justice Movements* (co-editor with Robert J. Brulle); *The Silicon Valley of Dreams: Environmental Injustice, Immigrant Workers, and the High-Tech Global Economy* (with Lisa Sun-Hee Park); and *Garbage Wars: The Struggle for Environmental Justice in Chicago.* He has served on the board of directors for the Center for Urban Transformation, Greenpeace USA, and International Rivers. He is currently the facilitator of the Minnesota Global Justice Project.

Dylan Powell is a community organizer from St. Catharines, Ontario. He started the media project/radio show *The Vegan Police* in October 2008 and has since gone on to co-found Marineland Animal Defense, a campaign dedicated to ending animal captivity at Marineland in Niagara Falls, Ontario, as well as the intersectionality-based Live Free Collective, a collective dedicated to highlighting the intersections of oppressions and working against them. Prisoner support has been a focus of his activism, and he has held fundraisers and provided support for numerous animal activists/liberations including the AETA 4, Walter Bond, the SHAC 7, and the Spanish 12. He also currently works with Josh Harper and others on The Talon Conspiracy, a free online archive of radical animal and earth liberation publications.

Will Potter is an award-winning independent journalist based in Washington, D.C., who focuses on "eco-terrorism," the animal rights and environmental movements, and civil liberties post-9/11. His reporting and commentary have appeared in *The Washington Post, Rolling Stone,* and *Democracy Now,* and he has testified before the U.S. Congress about his reporting. He has lectured at more than one hundred universities and public forums internationally about his work, and he is an advisory board member of the Rosenberg Fund for Children. His book, *Green Is the New Red: An Insider's Account of a Social Movement Under Siege,* was awarded a Kirkus Star for "remarkable merit" and named one of the best books of 2011 by *Kirkus Reviews.*

Ryan Shapiro is a longtime grassroots animal rights activist. Since the mid-1990s, Ryan has cocoordinated campaigns against factory farming, animal experimentation, the fur industry, circuses, whaling, and cetacean captivity. Ryan is a PhD candidate in the Department of

Science, Technology & Society at the Massachusetts Institute of Technology. Ryan's research explores the use of the rhetoric and apparatus of national security to marginalize animal protectionists as threats to American security from the nineteenth century to the present. As part of this research, Ryan has hundreds of Freedom of Information Act requests in motion with the FBI, and is currently suing the FBI for its failure to comply with the Freedom of Information Act. Ryan is also a plaintiff in *Blum v. Holder*, the lawsuit challenging the constitutionality of the Animal Enterprise Terrorism Act.

Wesley Shirley graduated with a PhD in Sociology from the University of Oregon in 2012 and now teaches at Lane Community College in Eugene, Oregon. His dissertation, "When Activism Is Terrorism: Special Interest Politics and the State Repression of the Animal Rights Movement," examined the AETA and similar laws as forms of state repression of social movements. He has been active in social justice movements for fifteen years, as well as played music in bands with an eye toward issues of social justice.

John Sorenson teaches critical animal studies, globalization, and anti-racism at Brock University in Ontario. He holds an honors BA and an MA from the University of Alberta, and a PhD in social and political thought from York University. His past research focused on the Horn of Africa, where he studied the experience of women in the Eritrean liberation struggle, and the African diasporic communities in Canada. He has been involved with a number of third world solidarity groups. His books *Imagining Ethiopia* and *Ghosts and Shadows* (with Atsuko Matsuoka) investigate the politics of national identity. His recent research concerns various ways of representing nonhuman animals. His most recent books are *Ape* and *About Canada–Animal Rights*.

Vasile Stanescu is an instructor in the Program of Writing and Rhetoric and a PhD candidate in the Program of Modern Thought and Literature at Stanford University. He serves, with Professor Helena Pedersen (Malmö University, Sweden), as co–senior editor of the Critical Animal Studies book series published by Rodopi Press. He also serves as the associate editor for the *Journal for Critical Animal Studies*. Stanescu has reviewed texts for the journals *Ethics and the Environment* and *Critical Sociology* as well as the books series Themes in 20th and 21st Century Literature and Culture. Stanescu has fifteen publications (current or forthcoming). In 2011, he received a grant from the Culture and Animals Foundation to help fund his current research on the intersection of critical animal studies and environmentalism.

Brad J. Thomson is a political organizer and legal worker in Chicago. He works as a paralegal and investigator at People's Law Office, a civil rights law firm that has represented political activists and victims of police brutality for over forty years. He was part of the legal team representing Scott DeMuth, an activist from Minneapolis charged with "animal enterprise terrorism" in Davenport, Iowa. As an organizer, Brad has been active in a number of radical and social justice organizations, including Food Not Bombs, the National Lawyers Guild, and the Civilian-Soldier Alliance, an organization of civilians supporting service members and veterans who oppose unjust wars and occupations. A supporter of animal rights, he has been vegan for over fourteen years and fosters rescued dogs.

Aaron Zellhoefer is a longtime campaigner and activist. His activism ranges from testifying in front of several members of Congress to engaging in civil disobedience. He is a champion for animal rights, gay rights, environmental justice, and the peace movement. His passion has taken him across the United States and to many foreign countries to fight for social justice. The *Toronto Star* called him President George Bush's worst nightmare. Aaron currently resides in Minneapolis, Minnesota, with his partner of eleven years, Kevin, and their rescued laboratory beagles, Junior and Raymond.

ABOUT THE PUBLISHER

LANTERN BOOKS was founded in 1999 on the principle of living with a greater depth and commitment to the preservation of the natural world. In addition to publishing books on animal advocacy, vegetarianism, religion, and environmentalism, Lantern is dedicated to printing books in the United States on recycled paper and saving resources in day-to-day operations. Lantern is honored to be a recipient of the highest standard in environmentally responsible publishing from the Green Press Initiative.

www.lanternbooks.com

CPSIA information can be obtained at www.ICGtesting.com
Printed in the USA
BVOW04s1951240714

360299BV00002B/8/P

9 781590 564301